The Psychology of Eyewitness Identification

ESSAYS IN COGNITIVE PSYCHOLOGY

North American Editors:
Henry L. Roediger, III, *Washington University in St. Louis*
James R. Pomerantz, *Rice University*

European Editors:
Alan D. Baddeley, *University of York*
Vicki Bruce, *University of Edinburgh*
Jonathan Grainger, *Université de Provence*

Essays in Cognitive Psychology is designed to meet the need for rapid publication of brief volumes in cognitive psychology. Primary topics will include perception, movement and action, attention, memory, mental representation, language and problem solving. Furthermore, the series seeks to define cognitive psychology in its broadest sense, encompassing all topics either informed by, or informing, the study of mental processes. As such, it covers a wide range of subjects including computational approaches to cognition, cognitive neuroscience, social cognition, and cognitive development, as well as areas more traditionally defined as cognitive psychology. Each volume in the series will make a conceptual contribution to the topic by reviewing and synthesizing the existing research literature, by advancing theory in the area, or by some combination of these missions. The principal aim is that authors will provide an overview of their own highly successful research program in an area. It is also expected that volumes will, to some extent, include an assessment of current knowledge and identification of possible future trends in research. Each book will be a self-contained unit supplying the advanced reader with a well-structured review of the work described and evaluated.

FORTHCOMING

Bahrick et al.: *Maintenance of Knowledge*
Butler & Kang: *The Mnemonic Benefits of Retrieval Practice*
Weaver: *Flashbulb Memory*

PUBLISHED

Schmidt: *Extraordinary Memories of Exceptional Events*
Lampinen, Neuschatz, & Cling: *Psychology of Eyewitness Identification*
Brown: *The Tip of the Tongue State*
Worthen & Hunt: Mnemonology: *Mnemonics for the 21st Century*
Surprenant & Neath: *Principles of Memory*
Kensinger: *Emotional Memory Across the Lifespan*

For updated information about published and forthcoming titles in the *Essays in Cognitive Psychology* series, please visit: **www.psypress.com/ essays**

The Psychology of Eyewitness Identification

JAMES MICHAEL LAMPINEN, JEFFREY S. NEUSCHATZ,
AND ANDREW D. CLING

Psychology Press
Taylor & Francis Group

New York   London

Psychology Press
Taylor & Francis Group
711 Third Avenue
New York, NY 10017

Psychology Press
Taylor & Francis Group
27 Church Road
Hove, East Sussex BN3 2FA

Printed in the United States of America on acid-free paper
Version Date: 2011912

International Standard Book Number: 978-1-84872-883-7 (Hardback)

Library of Congress Cataloging-in-Publication Data

Lampinen, James M.
   The psychology of eyewitness identification / James Michael Lampinen, Jeffrey S. Neuschatz, Andrew D. Cling.
      p. cm. -- (Essays in cognitive psychology)
   Includes bibliographical references and index.
   ISBN 978-1-84872-883-7 (hbk. : alk. paper)
   1. Criminal investigation--Psychological aspects. 2. Mistaken identity--Psychological aspects. 3. Eyewitness identification--Psychological aspects. 4. Memory. 5. Forensic psychology. I. Neuschatz, Jeffrey S. II. Cling, Andrew D. III. Title.

HV8073.5.L36 2012
363.25'8--dc23   2011036788

Visit the Taylor & Francis Web site at
http://www.taylorandfrancis.com

and the Psychology Press Web site at
http://www.psypress.com

CONTENTS

ACKNOWLEDGMENTS

The authors would like to thank Amber Culbertson-Faegre, Blake Erickson, Chris Peters, Lindsey Sweeney, and all the members of the Law and Psychology Lab at the University of Arkansas, and Stacy Wetmore, Devin Harker, and Will Exley from the University of Alabama in Huntsville, all of whom helped proofread sections of the manuscript. We would also like to thank Stephanie Drew from Psychology Press and Henry Roediger, series editor, for their help and patience in the process of shepherding this book through to the very end.

ABOUT THE AUTHORS

James Michael Lampinen is a professor of psychology at the University of Arkansas. He received his bachelor's degree in psychology from Elmhurst College and his PhD in cognitive psychology from Northwestern University. He then spent 2 years as a postdoctoral fellow at the State University of New York in Binghamton. Dr. Lampinen's research focuses on the subjective experience of false memories, mechanisms people use to avoid false memories, and applications of memory research to legal issues such as the accuracy of eyewitness identification and efforts to recover missing or wanted individuals (i.e., prospective person memory). Dr. Lampinen has published 45 book chapters and journal articles, has edited two books, and is under contract for a book on missing persons cases (Missing in America) and an introductory book on human memory (Memory 101). Dr. Lampinen is a recipient of the University of Arkansas' Outstanding Mentor Award and Fulbright College of Arts and Sciences' Master Researcher Award. He lives in Fayetteville, Arkansas, with his wife Stephanie.

Jeffrey S. Neuschatz received his BS at Roger Williams University in 1992 and his PhD at Binghamton University in 1999, and is associate professor and chair of the Psychology Department at the University of Alabama in Huntsville. Dr. Neuschatz is the coauthor of more than 30 scholarly works. His work has appeared in leading academic journals including *Law and Human Behavior* and *Journal of Experimental Psychology: Learning, Memory, and Cognition*. He is the recipient of the University of Alabama–Huntsville Foundation Award for Creative Achievement.

Andrew D. Cling received his AB at the University of Missouri at Columbia in 1979 and his PhD at Vanderbilt University in 1987, and is professor and chair of the Department of Philosophy at the University of Alabama in Huntsville. Dr. Cling's research in philosophy is currently focused on questions in the theory of knowledge. In particular, he is interested in a family of ancient skeptical paradoxes that seem to show that some of our core assumptions about having reasons for belief and good standards for intellectual judgment are inconsistent. Dr. Cling is also engaged in inter-disciplinary work on memory and eyewitness identification. Dr. Cling's papers have appeared in such journals as *Philosophy and Phenomenological Research, Synthese, Philosophical Studies, Philosophy of Science,* and *Philosophical Psychology.*

CHAPTER

Twenty-Seven Years

Twenty-seven years is an awfully long time. Twenty-seven years ago one of us was still in graduate school (AC), one of us was just out of high school (JL), and one of us had just had his bar mitzvah (JN). The Soviet Union was still considered the United States' chief nemesis, and Ronald Reagan was president of the United States. Twenty-seven years ago IBM had just released its XT personal computer, which came with a whopping 128 kB of memory and a floppy disk drive to boot. The World Wide Web was not yet invented, and cell phones were in their infancy. There was no Facebook. There was no Farmtown. There was no Wii.

In 27 years, a young adult, just out of high school, goes through a series of milestones that may include going to college, starting one's career, forming new friendships, travel, courtship and marriage, parenthood, and many other changes. One's hair can fall out. Or it can turn gray. In the United States, the average person lives 78 years (World Bank, 2010). Twenty-seven years is more than one third of the typical person's life and close to one half of the typical person's adult life.

For Michael Green, 27 years was the time of his longest nightmare (Solano, 2010). Back in 1983, four men abducted and sexually assaulted a woman in Houston. The men got away after a police chase, and investigators immediately started canvassing the area. They stopped males who matched the general description of the perpetrators and showed them to the victim to see if she could identify them. When Michael Green was stopped and shown to the victim, shortly after the crime, she failed to identify him as one of her attackers. But the police did not stop there. A week later, the victim was shown a photographic lineup that included a picture of Michael Green, as well as pictures of several other men. When the victim saw the lineup, she identified Green, even though a week earlier she had not. Later on, Green was put in a live lineup and shown to the victim again. She identified him again. At trial she indicated that she was absolutely certain that Green was her attacker. Based on her identification, Green was convicted and sentenced to 75 years in prison.

There were a number of reasons to be concerned about the victim's identification in this case. For one thing, shortly after her attack, when her memory was freshest, the victim failed to identify Green as her attacker. Then, a week later, when her memory was presumably less fresh, she did identify Green. Additionally, Green was shown to the victim multiple times, once shortly after the assault, once in a photo lineup a week later, then a bit later in a live lineup. This identification procedure is bound to lead to problems, because it makes it obvious to the witness who the police suspect of the crime. It may also result in an elevated feeling of familiarity with the suspect's face.

Despite problems with the identification procedure, the jury convicted Green. Unfortunately, the jury was mistaken. In 2010, new DNA tests were ordered in Green's case, and he was exonerated. An innocent man, he had spent 27 years of his life in prison. While in prison, his mother had died. He was not able to go to her funeral. Michael Green will never get those 27 years back.

To date, there have been 258 DNA exoneration cases in the United States (Innocence Project, 2010). That's 258 and counting. In the average case, the person exonerated spent 13 years in prison before being released. In 70% of the cases, the person exonerated was a member of a racial or ethnic minority group. Importantly, for the present book, a mistaken eyewitness identification was a contributing cause in more than 75% of these wrongful convictions (see Figure 1.1). Of the cases involving mistaken eyewitness identifications, more than one third of cases involved two or more witnesses making the same mistaken identification.

The 258 DNA exoneration cases likely represent the tip of the iceberg when it comes to wrongful convictions. About three quarters of DNA exoneration cases involve sexual assaults (Gross, Jacoby, Matheson, Montgomery, & Patel, 2005). This is because biological evidence is more likely to be available in sexual assault cases than in other types of cases. As eyewitness researcher John Tuttle put it, "Unless the guy robbing that 7-11 store gets pretty damned excited, he's not going to be leaving behind any biological fluids" (cited by Wells, n.d.-a). Without available biological evidence, there may be no way for individuals convicted of other types of crimes to establish their factual innocence. Given that rapists make up only 10% of the state prison population in the United States—and only one third of those cases involve sexual assaults by strangers—it has been estimated that the number of undetected wrongful convictions in the United States numbers in the thousands (Gross et al., 2005).

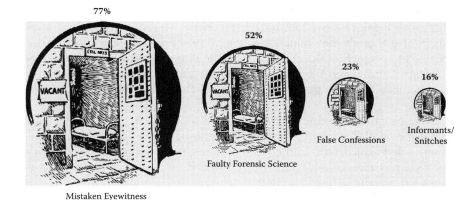

77%

52%

23%

16%

False Confessions

Informants/
Snitches

Faulty Forensic Science

Mistaken Eyewitness
Identifications

FIGURE 1.1   Contributing factors in the first 225 DNA exoneration cases. Percentages sum to more than 100% because in some cases more than one factor was involved. (*Source*: Based on data obtain from The Innocence Project at the Benjamin N. Cardozo School of Law at Yeshiva University, http://www.innocenceproject.org/understand/; clip art used to create the image obtained from the Open Clipart Library, http://www.openclipart.org; clip art image drawn by Johnny_automatic.)

☐ The Science of Eyewitness Identification

The science of eyewitness memory has been around for more than a century and in the past 30 years has produced a wealth of important findings that can be used by social policy makers to improve the criminal justice system. The focus of this book is on those variables that impact eyewitness identification accuracy. We are interested in cases where police show a witness one or more people and ask the witness to make an identification. There are different procedures that police can use in order to see if a witness can identify a suspect. For instance, in Michael Green's case, the first identification attempt involved a procedure called a *showup*. A *showup* is an identification procedure in which a witness is shown a single suspect and is asked if this is the person who committed the crime. Showups can be conducted live, as in Michael Green's case. These are sometimes called *corporeal showups*. Showups can also be conducted by showing the witness a photograph of the suspect. These are called *photographic showups*.

The second time the victim saw Michael Green, he was in a *lineup*. In a *lineup*, a witness is shown multiple people (often six) and is asked to indicate which individual, if any, committed the crime. A good lineup should have a single *suspect* and a number of *foils* (commonly five; foils are also sometimes called *fillers* or *distracters*). The suspect is the person who the police think might have committed the crime. The foils are known to be innocent, although they match the general description of the culprit. Foils are used to protect innocent suspects. If the lineup procedures are fair (see Chapters 2 and 4) and the suspect is innocent, a witness who makes a mistake is more likely to pick one of the foils than he or she is to pick the suspect.

Lineups can be conducted live or with a set of photos. Live lineups are sometimes called *corporeal lineups*, and photographic lineups are sometimes called *photoarrays*. In the United States, photoarrays are often made up of six pictures, arranged in two rows of three photos. These are sometimes informally referred to as *six packs*. In the United States, photoarrays are far and away more common than corporeal lineups (Fulero & Wrightsman, 2009). One reason for this is that it is typically much easier to put together the lineup when all you need to do is find photographs of foils who match the description of the culprit, as opposed to finding live people who match the description of the culprit. Additionally, under U.S. law, suspects in corporeal lineups have a right to counsel, whereas suspects in photoarrays do not (*United States v. Ash*, 1973).

For the most part, research psychologists study eyewitness memory by conducting experiments. In a typical eyewitness experiment, participants view a mock crime that may be in the form of a videotaped re-creation or a slide presentation, or may be staged live. In some experiments, participants are deceived into believing an actual crime has occurred (e.g., theft of a computer). In other experiments, participants know all along that it is just a simulation of a crime. Following the mock crime, there is usually a retention interval. The retention interval is simply the time that passes between the event and the attempted identification. Following the retention interval, the participants may be shown a lineup (or showup) and asked to make a decision. For half the participants, the lineup includes the person who committed the crime. This is called a *target-present lineup.* Target-present lineups mimic the situation where the police have a suspect, and the suspect is in fact guilty of the crime. For the other half of the participants, the lineup does not include the person who committed the crime. This is called a *target-absent lineup*. Target-absent lineups are meant to mimic the situation where the police have a suspect, but the suspect is in fact innocent of the crime. The advantage of using experimental techniques such as these is that they allow researchers to examine how accurate witnesses are under varying conditions. The researchers can measure the number of correct identifications of the suspect in the target-present lineup and the number of mistaken identifications of the suspect in the target-absent lineup and see what factors influence accuracy.

To give just one example, consider a clever study by Pigott, Brigham, and Bothwell (1990). They obtained the cooperation of bank managers at a number of different banks to conduct the study. At each bank, a volunteer entered the bank, went to the island where people fill out their deposit slips, and then went up to a teller and tried to cash an obviously forged postal money order. The money order was a $10 money order with an extra "1" written on it in ink so that it said $110. All the tellers who were approached in this way refused to cash the money order. The volunteer then acted irritated, took the money order back, and left the bank. The tellers informed their supervisors, and a few hours later a researcher posing as a plainclothes detective interviewed the tellers and showed them photoarrays that either included the culprit or did not include the culprit. The lineups had been constructed for the researchers by an actual police detective. When the tellers were shown the target-present lineup, the suspect was identified about half of the time. When the tellers were shown the target-absent lineup, an innocent person was mistakenly identified close to 40% of the time. Keep in mind that the tellers in this experiment thought that a real crime had occurred and that they were being interviewed by a real police officer.

In the past 30 years, hundreds of studies of eyewitness identification have been conducted. These studies shed light on the factors that can influence eyewitness accuracy. More importantly, the studies have had an impact on police practice, training, and policies (Wells et al., 2000). In the present book, we will be discussing some of the most important variables that have been identified by eyewitness researchers.

□ The Scope of the Problem

How big of a problem is mistaken eyewitness identification? There is no way to know for sure. According to survey research, eyewitness evidence plays a critical role in at least 77,000 criminal cases per year in the United States (Wells et al., 1998). Archival studies of actual eyewitness identification attempts have found that witnesses falsely identify foils around 20% of the time (Valentine, Pickering, & Darling, 2003). This number likely underestimates the number of foil identifications, because police sometimes record foil identifications by simply noting that the suspect was not identified (Wells, n.d.-a). This means that at least one out of five identification attempts results in the selection of an innocent person. If real witnesses to real crimes make the mistake of picking innocent foils, then real witnesses to real crimes undoubtedly also make the mistake of picking innocent suspects. After all, from a witness's point of view, an innocent foil and an innocent suspect are functionally equivalent (neither is the culprit).

In an attempt to provide a more precise answer to the question of how often witnesses identify innocent suspects, Levi (1998) derived an estimate of the probability that a suspect is guilty, given that the suspect has been chosen from a lineup, by using insights from probability theory (i.e., the Bayes theorem). First, consider a simplified case, where half of all lineups contain a guilty suspect and half of all lineups contain an innocent suspect (i.e., in the real world, there are just as many target-present and target-absent lineups). Statisticians would say the *base rate* for guilt is 50% and would denote it by saying p(G) = .50. Assuming that base rate, Levi pointed out that the probability of guilt, given that a suspect is chosen from a lineup, can be given by the following simplified version of the Bayes theorem:

$$p(G\,|\,C) = \frac{p(C\,|\,TP)}{p(C\,|\,TP) + p(C\,|\,TA)}$$

In this equation, p(G|C) (is the probability that the person is guilty given that they were chosen from a lineup, p(C|TP) is the probability of choosing a suspect from a target-present lineup, and p(C|TA) the probability of choosing a suspect from a target-absent lineup. Based on values taken from a number of published peer-reviewed studies, Levi estimated the probability of choosing the suspect from a target-present lineup was about 44% and the probability of choosing the suspect from a fair target-absent lineup was about 9.17%. So putting those values back into the equation, one gets the following:

$$p(G\,|\,C) = \frac{.44}{.44 + .0917} = .83$$

So if Levi's assumptions are correct, about 83% of the suspects identified from lineups are guilty and about 17% are innocent. That's quite a startling conclusion: Levi's calculations suggest that 17% of the suspects identified from lineups are innocent!

This value, of course, is just an estimate and depends on whether the right values were used for p(G), p(C|TP), and p(C|TA). Levi argued that the estimate is probably a conservative estimate. First, Levi argued that actual witnessing conditions are usually not as good as they are in laboratory studies. Thus, the actual value of p(C|TP) is probably less than 44% and the value of p(C|TA) is probably more than 9.17%. Second, the value given for p(C|TA) assumes that fair lineup procedures were being used, but this is not always the case in real life (see Chapters 2 and 4). Thus, p(C|TA) may be even higher. Levi argued that these considerations suggest that the actual rate of mistaken suspect identifications might be more than 17% in real-world lineups.

The estimate provided by Levi also depends heavily on the base rate of guilt. The base rate indicates what percentage of all police lineups actually includes a guilty suspect. You can see why base rates matter. If the base rate of guilt was 100%, then all suspect identifications would be correct identifications, even if witnesses made their decisions by rolling a six-sided die or reading chicken entrails. If the base rate of guilt was 0%, then all suspect identifications would be mistaken identifications. The basic principle is that, everything else being equal, the higher the base rate for guilt, the more likely it is that a suspect who has been identified by a witness is guilty. As p(G) increases, p(G|C) increases. Figure 1.2 shows the effects of base rates on the probability that someone is guilty, given that they have been chosen from a lineup (based on the estimates of p(C|TP) and p(C|TA) that Levi derived from prior research). Levi argued that the base rate of guilt may be less than 50%, because police may identify someone as a suspect simply because he or she matches the description and was in the area, resulting in many innocent suspects being put into lineups. That's certainly what happened in Michael Green's case.

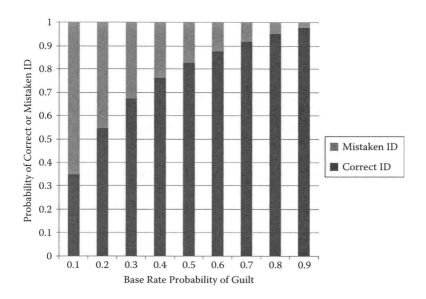

FIGURE 1.2 Conditional probability that suspect is guilty or innocent given that suspect was identified by a witness. The conditional probabilities are shown as a function of the base rate of guilt. Assumes values of p(C|TP) and p(C|TA) derived from Levi (1998).

☐ Plan for the Book

There is good reason to believe that there is a problem of mistaken identifications. We believe that the key to addressing this problem is to use psychological theory and research to develop practices and approaches that can be of service to the criminal justice system. In what follows, we describe some of that research. In Chapter 2, we describe basic psychological theory that relates to eyewitness identification. These theories cover the whole range of experimental psychology including perception, memory, and social reasoning. We next describe, in Chapter 3, some of the most important *estimator variables* that impact identification accuracy. An estimator variable is a variable that impacts witness memory but that the criminal justice system has no control over (e.g., how well lit the crime scene was, or how far away the perpetrator was). We then describe a range of important *system variables* that can have an impact on accuracy (Chapter 4). A system variable is a variable that impacts accuracy and that is under the control of the criminal justice system (e.g., the instructions given to the witness). Finally, we discuss what we refer to as *indicia of reliability* (Chapter 5). By indicia of reliability, we mean variables that are correlated with accuracy, even though they don't directly cause the witness to be accurate or inaccurate. For instance, on average, confident witnesses are more accurate than less confident witnesses. However, confidence does not cause the witness to be accurate. As we will see, factors like confidence are related to accuracy, but the relationship is imperfect and can sometimes be misleading.

In Chapters 6 and 7, we will move to applications of the broad body of knowledge developed by eyewitness researchers over the past 30 years. In Chapter 6 we will describe studies that have examined eyewitness identification accuracy in real-world settings. We will find that, for the most part, these studies of real-world witnesses tend to confirm the findings of laboratory studies. In Chapter 7, we will discuss the role of eyewitness experts as witnesses in the court system. We will find that the eyewitness expert has an important role to play in informing the court system about the factors that influence eyewitness memory.

☐ A Final Word

Sometimes, when talking to reporters or lawyers, the topic of eyewitness identification errors will come up. In such conversations, we sometimes hear that eyewitness testimony is notoriously inaccurate. As we have reviewed above, it is true that eyewitnesses can sometimes make grievous errors, and it is important to be aware of this fact. But to state that eye-witness testimony is error prone is to miss the point by means of over-simplification. If all we had to say was that eyewitnesses make errors, we wouldn't need to write a book. A brief article would do. And there wouldn't be a need for over 2,000 articles and counting on the topic of eyewitness testimony. An article or two would do.

The truth is more complex and nuanced than the simple conclusion that eyewitness reports are inaccurate. What researchers have found over the last three decades is that sometimes witnesses are accurate and some-times they are inaccurate, and that there is a set of variables that can be used to assess the likely accuracy of the witness (estimator variables) and inform police practice (system variables). This is an extraordinarily posi-tive message, because it suggests concrete steps that can be taken to help make the criminal justice system work better. When the wrong person is convicted of a crime, not only does an innocent person languish in prison, but also the actual culprit is free to commit additional crimes. That's why it's so important to get things right. This book is about how to get things right.

Theoretical Approaches to Eyewitness Identification

Famed social psychologist Kurt Lewin (1952, p. 169) once commented, "There is nothing so practical as a good theory." Most psychologists who do applied work understand well the interplay between application and basic psychological theory. Not only does basic research in human cognition and social processes inform our understanding of the performance of the eyewitness in choosing (or not choosing) someone from a lineup, but the reverse is also true. The applied questions that eyewitness researchers pose oftentimes provide new theoretical insights. A colleague in graduate school once said to one of us (JL), "In applied research you get your theoretical insights for free." That's part of what makes research on the topic of eyewitness identification so exciting and rewarding.

Another important fact about role theory in eyewitness research is that it is multifaceted. The theoretical issues that touch on the psychology of eyewitness identification run the gambit of human experimental psychology: memory, social influence, decision making, emotion, personality, and perception. All of these basic psychological mechanisms influence eyewitness identification. The current chapter provides background for issues that we will be reviewing in the subsequent chapters. It by no means covers all of the theoretical issues relevant to eyewitness identification. In our view, that would require a review of all of psychology. Rather, in this chapter we review some of the most important theoretical perspectives that relate to the accuracy of eyewitness identification. These ideas will be returned to again and again during the remainder of this monograph. This chapter is broken up into three main sections. First we discuss basic theory with regard to human memory that is useful for understanding eyewitness identification. Second, we discuss basic processes involved in human face perception and memory for faces. Third, we discuss theoretical frameworks that have been specifically designed to help us understand the nature of eyewitness identification.

☐ Human Memory

You are sitting on an old wooden bench at a bus terminal waiting for the 8:45 a.m. bus that is going to take you to Binghamton, New York, from Chicago. You are feeling a number of mixed emotions. On the one hand, you are looking forward to arriving in Binghamton, where you plan to spend a few days hanging out with old friends from graduate school. You are traveling to a 15-year reunion. On the other hand, it's going to be a long bus ride, 700 miles one way, and you're not looking forward to being on a crowded, smelly bus for that length of time. You obsessively check your coat pocket, making sure you haven't misplaced your bus ticket. A gentleman in a Chicago Bears knit cap approaches you, brandishes a silver gun, and politely asks you for your wallet. You comply, your heart racing. The man strolls off, looking back over his shoulder only once, as he makes his way out of the terminal. For a minute, you sit there in shock, not knowing what to do. You reach for your coat pocket and take out your cell phone to call 911. It looks like your trip is going to be delayed.

Basic Stages of Human Memory

The above example illustrates the type of situation that can happen in which eyewitness identification is going to be crucial. Once the police arrive, they will likely interview you. They will ask you what happened, what was stolen, what the gentleman looked like, what he was wearing, and a range of other questions. They might take you to the station and have you look through some mugshots. They might have you talk to a police artist to produce a composite of the thief. Or, if they catch someone who matches the general description you provided, the police might present you with a lineup or a showup (a one-person lineup).

What is interesting about all of this is that the robber is not there any longer. He is long gone. Yet, when the police ask you what the robber looked like, you are able to provide an answer. How does this occur? The answer must surely be that stored in the synapses of your brain is a mental representation of the event that just happened to you and what the robber looked like (Barsalou, 2008). That's what a memory is, a mental representation of a past event. This memory representation is not an exact or literal copy of what happened, and, in fact, it is well established that memory representations are subject to distortion (Lampinen, Neuschatz,

& Payne, 1998). Your accuracy when answering each of the questions that the police ask you depends crucially on this memory representation, the veridicality of the representation, your ability to access it, and your ability to reason with that representation once it has been retrieved.

Memory psychologists make distinctions between three basic stages of memory processing known as encoding, storage, and retrieval (Galotti, 2004). Encoding involves processing perceptual information (e.g., sounds, sights, smells, and contextual information) into a mental code that can be further processed. It is important to note that encoding is not a passive process, but rather involves selection and elaboration (Weinstein & Mayer, 1986). Selection occurs because people have limited attentional capacity (Kahneman, 1973). People are unable to process all of the environmental stimuli available at any given time. These capacity limitations require that people selectively attend to some information and ignore other information. Capacity is further limited by stress, pressure, and the need to engage in other activities. Because the encoding stage is selective, some information that may be relevant in later testimony is probably never mentally encoded at all. For instance, you would not be able to accurately answer a question about the culprit's shoes if you never really took note of his shoes.

In addition to being selective, the encoding stage of memory also involves elaboration. Elaboration involves interpreting events, making inferences, and drawing connections (Anderson, 1995). For instance, if you draw the inference that the perpetrator was a homeless person, then your memory for the perpetrator's actions and appearance may be colored by stereotypes you have about homeless people. This inference-making process is so commonplace that it typically happens automatically and without conscious effort. It is important to note that the information that actually gets encoded into memory is only that information that has been selected as well as elaborations that have been made on that information. Research indicates that people often have difficulty later distinguishing between what was actually experienced and the inferences that were made based on that information (Hannigan & Reinitz, 2001, 2003; Kleider, Pezdek, Goldinger, & Kirk, 2008; Lampinen, Faries, Neuschatz, & Toglia, 2000; Singer & Remillard, 2008). This tendency to confuse inferences that one made with events as they actually happened makes memory subject to distortion (Chan & McDermott, 2006; Erskine, Markham, & Howie, 2001; García-Bajos & Migueles, 2003; Greenberg, Westcott, & Bailey,1998; Lampinen et al., 1998; Roediger & McDermott, 2000; Tuckey & Brewer, 2003).

The storage phase involves retaining information in memory after encoding (Anderson, 1995). For instance, as a witness you would likely encode a variety of details into your memory representation for the above event. However, it is likely that several minutes would pass before the police arrived to take your report. During that time period, the information would need to be retained in your memory. After the initial police report is taken, you might be called on to answer questions again once a suspect had been caught. This may be days, weeks, or months later. Before trial the prosecutor might review your testimony with you. If the case goes to trial, you would be called on to answer questions under oath. You might recall the event in other circumstances too. For instance, you might recount the event in order to explain to your friends and relatives why your trip to Binghamton had been interrupted. In between each of these remindings, a representation of the details of the event would have to be stored in your memory. Research indicates that while in storage, memories are subject to distortion in the form of postevent information (Lindsay, 1993; Loftus, 1991; Okado & Stark, 2005). Postevent information is information that a person encounters after an event that is relevant to the event. For instance, a witness may read newspaper accounts of the crime or may hear what other witnesses said about the crime. Each of these encounters may provide details that become incorporated into the witness's memory for the event.

The final stage of memory is known as retrieval (Shiffrin & Atkinson, 1969). According to cue-dependent theories of memory, the act of retrieval will occur successfully only to the extent that contextual details that were available at the time of the original event are reactivated in the person's mind at the time he or she is trying to remember the event (Reingold, 2002; Tulving & Thompson, 1973). In other words, you will remember an event best when you are able to re-create in your mind the full context of the original event that you are trying to remember. The more contextual details, the better. The notion that retrieval depends crucially on the quality of the contextual cues available at retrieval provides some of the theoretical grounding for the cognitive interview technique developed by Fisher and Geiselman (1992; see Chapter 4 for a fuller description). Recommendations that have been developed by the U.S. Department of Justice regarding the interviewing of eyewitnesses explicitly recognize the fact that accurate memory depends on maximizing the number of retrieval cues available to the witness (Technical Working Group, 1999).

The retrieval stage of memory is also a time when memories are subject to distortion. In fact, the very word *retrieval* is misleading. A more apt word is *reconstruction* (Lampinen & Neuschatz, 2008). Consider the description of remembering offered by Sir Frederic Bartlett (1932) in his classic book *Remembering: A Study in Experimental and Social Psychology*:

> Remembering is not a completely independent function, entirely distinct from perceiving, imaging, or even from constructive thinking, but it has intimate relations with them all.... One's memory of an event reflects a blend of information contained in specific traces

encoded at the time it occurred, plus inferences based on knowledge, expectations, beliefs, and attitudes derived from other sources.

As Barlett's description implies, when you remember an event, you make use of a number of different types of information. You use knowledge structures called *scripts* and *schemas* that provide information about what typically happens during an event (Bower, Black, & Turner, 1979). For instance, your script for going to a baseball game might include knowledge that baseball games include a seventh-inning stretch and that people often order hot dogs at baseball games. Reconstruction also makes use of postevent information (Loftus, 1979). For instance, after leaving a baseball game you may read about it in the newspaper the next day, or may talk to a friend who was also at the game. Memory reconstruction can also lead to borrowing specific details from one event and incorporating them into one's memory for a related event (Odegard & Lampinen, 2004). For instance, you may remember an obnoxious fan screaming obscenities at one baseball game, when in fact the obnoxious fan screamed obscenities at a different baseball game. In attempting to remember the baseball game, you would *reconstruct* the event by combining information from all of these sources. Thought of in this way, remembering is a dynamic decision-making process that attempts to approximate the past by making use of all available information stored in memory to create a version of the past that is maximally coherent (see the Appendix for some philosophical implications of this view).

A good analogy that has been made by a number of different people is that the act of reconstruction is a lot like a paleontologist trying to make sense of a bunch of dinosaur bones, given a limited fossil record. Here is how Daniel Schacter (1996) described the process:

> For the paleontologist, the bone chips that are recovered on an archeological dig and the dinosaur that is ultimately reconstructed from them are not the same thing: the full blown dinosaur is constructed by combining the bone chips with other available fragments, in accordance with general knowledge of how the complete dinosaur should appear. Similarly, for the rememberer, the engram (the stored fragment of an episode) and the memory (the subjective experience of recollecting a past event) are not the same thing. The stored fragments contribute to the conscious experience of remembering, but they are only part of it. (pp. 69–70)

So "retrieving" an event is actually "reconstructing" the event. Recent research has shown that details from one event can be incorporated into memories for another event, in a process called *content borrowing*, to create vivid but false memories (Lampinen, Meier, Arnal, & Leding, 2005; Lampinen, Ryals, & Smith, 2008). And, indeed, recent evidence from neuroscience has shown that memories can oftentimes be quite labile during the retrieval stage (Lopez, 2000).

Varieties of Human Memory

In addition to the distinction between different functional stages of memory, memory psychologists also recognize a variety of different types of memory. Perhaps the best known of these distinctions was made in a classic paper by Atkinson and Shiffrin in the late 1960s (Atkinson & Shiffrin, 1968). According to Atkinson and Shiffrin's theory, representations of events go through three separate memory buffers known as *sensory memory*, *short-term memory*, and *long-term memory* (see Figure 2.1). In the above example, when the man approaches you with a gun, an image of the man's face is perceptually processed and stored in a memory buffer for a fraction of a second. This memory buffer is known as sensory memory and includes the basic perceptual details of the event. According to Atkinson and Shiffrin, some information from the sensory memory buffer is then transferred into short-term memory. Short-term memory stores information for a few seconds unless it is actively rehearsed. One major limitation on human cognition is that short-term memory has a limited capacity. For instance, it is typically estimated that a person can hold around seven items in short-term memory at a time (Miller, 1956). Because of this limitation, only a fraction of the information in sensory storage actually gets passed to short-term memory for detailed analysis. Finally, when information in short-term memory is processed at a sufficient level of depth, it can be passed on to long-term memory. Long-term memory contains information from one's entire life, and some psychologists even believe

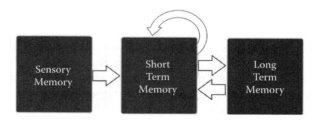

FIGURE 2.1   Components of the Atkinson and Shiffrin (1968) model of memory. (*Source*: Atkinson, R. C., & Shiffrin, R. M. (1968). Human memory: A proposed system and its control processes. In K. W. Spence & J. T. Spence (eds.), *The psychology of learning and motivation* (Vol. 1, pp. 89–195). New York: Academic Press.)

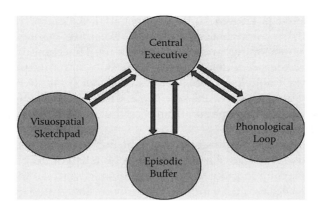

FIGURE 2.2 Components of the working memory model. (*Source*: Based on figure originally presented by Baddeley, A. D. (2000). The episodic buffer: A new component of working memory? *Trends in Cognitive Science, 4*, 417–423.)

that every piece of information that has ever been passed on to long-term memory is still stored in long-term memory (Shiffrin & Atkinson, 1969; Tulving, 1974; but see Loftus & Loftus, 1980). Long-term memory, according to this theory, is subject to retrieval failure. That is, although the relevant information may be present in long-term memory, without the appropriate retrieval cues, the information may never be retrieved.

Many of the details in Atkinson and Shiffrin's (1968) model have been contested, but the model still provides a nice way of thinking about the basic way human memory is organized. Subsequent research also elaborated on many of the ideas in the model. For instance, Baddeley and Hitch (1974) described a model of working memory that in many ways has replaced Atkinson and Shiffrin's (1968) simpler idea of how short-term memory works (see Figure 2.2). The Baddeley and Hitch (1974) model made two important contributions to our understanding of memory. First, at a functional level, Baddeley and Hitch (1974) argued that working memory was the place where problem solving and decision making occurred. That is, working memory, as the name implies, was the place where the actual work of reasoning with mental representations and memories happens. So when the police ask you which direction the perpetrator came from, you might replay the scene in your mind's eye. That replay of the event would be occurring in working memory. The second contribution of Baddeley and Hitch's (1974) model is that it held that working memory is actually made up of three components. One component of working memory processes primarily verbal information. This component is known as the *phonological loop* (Baddeley, Gathercole, & Papagno, 1998). Another component of working memory primarily processes visual information.

This component is known as the visuospatial sketchpad (Logie, 1995). Finally, another component is involved in executive management of the whole system, reasoning, and decision making. This component is called the *central executive* (Baddeley, 1996). About 30 years after proposing the original theory, Baddeley (2000) proposed another component of working memory that he termed the *episodic buffer*. The episodic buffer is responsible for combining information from the other buffers into a unified conscious experience.

When the attacker approaches you in the bus terminal, you register his face in the visual spatial sketchpad. When he tells you to give him your money or he's going to shoot you, you process his words in the phonological loop. The verbal and visual information are integrated into a unified perceptual experience within the episodic buffer. When you decide on your course of action (i.e., comply with his demands), you are likely using the central executive.

Theorists have also made distinctions among different types of longterm memory. The best known of these is the multiple memory system proposed by Endel Tulving (Tulving, 1972, 1983, 1999). According to Tulving, long-term memory can be thought of as being made up of three partially overlapping systems. The first of these is *procedural memory*. Procedural memory stores information about how to perform physical and mental tasks such as swinging a golf club, doing long division, or taking your wallet out of your pocket to hand to a robber. *Semantic memory* stores factual information that lacks details about where that information was encountered. For instance, you might know that Columbus traveled to America thinking he was en route to India, but it is unlikely that you remember the specific event of learning that information. It is just a fact that you know. Similarly, you know your name, but you almost certainly don't remember the specific event wherein you first learned your name. Lastly, Tulving argued that there is a memory system known as *episodic memory*. Episodic memory involves memories for specific events from your life, such as the last movie you went to, the time you got robbed at the bus station in Chicago, or the jerk yelling obscenities at the baseball game. Tulving (2002) has referred to episodic memory as a kind of "mental time travel" because it involves mentally re-creating the original event. What the eyewitness is typically remembering are details about specific events that occurred at a particular time and place. Consequently, almost all research on eyewitness memory involves episodic memory.

Signal Detection Theory

In addition to making distinctions between different stages of memory processing and different types of memory storage, an understanding of eyewitness memory requires a understanding of how psychologists think about the basic processes involved in making memory judgments. Imagine that the police approach you some time after the incident at the bus station and show you a picture of an individual that they suspect may be the culprit (i.e., showup; Steblay, Dysart, Fulero, & Lindsay, 2001). You are asked, "Is this the person who robbed you?" How do you make the decision?

One important theory that can be useful in analyzing these situations is signal detection theory (Parks, 1966). To illustrate signal detection theory, imagine you decide to conduct the following experiment. You obtain a sample of participants, and each participant is shown yearbook-style photographs of 50 people. Each picture is shown for 2 seconds, and you ask the participants to try to remember the faces they are shown. Participants then engage in an unrelated task for 10 minutes (known as the *retention interval*). After the retention interval, you give them a test. The test is made up of 100 pictures. Fifty of the pictures are of the people that had just been studied (*old* pictures), and 50 pictures are of never-before-seen people (*new* pictures). For each picture, you ask your participants to indicate whether the picture is *old* or *new*. Tests like these are called *old/new recognition tests*.

Given the setup of your experiment, there are four possible outcomes. You can see these outcomes in Figure 2.3.

- Participants can say "old" when an item really is old. These correct responses are called *hits* by memory psychologists. In eyewitness research, this is similar to a witness who correctly identifies the culprit.
- Participants can say "old" when an item is really new. These incorrect responses are called *false alarms* by memory psychologists. In eyewitness research, this is similar to a witness who mistakenly identifies an innocent person.
- Participants can say "new" when an item is really old. These incorrect responses are called *misses* by memory psychologists. In eyewitness

	Face was seen	Face was not seen
Witness says, "I saw that face."	HIT	FALSE ALARM (FA)
Witness says, "I didn't see that face."	MISS	CORRECT REJECTION

FIGURE 2.3   Possible outcomes on an old/new recognition test.

research, this is similar to a witness who fails to identify the culprit and the guilty person consequently goes free.

• Lastly participants can say "new" when an item really is new. These correct responses are called *correct rejections*. In eyewitness research, this is similar to a witness who correctly says the culprit is not there.

Typically, memory researchers report only the *hit rate* and the *false alarm rate*, because the miss rate and correct rejection rate can be derived easily from the hit and false alarm rates. For instance, if there were 50 previously studied pictures and the participant had 40 hits, then there must have been 10 misses. And if there were 50 pictures that were not studied, and the participant had 20 false alarms, there must have been 30 correct rejections.

So what kinds of mental gyrations do people go through to decide whether or not an item was studied? According to signal detection theory, when an item such as a picture is shown on a recognition memory test, that item is compared to representations stored in memory. If an item on the memory test is very similar to one or more items stored in memory, it will produce a strong subjective sense of *familiarity* or *memory strength*. If an item on a memory test is not very similar to anything in memory, it will produce a weaker feeling of familiarity or memory strength. It is important to note that both *old* items and *new* items will produce some sense of familiarity that can be thought of as varying along a continuum from weak to strong.

When considering the entire set of items, both the familiarity of the new items and the familiarity of the old items will be normally distributed, with the old items being more familiar on average than the new items, but with some overlap existing between the distributions. You can see a graphical depiction of this situation in Figure 2.4.

The average familiarity of the old items will be greater than the average familiarity of the new items, but the trick is to decide for any particular item whether it is old or new. The better the person's memory, the further apart these two distributions will be, and the easier it will be for the person to distinguish between the old and the new items. In signal detection theory, the distance between the two distributions is known as d′ (pronounced *D prime*). Technically, d′ is the distance between the distributions measured in standard deviation units. Large values of d′ reflect good memory (see Figure 2.5). Small values of d′ reflect poor memory. A participant who is completely incapable of distinguishing old items from new items would have a d′ score of 0. A participant who has a great memory might have a d′ score of 1 or 2 or 3. If a participant had more false alarms than hits, they would have a negative d′ score.

The measure of memory strength in signal detection theory (d′) is only part of the story. According to signal detection theory, a participant's task on a recognition memory test is difficult and ambiguous. This is because

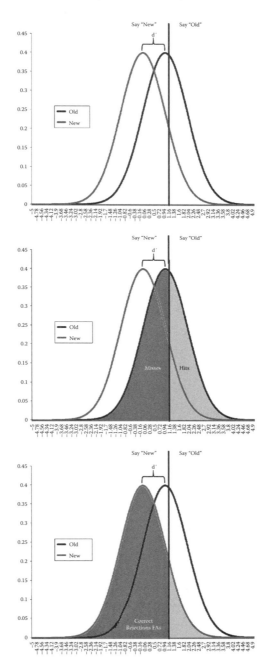

FIGURE 2.4   Signal detection theory.

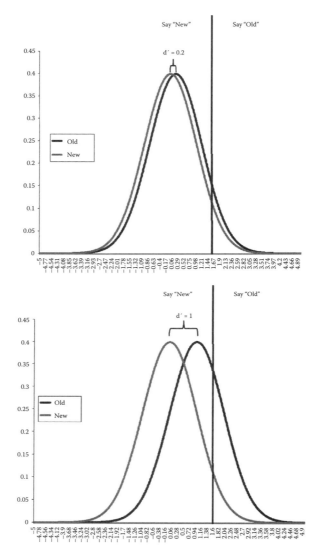

FIGURE 2.5 Graphs illustrating changes in d' in signal detection theory. The top figure illustrates poor memory and a low value for d'. The bottom figure shows someone with better memory and a higher value for d'.

the distributions for the two types of items (old items and new items) overlap. Overall, old items are more familiar than new items, but some new items are more familiar than some old items. Because of this, participants have to decide how much familiarity a face has to have before they are

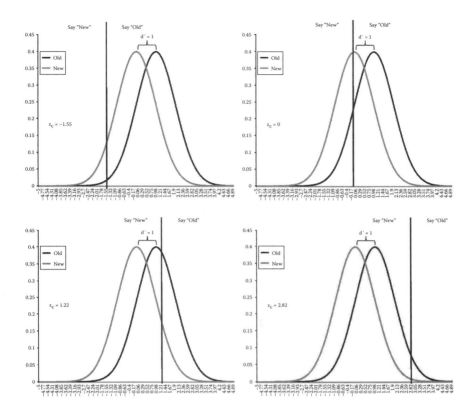

FIGURE 2.6 Graphs illustrating changes in response criterion in signal detection theory. Graph on top left illustrates a very liberal decision criterion. Graph on bottom right illustrates a very conservative decision criterion.

willing to say it was studied. This is known as the participant's *response criterion* (sometimes this is called the *response bias*). The response criterion is shown in the graphs as a straight horizontal line indicating the familiarity that is needed before the participant will indicate that an item was studied. Anything that is more familiar than the criterion will be called "old." Anything less familiar than the criterion will be called "new."

The placement of the response criterion is up to the individual. You can see the consequences of setting different response criteria in Figure 2.6. Participants can decide to be very liberal, and respond "old" even if the degree of familiarity is relatively low. This will increase the proportion of hits, but will come at a cost of more false alarms. A participant might decide to be very conservative and respond "old" only when the degree of familiarity is very high. This will limit false alarms but come at the cost of fewer hits. Or a participant may adopt a neutral response criterion and split the difference between the two types of errors.

According to signal detection theory, a particular participant's performance on an old/new recognition test is characterized both by how good the participant's memory is (i.e., d′) and by the response criterion they decide to use.

Imagine you do the study where students study yearbook photos. After the study phase and retention interval, you hypnotize half of the participants in an attempt to improve their memories (see Chapter 4). You then give them an old/new recognition test. Imagine that the hit rate for students who were not hypnotized is 60% and the hit rate for those who were hypnotized is 80%. Considered in isolation, that sounds like the hypnosis was a pretty big help. However, if you find out that the false alarm rate in the no-hypnosis group is 5% and the false alarm rate in the hypnosis group is 15%, you might change your mind. From the standpoint of signal detection theory, we want to know if those differences reflect changes in memory strength, changes in the response bias, or both. Luckily signal detection theory makes it possible to estimate memory strength (d′) by looking at the hit rates and false alarm rates combined. Details of the calculations can be found in Snodgrass and Corwin (1998) as well as several other references. In this example, we can calculate d′ for the hypnosis group as 1.88, and we can calculate d′ for the not-hypnotized group as 1.90. So in this hypothetical example, hypnosis had no appreciable effect on memory. It changed only the response criterion that participants were setting. Participants set a more liberal response criterion when they were hypnotized. This led to more hits and more false alarms in our hypothetical example.

Throughout chapters later in this monograph, we will make use of insights from signal detection theory. It is important to note that memory researchers sometimes debate some of the technical details underlying signal detection theory (Ratcliff, Sheu, & Gronlund, 1992; Singer, 2009; Yonelinas, 1994). Those debates are important, but are beyond the scope of the current volume. For the current volume, the most important point is that signal detection theory provides us with a way of estimating memory strength and response criterion, with large values of d′ reflecting better memory.

Dual Process Theories

Signal detection theory is a useful starting point for understanding how eyewitness memory works. However, one limitation of signal detection theory is that it fails to fully account for the variety of different memory experiences that people have. In signal detection theory, memory is seen as being represented along a single dimension of memory strength or familiarity. Many memory theorists believe that this is an oversimplification (Diana, Reder, Arndt, & Park, 2006; Jacoby, 1991; Joordens & Hockley, 2000; Lampinen, Watkins, & Odegard, 2006; Mandler, 1980; Yonelinas, 1994). These theorists think it makes sense to distinguish among qualitatively different types of memory. The best known of these theories posit the existence of two qualitatively distinct memory processes. Thus, these theories are known as *dual process theories*.

One of the most influential dual process models was proposed by George Mandler (1980). According to Mandler, recognition memory (such as recognizing a face) can occur in two distinct ways: recall and familiarity. *Recall* involves the conscious re-experiencing of the item in the context in which it was originally experienced. For instance, a student once told one of us (JML) that he could remember the exact wording of the lame joke one of us (JML) told when introducing a concept in class. Mandler distinguished this type of recognition memory from what he called familiarity. *Familiarity* involves a feeling or intuition that the item was previously presented, in the absence of an exact memory for the context in which the item was presented. Mandler gave the example of seeing someone on a bus, knowing that you have seen the person before, but not being sure exactly where you know them from (a common experience for most of us). According to Mandler, feelings of familiarity occur because the individual features that make up the item are tightly bound together in memory. Thus, when you see the person on the bus, you know that you have previously seen that exact combination of eyes, nose, mouth, facial shape, hairline, and so on, but you cannot recall exactly where you saw that person before. Mandler called these types of associations *intra-item associations*, that is, associations between the features that make up the item. In recall, recognition of the item occurs because there is a tight connection between the individual item and the context in which it was originally encountered. Thus, when you see the person's face, you can also remember that you saw the person at a Halloween party and that the person was dressed as Humpty Dumpty and made a drunken fool of himself. Such connections between the item and the context in which the item occurred are known as *inter-item associations*.

Mandler's view of memory was influential and led to the development of other important dual process models. One of the most influential was Jacoby's (1991) *process dissociation model*. According to Jacoby, remembering an item in the context of its original occurrence can be thought of as *recollection*, whereas having a feeling that an item was previously presented devoid of the context can be thought of as *familiarity*. One important concept that Jacoby introduced was the idea that familiarity, at least some of the time, occurs because prior experience with an item makes the perceptual processing of that item easier in the future (Jacoby & Dallas, 1981). Jacoby referred to this idea as *perceptual fluency*. Mental processing of any individual item (e.g., a face, word, or song) requires some time and effort from your perceptual system. However, when you are presented with an item that you have previously experienced, it is a little easier for your perceptual system to process the item on the second go around. You are not consciously aware of this increased fluency of processing; however, subjectively the increased ease of processing gives rise to a subjective feeling of familiarity. Jacoby thus argued that recognition memory sometimes involves an inference that we make based on how easy or difficult it is to perceptually process an item.

Another important contribution of process dissociation theory is that it provides a technique for teasing apart the contributions of recollection and familiarity. The basic principle is that recollection allows you to make a response that depends upon the context in which the item was presented, whereas familiarity does not allow this kind of context-dependent response. For instance, imagine I show you pictures of 100 people. Half of the people are holding guns (i.e., bad people), and half of the people are holding kittens (i.e., nice people). Imagine that when you return to the lab on the following day, I show you 200 pictures of people who aren't holding anything. One hundred of the pictures are pictures of the people you saw the previous day. One hundred of the pictures are of completely new people. As I show each picture, I ask you to say "yes" only to people who were holding guns. Successful performance of this task requires conscious recollection. That is, you have to remember not just that a particular face was presented but also that it was presented in the context of a gun.

Jacoby (1991) used this insight to create a formal way of measuring recollection and familiarity called the *process dissociation procedure*. The process dissociation procedure takes advantage of the *logic of opposition*. Participants take two kinds of tests, called *inclusion* and *exclusion* tests. Given the example we have been working with, the two tests might be set up as follows.

- *Inclusion test*: The test is made up of 50 nice people, 50 bad people, and 100 new people. You are asked to say "no" to any person whose picture was not shown on the previous day. You are asked to say "yes" to any person whose picture you saw the previous day, regardless of whether they were holding a gun or a kitten. Thus you should *include* both people who were holding guns and people who were holding kittens.
- *Exclusion test:* This test is made up of 50 good people, 50 bad people, and 100 new people. You are asked to say "yes" to any person who you saw holding a gun the previous day, and to say "no" to anybody

who was holding a kitten or anybody whose picture wasn't present at all. Thus you should *exclude* people who were holding kittens but *include* people who were holding guns.

The key measure is how often you say "yes" to the people who had been holding kittens. Here's why: If you are using conscious recollection, you should respond differently on the inclusion test and the exclusion test to the people who were holding kittens on the previous day. On the inclusion test, you should say "yes" to people who were holding kittens, whereas on the exclusion test, you should say "no" to people who were holding kittens. Performing this task requires recollection, because *recollection* is defined as remembering the context in which an item was presented.

In Figure 2.7, the Venn diagrams are drawn to illustrate the probability of saying "yes" in response to a person you saw holding a kitten on the previous day. In the inclusion condition, you should include a person holding a kitten if he or she is familiar. You should also include a person holding a kitten if you consciously recollect him or her holding the kitten. Thus, both of the circles are shaded. In the exclusion condition, you should include people if they seem familiar, but you should exclude them if you can consciously recollect that they were holding a kitten. By inspecting the Venn diagrams you can see that, according to the theory, the probability of conscious recollection (R) is simply the difference between saying "yes" to people who were holding kittens in the inclusion (I) and exclusion (E) conditions:

$$R = I - E \qquad\qquad (2.1)$$

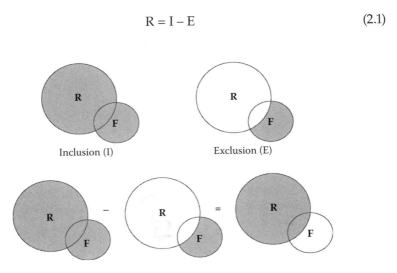

FIGURE 2.7   Estimating recollection using the process dissociation procedure.

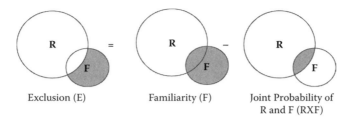

Exclusion (E)   Familiarity (F)   Joint Probability of
                                                R and F (RXF)

FIGURE 2.8   Estimating familiarity using the process dissociation procedure.

Let's say that when people are shown pictures of individuals they had previously seen holding kittens, they say "yes" to those pictures 60% of the time in the inclusion condition and 20% of the time in the exclusion condition. Then, according to the logic of opposition, people are consciously recollecting the context of the pictures 40% of the time (60 − 20 = 40).

It is also possible to estimate familiarity. To do so, you need to know a little probability theory and you need to apply a little algebra. First, examine that portion of the Venn diagrams where the R circle and the F circle overlap. That's called the *joint probability* of R and F. Simply put, it's the probability of both recollection and familiarity occurring at the same time. When two events are independent (i.e., they don't influence each other), the joint probability of two events is equal to the product of their individual probabilities. In other words, the probability that both recollection and familiarity will occur at the same time is the probability of recollection occurring multiplied by the probability of familiarity occurring. The situation is shown in Figure 2.8.

The equation corresponding to the situation illustrated in Figure 2.8 is

$$E = F - RF \tag{2.2}$$

When you solve for F, the equation becomes

$$F = E / (1 - R) \tag{2.3}$$

Earlier we had said that the probability of saying "yes" in the exclusion condition was 20% (.20), and we estimated recollection to be 40% (.40). So our estimate of familiarity becomes

$$F = 0.20 / (1 - 0.40) = .3333 \text{ or } 33.33\% \tag{2.4}$$

So in this hypothetical example, if you are shown a picture on a memory test, there is a 33.33% chance that it will produce a feeling of familiarity in you that will be sufficient to allow you to recognize that it was on the study list the previous day. And there is a 40% chance that you will consciously recollect the context in which the face was presented.

The distinction between recollection and familiarity is an important one for a couple of different reasons. First, it is typically important that a witness not simply recognize a person but also be able to recognize the context in which he or she saw that person. For instance, in a phenomenon known as *unconscious transference*, an innocent person seen in one context may mistakenly be remembered as having been seen committing the crime (Phillips, Geiselman, Haghighi, & Lin, 1997; Ross, Ceci, Dunning, & Toglia, 1994).[1] Second, recollection is usually associated with higher levels of subjective confidence than is familiarity (Yonelinas, 2001). Confidence is one of the best predictors of jurors' judgments of the credibility of a witness (Cutler, Penrod, & Dexter, 1990; Fox & Walters, 1986; Lindsay, Wells, & Rumpel, 1981).

In many cases, researchers may not want to use the process dissociation procedure to estimate recollection. For one thing, one needs a large number of observations to get estimates using the technique. For another, the technique is controversial among memory psychologists (in particular, the assumption that recollection and familiarity are independent is a point of contention) (Curran & Hintzman, 1995; Dodson & Johnson, 1996; Graf & Komatsu, 1995; for replies, see Jacoby, 1997; Jacoby, Yonelinas, & Jennings, 1997). Because of this, alternative methods of measuring recollection and familiarity are sometimes used. One of these methods is called the *remember/know technique* (Gardiner, 1988; Gardiner & Java, 1990, 1991; Lampinen, Copeland, & Neuschatz, 2001; Lampinen, Faries, Neuschatz, & Toglia, 2000; Neuschatz et al., 2004; Rajaram, 1993, 1998; Tulving, 1985). In the remember/know technique, participants are asked to indicate whether an item is old or new. If they say it is old, they are asked whether they can recall specific details of the item's previous presentation, or if they believe the item is old for some other reason (e.g., it just seems familiar). If a participant believes that he or she can recall specific details of the item's presentation, then he or she makes a *remember* judgment. If a participant believes an item is old, but does not remember anything specific about the item's presentation, the participant makes a *know* judgment. Thus remember judgments can be used to indicate conscious recollection, whereas know judgments are used to indicate feelings of familiarity. Remember/know judgments provide an alternative way of measuring recollection and familiarity based on participants' self-reports. Of course, self-report data are open to challenge, and so the best approach is to come at the question from a variety of different perspectives and to seek converging evidence (Lampinen, Neushatz, & Payne, 1998).

☐ Theories of Face Perception and Memory

In the "Human Memory" section of this chapter, we described some basic theoretical views of human memory that are useful for understanding the applied issue of eyewitness identification. These theories concerned human memory writ large. However, the focus of the present monograph is specifically on the problem of eyewitness identification. Eyewitness identification typically deals with seeing a face in one context and then recognizing that face in a slightly different context. Because of this, it is useful for someone interested in eyewitness identification to have some basic knowledge of the processes involved in recognizing people's faces.

Functional Accounts of Face Processing

Faces are complex and highly socially relevant stimuli (Bruce, 2002). Faces are important because they convey information about gender, age, ethnicity, health, emotion, and personal identity (Donath, 2001). Moreover, faces are dynamic entities. They change as we move (O'Toole, Roark, & Abdi, 2002; Roark, Barrett, Spence, Abdi, & O'Toole, 2003) and change across time as we age (Sadler, 1986; Taylor, 2001). Yet from one viewing to the next, there are things about our faces that remain the same and allow for identification. Theories of facial perception need to account for all of these aspects of face perception.

A useful functional account of all of these components of the face-processing problem was developed by Bruce and Young in 1986. According to the Bruce and Young framework, face processing involves a set of processing modules that operate on seven distinct kinds of facial codes. The facial codes proposed in the framework are pictorial codes, structural codes, visually derived semantic codes, identity-specific semantic codes, name codes, expression codes, and facial speech codes. The *pictorial code* simply describes the person's face as a picture. The pictorial code for a face is much like the visual representation of any sort of object. Structural codes provide *configural information* about the person's face, such as the distance between the eyes or the relative symmetry of the face as a whole. As we will see in this section, evidence indicates that this sort of configural information is crucial for facial recognition. *Visually derived semantic codes* include information about the person's characteristics, such as gender, age, attractiveness, and so on. *Identity-specific semantic information* includes information specific to individuals, such as what they do for a living or where they are typically encountered. As the name implies, *name codes* provide information about the names that are associated with particular faces. *Expression codes* represent the

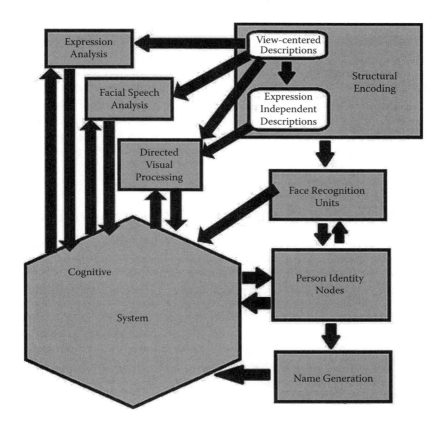

FIGURE 2.9   Bruce and Young's (1986) theory of face perception. (*Source*: Based on figure originally presented in Bruce, V., & Young, A. (1986). Understanding face recognition. *British Journal of Psychology, 77,* 305–327.)

emotional expressions associated with people's faces. Finally, Bruce and Young noted that we also represent speech-related visual information in what they called a *facial speech code*.

According to the framework, these seven types of codes are used by a set of modules (shown in Figure 2.9) in order to make different types of perceptual judgments about faces. In particular, for tasks in which recognition of the face is crucial (e.g., that was the person who robbed me at the bus terminal), facial recognition begins by developing a viewpoint-dependent representation of the person's face. This viewpoint-dependent representation is then converted to a more abstract, expression-independent structural code. Once this structural code is developed, the information is compared to information stored in face recognition units. Face recognition units represent particular previously seen faces. These units become active when the current face being judged has a similar structural representation. When a particular face unit becomes sufficiently activated, it may activate a particular person identity node containing identity-specific semantic information about the person we have just encountered. Finally, the foregoing activation may also lead to the activation of a name node allowing us to provide a name for the individual being identified. The model proposed by Bruce and Young (1986) has considerable appeal as a heuristic for thinking about the steps involved in face processing and how facial recognition can fail.

Holistic Processing and Featural Processing of Faces

A great deal of evidence indicates that face processing involves both the local identification of individual facial features and the processing of higher order configural information (Bruce, Doyle, Dench, & Burton, 1991; Cabezza & Kato, 2001; Farah, Wilson, Drain, & Tanaka, 1998). *Configural information* refers to how individual parts of a face are related to one another. This configural information allows for face recognition to occur holistically rather than by analyzing each individual facial feature one at a time. The terms *configural* and *holistic* are often used interchangeably, but it is important to note that there are distinctions in the terms that are important. *Holistic processing* basically refers to any type of processing where the unit of analysis is the face as a whole. For instance, holistic processing may involve noting the symmetry of the face (Chen, Kao, & Tyler, 2006), information about the relative locations of different parts of the face (Burton, Bruce, & Johnsonton, 1990), or even characteristics such as attractiveness, honesty, or kindness (Frowd, Bruce, & Hancock, 2008). The term *configural*, on the other hand, refers more specifically to relational information between the parts of the face. Configural processing often is holistic, in that it may take into account the face as a whole, but may also involve lower order relations such as how far apart the person's nostrils are. Such information is relational, and hence configural, but it does not deal with the face as a whole.

A number of different types of experimental paradigms have been used to examine the degree to which holistic information is used in facial recognition. The classic demonstration of the importance of holistic information in face processing is the inverted face effect (Diamond & Carey, 1986; Passarotti, Smith, DeLano, & Huang, 2007; Taylor, Batty, & Itier, 2004; Sekunova & Barton, 2008; Yin, 1969). You can see what the materials for these kinds of experiments look like in Figure 2.10. In these studies, participants are presented with a target face that is either in an upright orientation or an upside-down orientation. Following a brief delay, participants

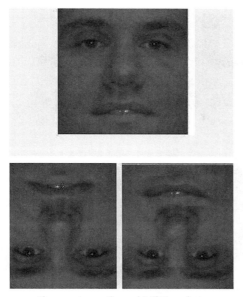

Flip over to see the real Jeff Neuschatz

FIGURE 2.10   Illustration of the inverted face paradigm.

make a recognition judgment of an upright or upside-down picture. Research indicates that when making judgments about the upside-down pictures, recognition is slower and less accurate. Studies have shown that the decreased performance when faces are inverted occurs due to changes in configural information. For instance, Leder and Bruce (2000) digitally varied either the bushiness of the eyebrows (local feature) or the distance between the eyes (configural feature). Changes in configural information were harder for people to spot in upside-down pictures than were changes in local feature information.

Another design which has been used to good effect to study holistic processing is the composite face design (Cheung, Richler, Palmeri, & Gauthier, 2008; Gauthier & Bukach, 2007; Goffaux & Rossion, 2006; McKone, Kanwisher, & Duchaine, 2007). In this design, participants are presented with pictures in which the top half of one person's face is combined with the bottom half of another person's face. You can see sample stimuli in Figure 2.11. A line separates the two halves, resulting in an illusion that it is a single person's face. In a typical experiment, participants are shown composite faces for a brief period of time, followed by a visual mask. Participants are then shown a composite face in which the entire face matches, half the face matches (either the top half or the bottom half), or none of the face matches. The participant's task is to indicate if a specific

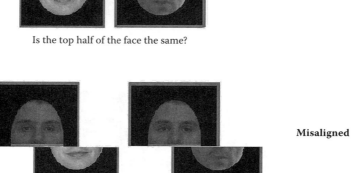

Is the top half of the face the same?

Aligned

Is the top half of the face the same?

Misaligned

FIGURE 2.11 Illustration of the composite face paradigm. In this example, participants would be asked if the top halves of the composite faces match. In all cases, the bottom halves of the face do not match.

half of the face matches. For instance, participants might be asked, "Does the top half of the face match?" Imagine you are shown such a composite face and are then shown a new composite face in which the top half matches and the bottom half does not match. You are asked to indicate whether the top half of the face matches the picture you just saw. To the extent that you are relying on holistic processing, this task should be difficult, because the face as a whole does not match, interfering with your ability to recognize that the individual features in the top half of the face do match. Indeed, this is what researchers have typically found. Participants performing this task show impaired performance when measured by both accuracy and response time. The effect can further be demonstrated by misaligning the two halves of the composite, as shown in Figure 2.11 (Goffaux & Rossion, 2006; Hole, 1994; Hole, George, & Dunsmore, 1999; Le Grand, Mondloch, Maurer, & Brent, 2004; Michel, Rossion, Han, Chung, & Caldara, 2006; Robbins & McKone, 2007; Young, Hellawell, & Hay, 1987). When the two halves of the face are misaligned, it eliminates the holistic information and the task of matching just the top half of the face becomes pretty easy.

Evidence indicates that configural information greatly aids recognition of faces. For instance, Davidoff and Donnelly (1990) presented participants with intact faces or faces in which the location of the parts were scrambled and found that recognition of faces was impaired when the parts were scrambled. Moreover, it has been found that providing verbal descriptions of faces can sometimes impair recognition of those faces, a finding termed the *verbal overshadowing effect* (Schooler & Engstler-Schooler, 1990). Evidence indicates that part of the reason verbalization can impair face recognition is because verbal descriptions typically focus on individual facial features, thus impairing recognition of configural information (Fallshore & Schooler, 1995).

Other studies have also been performed to assess the importance of configural information. For instance, researchers have used computer software programs to change the location of facial features by a small number of pixels (Freire & Lee, 2001). Thus the new pictures are identical to the old pictures with regard to local featural information, but vary slightly in their configural information. Research indicates that people are quite good at picking up even small changes in configural information. Taken together, all of this research suggests that both featural information and configural information are used in face recognition. However, configural information appears to be especially important. These results will have important implications for our understanding of the ability of witnesses to recognize perpetrators from lineups.

Neurobiology of Face Perception

In parallel with the important work being done on functional accounts of human face processing, neuroscientists have made major advances in understanding how the brain processes information about faces (Bruce & Young, 2000; Grill-Spector, Knouf, & Kanwisher, 2004; Kanwisher, McDermott, & Chun, 1997; Servos, Engel, Gati, & Menon, 1999; Xu, 2005). Like all visual stimuli, information needed to recognize a face is first processed in the retina, where the information is then sent to the lateral geniculate nucleus of the thalamus and then to the primary visual cortex in the occipital lobe of the cerebral cortex (Enns, 2004; Martin, 1994). The primary visual cortex is known to have detailed maps of visual space in which different locations in space are represented by particular groups of neurons (known as *cortical columns*). Additionally, particular collections of neurons (known as *feature detectors*) are known to respond preferentially to particular orientations of lines (Hubel & Wiesel, 1959, 1962). Thus, at its earliest stop in the visual cortex, a detailed mapping of facial features is represented by collections of neurons that indicate the orientations of lines that make up the person's face.

From the primary visual cortex, visual information is sent to a number of different submodules. However, neuroscientists have noted that there appear to be two parallel pathways leaving the primary visual cortex

(Ettlinger, 1990; Goodale & Milner, 1992; Mishkin & Ungerleider, 1982). One pathway sends information up toward the parietal lobe and represents information about object locations and about how the person can interact with the object. This is the *where/how pathway* (also known as the *ventral route*). The other pathway sends information toward the temporal lobe and represents information about object identity. This is the *what pathway* (also known as the *dorsal route*). In particular, it is known that an area known as the inferotemporal cortex is especially important for object recognition, including the recognition of faces. In early studies, for instance, Klover and Bucey (1938) found that if this area was destroyed in monkeys, the monkeys lost the ability to recognize common objects. This work was later extended by Gross, Roch-Mirranda, and Bender (1972). They recorded the activity of particular groups of cells in the inferotemporal cortex of monkeys. They found that there were some cells that appeared to be specialized to recognize particular types of objects. For instance, some cells responded only when the monkeys were shown a silhouette of a hand. Other cells responded only to faces. There were even cells that appeared to respond to the presentation of a toilet brush that the monkeys frequently saw.

With regard to recognition of faces, it appears that a particular part of the inferotemporal cortex known as the *fusiform face area* (FFA; see Figure 2.12) is specialized for the recognition of faces (Kanwisher, McDermott, & Chun, 1997). In studies with monkeys, the FFA shows activation only to intact faces and does not respond to jumbled faces or other

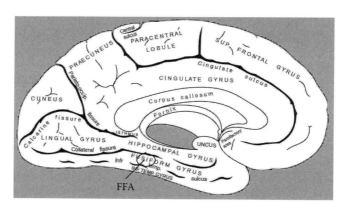

FIGURE 2.12   This drawing shows the medial surface of one cerebral hemisphere with the approximate location of the fusiform face area (FFA) indicated. The exact location of the FFA varies from individual to individual but is typically located along the midfusiform gyrus. (*Source*: Obtained at WikiCommons. Drawn by Mysid, based on the online version of the 1918 *Gray's Anatomy.*)

complex stimuli (Haxby, Hoffman, & Gobbini, 2000). In fact, humans with damage to the FFA show deficits in face recognition known as *prosopagnosia* (Barton, Press, Keenan, & O'Connor, 2002; Mayer & Rossion, 2007). The evidence from neuroscience makes it clear that when witnesses are processing a culprit's face, this information processing is occurring in the FFA as well as related cortical areas.

Face Space Theory

Before leaving the topic of research on face perception, one last theory is important for our understanding of eyewitness identification. To most people it seems like common sense that some faces are just easier to remember than other faces. Some people just stand out in the crowd. Such faces are referred to as *distinctive* (Metzger, 2006). But what exactly is meant by saying that a face is distinctive? One important theory that has been used to try to explain this concept is Valentine's (1995) *face space theory*. The concept behind face space theory is that individual faces that one has encountered are stored in memory as exemplars. The exemplars can be thought of mathematically as inhabiting a kind of multidimensional space. Exemplars are stored around the prototypical face with faces that are more distinct being further away from the prototype. These distinctive faces are easier to recognize because there are fewer similar faces surrounding them in the face space and so there is a lower risk of mixing up the face you saw with another similar face. Valentine's theory has been used in a number of different contexts, including in attempting to explain the finding that members of other races are more difficult to recognize than members of one's own race (Valentine, 1991). According to Valentine's theory, this occurs because the dimensions along which members of other races vary are different from the dimensions along which one's own race varies (see Figure 2.13). Member of other races therefore end up being clustered very close together, making it difficult to make distinctions among the exemplars.

Conceptions of the Lineup Task

The theoretical accounts described thus far are basic theories of memory and perception. At a general level, it is useful for anyone interested in the science of eyewitness identification to have a basic understanding of these theories. However, as research on eyewitness identification heated up in the 1970s and 1980s, specific theoretical frameworks were developed that were specifically applied to the task of making identifications in lineups

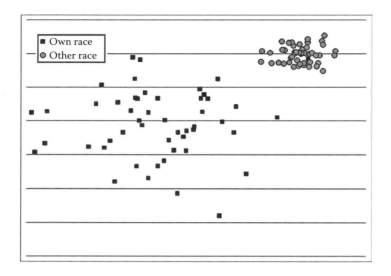

FIGURE 2.13   Illustration of Valentine's "face space" theory.

and photospreads. These frameworks are also extremely important for understanding the research presented in the rest of this monograph.

Lineup as Experiment Analogy

An important initial task for anyone interested in applying basic research in perception and memory is to do an analysis of the underlying task that is under investigation. This task analysis guides research and theorizing in the domain. In the case of research on eyewitness identification, the task analysis requires a basic understanding of what goes on in the course of conducting a lineup. In a useful analogy, Wells and Luus (1990) argued that the lineup can be fruitfully understood as similar to an experiment. In a scientific investigation, one usually begins with a hypothesis. The hypothesis is often generated based on previous research and findings. In fact, the scientific investigator often has reason to believe that the hypothesis is true, even if those reasons amount to mere intuition. Importantly, the scientific researcher does not *know* for sure that the hypothesis is true. In fact, the whole point of conducting the experiment is because one does not know for sure that the hypothesis is true.

In a police investigation, the situation is similar. When police are investigating a crime, they will typically generate one or more hypotheses about who committed the crime. The hypothesis is generated during the course of the investigation. For instance, in a murder investigation, police may generate information that a particular person had recently had a heated argument with the murder victim. That, quite reasonably, leads the police investigator to form a hypothesis that the person who had the argument with the victim is the person who committed the murder. That person becomes a suspect. When the police identify someone as a suspect, they are basically forming a hypothesis. Like a scientific hypothesis, the police don't know for sure that the suspect is the one who committed the crime. In fact, that is why the lineup is conducted: to test the hypothesis.

Once a scientific investigator generates a hypothesis, they come up with a way of testing the hypothesis. The preferred method of testing a hypothesis is to conduct an experiment. An experiment is basically a situation created by the experimenter designed to see whether or not the hypothesis really holds. For instance, if an experimenter believes that a particular drug will decrease flu symptoms, they provide people who have the flu with the drug and see if their symptoms are alleviated. In actual practice the experimenter needs to worry about biases that might creep into the experiment. For one thing, someone with the flu will typically show a decrease in symptoms over time even if nothing is done. Thus a control condition is needed, in which people with the flu do not get the active drug. In order to say that the drug really controls flu symptoms, the researcher would have to show that the patients who take the drug do better than the patients who don't take the drug. It is also possible that patients who get the drug may end up convincing themselves they are feeling better just because they are being treated. This is known as a *placebo effect*. Because of that, people in the control conditions of experiments like these are usually given an inactive pill called a *placebo*. Importantly, the patient does not know whether he or she is getting the actual drug or the placebo, and the research assistant who is administering the drug does not know who is receiving the actual treatment. Such designs are called *double-blind*, and they are designed to prevent either the researcher or the participant from inadvertently biasing the results.

Police investigators are in a similar situation when they conduct a lineup. Police have a hypothesis that the suspect is the person who committed the crime. But they do not know for sure if this is true. The lineup is much like an experiment. If the suspect really is guilty, then you would expect that the witness will pick the suspect out of the lineup. That would provide evidence consistent with the hypothesis. However, just like in an experiment, it is important for a lineup to have control conditions. This is because a witness may pick someone out of a lineup, even if he or she did not commit the crime. In a typical lineup, the *foils* serve as the control condition. *Foils* are members of the lineup who match the general description of the perpetrator but who are known by police to be innocent.[2] Thus, if a witness picks one of the foils, one knows that the witness is in error. Other controls have also been suggested by eyewitness researchers. For instance, some researchers have suggested the use of a *blank lineup* (Wells, 1984). A blank lineup is made up entirely of foils. The witness is first shown the blank lineup. If the witness picks someone out of this lineup, then the police have established that the person is an unreliable witness. If the witness does not pick someone out of the blank lineup, the witness is then shown the actual lineup. Just like in an experiment, it has also been argued that *double-blind procedures* should be used (Wells & Seelau, 1995). This means that the witness should not be told which member of the lineup is the suspect. It also means that the person administering the lineup should not know who the suspect is. The idea is that by administering the lineup in a double-blind manner, there is no way for the police investigator to inadvertently bias the witness's choice. The lineup as experiment analogy provides a useful way of thinking about lineups. The framework is an important one to keep in mind in reviewing the rest of this monograph.

System Variables and Estimator Variables

Another framework that has proven fruitful for eyewitness researchers was a distinction made by Wells in a 1978 article in *American Psychologist*. Wells pointed out that there are a number of different variables that are known to influence eyewitness identification accuracy. Additionally, there are a potentially boundless number of additional variables yet to be discovered. Given those facts, and given that one cannot do everything all at once, Wells (1978) asked the question of how eyewitness researchers should prioritize their research agenda. In providing his answer to that question, Wells pointed out that one could usefully classify the variables that affect eyewitness accuracy into two categories: *system variables* and *estimator variables*.

System variables refer to that set of variables that the criminal justice system has control over. For instance, in administering a lineup, police have control over how many foils to include in the lineup, what instructions to give the witness, how they go about choosing the foils, and so on. *Estimator variables* refer to that set of variables that are likely to influence witness accuracy, but that the criminal justice system has no control over. For instance, the length of time the witness has to view the culprit, the lighting conditions at the time of the crime, how far away the witness was, the race and gender of the witness, and whether the suspect was wearing a disguise are all estimator variables. Estimator variables are important variables that influence accuracy, but police cannot really do anything about them.

In his influential article, Wells argued that, as a starting point, it was more useful for eyewitness researchers to concentrate on system variables. Concentrating on system variables would allow researchers to be proactive in being able to suggest to law enforcement practical things that they could do to increase identification accuracy. Estimator variables are also important, because they allow researchers to know which identifications are likely to be reliable. In looking at the system variable–estimator variable distinction, it is useful to consider how eyewitness evidence is similar to physical evidence like fingerprints or DNA. The reliability of physical evidence depends crucially on whether the detective or criminalist who collects the evidence follows proper protocols so as to avoid contaminating the evidence. However, the reliability of physical evidence may also be influenced by factors that are completely outside of the control of the police. For instance, a culprit may wear gloves, may leave only a partial print, or may set a fire that compromises the physical evidence. DNA evidence may be compromised by the passage of time and decay of the biological evidence. It is important for criminalists to understand these factors so that they know how reliable their evidence is likely to be.

Relative and Absolute Judgment Strategies

Another important theory that was developed to help understand lineup performance in particular is the distinction between relative and absolute judgment strategies (Wells, 1984). According to this view, when a witness views a lineup, he or she will sometimes evaluate the lineup members by comparing lineup members with each other. These judgments are known as *relative judgments*. A witness following a relative judgment strategy compares and contrasts lineup members, trying to find the lineup member that comes closest to matching his or her memory for the event. Using a relative judgment strategy is likely to produce acceptable results when the police have the right suspect. After all, the actual culprit is, in all likelihood, going to provide the best match to the witness's memory, and is thus likely to be correctly chosen by a witness using a relative judgment strategy. The problem occurs when the suspect is actually innocent, when the police investigator's hypothesis about who committed the crime is in error. Wells pointed out that in this circumstance, even though the culprit is not present in the lineup, some lineup member will be a better match to the witness's memory than all the other lineup members. Thus, a witness making a relative judgment is likely to pick someone. In terms of the signal detection analysis we discussed earlier, a witness using a relative judgment strategy is likely to have a liberal response bias.

By contrast, a witness using an *absolute judgment strategy* views each member of the lineup independently and makes a decision as to whether or not that lineup member is the culprit. Thus each individual lineup member is compared to the witness's memory and an absolute decision is made for that lineup member. If the culprit is present in the lineup, it is likely that the culprit will be chosen, because that person is likely to be a very good match to what is in the witness's memory. However, if the suspect is innocent, it is more likely that the witness will reject the lineup altogether, because nobody in the lineup will be an especially good match. Indeed, research indicates that self-reported use of a relative judgment strategy is associated with more false identifications than is self-reported use of an absolute judgment strategy (Dunning & Stern, 1994).

Recently, Clark (2003) developed a computer simulation of relative and absolute judgment strategies called the *WITNESS model*. The model begins with a relatively simple way of simulating long-term memory for faces. It assumes that memories for faces can be thought of as being made up of groups of features that are stored in long-term memory. Quite reasonably, the WITNESS model assumes that the representations stored in long-term memory are incomplete (i.e., they are missing features) and error prone (i.e., sometimes the wrong feature is stored). For instance, imagine the perpetrator has a fair complexion, dark brown hair, brown narrow eyes, a bulbous nose, thin lips, a square jaw, and a bushy uni-brow. The representation stored in memory may be missing the fact that the culprit had thin lips and may have miscategorized the culprit's hair as black rather than brown. When memory is probed, the witness examines the members of the lineup to determine how similar they are to the representation of the culprit that is stored in memory.

First consider how the WITNESS model would account for an absolute judgment. For each member of the lineup, the person determines how similar that lineup member is to the representation stored in memory. One of the members of the lineup is necessarily a better match than any of the other members of the lineup. If the match between that lineup member (the best match) is above the response criterion the witness sets, they will select that member of the lineup. If even the best match is below the witness's response criterion, they will reject the lineup altogether and tell the police that none of the lineup members looks familiar.

Now consider how the WITNESS model would account for a relative judgment. Again, for each member of the lineup, the person determines how similar that lineup member is to the representation stored in memory. Again, one of the members of the lineup will be a better match than all the other lineup members. Someone using a relative judgment strategy will select that person from the lineup if they are a much better match than the next best match. That is, the decision is based on the two best matches, and the best match is chosen if it is much better than the next best match. The WITNESS model also envisions situations in which witnesses use a combination of both strategies, making their decisions based on a weighted sum of the two types of evidence.

As we will see in the chapter on system variables (Chapter 4), the relative judgment–absolute judgment distinction has been influential among researchers trying to develop better methods for police conducting line-ups. In particular, relative judgment strategies are seen as being error prone. As a consequence, researchers have tried to develop techniques that discourage the use of relative judgment strategies in favor of absolute judgment strategies.

Evaluations of Lineups

A final area of both theoretical and practical importance deals with measures designed to evaluate the goodness of a lineup. In this regard, we are going to discuss two main types of measures: *lineup fairness* and *diagnosticity*. To get an idea for what is meant by lineup fairness, consider the following case from the state of Texas in 1995 (Wells, n.d.-b). In the case, a witness had described the perpetrator of the crime as an African American male. The witness was later shown a lineup. The lineup was composed of six men. One of the men was a black male. The rest were Hispanic males. Although this seems shockingly inappropriate, it is useful to consider why it is inappropriate. First, the witness was brought to the police station and reasonably believed that the police had a suspect (i.e., someone who they had reason to believe was guilty of the crime). Second, only one of the people in the lineup could possibly be the suspect, because only one person in the lineup bore any resemblance to the description the witness had previously given of the culprit. The police were telegraphing to the witness who they suspected of the crime. It would not be surprising, given those circumstances, for the witness to select the suspect. Consider the situation from the point of view of the lineup as experiment analogy. The foils in a lineup are meant to serve as a kind of control condition, so that if a witness is prone to guessing, the errors are drawn away from the suspect and toward the known innocent foils. In an unfair lineup, the foils are implausible, and so if a witness is prone to guessing, they are likely to guess the suspect.

A variety of different measures of lineup fairness have been suggested over the years. The best known of these is the *functional size* of the lineup (Wells, Leippe, & Ostrom, 1979). To get a sense of what is meant by functional size, it is useful to contrast it with the *nominal size* of a lineup. The nominal size of a lineup is simply the number of people who are present in the lineup. For instance, in a typical police lineup a witness may be shown one suspect and five foils. The nominal size of such a lineup is six. If such a lineup is fair, then the probability of picking an innocent suspect (given that the witness picks anybody) should be about one in six. In other words, if the suspect is innocent, the witness should be just as likely to pick any of the foils as he or she is to pick the suspect. Now consider the lineup from Texas. In that lineup, there was one suspect and five foils. However, only the suspect was a plausible choice given the witness description. There were six people in the lineup, but in reality it was as if the actual size of the lineup was one. Eyewitness researchers would say that the *nominal size* of the lineup was six, but the *functional size* of the lineup was one.

Consider another example that illustrates the concept of functional size (Wells et al., 1979). Imagine there is a bank robbery by a white female, in her early 30s, with blond hair and a medium build. The police identify a suspect and show a fair six-person photoarray to the witness. Because we posited a fair lineup, we can say that the functional size of the lineup is six and the nominal size of the photospread is six. If the suspect is innocent, but the witness decides to make a choice, there is only one chance in six that the witness will mistakenly choose the suspect. So far, so good.

Now imagine the following alternative. I start with the six-person lineup, as above, but I replace three of the foils with a Hispanic man in his late 80s, an African American woman in her 60s, and a picture of an espresso machine. The lineup still contains six choices (nominal size = 6), but it contains only three blond women in their early 30s. Clearly, in this case, the lineup provides no more protection to the innocent suspect than would a three-person lineup (functional size = 3). If the suspect is innocent, but the witness decides to make a choice, there is now one chance in three that the witness will choose her.

In an actual case, lineup bias can occur in more subtle ways. For this reason, the functional size of a lineup can sometimes be determined by making use of what has been called a *mock witness paradigm* (Wells et al., 1979). In the mock witness paradigm, an expert witness, usually a researcher with expertise in eyewitness memory, first obtains a copy of the lineup or photospread that was shown to the actual witness. The expert also obtains the witness's description of the perpetrator that was given prior to the lineup or photospread. A sample of participants is then obtained who did not witness the original crime and who have never seen the suspect or the foils. These mock witnesses are given the witness description, and based on that description alone, they are asked to indicate who they think the suspect is.

To see how this works, imagine a witness is shown a six-person lineup and picks the suspect out of the lineup. The defense becomes concerned that the lineup may not be a fair lineup. They hire a defense expert who obtains the witness's pre-lineup description of the perpetrator, and they obtain a copy of the photospread used for the identification. One hundred participants are obtained. The participants are provided with the witness's description of the perpetrator and are asked, based on that description alone, who they think the suspect is. Seventy-five of the mock witnesses pick the suspect (suggesting that it is an unfair lineup). In evaluating the results of this assessment of lineup fairness, consider the following:

1. The mock witnesses did not see the actual crime. If the lineup was fair, they should only pick the suspect one sixth of the time (p = .167).
2. In fact, the witnesses picked the suspect 75% of the time (p = .75).
3. The nominal size of the lineup is six, but based on the mock witness paradigm it is as if the lineup contained only 1.33 people (functional size = 1/.75).

The functional size of a lineup provides a useful index of lineup fairness. In practice, of course, exactly what the functional size of a lineup should be is a matter of social policy not science. Nevertheless, functional size provides a nice heuristic that legal decision makers can reason with. For instance, if the nominal size of a lineup is eight, but the functional size is two, it might be useful to entertain the question of whether one would consider a two-person lineup an adequate protection against the fallibilities of human memory.

Another important way of evaluating lineups concerns the diagnosticity of the identification. The reader will remember that a well-conducted police lineup is made up of a single suspect and several foils (Wells & Luus, 1990). In some situations, the suspect actually is the person who committed the crime. Such lineups are called *target-present lineups*. In other situations, the suspect is not the person who committed the crime. Such lineups are called *targe-absent lineups*. When eyewitness researchers conduct experiments, they know whether they are showing an experimental participant a target-present lineup or a target-absent lineup. The police, of course, don't know whether they are dealing with a target-present lineup or a target-absent lineup. In fact, the whole point of conducting a lineup is to help determine whether the suspect committed the crime or whether the suspect is innocent.

What legal decision makers want to know is whether the person who was identified committed the crime. A witness's identification of a suspect (and, to some extent. a non-identification) provides data that are relevant to that question. As a consequence, the most helpful information that psychologists can provide law enforcement is an estimate of how likely it is that a suspect is guilty given that the suspect has been identified by the witness. In other words, what are the odds that a person is guilty, given that the witness picked him or her out of the lineup? An index used to assess this likelihood is called the *diagnosticity of the lineup* (Clark, Howell, & Davey, 2008).

Diagnosticity is estimated by combining information from target-present lineups and target-absent lineups. In looking at responses to target-present lineups, the main measure we are going to be interested in is the percentage of correct identifications of the suspect from the lineup. In looking at target-absent lineups, the situation is a little more complex. Because police lineups are typically made up of one suspect and a number of innocent foils, there are two types of false identifications that can be made in a target-absent lineup. First, the witness might falsely identify the suspect from the lineup (i.e., false suspect identification). Second, the witness might falsely identify one of the foils (i.e., false foil identification). False identification of a suspect from a lineup is typically seen as more troubling and potentially dangerous than the false identification of a foil. When a foil is falsely selected it is a mistake, but nobody is put at risk of going to prison. No harm no foul, so to speak.

In some of the studies we describe in the present monograph, the researchers did not distinguish between the false identification of suspects and the false identification of foils. Nobody in the target-absent lineup was designated as the suspect per se. In those cases, it is often informative to calculate an estimate of the proportion of *false suspect identifications*. To do so, we will simply take the overall rate of mistaken selections from target-absent lineups and divide it by the number of people in the lineup (i.e., the *nominal size*). For instance, if witnesses are shown a target-absent lineup made up of six people, and 60% of the time witnesses identify someone from the target-absent lineup, then the *estimated false suspect identification* rate would be 10% (60% divided by 6). That is, the percentage of overall false identifications was 60%, but if the lineup was a fair lineup, it is likely that the rate of *false foil identifications* would be 50% and the rate of *false suspect identifications* would be 10%.

The diagnosticity of a lineup is defined as the *correct identification rate* in target-present lineups divided by the *false suspect identification rate* in target-absent lineups (or, if that is not available, the estimated false suspect identification rate).

$$\text{Diagnosticity} = \frac{\text{Correct IDs}}{\text{False Suspect IDs}}$$

$$(2.5)$$

Diagnosticity tells you how much more likely it is that the suspect is guilty than not guilty, given that the suspect has been identified by the witness.

For instance, assume that the suspect is correctly identified 80% of the time in a six-person target-present lineup and that *someone* is incorrectly identified 60% of the time in a six-person target-absent lineup. As we just noted, to estimate the rate at which suspects would be falsely identified in a fair target-absent lineup, we would take 60% and divide it by 6, providing us with an estimated false suspect identification rate of 10%. The diagnosticity of the identification would then be 80/10 or 8. In other words, if a suspect is identified by a witness, it is eight times more likely that the suspect is guilty than not guilty (assuming equal base rates and a fair lineup). Or, put another way, there are eight chances in nine that the person is guilty and one chance in nine that the person is innocent.

Ideally, you would like to use the actual false suspect identification rate, if it is available, rather than the estimated suspect identification rate to determine diagnosticity. However, when the actual false suspect identification rate is not available, the estimated rate can still provide a useful estimate of diagnosticity, based on the assumption of a fair lineup. And, of course, the fairness of the lineup itself is a factor that influences diagnosticity.

☐ Summary and Conclusions

The information covered in this chapter provides a very brief overview of theoretical issues that are of importance to eyewitness researchers. We consider the information we covered in the present chapter the minimal information that is needed to fully appreciate the rest of the monograph. In the chapters that follow, we apply these issues in trying to understand the current state of knowledge concerning estimator variables and system variables.

☐ Endnotes

1. As we will see in Chapter 4, there is a good deal of debate about the exact mechanism responsible for this finding.
2. Foils are also sometimes called *fillers,* and we will use both terms interchangeably throughout this book.

CHAPTER

3

Estimator Variables

In 1972, the Supreme Court ruled on the case of *Neil v. Biggers*. Mr. Biggers was accused of taking his victim into the woods and raping her. Although the crime occurred at night, the court record revealed that there had been a full moon and that the attack had lasted for over one half hour. The victim described her assailant to police, telling them that he was a black teenager, was overweight, and had a youthful voice. She was unable to pick anyone out of the mug books she was initially shown. However, 7 months later, police staged a live showup with Mr. Biggers. Recall from Chapter 1 that a showup is an identification procedure in which the witness is shown a single person and is asked if that person is the culprit. The victim positively identified Mr. Biggers from the showup. She indicated that she was confident in her identification. Mr. Biggers was subsequently convicted.

The identification procedure used in this case was questionable. The witness was shown a single person (i.e., a showup) and was asked whether Mr. Biggers was her attacker. As we will discuss later, showups, especially when conducted after a long delay, are a suggestive technique and create the risk of false identification (Yarmey, Yarmey, & Yarmey, 1996). The use of a showup in this case was not only suggestive but also needlessly suggestive. The showup occurred 7 months after the crime. Certainly the police could have taken the time to construct a fair lineup with five or more foils in order to provide some safeguards against a false identification. Mr. Biggers's attorneys appealed the conviction. The case eventually made its way onto the docket of the U.S. Supreme Court. The Court agreed that the use of the showup was not the best of approaches. However, they concluded that, given the *totality of the circumstances*, the identification was still likely to be reliable. What were the "totality of the circumstances"? The witness had paid attention to her attacker's face. She was confident in her identification. She had a good view of her attacker. She had a long time to look at him. The amount of time that had passed between the crime and the identification was not too long for an accurate identification. Her description of her attacker matched the person she identified.

These general principles were later reaffirmed in *Manson v. Braithwaite* (1977). *Manson v. Braithwaite* (1977) created a two-pronged test for whether or not an identification should be excluded (Wells & Quinlivan, 2009). First, the judge is to decide whether or not the identification procedure used in the case was needlessly suggestive. If the judge rules that the procedure used was suggestive, the judge then has to decide whether the witnessing conditions, taken as a whole, would nevertheless tend to produce a reliable identification. These two cases are an important part of American jurisprudence. Taken together, the cases concluded that system variables (e.g., the use of a showup) may be unimportant if the witness's ability to view and remember the crime is otherwise likely to be good. Many of the factors that the Court emphasized are referred to as *estimator variables* by eyewitness researchers (Wells, 1978). An estimator variable is a variable that is likely to influence the accuracy of an eyewitness, but that the criminal justice system (e.g., police and prosecutors) has no control over. Police investigators do not have any say over what the lighting conditions were when the crime occurred. Police investigators cannot control how much attention the witness paid at the time of the crime. Police have no control over the gender or ethnicity of the perpetrator, how afraid the witness was, whether the witness was intoxicated, and so on. These factors could arguably influence the accuracy of an eyewitness, but the police do not have any control over them. Like other forms of evidence, the quality of eyewitness evidence may be of variable quality despite the best efforts on the part of investigators to accurately collect and preserve the evidence. The best the legal system can do is to take these factors into account in determining how much weight to give to the witness's testimony or, in extreme cases, exclude the identification if the risk of error is too high.

We can think of estimator variables as belonging to several different classes. Some estimator variables reflect *characteristics of the witnessing situation.* These include things like lighting, distance, view, type of crime, presence or absence of a weapon, and so on. Other estimator variables reflect *characteristics of the witness.* Is the witness old or young? Do they have any health conditions? Were they intoxicated at the time of the crime? What are their general visual abilities? Estimator variables may also reflect *characteristics of the perpetrator.* Were they wearing a disguise? Has their appearance changed greatly between the time of the crime and the time of the lineup? How visually distinctive is the person's appearance? There are also estimator variables that involve an *interaction between characteristics of the witness and characteristics of the perpetrator.* Perhaps best known among these is the ubiquitous own-race bias. The own-race bias is the finding that people recognize members of their own racial or ethnic group better than members of other racial or ethnic groups (Meissner & Brigham, 2001). Other similar interactive effects occur, most notably the own-age bias (Anastasi & Rhodes, 2006).

In the present chapter we will examine each of these classes of estimator variables, discussing some of the salient factors that influence eyewitness identification accuracy. We will discuss some of the implications of these findings for the legal system, as well as theoretical accounts of some of the salient effects. Last, we will talk about the importance of estimator variables for eyewitness experts and the legal system.

☐ Characteristics of the Situation

The first set of estimators we are going to review in this chapter are factors that vary across witnessing situations. Characteristics of the situation include things like lighting, distance, viewing time, stress, and so on. It is important to note that oftentimes police do not have precise information about witnessing conditions and instead must rely on the witness's memory to estimate these variables (Lindsay, Semmler, Weber, Brewer, & Lindsay, 2008). This, of course, provides additional complications. For instance, a witness who says they were 10 yards away from the perpetrator may instead have been 15 yards away. A witness who says they saw a perpetrator for 10 minutes may have seen the perpetrator for only 6 minutes. Thus, as a practical matter, it is important for police to try to document the actual witnessing conditions, and if they are unable to do so, to take into account that the witness may not have perfect memory for those circumstances.

Illumination

Basic accounts of perception, as well as common sense, tell us that the degree of illumination should influence the ability of witnesses to accurately remember a person's face (e.g., Johnson, 1976). Visual perception depends on quanta of light (i.e., photons) reflecting off of a surface (i.e., the perpetrator's face) and eventually activating the photoreceptors on the witness's retina (Mather, 2008). The less light that is present in a situation, the more visual perception should be impaired, and the less accurate one would expect eventual recognition to be. There are two types of photoreceptors in the human eye (cf. Enns, 2004), cones and rods. Cones are concentrated in the fovea and are phototopic. That is, they specialize in bright lighting conditions. Rods are more broadly dispersed but are absent from the fovea. They are scotopic. That is, they specialize in dim lighting conditions. One consequence of this is that under bright lighting conditions, a witness will primarily be relying on cone vision, whereas under dim lighting conditions, a witness will primarily be relying on rod vision.

Cones and rods also differ considerably in their ability to detect fine details (Goldstein, 2007). There is a six-to-one mapping between cones and the ganglion cells of the optic nerve, and in the fovea, the mapping is one to one. Thus, the foveal cone vision that predominates in bright lighting conditions provides fantastic spatial resolution. Cone circuits also show evidence of lateral inhibition, which sharpens contours and thus aids in the detection of edges. Moreover, approximately 9% of the primary visual cortex is devoted to processing information from the fovea, even though the fovea makes up only 0.01% of the retina (Goldstein, 2007). Rods, because they are specialized for dim lighting (i.e., scotopic vision), show greater spatial and temporal convergence. More than 100 rods feed into every ganglion cell of the optic nerve. This allows the rods to pool their resources, combining information across space to allow for vision even under dim lighting conditions. However, this pooling of resources comes at a cost of decreased spatial resolution. Rods also take longer to respond than cones do in order to pool information across time. This, again, aids vision in dim lighting conditions but also comes at a cost. If an object is moving, or if the eye itself moves, the image will appear blurry. The situation is rather like a camera with a slow shutter speed. The slow shutter speed allows more light to accumulate, which provides more information about the image being viewed, but any movement will cause the image to appear blurry.

Sudden changes in lighting are also likely to cause problems for eyewitnesses. The reader has probably had the experience of coming into a dark room after being out in the bright sunshine. Vision is very poor in this situation because the eye needs time to adjust to the sudden change in illumination. This process is called *dark adaptation* (Goldstein, 2007). Photoreceptors respond to light by means of a chemical reaction in a molecule called *rhodopsin*. When light hits a photoreceptor, the molecule changes its shape and this causes an enzyme cascade that ultimately results in a signal being sent to the visual centers of the brain. Because rods are very sensitive to light, their supply of rhodopsin gets used up quickly under bright lighting conditions in a process called *bleaching*. The rhodopsin gets regenerated, but when the lighting is bright the rods' supply of rhodopsin gets used faster than it can be regenerated. That's why, under bright lighting conditions, virtually all vision is cone vision. When you move from a brightly lit area to a dimly lit area, the cones function poorly because cones need a lot of light to function well. But the rods cannot respond either; because they are out of rhodopsin, they are bleached. As a consequence neither the rods nor the cones are functioning optimally and vision is impaired. The eye adapts to this situation, but this takes time. Dark adaptation actually involves two processes. The cones themselves appear to adapt to the change in illumination by becoming somewhat more sensitive to light. This process is pretty quick, with the cones reaching their maximum sensitivity in around 10 minutes. At the same time, the rods are having their supply of rhodopsin refilled so that they can function at maximum capacity. This process is slower and takes about 20 minutes. Thus a witness who views a crime after they have moved from a bright environment into a darker environment is at a relative disadvantage, and the window that this disadvantage operates under is approximately 20 minutes.

Not only does the overall level of illumination influence recognition of faces, but so does the direction of illumination. If a face is illuminated from one direction during the witnessed event, and lit from a different direction during the lineup or photospread, it may be difficult for the witness to match the target to the representation of the perpetrator stored in memory. In one study, Braje, Kersten, Tarr, and Troje (1998) had participants make same/different judgments for pairs of faces presented sequentially. For some pairs of photographs, the faces were illuminated from the same direction. For other pairs of photographs, the faces were illuminated from different directions. Recognition performance declined when the faces were lit from different directions. Cast shadows also impaired recognition performance. Other researchers have produced similar results (Braje, 2003; Liu, Collin, Burton, & Chaudhuri, 1999).

These basic facts about visual perception predict that eyewitness accuracy will be impaired when illumination is poor. Experimental research confirms these claims. For instance, DiNardo and Rainey (1989) showed participants 10 photographs for 3 seconds a piece in either dim lighting or bright lighting conditions. The participants were then tested with 40 photographs for an old/new recognition test under the same lighting conditions. Recognition performance was better when bright lighting was used than when dim lighting was used. In follow-up research, DiNardo and Rainey (1991) crossed illumination at study and illumination at test and found that both independently influenced recognition performance.

In an attempt to more precisely determine how well people can recognize unfamiliar individuals under different lighting conditions, Wagenaar and Van der Schrier (1996) simulated situations in which witnesses viewed an individual at one of nine different illuminations varying from 0.3 lux to 3000 lux. Point three lux is the approximate illumination one would expect for a night with a full moon, and 3000 lux is the amount of illumination one would expect during daylight on a day with a few clouds. Participants viewed photographs of individuals under differing lighting conditions and then were presented with either target-present or target-absent lineups.

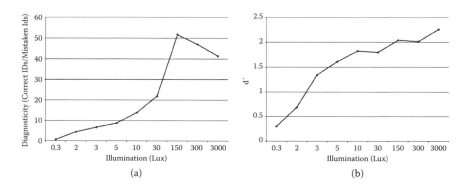

FIGURE 3.1   Effects of illumination on diagnosticity (a) and d′ scores (b) in Wagenaar and van der Schrier (1996). Results are collapsed across the different distances used in the study. (*Source*: Based on data presented in Wagenaar, W. A., & Schrier, van der J. H. (1996). Face recognition as a function of distance and illumination: A practical tool for use in the courtroom. *Psychology, Crime & Law, 2,* 2321–2332.)

Wagenaar and Van der Schrier (1996) presented their data using estimates of diagnosticity and d′ scores. Recall from Chapter 2 that d′ is a measure of memory strength used in signal detection theory. Large values of d′ indicate strong memory. We also introduced the concept of diagnosticity in Chapter 2. Diagnosticity is the ratio of correct identifications to mistaken identifications. Large diagnosticity values indicate that when a suspect is identified, it is very likely the suspect is guilty. For instance, a diagnosticity of 5 means that the odds are 5 to 1 that the suspect is guilty, if the suspect has been picked from a lineup.[1] In Figure 3.1 we collapsed the results across the different distances used in the study so that you can clearly see the overall effect of lighting on diagnosticity and d′. As lighting conditions improved, there was a fairly steep increase in recognition memory abilities. Wagenaar and Van der Schrier (1996) suggested what they called the "rule of 15." According to this rule, acceptable levels of accuracy require illumination of at least 15 lux and distances of no more than 15 meters. They based this claim on estimated diagnosticity, which they argued was unacceptably low when illumination dropped below 15 lux.

These studies all support the general contention that degree of illumination sets hard limits on the recognition accuracy of eyewitnesses. It is important to note, however, that the research conducted to date has primarily examined the effects of illumination on recognition of faces that were viewed as photographs. There is a clear need to examine the effects of illumination in simulated crime paradigms, where the witness sees an actual person at varying levels of illumination.

Distance

It seems like common sense that the further away a witness is from the perpetrator of a crime, the less likely the witness will be to accurately recognize that individual. However, this does not stop prosecutors from occasionally relying on witnesses whose only view of an event was from a very long way away. Loftus and Harley (2005) described a case in which a positive identification was made by a witness who was 450 feet away at the time of the event. As they point out, this is equivalent to being able to identify someone who you had seen behind home plate when you were in the center field stands at a baseball game.

The effect of distance on face perception follows naturally from very basic concepts in perceptual psychology and geometric optics. The size an image casts on the retina is a function of the size of the actual object and how far away that object is from the viewer (Goldstein, 2007). The further away something is, the smaller an image it will cast. Because there are a finite number of photoreceptors on the retina, larger images have more photoreceptors devoted to them than smaller images, making larger images more distinct and visually detailed. The same thing is true for your digital camera. The picture your digital camera takes has a certain number of pixels. Smaller images have fewer pixels devoted to them. This is why simply enlarging a small digital image does not always work out so well. You just end up with a big pixilated image.

Typically, perception researchers describe the size of an image on the retina in terms of the *degrees of visual angle*. The concept of visual angle sometimes sounds odd to people when they first encounter it, but it is actually pretty straightforward. The retina is roughly spherical. So if one is looking at a person's face, the image on your retina will actually be curved. *Visual angle* refers to the angle that produces that arc (see Figure 3.2). If you have two different-sized objects that are the same distance from an observer, the larger object will result in a larger visual angle. Similarly, if you have two objects that are the same size but are different distances from an observer, the object that is closer will produce a larger visual angle.

Visual angle (θ) can be calculated, if you know the length of the object (L) and the distance of the object from the observer (D) by using some trigonometry that your high school teachers told you would be important one day. Here is the equation:

$$\theta = 2 \arctan\left(\frac{L}{2D}\right) \qquad (3.1)$$

This equation is a useful one for the eyewitness expert to know, because it provides an upper threshold on the level of detail that can be accurately

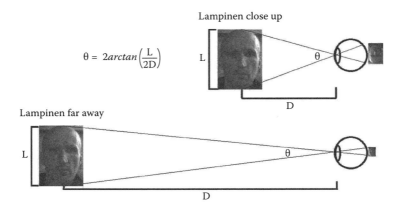

$$\theta = 2arctan\left(\frac{L}{2D}\right)$$

FIGURE 3.2 Illustration of the effect of distance (D) on visual angle (θ). Visual angle is a measure of the size an image casts on the retina. At any distance, larger objects result in greater visual angles. For any sized object, greater distances result in smaller visual angles.

perceived by the witness. To see why this is so, we will first solve the equation for L (i.e., the length of the object).

$$L = 2D * Tan\left(\frac{\theta}{2}\right) \tag{3.2}$$

The maximum cone density in the fovea is slightly less than 160,000 cones per square millimeter (Goldstein, 2007). That means a square millimeter smack dab in the middle of the fovea will be about 400 cones wide by 400 cones high. One degree of visual angle takes up about 0.30 mm (Goldstein, 2007). So a square that is one degree of visual angle by one degree of visual angle will be made up of approximately 120 cones by 120 cones. Estimates of visual acuity indicate that people with normal vision are unable to make out details smaller than about 1/60 of a degree of visual angle under ideal conditions (Foley & Matlin, 2010). Because a witness cannot discriminate details smaller than 1/60 of a degree of visual angle, an image that is exactly one degree of visual angle by one degree of visual angle would be represented in the brain by at most 60 × 60 pixels of information.

So let's apply this to the example from Loftus and Harley (2005). They described a case where an eyewitness was 450 feet away from the perpetrator (D = 5400 inches). The smallest detail that a person can detect is 1/60 of one degree ($\theta = 1/60$). We can apply Equation (3.2) to determine the smallest detail that someone at that distance would be able to detect:

$$L = 2(5400\,\text{inches}) * \left(\frac{(1/60)\,\text{degree}}{2} \right) = 1.57\,\text{inches} \qquad (3.3)$$

In other words, under the best circumstances, a witness who is 450 feet away from a perpetrator would not be able to make out details any finer than 1.57 inches. The typical adult male face is about 6 inches wide and 8.6 inches high (Poston, 2000). So at a distance of 450 feet away, the visual centers of the brain would essentially be presented with an image that was 3.82 pixels wide (6 ÷ 1.57) by 4.58 pixels high (8.6 ÷ 1.57). If a perpetrator's face was completely rectangular, then there would be 4.58 × 3.82 = 17.50 pixels of visual information available for the face at that distance. If one assumes instead that the shape of a face is roughly oval, then one can use the equation for the area of an oval to determine the number of pixels of visual information:

$$A = \left(\frac{h}{2} \right)\left(\frac{w}{2} \right)\pi \qquad (3.4)$$

$$A = \left(\frac{4.58}{2} \right)\left(\frac{3.82}{2} \right)3.14 = 13.74\,pixels \qquad (3.5)$$

One can imagine the witness in court: "That's him! I'd recognize those 14 pixels anywhere!"[2]

The idea that the images produced by faces become increasingly pixilated fits in well with Loftus and Harley's (2005) *distance as filtering hypothesis*. According to this account, distance acts analogously to a filter that selectively filters out high-frequency spatial information. Spatial frequency can best be understood in terms of gratings such as those shown in Figure 3.3 (Goldstein, 2007). A high spatial frequency grating is one in which light and dark areas alternate quite a bit for any given distance (usually expressed as the number of alterations per degree of visual angle). A low spatial frequency grating is one in which the light and dark bars alternate less often for any given distance. When spatial frequency gets too high, people fail to see contrast at all and merely see a uniform gray field.

A mathematical theorem called Fourier's theorem showed that any visual image can be represented as a combination of a set of gratings such as these (Goldstein, 2007). In fact, there is evidence that the brain represents faces in just this way (Näsänen, 1999). Loftus and Harley (2005) argued that distance filters out high spatial frequency information, leaving only lower spatial frequency information. Because perception of fine-grained details requires high spatial frequencies, we lose the ability to see fine-grained details as distance increases.

Spatial Frequency

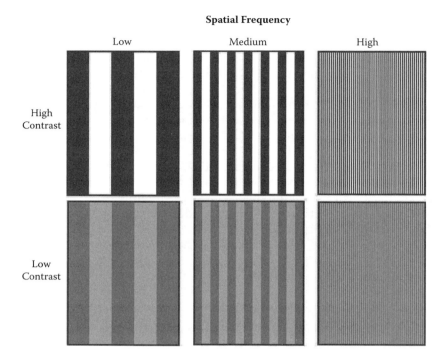

FIGURE 3.3 Square wave gratings illustrating the concepts of contrast and spatial frequency. *High contrast* refers to larger differences between light and dark regions. *Spatial frequency* refers to how often light and dark regions alternate.

Wagenaar and Van der Schrier (1996) assessed the effects of distance on eyewitness identifications. Participants saw photographs that varied in size to simulate viewing perpetrators at varying distances. Photographs were enlarged such that the degrees of visual angle produced by viewing the photograph in the experimental setting matched the degree of visual angle that would be produced by viewing the face at the specified distance. Following the viewing of each photograph, participants were presented with a target-present or target-absent photo lineup. Estimated d′ values for different distances are depicted in Figure 3.4. Wagenaar and Van der Schrier (1996) concluded that recognition of unfamiliar faces was likely to be unacceptably poor at distances over 15 meters, even under the best of circumstances (e.g., optimal lighting, immediate testing, and no change in appearance of the perpetrator).

More recently, Lindsay, Semmler, Weber, Brewer, and Lindsay (2008) conducted a study on the effect of distance on eyewitness memory, using actual people as the targets. More than 1000 participants were approached

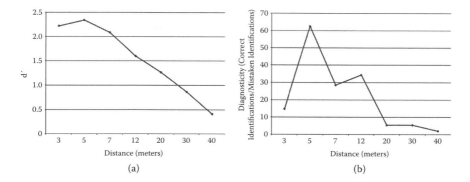

FIGURE 3.4 Effects of distance on d' (a) and diagnosticity (b) in Wagenaar and van der Schrier (1996). Results are collapsed across the different distances used in the study. (*Source:* Based on data presented in Wagenaar, W. A., & Schrier, van der J. H. (1996). Face recognition as a function of distance and illumination: A practical tool for use in the courtroom. *Psychology, Crime & Law, 2,* 2321–2332.)

on the street during daylight hours and were asked to observe an individual for 10 seconds. The target individual was either close (distances between 5 and 15 meters) or far away (distances between 20 and 50 meters). All participants were then shown either a target-present or target-absent lineup. The results indicated that performance declined substantially at the longer distances. Most of the targets (61.07%) were correctly identified from target-present lineups when the targets were close, but a minority of targets was correctly identified when the target had been far away (36.77%). False identifications in the target-absent lineup were 48.6% when the target had been close and 53.33% when the target individual had been far away. Recall that in an actual police lineup, the lineup is made up of one suspect and a number of foils (foils are known to be innocent). Because of that, it is common to divide the false identification rate by the size of the lineup to get an idea of how often innocent suspects would be falsely identified (assuming a fair lineup). When the researchers did so, they found that the estimated false suspect identification rates were 8.1% when the target had been close and 8.88% when the target had been far away. As can be seen, the effect of distance on recognition accuracy had the largest impact on the rate at which guilty suspects were chosen in the target-present lineups.

So what are the implications of this for police and the courts? As noted above, when thinking about the practical implications of a variable on eyewitness identification, a useful index is the diagnosticity of the lineup. *Diagnosticity* is the ratio of correct suspect identifications to false suspect identifications. It tells you how much more likely it is that someone is guilty than that they are innocent, given that they were identified. At close distances, the diagnosticity observed in the Lindsay et al. (2008) study was about 7.54 (61.07/8.1). In other words, if a suspect was identified, it was 7.54 times more likely that the person was the target than that they were not the target. At longer distances, the diagnosity was much lower, only 4.14 (48.6/8.88). In other words, if a suspect was identified, it was 4.14 times more likely that the person was the target than that the person was not the target. Lindsay and colleagues concluded that identifications were less reliable at longer distances. However, contrary to Wagenaar and Van der Schrier (1996), they argued that 15 meters did not provide a cutoff beyond which identification accuracy was unacceptable. Rather, they suggest that the courts simply use information about distance to weigh some testimony more than others.

There is one other important factor to note from the Lindsay et al. (2008) study. As the authors pointed out, sometimes the only information available about the distance a witness was away from a perpetrator comes from the witness's memory. However, distance estimates are oftentimes unreliable and can underestimate the actual distance. To examine this issue, Lindsay et al. asked their participants to estimate the distance they were from the target, either while the target was present or from memory. They found that participants frequently underestimated actual distances and that errors were especially frequent when the estimate relied on memory.

Viewing Time

Another variable that is likely to influence the accuracy of a witness's identification is the amount of time the witness was exposed to the perpetrator's face. In some eyewitness situations, the witness may catch only a fleeting glimpse of the perpetrator. In others, the witness may be exposed to the perpetrator for an hour or more. A commonplace assumption in many perceptual theories is that the visual system samples information from the environment over time (e.g., Lamberts & Freeman, 1999). Brief exposures result in a sparser sampling of information and thus should result in poorer memory.

For instance, DiNardo and Rainey (1991) had participants study a group of photographs. Each photograph was presented for either 1.5 seconds or 5 seconds. Participants were then presented with a mixture of old and new photographs. The results showed a definite advantage for photographs that had been studied for longer periods of time. Correct recognition of presented photos (i.e., hits) was 82.75% in the 5-second condition and 76.75 in the 1.5-second condition. False recognition of nonpresented photos (i.e., false alarms) was 15.75% in the 5-second condition and 19.67% in the 1.5-second condition. Longer exposures led to more hits and fewer false alarms. These results match most people's intuitions that longer exposures should result in better memory.

However, a review of the literature on face memory by Shapiro and Penrod (1986) suggests that the relationship between exposure duration and face recognition accuracy is not always simple. In their review, they found that increases in exposure duration can sometimes result in both increased correct recognition of previously seen faces and increased false recognition of new faces. Read (1995) further tested this notion in a field study in which participants interacted with a store clerk for either a short period of time (< 1 minute) or a long period of time (4–12 minutes). In addition to exposure duration, Read varied the similarity of the lineup photos to the confederate's appearance at the time of the interaction. In particular, at the time of the interaction with the store clerk, the confederate had been wearing glasses and had worn her hair down. In the high-similarity condition, all the photographs in both the target-present and target-absent lineups showed women who matched the general description of the confederate and who wore glasses and had their hair down. In the low-similarity condition, the same women were shown, but without glasses and with their hair worn up.

The low-similarity condition worked out as one might expect (Figure 3.5A). Longer exposures led to more correct identifications in the target-present lineups and fewer false identifications in the target-absent lineups. However, in the high-similarity conditions, things were different (Figure 3.5B). Longer exposure durations were associated with more correct identifications in the target-present lineups but were also associated with more false identifications in the target-absent lineups. Not only that, the diagnosticity of the lineup was *much* better in the low-exposure duration condition. Longer exposure duration may typically help witnesses, but under conditions of very high levels of contextual similarity, exposure duration may actually increase the likelihood of false identifications and *hurt* the diagnosticity of the lineup.

Why? Read (1995) advanced the following explanation. First, under conditions of high contextual similarity, participants in both the target-present and target-absent conditions are likely to experience a strong sense of familiarity. All the members of the lineup will kind of look familiar to the witness because they all match the general description of the perpetrator and they all are similar to the perpetrator in terms of hairstyle, wearing glasses, and so on. This high degree of contextual similarity occurred in both the target-present and target-absent lineups. Read proposed that this heightened familiarity might have caused the witnesses to conclude that *someone* in the lineup must be the culprit. Not only that, Read proposed that in the long-exposure-duration condition, people might have drawn the conclusion that they *should* be able to identify someone. As a consequence, longer exposure durations combined with contextual similarity

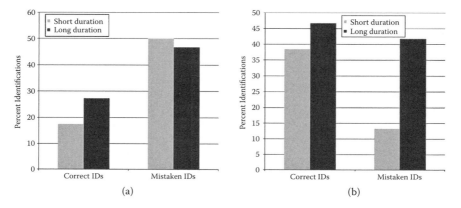

FIGURE 3.5   Effects of viewing time on eyewitness identification accuracy in Read (1995). Figure (a) shows the low-similarity condition. Figure (b) shows the high-similarity condition. Correct identification reflects identification of suspect in target-present lineups. Mistaken identification reflects overall identification rate from target-absent lineups. (*Source*: Based on data presented in Read, J. (1995). The availability heuristic in person identification: The sometimes misleading consequences of enhanced contextual information. *Applied Cognitive Psychology, 9,* 91–121.)

led to more mistaken identifications in target-absent lineups. Read (1995) suggested that another way of thinking about the results is in terms of the *availability heuristic* (Tversky & Kahnemann, 1973). According to the availability heuristic, we tend to think events are probable when we find it easy to generate information about the events. Read (1995) argued that in the long-exposure-duration conditions and high-similarity condition, contextual details were highly available in memory and led people to conclude that someone in the lineup must be the guilty party.

In a more recent study by Memon, Hope, and Bull (2003), young adult and elderly participants watched a videotape of a robbery. In one version of the videotape, the perpetrator's face was visible for approximately 45 seconds. In the other version, the perpetrator's face was visible for only 12 seconds. After viewing the video, participants were presented with either a target-present or target-absent lineup. The results were consistent with increased exposure duration being associated with more accurate eyewitness identifications. First, for both young adults and elderly, there was a large effect of exposure duration on the correct identification of suspects in the target-present lineups. For the young adult participants, the perpetrator was correctly identified only 29% of the time when he was visible for only 12 seconds in the film. When the perpetrator was visible for 45 seconds, the correct identification rate jumped to 95%. Similar large increases in accuracy at longer exposure durations occurred for the elderly witnesses.

To get a sense of the size of this effect, consider again the concept that we have called *diagnosticity*, which is the ratio of correct suspect identifications in target-present lineups to false suspect identifications in target-absent lineups. For young adults, in the short-exposure condition, the diagnosticity was 1.93. In other words, given that a suspect was selected, that person was 1.93 times more likely to be a guilty suspect than an innocent suspect. When exposure duration increased to 45 seconds, the diagnosticity increased to 13.90. Given that a suspect was selected in the long-exposure condition, it was almost 14 times more likely that the person was a guilty suspect than an innocent suspect. Thus there was a large and forensically meaningful difference between the accuracy of witnesses exposed to a culprit for a short time and the accuracy of witnesses exposed to a culprit for a somewhat longer time.

So what are we to make of these findings? First, with regard to basic perceptual and cognitive processing, it seems reasonable to conclude from these data that memory for faces should be improved with longer exposure durations. That is, increased viewing time should lead to better memory records. However, increased viewing times may, under certain circumstances, change the metacognitive assumptions made by witnesses, making it less likely that they will reject a lineup. This can actually *increase* errors.

One thing is for certain: Long viewing times do not guarantee that an eyewitness will make an accurate identification. For instance, Morgan et al. (2007) tested the eyewitness accuracy of military recruits who had been subjected to interrogations lasting approximately 40 minutes. Despite the relatively long exposure to their interrogators' faces, accuracy was not particularly good. We also know from DNA exoneration cases that long viewing times do not guarantee accuracy. For instance, one of the best known DNA exoneration cases involved Jennifer Thompson. Thompson was a victim of a brutal rape that occurred in 1984. During the course of the attack, Thompson made a conscious effort to look at her attacker's face and had an opportunity to view her attacker's face for a full half hour. Thompson managed to escape and later identified Ronald Cotton as her attacker. Cotton always maintained his innocence; however, based largely on Thompson's testimony, Cotton was convicted. He spent over a decade in prison, but was eventually exonerated based on new DNA techniques (Thompson, 2009). Despite the half hour viewing time, and Thompson's best attempts to remember her attacker's face, she still ended up making an incorrect identification.

Passage of Time

Perhaps one of the most famous findings in the history of research on memory is Ebbinghaus's (1885/1913) famous forgetting curve (see Figure 3.6). Ebbinghaus, using himself as a subject, memorized strings of nonsense syllables and then tried to relearn those nonsense syllables after varying amounts of time. His measure of retention was how much less time it took him to relearn the string of nonsense syllables the second go around. What Ebbinghaus discovered was a smooth exponential forgetting curve, in which memory sharply declined immediately after the original learning trials and then declined more slowly as the retention interval increased. Given how influential this finding was among psychologists, it is not surprising that most memory psychologists believe that eyewitness identifications

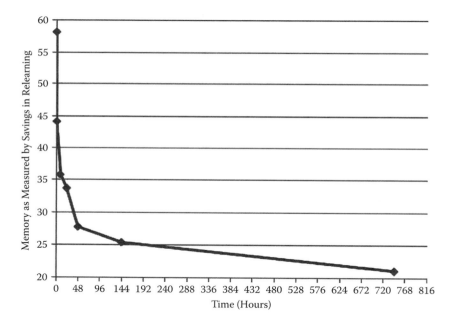

FIGURE 3.6 Ebbinghaus's (1913) forgetting curve. Ebbinghaus measured memory in terms of "savings in relearning," which was defined at how much quicker he could learn a list of nonsense syllables after having previously learned it. Savings in relearning was measured as a percentage change. For instance, if it originally took you 10 minutes to learn a list and later you could relearn it in 8 minutes, the savings in relearning would be 20%. (*Source*: Based on data presented in Ebbinghaus, E. (1885/1913). *Memory: A study in experimental psychology*. New York: Columbia University Press.)

are likely to be less accurate if a witness is questioned long after a crime occurred (Kassin, Ellsworth, & Smith, 1989; Kassin, Tubb, Hosch, & Memon, 2001).

A number of studies have examined the effects of retention interval on memory for faces. One fairly typical study was conducted by Metzger (2006). During a study phase participants studied 24 black-and-white year-book photos that were projected onto a screen in the experiment room for 5 seconds each. Half of the photographs had been previously rated as being highly distinctive, and half were less distinctive. Participants were tested either immediately, after 3 weeks, after 6 weeks, or after 12 weeks. The test consisted of 48 photographs. Half of the photographs had been previously studied (targets), and half of the photographs had not been previously studied (foils). As with the targets, half of the foils were photographs that had been previously rated as being highly distinctive, and half of the foils were photographs that had been rated as being less distinctive. For each photograph, participants simply indicated whether it was old (i.e., previously studied) or new (i.e., not previously studied). Participants also indicated their confidence using a 4-point confidence scale.

Metzger analyzed the results by calculating d' scores for each participant. Recall that d' is an index of recognition memory that provides an estimate of how much more familiar studied items seem to participants than unstudied items. Large d' scores indicate better memory. For both the distinctive and the less distinctive faces, memory quickly deteriorated as the retention interval increased. Consider the results for the visually distinctive faces. When memory was tested immediately after viewing the photographs, the mean d' score was 2.66, but after 12 weeks, d' fell to .74. The same pattern was observed for the less distinctive faces, although the drop was less dramatic, because the less distinctive faces were not recognized as well to start with.

These findings from basic face memory research suggest that memory for faces declines with time and that there is substantial forgetting of faces after 12 weeks. However, even after 12 weeks, performance was better than chance. These results are informative for eyewitness researchers and law enforcement. For a perpetrator with a highly distinctive face, a witness who makes an identification immediately after the crime can be highly reliable. After 3 months, identification accuracy is likely to decline substantially. The identification will not be informationally worthless, however. The investigator should be cautious though, because even for a highly distinctive face, accuracy is likely to be low and there is a substantial chance of a false identification.

Although studies such as these provide useful information about recognition memory of faces, it is important to note important differences between such studies and actual eyewitness identification procedures. First, most face recognition studies involve studying a large number of faces and being tested with a large number of faces. A typical crime involves a much smaller number of perpetrators, and often only one. Second, eyewitness identification usually involves picking a person from a lineup, and in a well-conducted lineup, the witness is told that they are free to reject the lineup altogether. Because of this, it is always important to test the generalizability of findings using more realistic eyewitness scenarios.

In one recent study, Memon, Bartlett, Rose, and Gray (2003) compared lineup performance of younger and older witnesses. Participants viewed two videotapes, one showing a young adult perpetrator and one showing an elderly perpetrator. The participants were then shown two lineups, one 35 minutes after the videotape and the other one week after viewing the videotape. For the current section, the results of most interest concern the effects of retention interval on witness accuracy. The one-week delay had very little effect on lineup accuracy for the young adult witnesses. Correct identification in the target-present condition decreased only slightly and not significantly, and false identifications also decreased slightly. For the elderly witnesses, the story was different. The one-week delay produced a substantial decline in correct identifications in target-present lineups, down from about 40% correct IDs to around 15% correct IDs.

Results of studies such as these were recently reviewed in a comprehensive meta-analysis by Deffenbacher, Bornstein, McGorty, and Penrod (2008). Their analysis involved combing the results of 39 studies that examined the effect of retention interval on memory for faces. The studies that were included were both old/new recognition studies and eyewitness identification studies that involved simulated lineups or showups. Although the review included an occasional study that found no significant effect of retention interval, the overall finding was that longer retention intervals result in poorer face memory and worse lineup performance. The meta-analysis found that the mean effect size was .38. An effect size provides an index of how strongly two variables are related. An effect size of .38 indicates a moderate relationship between the independent variable (i.e., time) and the dependent variable (i.e., accuracy) (Cohen, 1988).

Deffenbacher et al. (2008) went beyond merely establishing that time delay impairs eyewitness accuracy to examine the nature of the relationship between time delay and accuracy. The starting point of their analysis was Wickelgren's (1974) theory of forgetting. According to Wickelgren's theory, forgetting over time occurs for two reasons. First, some forgetting occurs due to the interference that arises from encountering other similar items. Thus, as time passes, the witness encounters other individuals, who may be similar in appearance to the perpetrator; these other similar individuals may make it more difficult to remember the perpetrator. Second, Wickelgren assumed that memory representations (i.e., traces) decay over time. *Decay* essentially implies that the features that make

up the representation become less tightly bound, making it more difficult later on to reconstruct the original representation. Lastly, Wickelgren
introduced the concept of *fragility*, which represents the degree to which
a particular memory trace is subject to forgetting. In other words, some
stimuli are less distinctive and are likely to be forgotten relatively quickly,
whereas others are more distinctive and are likely to be forgotten relatively slowly. Wickelgren's theory thus examined memory as a function
of the initial strength of the memory, the fragility of the memory trace,
the degree of decay over time, and the degree of interference over time.
Wickelgren provided a formal mathematical model of the relationships
between these variables. The specific form of the forgetting function is
given by the following equation:

$$m = \frac{L}{t^D e^{It}} \tag{3.6}$$

In Equation (3.6), **m** represents how strong the person's memory for the
event is currently, **L** represents the initial memory strength, **t** represents
time measured in seconds, **D** represents forgetting due to decay, **I** represents forgetting due to interference, and **e** is a mathematical constant
that may be familiar to some readers from their high school and/or college math classes. It is the base of the natural logarithm and is equal to
approximately 2.72.

The equation looks intimidating, but it is possible to get a basic sense
of what it is saying by examining what is likely to happen as the parameters of the function change. First, note that the numerator, **L**, indicates
the initial memory strength. As time passes, that initial memory strength
is getting divided (i.e., made smaller) by numbers that vary as a function
of how much time has passed. As more time passes, the initial memory
strength (**L**) is being divided by bigger and bigger numbers, making the
current memory strength (**m**) smaller and smaller. Recall that **D** indicates
the effects of simple decay on memory. Imagine that **D** is equal to 1. Then,
after 2 seconds have passed, the memory strength would be cut in half;
after 3 seconds have passed, memory strength would be cut by one third;
after 4 seconds have passed, memory strength would be cut by one fourth;
and so on. Smaller values of **D** represent less pronounced effects of decay
on memory strength because **t** is being raised to a smaller power. One can
interpret the **I** parameter in a similar way. In this part of the equation,
the base of the natural logarithm (**e**) is being raised to the **It** power. The
greater the value of the interferences parameter (**I**) and the more time that
passes (**t**), the larger the resultant value e^{It} becomes. And as e^{It} gets larger
and larger with the passage of time, the denominator of the equation gets
bigger and the memory strength (**m**) gets smaller and smaller.

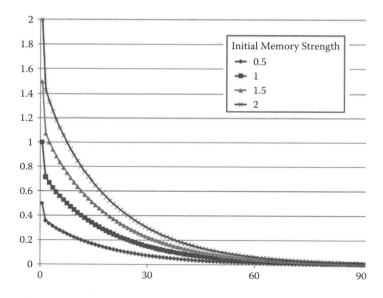

FIGURE 3.7 Illustration of the effect of the passage of time on memory according to Wickelgren's forgetting function. The y-axis shows d' scores, and the x-axis shows days that have passed since initial exposure.

Deffenbacher et al. (2008) used this function to fit data from eight different studies and found that it provided a good account of forgetting for faces. They also provided estimates of the parameters that might be reasonable to assume for forgetting due to decay (.025) and forgetting due to interference (6×10^{-7}). The results provide a nice theoretical account of how delay affects eyewitness identification accuracy. In Figure 3.7, we used these estimates to plot out the projected memory (d') as a function of time, based on different initial levels of memory strength. You can see in this graph that as time passes, there is initially a very rapid drop in memory, which then levels off as more time passes.

Arousal and Stress

As we have just seen, eyewitness identification is influenced by basic facts about perception and memory. However, eyewitness testimony also has an emotional component that is important for the researcher and practitioner to consider. Some crimes are extremely stressful, such as witnessing a bank robbery, whereas other crimes are relatively less stressful, such as someone trying to pass a forged check. Stressful events produce both physiological and psychological changes that occur as an attempt on the part of the body to allow the person to cope with the situation (Costanzo, 2007). These changes are mediated by activation of the sympathetic branch of the autonomic nervous system. Stress results in the release of the hormones cortisol and adrenalin from the adrenal gland. The hormones result in heightened alertness, increased heart rate and blood pressure, as well as cognitive and emotional changes.

The effects of stress on memory and cognition are multifaceted, diverse, and complex. For instance, it is known that exposure to cortisol can impair long-term memory formation (Lupien & McEwen, 1997). In one study, Newcomer et al. (1999) demonstrated that participants given high doses of cortisol for several days showed major impairments in the ability to form long-term memories. Moderate doses of cortisol or durations shorter than 4 days did not produce this effect. Other work has shown that long-term exposure to cortisol may actually damage the hippocampus, the brain region responsible for long-term memory formation (Sapolsky, Krey, & McEwen, 1985).

There is a large amount of literature on the effect of stress on memory in general and on eyewitness identification accuracy in particular. As Deffenbacher, Bornstein, Penrod, and McGorty (2004) have recently noted, every possible relationship has been observed. Some studies have found that stress is associated with impaired eyewitness identification accuracy. Other studies have found that stress is associated with improved eyewitness identification accuracy. Still other studies have produced null effects. However, the preponderance of evidence now available indicates that very high levels of stress are associated with decreases, sometimes substantial decreases, in eyewitness identification accuracy.

As an example of a study showing substantial impairment in identification accuracy following a stressful event, consider this recent study by Morgan et al. (2004). Participants were military personnel who were subjected to simulated interrogations as part of their training. In the high-stress version of the interrogation, the participants had to endure physical confrontations with their interrogators. In the low-stress version of the interrogation, the interrogators simply tried to trick the participants into revealing information. Twenty-four hours after the training exercise was completed, participants were shown a live lineup, a simultaneous photo lineup, or a sequential photo lineup. High stress clearly impaired eyewitness identification accuracy. Consider the performance in the simultaneous photospread. Correct identifications from the target-present lineup in the low-stress condition were 76% compared to only 34% in the high-stress condition. False identifications in the target-absent lineup were 12% in the low-stress condition and 68% in the high-stress condition.

In another recent study, Valentine and Mesout (2009) took advantage of a naturally occurring event that included a fear-provoking component.

They examined the identification accuracy of visitors to the London Dungeon, an interactive tourist attraction featuring scenes of medieval torture. One part of the tour includes the Labyrinth of the Lost. In the Labyrinth of the Lost, patrons walk through a large mirrored maze and are confronted by various frightening characters who jump out at them unexpectedly. In the study, patrons who were visiting the London Dungeon were asked to wear heart rate monitors as they made their way through the dungeon. While in the labyrinth, a man wearing a hooded robe jumped out in front of them and blocked their path. The participants subsequently reported the level of anxiety they had experienced, and these self-reports were confirmed with data from the heart rate monitors. Participants were then asked to make an identification from a nine-person target-present lineup. Participants who scored above the median in self-reported anxiety were correct only 17% of the time, which is only a little better than chance (11.11%). Participants who scored below the median in self-reported anxiety were correct 75% of the time.

Despite these findings, some studies of the relationship between stress and identification accuracy have produced null effects. For an example of a study that found no relationship between degree of stress and identification accuracy, consider the study by Clifford and Hollin (1981). Participants watched videos depicting a violent purse snatching or a similar videotape in which a man asks for directions. Participants were later asked to answer questions about the event and were also presented with a target-present photo lineup. Although eyewitness identification accuracy was lower for participants who viewed a violent video (23.33%) than for participants who viewed a nonviolent video (30%), the difference was not statistically reliable. This latter finding may reflect a lack of power as only 60 participants took part in the study. Of course, it is important to note that even though the result was a null effect statistically, the pattern was consistent with stress impairing identification accuracy.

One way of accounting for the effects of stress on eyewitness memory is in terms of the Yerkes–Dodson Law (1908). According to this account, memory performance will be best under moderate amounts of physiological arousal, and under extremely high levels of arousal or extremely low levels of arousal memory will be poor. At very low levels of arousal, attention is unfocused, and consequently relevant details of the event are likely to be missed. The person is just kind of zoning out (like the students in our lectures). Moderate levels of arousal lead to better attentional focus and improved memory. The person is alert and can concentrate on what is relevant. However, at high levels of arousal, such as those experienced by a witness to a violent crime, memory may be impaired. Arousal and stress get so intense that the person is overloaded and cannot attend well to the relevant aspects of the event. The Yerkes–Dodson Law is typically

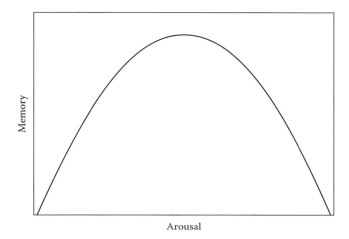

Memory

Arousal

FIGURE 3.8   Illustration of the Yerkes–Dodson Law.

depicted as an inverted U-function where moderate levels of arousal result in the best memory performance (see Figure 3.8).

Of course, this begs the question as to how much stress is an optimal amount of stress and the answer appears to be that it depends a great deal on the specifics of the situation, the person, and the types of details being tested. These issues are explored most fully in Easterbrook's (1959) *cue utilization hypothesis*. According to this hypothesis, high levels of stress narrow the focus of attention to a small number of details. This has sometimes been called *attentional tunneling*. Importantly, attentional tunneling can lead to a focus on either external features of the environment (e.g., the attacker) or internal details related to the person's own mental state (e.g., thoughts such as "I'm going to die"). If witnesses focus their attention on their own internal states, they will have little attention to devote to the face of the perpetrator, resulting in poor memory later on. Additionally, if witnesses focus their attention on a weapon or fear in the faces of other victims, they will have relatively less attention to focus on the perpetrator's face. Eyewitness researchers have shown that stress appears to narrow attention to central aspects of the event to the detriment of more peripheral aspects of the event. Consistent with this view, it has been found that eyewitnesses to stressful events may have preserved memory for central details but impaired memory for peripheral details (Christianson, 1992).

Thus the theoretical understanding of stress and memory outlined so far leads to predictions that are not as simple as saying stress impairs memory. Indeed, relative to very low-stress situations, moderate levels of stress may improve memory. However, very high levels of stress will likely impair memory. Moreover, stress should have a larger impact on the less central details of an event. The effects may also depend a great deal on what aspect of the external or internal environment the witness chooses to focus on under the demands of attentional tunneling.

Deffenbacher (1994) proposed that it is important to distinguish between different aspects of the stress response. In particular, he argued that it is important to distinguish between cognitive anxiety and somatic anxiety. *Cognitive anxiety* refers to that aspect of stress that involves worry. *Somatic anxiety* refers to the person's perception of the physiological arousal that accompanies stress. Based on Fazey and Hardy's (1988) *catastrophe model of anxiety*, Deffenbacher proposed that when cognitive anxiety is relatively high, increases in somatic anxiety should lead to gradual increases in performance, but only up to a certain breaking point. When that breaking point is reached, there is not a gradual decline in performance (as in the Yerkes–Dodson Law) but rather a catastrophic breakdown of the entire system leading to a large sudden drop in performance. In a recent meta-analysis, Deffenbacher et al. (2008) have shown that the emerging consensus is that high levels of stress, producing both high levels of cognitive anxiety and high levels of somatic anxiety, result in decreased eyewitness identification accuracy. Indeed, Deffenbacher et al. reviewed 27 published tests of the relationship between anxiety and eyewitness identification accuracy. In eight of those comparisons, effect size estimates indicated that accuracy was greater in the high-stress condition (although usually not significantly so), and in 19 cases accuracy was higher in the low-stress condition. Moreover, the deleterious effects of stress on memory were greatest for studies that utilized staged crimes as opposed to more artificial videotaped or slide presentations. Overall, then, the effects of high levels of stress, including both high levels of cognitive anxiety (i.e., worry) as well as somatic anxiety (i.e., the perception of physiological arousal), appear to be associated with reduced eyewitness identification accuracy under most circumstances.

Presence of a Weapon

A related factor that has been implicated in the accuracy of eyewitness identification is whether or not a weapon was present in the crime (Pickel, 2007). In particular, it has sometimes been found that the presence of a weapon can impair the accuracy of eyewitness identifications from line-ups or the accuracy of witness descriptions (Loftus, Loftus, & Messo, 1987). This finding has been referred to as the *weapon focus effect*. The basic claim is that the presence of a weapon captures the witness's attention, thus leaving less attention available to process the perpetrator's facial features or other important aspects of the event.

In one of the first scientific studies of the weapon focus effect, Johnson and Scott (1976, cited in Loftus et al., 1987) created a staged event. In one version of the event, participants in a waiting room heard a conversation and then saw a man enter the room holding a grease pen. In the weapon focus condition, participants in a waiting room heard an argument and then saw a man enter the room holding a bloody letter opener. Participants were later asked to make an identification from a group of 50 pictures. Participants in the weapon focus condition were less accurate (33%) than were participants in the control condition (49%).

In a later study, Loftus et al. (1987) showed participants a slide presentation of a man at a fast-food restaurant. In one version of the slides, the man handed the cashier a check and was then given money in return. In the weapon focus condition, the man pulled a gun on the cashier and was given money in return. Participants were later shown an eight-alternative target-present lineup. Participants were more accurate in the control condition (38.9% in Experiment 1 versus 35% in Experiment 2) than in the experimental condition (11.1% in Experiment 1 versus 15% in Experiment 2). In addition, participants in the weapon focus condition were less accurate on memory questions about the perpetrator (e.g., describe the perpetrator's hair) than were participants in the control condition, although this effect was statistically reliable only in Experiment 2. In addition to measuring the accuracy of participants' memories, Loftus et al. (1987, Exp. 1) also recorded participants' eye movements as they viewed the slides. The results of this analysis revealed that participants fixated on the weapon more often than they did on the check, and the total length of time they fixated on the weapon was longer than the total length of time they fixated on the check. These results support the idea that the presence of a weapon captures attention.

Another early study used a face recognition paradigm to investigate the role of weapon presence on memory for faces (Tooley, Brigham, Maass, & Bothwell, 1987). Participants viewed 24 slides that showed full-body views of men standing at a convenience store. Half of the slides showed Caucasian males, and half showed African American males (participants were predominantly Caucasian). In addition, in half of the slides the men were holding a weapon, and in half of the slides the men were holding some other object. Prior to viewing the slides, participants were told to focus on (a) each person's face, (b) each person's hand, (c) the background of each slide, or (d) whatever they felt like focusing on. In addition to these manipulations, the researchers artificially increased arousal in some participants by means of white noise and by telling them that during the presentation phase they might receive an electric shock. After the presentation phase, participants took an old/new recognition test. The test included the 24 targets that had been previously seen, but they were wearing different clothing than they had previously worn. Intermixed with the targets on the recognition test were race-matched foils. For each photograph, participants indicated whether that individual had been previously presented during the study phase.

Results were analyzed by means of d′ scores (see Chapter 2). Not surprisingly, participants in the face focus condition (M = .56) outperformed participants in the other conditions (M =.22 hand focus; M = .28 background focus; M = .26 free focus). There was also evidence of a same-race bias as memory was better for Caucasian pictures (M = .38) than African American pictures (M = .28). Importantly, there was evidence of a weapon focus effect as memory was significantly worse for pictures of men who had been holding weapons (M = .31) than it was for men who had been holding other objects (M = .35). The difference in mean d′ was only .04, making it a small effect in absolute terms. However, the difference was statistically reliable. In addition, Tooley et al. (1987) pointed out that the weapon effect accounted for only 1.6% of the variance in recognition accuracy.

There has been some debate about the cause of the weapon focus effect. One early explanation (Loftus et al., 1987) focused on the notion that weapons are threatening and likely to produce emotional arousal. In particular, Loftus et al. (1987) conceptualized the weapon focus effect in terms of Easterbrook's (1959) cue utilization hypothesis. According to this account, when someone views a scene containing a weapon, it produces stress, which narrows the person's focus of attention to the source of that stress (i.e., the weapon), leaving less processing resources to encode features of the perpetrator's appearance.

Shortly after these initial studies, Kramer, Buckhout, and Eugenio (1990) presented some evidence consistent with the emotional arousal account. Participants viewed slides depicting an assault in which the perpetrator hits an individual over the head with a glass bottle following a dispute at a card game. In the weapon-visible condition, a man enters the room brandishing the bottle, curses the victim, and then breaks the bottle over his head. In the weapon-hidden condition, a man enters the room with something held behind his back, curses the victim, and then hits him over the head with the bottle that had been hidden behind his back. Results indicated that memory for facial details were superior when the weapon was hidden prior to the assault than when it was visible. Moreover, self-reported anxiety was higher in the weapon-visible condition and was negatively correlated with description accuracy.

Other researchers have argued that the weapon focus effect can be explained by the novelty of the weapon. Support for the novelty account has been produced in a number of innovative experiments by Pickel and colleagues (Pickel, 1998, 1999; Pickel, Ross, & Truelove, 2006). In a direct comparison of the role of novelty and threat, Pickel (1998) presented participants with a videotape of a scene inside a hair salon. A target individual in the scene was shown holding an object that varied in both threat and situational novelty. The high-threat and low-novelty condition showed the target holding a pair of scissors. The high-threat and high-novelty condition showed the target holding a handgun. The low-threat and high-novelty condition showed the target holding a chicken (!). The low-threat and low-novelty condition showed the target holding a wallet. In addition, there was a control condition in which the target individual was not holding anything. The results indicated that memory for details of the target person's appearance were significantly influenced by the novelty of the object they were holding, but were not significantly influenced by the level of threat of the object. In particular, more details were remembered in the conditions where the object was low in novelty (M= 8.33 details) than in the conditions where the object was high in novelty (M = 7.52 details). In other research, Pickel (1999) found that a weapon focus effect occurs in situations where the presence of a gun is unexpected, but does not occur in situations where the presence of a gun is expected. Furthermore, witness accuracy is poorer when people view individuals who are holding objects that are inconsistent with their occupations, suggesting that the presence of a novel object is sufficient to produce a decrease in memory for the target individual.

In other studies, the role of novelty and threat has been more ambiguous. In one study, participants viewed a videotape that showed a scene in an office in which a man enters holding a briefcase (Mitchell et al., 1998). In the *control condition*, the man simply shakes hands with two men inside the office. In the *novel object condition*, the man takes a stalk of celery out of his briefcase and shows it to the men inside the office. In the *weapon–no threat condition*, the man takes out a gun and shows it to the men inside the office in a nonthreatening manner. The video was filmed in such a way that this was a friendly interaction in which the gun was merely being shown to the other men. In the *weapon-threat condition*, the man takes out a gun and points it in a threatening manner at the men inside the office. Following the presentation of the videotape, participants answered questions about the film, including specific questions concerning the "perpetrator" and his appearance.

If one looks at the overall pattern of effects, the results are quite intriguing. Witness performance was lowest in the condition in which the "perpetrator" was holding the celery (58%), and this value did not significantly differ from performance in the weapon-threat condition (60%). Performance was better in the control condition (69%) and the weapon–no threat condition (70%). The results appear to be consistent with the idea that both novelty and threat may be relevant. The novel object condition did worse than the control condition, supporting the idea that novelty matters. The presence of a weapon decreased performance, but only when the weapon was used in a threatening manner. This seems to support the idea that threat matters. However, although the results of this study are provocative, they are not definitive. First, although the novel object condition and the weapon-threat condition produced similar results and were not significantly different from one another, the weapon-threat condition was only marginally significantly different from the control condition (p = .08). Second, if the weapon focus effect occurs via novelty, then it seems strange that the effect did not occur in the weapon–no threat condition. Intuitively, it seems odd that someone would walk into an office and take a gun out of their briefcase for whatever reason. Third, although Mitchell et al. collected ratings of participant's emotional responses, the results of those ratings were not especially informative. For instance, the novelty account would presumably predict higher ratings of surprise for the novel object than for the other object. Yet inferential tests revealed no significant effect of condition on ratings of surprise. Similarly, the threat account would predict higher ratings of anxiety, fear, and so on in the weapon-threat condition, and yet again, there were no significant effects of condition on these ratings.

More recently, Hope and Wright (2007) argued that both novelty and threat may play a role in the weapon focus effect. Participants in this study viewed a series of slides while also performing an attention-demanding ongoing task. The slides showed a man entering a grocery store. In the critical slides, the man was shown holding either a neutral object (i.e., wallet), an unusual object (i.e., a brightly colored feather duster), or a weapon (i.e., a gun). Participants later answered a series of 22 questions about the slides and rated their confidence in response to each question. Performance on the ongoing task was worse in the novel object and weapon condition than in the neutral condition, suggesting that the presence of a novel object or weapon captures attention. With regard to memory accuracy, performance in the novel object condition and the weapon condition was significantly worse than performance in the neutral object condition. The novel object and weapon conditions did not significantly differ from one another with regard to accuracy. However, participants in the weapon condition were significantly less confident than were participants in the novel object condition. Hope and Wright (2007) argued that when a sensitive measure is used (i.e., confidence), it is possible to demonstrate that the memory impairment produced by the presence of a weapon is greater than what one would expect based on novelty alone.

These theoretical issues are not yet fully resolved. However, in addition to the theoretical account of the weapon focus effect, there are a number of other pragmatic issues that are important to consider. For instance, most studies of the weapon focus effect have relied exclusively on target-present lineups. More needs to be known about what effect weapon focus might have on target-absent lineups. Additionally, the effect of the presence of a weapon on eyewitness identification is often quite small. Oftentimes researchers fail to find any effect at all on eyewitness identification. More often, the effect of weapon focus appears in accuracy scores for memory questions about the perpetrator and the event (e.g., "What color were the perpetrator's eyes?" or "About how tall was the perpetrator?"). Indeed, an early meta-analysis by Steblay (1992) estimated the effect size of weapon focus on lineup accuracy to be only .13, a reliable but rather small effect. For description questions, Steblay (1992) estimated an effect size of .55, in the moderate effect size range. Another issue that is of importance has to do with the lack of naïve realism in most weapon focus studies. In actual eyewitness situations, a witness is oftentimes personally threatened by the presence of the weapon. At the very least, they are likely to believe that *someone* might be injured or killed by the weapon. However, for ethical reasons, most studies of the weapon focus effect have presented partici-pant witnesses with videotape or slide presentations in which no personal threat is likely to be experienced. This makes a full test of the weapon focus effect difficult. Maass and Kohnken (1989) developed an interesting way of addressing this problem. Participants in the study were told they were taking part in a study of physical activity and emotional well-being. Participants were seated in a recliner and after waiting for a period of time were approached by a female experimenter. In the "weapon" condition, the experimenter was holding a syringe with a 5 centimeter long needle. In the control condition, the experimenter was holding a pen. In each con-dition, half of the participants were told that they would receive an injec-tion. Participants were later tested for their memory of the confederate. Presence of the syringe resulted in lower lineup accuracy relative to the control condition, although the verbal threat had no effect. It is possible that the verbal threat had no effect because the very presence of a syringe may be experienced as threatening. Although the weapon focus effect has received a fair amount of attention, clearly additional work needs to be done to address these and other questions.

Seriousness of the Crime

Other situational variables have also been examined by eyewitness researchers. For instance, it seems reasonable that the degree of atten-tion paid to a crime would depend on how serious the crime is. Leippe, Wells, and Ostrom (1978) examined this possibility by staging a crime for participants in which either a small amount ($1.50) or a large amount ($50) of money was stolen. For half of the participants, the amount of money stolen was not known until one minute after the theft. For the other half of the participants, the amount of money being stolen was known during the theft. Participants were later shown a six-person target-present lineup. For participants who had foreknowledge of the amount of money involved, crime seriousness significantly predicted accuracy. Participants in the serious crime condition were accurate 56% of the time, whereas participants in the less serious crime condition were accurate only 19% of the crime. When participants lacked foreknowledge of the amount of money being stolen, crime seriousness had no significant effect on accuracy.

☐ Characteristics of the Witness

Characteristics of the witness have also received some attention from eyewitness researchers. Witness characteristics include things like age, personality characteristics, whether the witness was a victim or bystander, as well as general cognitive abilities. With the exception of age, witness characteristics are relatively understudied. However, they are an important matter for police and eyewitness experts to take into account when estimating the likely accuracy of a witness's identification. Witness characteristics also include factors such as gender and race; however, those issues will be dealt with separately when we discuss interactions between witness characteristics and perpetrator characteristics.

Victim Versus Bystander Witnesses

A few studies have examined differences between witnesses who were bystanders to a crime and witnesses who are victims of the crime. In one study to examine this issue, Kassin (1984) had pairs of students engage in a risk-taking game that involved a cash payoff. The students were sitting across the table from each other and perpendicular to the door. During the course of the experiment, an individual entered the room and stole the money from one of the participants. Thus, one of the participants was a victim (his or her money was stolen), whereas the other participant was a bystander (he or she saw the other participant's money being stolen). Participants were later shown a seven-person target-present photospread and were asked if they could identify the person who stole the money. About half of the *bystander witnesses* were able to correctly identify the thief, whereas none of the *victim witnesses* correctly identified the thief. Kassin (1984) accounted for the results by arguing that the victims experienced greater emotional arousal and this impaired their memory for the perpetrator.

Similar results were obtained by Hosch, Leippeioni, and Cooper (1984). At the start of the experiment, the experimenter placed a calculator on the table in front of the participants. The experimenter told the participants that they would not need their watches during the experiment and asked them to remove their watches and place them in a box on the table. The participants complied. Participants then completed a questionnaire. After 75 seconds had passed, a confederate, who had been pretending to be one of the participants, got up and walked in front of the other participants. In the bystander witness condition, he picked up the experimenter's calculator and said that he had always wanted a calculator like that one, and then he ran out of the room with it. In the victim witness condition, the confederate picked up the box of watches, said he had always wanted watches like those, and then ran out of the room with the participants' watches.

The participants were later interviewed under the belief that they were witnesses to an actual crime (i.e., they were not told that the crime had been staged until after the experiment was over). Participants were then provided with a five-person target-present lineup. Correct identification of the thief was greater for the bystander witnesses (52.38%) than for the victim witnesses (36.84%), although the difference was not statistically reliable (presumably due to the relatively small number of participants). Given how little research has examined this distinction and how important the distinction is in real-life forensic settings, more work needs to be done to address differences between victims and bystanders. In particular, it may be that different approaches need to be taken with victim and bystander witnesses in order to maximize lineup performance.

Elderly Witnesses

It is well known that older adults suffer deficits in memory relative to younger adults (Light, 1991). Elderly participants show deficits in both working memory (Salthouse & Babcock, 1991) and long-term memory (Poon, 1985) relative to younger adults. These deficits are especially likely to influence long-term episodic memories. Elderly adults are known to be especially susceptible to source monitoring errors that impair their ability to remember the context in which events occurred and are also more susceptible to leading or biased questioning (Mitchell, Johnson, & Mather, 2003). These deficits are likely linked to broader deficits in binding together information into a single memory representation (Lyle, Bloise, & Johnson, 2006). Elderly participants also show deficits in their ability to inhibit irrelevant information, which may make them more prone to the effects of interference (Collette, Germain, Hogge, & Van der Linden, 2009).

These general memory deficits appear to affect the ability of elderly witnesses to make accurate identifications. One relevant source of evidence comes from studies of face recognition. These studies typically use an old/new recognition paradigm. Participants are shown some pictures of individuals for study. At test, they are shown some previously studied individuals and some new, previously unstudied individuals. The participant's task is to indicate which pictures are old and which pictures are new. Facial recognition studies tend to show that elderly participants perform more poorly than younger adults (Ferris, Crook, Clark, McCarthy, & Rae, 1980). For instance, Savaskan and colleagues (2007) tested young adults (20–40 years old), elderly adults (60–80), and very old adults (>80) in a facial recognition paradigm. Participants were shown 30 photographs of individuals between the ages of 20 and 65 with happy or angry facial expressions. After a 10-minute retention interval, participants were shown 60 photographs, half of them previously studied individuals and half of them previously unstudied individuals. All test photographs showed the individuals with a neutral expression. Participants were asked to indicate if the individual had been previously shown to them, and if so, whether their expression had been happy or angry. Recognition memory was measured in terms of d′. With regard to overall accuracy, young adults ($M_{d′}$ = 1.597) and elderly adults ($M_{d′}$ = 1.214) did not significantly differ; however, both groups performed significantly better than the very old group ($M_{d′}$ = .724). Additionally, all participants were more likely to remember the happy faces than the angry faces. The ability to remember the exact facial expression was relatively poor for all groups and worst for the very old group.

The results of this study are interesting in that they suggest an important distinction between elderly participants who are younger than 80 and those who are older than 80. Additionally, some recent research suggests that elderly adults have more difficulty recognizing that faces are the same when seen from different points of view. Habak, Wilkinson, and Wilson (2008) presented young adult and elderly participants with a stimulus face followed by a test face. The stimulus face was presented for a variety of different exposure durations. Sometimes the stimulus and test faces were identical. For instance, if the face was shown in a frontal shot during the stimulus presentation, it was also shown as a frontal shot during the recognition probe. In other cases, the orientation of the face was different on the test than it was when it was studied. For instance, if the face was shown in a frontal shot when it was studied, it was shown rotated by 20 degrees on the test. Elderly had largely preserved perceptual recognition of faces when the faces were presented in identical orientations, but they showed large deficits in recognition when the orientation of the face was changed. Thus, one reason that elderly might have difficulty in eyewitness identification situations is because they have difficulty making connections between various views of the same face. These results suggest that facial memory in the elderly may be more viewpoint dependent. Research by Bartlett and Leslie (1986) has shown that elderly participants who are shown multiple pictures of the same targets taken from several camera angles do as well as high school–aged participants on later facial recognition tests.

Studies of the performance of elderly witnesses in staged crime tasks have also been conducted. In one early study, Yarmey and Kent (1980) compared elderly participants (aged 65–90) with a group of younger participants (aged 15–26). Participants viewed a staged crime in which a male perpetrator assaulted a victim and stole his wallet. Participants completed an old/new recognition test for the perpetrator, victim, and two bystanders. Older participants provided less information when asked to recall details about the crime; however, their recognition memory for the perpetrator and victim did not significantly differ from the recognition memory of younger adults. Younger adults, however, were better at recognizing the bystanders. These results suggest that there are circumstances where young adults and elderly participants can perform similarly on eyewitness tasks; however, one should be cautious in interpreting these results given that the recognition task did not actually involve a lineup in the traditional sense.

In a more recent study, Memon, Bartlett, Rose, and Gray (2003) presented participants with two videotapes depicting staged crimes. One videotape showed an elderly perpetrator. The other videotape showed a young adult perpetrator (see the section in this chapter on own-age bias). Participants were shown two lineups after a short delay of 35 minutes or a long delay of one week. Some participants were presented with target-present lineups, and some were presented with target-absent lineups. In the target-present lineup, young adults made more correct identifications than elderly witnesses, but only for the lineup that included the young adult perpetrator. There were not significant differences in correct identifications for the lineup that included the elderly perpetrator. In the target-absent lineup, elderly participants were more likely to make false identifications than were younger adults. This was especially true for the young adult lineup and after the longer delay.

The pattern of results collectively suggests that elderly witnesses are more prone to making false identifications than are younger witnesses; however, the magnitude of the problem depends on the time delay and the age of the perpetrator. Moreover, one needs to be especially cautious when the witness is very old or suffers from dementia.

Child Witnesses

The past two decades saw an explosion of interest in the memory abilities of children in general and the reliability of children as witnesses more particularly (Ceci & Bruck, 1993). The latter trend was driven partly by a series of high-profile cases involving accusations of child sexual abuse at day care centers, and concerns that some of these accusations may have arisen as a consequence of suggestive questioning techniques. Much of the research on child witnesses has focused on their suggestibility (Ceci & Bruck, 1995). An early finding was that preschool-aged children are more prone to being misled by suggestive questioning than are older children and adults. This is at least partly due to the fact that younger children are more prone to trust adult authority figures and, as a consequence, incorporate their suggestions into their memories (Lampinen & Smith, 1995). There is also a large body of evidence demonstrating that as children get older, they improve in their ability to process both the verbatim details of events and the overall gist of events (Brainerd, Reyna, & Ceci, 2008; Lampinen, Leding, Reed, & Odegard, 2006). This body of research has been important in providing the courts as well as interviewers with information about children's memory for events. However, relatively less research has focused on children's abilities with regard to lineup identifications. As in the other areas we have discussed, one fruitful place to start is to look at children's perception and memory for faces in general, as these form basic building blocks with regard to lineup performance.

Face recognition research has generally found that the ability to recognize unfamiliar faces increases as a function of age, reaching adult levels at around the age of 14 (Freire & Lee, 2001). Diamond and Carey (1977) argued that face recognition improves with age, partly because children show a shift from featural processing to configural processing that is not fully completed until around the age of 10. The claim is not that holistic processing of faces is entirely absent in children. Indeed, there is evidence that even infants have some ability to process faces configurally (Maurer & Barrera, 1981). Rather the claim is that, prior to the age of 10, children are less adept at configural processing of faces than are adults, and thus young children rely more on featural encoding than do adults.

As we discussed in Chapter 2, evidence for holistic processing is often examined by making use of a face inversion paradigm. Participants are asked to recognize faces that are presented upright on some trials and upside-down on other trials. The assumption is that inverting faces makes it more difficult to process them holistically. The differences in reaction time and/or accuracy for the upright versus inverted faces thus provide an index of holistic face processing. Supporting the view that holistic processing improves with age, Goldstein (1975) found that face inversion effects occur in children, but that they are smaller in magnitude than they are for adults.

Other evidence offered for the developmental shift hypothesis comes from studies of children's responses to paraphernalia (Carey & Diamond, 1977; Diamond & Carey, 1977; Freire & Lee, 2001). Paraphrenalia are articles like clothing, jewelry, glasses, and so on that are not part of a person's face per se. It has been argued that children's reliance on paraphernalia to make face recognition judgments shows that they have a general strategy of relying on individual features when recognizing faces. In one study, Diamond and Carey (1977) showed children pictures and then asked them to indicate which of two individuals they had previously seen. When the children studied the faces, the target individual was shown wearing a piece of paraphernalia such as a scarf. On the test, the target individual was not wearing that item, but the foil was. Diamond and Carey showed that young children were especially likely to falsely pick the foil if the foil was shown wearing the paraphernalia that had been previously worn by the target. Later research showed that this effect was especially likely to occur when the targets and foils were highly similar and when the article of clothing was very distinctive (Flin, 1985). This tendency of children to pick an individual based on superficial similarities is important to consider when evaluating children eyewitness identification.

More recent research has tended to favor the view that configural processing of faces comes online early and is at near adult levels by preschool. For instance, Baenninger (1994) created stimuli in which faces were presented as intact wholes or in which the locations of features were swapped, thus changing the configural information. For instance, a photograph would be presented for study in its normal version. The test items included a target and foil. In one version, the targets and foils would be presented as normal intact faces. In other conditions, the location of the features were swapped (either two features were swapped or three features were swapped depending on the condition). The logic was simple. In the conditions where the features were swapped, all the individual features were still present. Thus, if someone was merely relying on matching features, recognition should be as good in these conditions as in the control condition. However, if one was relying on configural information, performance should be much worse when the location of the features was swapped. Participants in the study were 8 years old, 11 years old, and adults. Results indicated that children as young as 8 years old showed large decreases in accuracy when the locations of the features were swapped, indicating that even the 8-year-olds were using configural processing.

Other research has examined children even younger than 9 years old. For instance, Freire and Lee (2001) presented children between the ages of 4 and 11 with a target picture for study. Five seconds later, they were shown four pictures. The four pictures included the target individual and three foils. The foils were created by taking the original target image and manipulating the configuration of the features in the face by means of a computer program. The program moved the location of the mouth three pixels up or three pixels down, and moved the location of the eyes two pixels inward or two pixels outward. Thus the new pictures were realistic-looking photographs that retained the exact same features but put those features in a new configuration. Children of all ages performed better than chance, suggesting that all of the children made some use of configural information to perform the task. There was some evidence that children improved as they got older; however, the effect of age was not significant, possibly due to a lack of statistical power (only 10 children in the oldest age group).[3]

Other recent evidence suggests that children are adept at configural processing of faces by the early preschool years. Cassia, Picozzi, Kuefner, Bricolo, and Turati (2009) examined configural processing in children using the *composite face paradigm*. In the composite face paradigm, participants are presented with a face for study and are then presented with a composite face made up of the top half of one face and the bottom half of another face. Participants are then asked whether to make a recognition decision based on only half of the face. For instance, they might be asked, "Does the top half of this face match the top half of the face you just studied?" If faces are being processed holistically, then this task should be difficult, because the holistic representation of the composite face will fail to match the holistic representation of the original face. It will produce a strong sense of mismatch at the holistic level, even if the top half of the original face matches the top half of the test face. This composite condition is compared to a condition in which the two face halves are presented, but they are offset from one another so that the top half of the composite face is shifted to the right and the bottom half of the composite face is shifted to the left. This offset of the two faces should eliminate the use of holistic processing. Evidence for holistic face processing comes from a finding that people are faster and more accurate when presented with the offset composite faces than they are when they are presented with the composite faces where the two halves are lined up. Cassia et al. (2009) found that this effect occurred for both 5-year-olds and adults and that the effect was of similar magnitude for the two groups. In follow- up experiments, they found that children as young as 3½ showed evidence of holistic face processing using the composite face paradigm. Thus, although there may be some improvement in the use of configural information as children age, some ability to make use of configural information is present at an early age.

We next turn to research on children's performance more specifically in eyewitness identification tasks. In one early study, Brigham, Van Erst, and Bothwell (1986) exposed children who were in the fourth, eighth, and 11th grades to a staged theft of a cassette tape recorder. Following the staged theft, children were interviewed and were presented with a six-person target-present lineup. Overall, children did reasonably well, but the eighth graders (93%) and 11th graders (88%) did significantly better than did the fourth graders (68%) in correctly picking the culprit out of a target-present lineup. Other research by Leippe, Romanczyk, and Manion (1991) has also found evidence of improved eyewitness performance with age. In their study, children who were 5–6 years old and 9–10 years old were compared to adults with regard to their performance on two lineups. Participants interacted with a man who gave them a "skin test," which required an interpersonal touch. The task lasted 6 minutes. At one point during the task, a female intruder interrupted the session. Participants were later interviewed and shown two lineups, one for the "toucher" and one for the "intruder." For the toucher, some participants received target-present lineups, whereas other participants received target-absent lineups. The intruder lineups were always administered as target-present lineups.

Adults made more correct identifications of both the "toucher" and the "intruder," and fewer false suspect identifications of the "toucher" than did children in either age group. For the "toucher," adults correctly identified the target 93.3% of the time in target-present lineups compared to 78.6% of the time for 5–6-year-olds and 62.5% of the time for 9–10-year-olds. In the target-absent lineups, false identifications were 8.3% for adults (an estimated suspect identification rate of 1.38%), 33.3% for 5–6-year-olds (estimated suspect identification rate of 5.55%), and 13.3% for 9–10-year-olds (estimated suspect identification rate of 2.22%). This translates into estimated diagnosticity ratios of 67.44 for adults, 14.16 for 5–6-year-olds and 28.20 for 9–10-year-olds. In other words, if an adult identified someone, it was close to 70 times more likely that the person was the target than that they were not the target. When a 5–6-year-old identified someone, it was about 14 times more likely that they were the target than that they were not the target.

It is noteworthy, in this study, that the differences between children and adults were reflected in both the correct identification rate and the false choosing rate. Indeed, a major focus of research on children's lineup identifications concerns a tendency of children to *yeasay*, that is, to choose *someone* from the lineup. For instance, Beal, Schmitt, and Dekle (1995) found that not only did kindergarteners often identify someone from a target-absent lineup, but they even did so after previously identifying someone else from a target-present lineup(!). A meta-analysis by Pozzulo and Lindsay (1998) found that children and adults tend to perform similarly in target-present lineups, but children make many more false identification errors in target-absent lineups. Several attempts have been made to reduce this bias. Beal et al. (1995) allowed children to reject lineups by making a nonverbal response and found that this manipulation did not reduce false identifications. Parker and Ryan (1993) reported some evidence that sequential lineups can reduce false identifications by both children and adults; however, these findings were not statistically reliable. One potential procedure that has shown some success in decreasing false identifications is called the *elimination lineup*. In an elimination lineup, children are asked to eliminate lineup members until only one is left. The children are then asked if this remaining lineup member is the target. Pozzulo and Lindsay (1999) found that elimination lineups decreased children's false identifications without reducing their correct identifications in target-present lineups.

General Cognitive and Perceptual Abilities

Eyewitness identification involves a set of complex perceptual, cognitive, and decision-making abilities. It is reasonable, therefore, that indexes of basic performance on these skill sets might influence eyewitness identification accuracy. One obvious variable that may influence eyewitness identification accuracy is basic abilities in face recognition. Morgan et al. (2007) examined this issue in a study of military personnel involved in survival training. The personnel went through mock interrogations. Forty-eight hours later, the personnel attempted to identify their interrogator from a 10-person sequential lineup. For some of the participants, the interrogator was present in the lineup, and for others the interrogator was not present. Morgan et al. (2007) also administered a standardized test of face recognition, the Weschler Face Test (1997). The Weschler Face Test is a standardized test of face memory in which participants are presented with 24 target faces for study and are then asked to make old/new judgments for a set of 48 faces, half of which are old and half of which are new. Results indicated a significant correlation between performance on the Weschler Face Test and eyewitness identification accuracy. These results suggest that general variations in memory for faces may be useful predictors of the accuracy of eyewitnesses for actual stressful events.

Intellectual Disabilities

Police at times may also be called on to collect eyewitness identification evidence from individuals with intellectual disabilities.

In a recent study, adults with intellectual disabilities (IQ measured to be between 50 and 75) were compared with adults without intellectual disabilities (Ericson, Isaacs, & Taylor, 2003). Control participants were drawn from two groups. One group of participants was made up of college students. Another group of participants was adults with only a high school education. Participants were shown a video of a purse snatching at a garden center. One version of the film clearly and distinctly showed the perpetrator and the crime. A second version of the film was less clear, and the perpetrator was shown less distinctly. A third version of the film showed the event in an ambiguous manner. Participants were then shown either an eight-person target-present lineup or eight-person target-absent lineup. In target-present lineups, the correct identification rate was similar for intellectually disabled participants (M = 23.33% collapsed across version of film) and for control participants (M = 21.67% collapsed across control groups and version of film). In target-absent lineups, by contrast, false identifications were significantly more common among intellectually disabled participants (M = 55% collapsed across version of film) than for control participants (M = 24.17% collapsed across control groups and version of film). Given that the researchers used an eight-person lineup, the estimated rate at which innocent suspects would be identified was 6.88% for the participants with intellectual disabilities (55%/8) and 3.02% (24.17/8) for control participants. Note that this corresponds to estimated diagnosticity ratios of 3.39 for participants with intellectual disabilities and 7.17 for control participants. These results suggest that care needs to be taken when collecting identification evidence from witnesses with intellectual disabilities, especially with regard to avoiding false identifications.

Sleep

Recent research suggests that sleep deprivation may also influence the ability of a witness to identify a suspect. In one study, participants were either sleep deprived (36 hours of sleep deprivation) or not sleep deprived. In each group, half of the participants were given caffeine prior to testing and half were not. Participants in all conditions viewed two sets of 12 photographs of faces. Following a 5-minute retention interval, participants took a recognition test made up of 48 photographs. For each photograph, they made old/new judgments as well as source memory judgments (was the face from the first list or the second list?). Sleep deprivation had no influence on recognition memory, but did appear to impair source memory. Caffeine improved source memory in the sleep-deprived group, but still did not bring their performance up to the level of the controls. Another interesting finding in this study was that sleep-deprived subjects had an inflated sense of confidence in their recognition of faces. Although this study is provocative, it is important that additional research be conducted to confirm and extend these findings.

Intoxication

It is not unusual for police to interview witnesses who viewed a crime while they were under the influence of alcohol (Yuille, 1986). Because alcohol can impair cognitive functioning, it is possible that witnesses who view an event while intoxicated will show impaired performance.

According to Steele and Joseph (1990), intoxicated individuals show impaired attentional abilities, which they called *alcoholic myopia*. In one recent study, Dysart, Lindsay, MacDonald, and Wicke (2002) had two female confederates approach customers at a local bar to participate in a study. After a 12-minute filler period, the researchers measured the blood alcohol levels of the customers. Customers were then shown a picture (i.e., a photo showup) and were asked if the picture was of one of the women who had recruited them. In some cases it was, and in some cases it wasn't. One week later, participants were shown a six-person photo lineup. For some participants the lineup included one of the confederates (target present), but for other participants it did not (target absent). The researchers found that increased blood alcohol resulted in more false identifications in the target-absent showup condition. There was no effect of blood alcohol levels in the target-present showup condition. These results are striking. Intoxicated witnesses were more than twice as likely to falsely identify an innocent suspect in a showup. And, indeed, the diagnosticity of their identifications was only 1.12. Strikingly bad! In other words, if a drunk identifies someone in a showup, it is about as likely that the person is innocent as that they are guilty.

These findings raise additional questions. On the one hand, the impairment may occur because intoxication impaired the encoding of information at the time of the original event. The alcoholic myopia view predicts that alcohol limits attentional resources, which should lead to impoverished encoding of information. Alternatively, the effect may have occurred due to impaired decision processes during the showup itself. This too is plausible. It is well known, for many of us by means of our own single-subject research, that alcohol can impair decision making. At any rate, it appears to be a very bad idea to conduct a showup with an intoxicated witness.

Research by Yuille and Tollestrup (1990) provided some support for the view that alcohol hurts eyewitness memory by impairing the encoding of information. In this study, participants watched a staged crime. Some of the participants viewed the crime while under alcohol intoxication, whereas other participants viewed the staged crime while sober. After a one-week delay, participants were presented with either a target-present or target-absent lineup. Alcohol intoxication had no effect on accuracy in target-present lineups, but led to an increase in false identifications in the target-absent lineup. Because the participants were not drunk at the time of the identification procedure, this suggests that alcohol impairs the encoding of distinctive facial details that can be used to later identify the perpetrator of a crime.

Alcohol is not the only intoxicant that may influence eyewitness accuracy. It is well known that marijuana intoxication can impair memory generally. For instance, Miller, McFarland, Cornett, and Brightwell

(1977) found that marijuana intoxication at time of study resulted in decreased free recall of words. Yuille, Tollestrup, Marxsen, Porter, and Herve (1998) examined the role of marijuana intoxication on eyewitness memory. In the study, participants were enrolled in a research study on the effect of marijuana. Participants were asked to smoke either a marijuana cigarette or a placebo cigarette in which the active ingredient of marijuana (THC) was removed. After smoking the cigarette, a confederate entered the room and complained that they detected the odor of marijuana. The confederate threatened to call the police, and even after they were shown documentation that the police approved of the study, the confederate continued to act pissy with the researchers. After the confederate left, participants were asked a series of questions about the incident. One week later, participants returned to complete a second interview, and they viewed an eight-person target-present or target-absent photospread. On the immediate interview, participants in the marijuana group produced less information than participants in the placebo group. However, there was not a significant difference between the two groups after one week on either the interview questions or the lineup identification task. It should be noted, however, that the relatively small number of participants in the study precludes any firm conclusions. Given the forensic relevance of interviewing witnesses who have used marijuana, further research is certainly warranted.

Glucose Enhancement

Memory researchers have found recently that memory and cognition fluctuate as a function of changes in blood glucose levels (Benton, Owens, & Parker, 1994; Hall, Gonder-Frederick, Chewning, & Silveira, 1989; Morris, 2008). Early research demonstrated this effect with verbal materials such as words and paragraphs. This effect may be mediated by the effect that glucose consumption has on attention (Sunram-Lea, Foster, & Durlach, 2002). The same thing seems to be true for face recognition. Metzger (2000) tested young adults who were asked to drink lemonade sweetened with either sugar (50 mg glucose) or an artificial sweetener (23.7 mg saccharine). Participants studied a series of faces and then took an old/new recognition test for those faces. Glucose consumption had no effect on hit rates, but significantly decreased the false recognition of nonpresented faces. Metzger and Flint (2003) later extended this finding, showing it occurs for both healthy young adults and patients with Alzheimer's disease. This finding suggests that a witness experiencing low blood sugar at the time of an event might show impaired eyewitness accuracy. However, more research needs to be conducted on this topic specifically in the context of eyewitness identification procedures.

Personality and Cognitive-Style Variables

Some researchers have examined the role of personality differences and differences in cognitive style on eyewitness performance. One potential source for individual difference variables that might predict eyewitness accuracy comes from the Big 5 or OCEAN theory of personality (Costa & McCrae, 1992; Goldberg, 1990; Jones, 1990). According to the OCEAN theory, personality can be characterized along a set of five basic continuous dimensions: *openness to experience, conscientiousness, extraversion, agreeableness,* and *neuroticism.* Not all of these dimensions have been studied in the context of eyewitness identification or even face memory, and those that have been studied have not always panned out. For example, Clifford and Scott (1978) examined the relationship between introversion/extroversion and the accuracy of eyewitness descriptions and found no significant correlation. However, some research does suggest that neuroticism might be related to eyewitness identification accuracy. *Neuroticism* refers to the degree of emotional stability that a person has, including how well they perform under stress. Bothwell, Brigham, and Pigott (1987) reasoned that participants high in neuroticism should perform acceptably under conditions of low arousal, but might be impaired under the high-arousal conditions that characterize some crimes. A research assistant in a white lab coat took each participant's pulse and then led them to a testing room, where they were seated by a table. In the low-stress condition, nothing of note was on the table. In the moderate-stress condition, an empty syringe package was on the table. In the high-stress condition, an unused syringe package was on the table. The research assistant then took the participant's pulse again. Participants were later shown a target-present or target-absent lineup in which they were asked to identify the research assistant. The findings indicated that participants high in neuroticism showed poor identification accuracy when arousal levels were high. For participants who were low in neuroticism, the reverse was true. High levels of arousal were associated with better memory. This study provides suggestive evidence that neuroticism may be a relevant factor for investigators to consider when evaluating eyewitness accuracy, and that the effect of neuroticism on accuracy may interact with the degree of emotional arousal evoked by the crime.

Another individual difference variable that has received some support is field dependence (Witkin, Moore, Goodenough, & Cox, 1977). *Field dependence* refers to the tendency of individuals to think globally versus analytically. Field-dependent individuals process information in a holistic fashion, whereas field-independent individuals are more adept at breaking stimuli into their constituent parts. Field-dependent individuals also tend to be more guided by social information than are field-independent individuals (Eagle, Goldberger, & Breitman, 1969).

Field dependence can be measured in a couple of different ways. One measure is the rod and frame task (Cross, Schuck, & Dannemiller, 1972). In the rod and frame task, participants in a darkened room are shown a luminous bar inside a luminous frame. The frame is tilted, and the participant's job is to adjust the rod until it is upright. Doing so requires ignoring the tilted frame that the bar is inside of. Field-dependent individuals have more trouble with this task because they view the stimuli holistically and have more difficulty separating the parts. Another task used to measure field dependence is the embedded figure task (Witkin, Oltman, Raskin, & Karp, 1971/2002). In the embedded figure test, participants are shown complex geometric figures and are asked to find simpler figures embedded within that larger figure. Like the rod and frame test, the embedded figure test requires that the participant ignore the pattern as a whole and focus instead on the individual parts that make up the figure. Field-dependent individuals find this more difficult than field-independent individuals.

These distinctions have led some researchers to predict that face memory generally, and eyewitness identification in particular, should be superior in field-dependent individuals. As we saw in Chapter 2, face processing optimally involves holistic processing of information, which field-dependent individuals have a preference for. Moreover, faces are the ultimate socially relevant stimuli, which field dependents have more interest in. Some research in the face recognition literature supports the notion that field dependence is associated with superior memory for faces. In one study, Crutchfield, Woodworth, and Albrecht (1958) gave the rod and frame test to Air Force pilots. Pilots were then shown photographs of individuals who had gone to the same assessment center as them, as well as other individuals who had gone to the assessment center with a different cohort. They were asked to pick out those photographs of individuals whom they recognized from the assessment center. The pilots who had scored highest on field dependence, as measured by the rod and frame task, were more accurate on the picture recognition test.

In another study, Messick and Damarin (1964) presented participants with pictures of 79 individuals and asked the participants to rate their age and whether they resembled anyone they knew. Two hours later, participants were presented with 40 pictures (20 old and 20 new) and were asked to indicate which of the pictures they had previously seen. All the participants also completed an embedded figures test. Messick and Damarin (1964) did not report hit and false alarm data separately; however, overall accuracy was negatively correlated with performance on the embedded figure test, indicating that recognition of the faces was superior in participants who were high in field dependence (recall that high field dependence is indexed by poor performance on the embedded figures test).

Not all researchers, however, have found evidence for a relationship between field dependence and eyewitness accuracy. For instance, Hoffman and Kagan (1977) presented participants with pictures for study and then assessed their memory using an old/new recognition test. Field dependence was measured using both the rod and frame task and the embedded figures test. Contrary to the findings reported above, field-independent participants performed better than field-dependent participants. Other researchers have reported similar findings (e.g., Adcock and Webberley, 1971). It is possible that field-dependent individuals may perform better on face recognition tests, but only when the task requires incidental learning. Indeed, a major review of the literature by Goodenough (1976) concluded that field-dependent individuals tend to do better on memory tasks that involve incidental learning because they attend to socially relevant cues automatically.

A third individual difference variable that may have some effect on eyewitness identification accuracy is self-monitoring. Self-monitoring is a personality variable that indicates the degree to which people monitor their own behavior to make sure that it conforms to societal norms and expectations. According to Snyder (1974), people who are high in self-monitoring show a great deal of concern with how others are evaluating them and act in a way so as to form favorable impressions in others. Low self-monitors show less concern with what others are thinking of them and are less concerned with forming favorable impressions. These observations led Hosch, Leippeioni, and Cooper (1984) to predict that high self-monitors would be more likely to be influenced by biased lineup instructions. To test this hypothesis, the experimenters created a staged crime in which a perpetrator stole either the participant's watch or a calculator that belonged to the experimenter. Police investigators took the witness's statement and administered a lineup using either biased or unbiased lineup instructions. The biased instructions implied that the perpetrator was in the lineup; the unbiased instructions indicated that the perpetrator may or may not be in the lineup. First, consider the lineup rejection rates of the high self-monitors. When given lineup instructions suggesting that the perpetrator was in the lineup (i.e., biased instructions), high self-monitors rejected the lineup only 4.3% of the time. When given lineup instructions suggesting that the perpetrator may or may not have been in the lineup (i.e., unbiased instructions), high self-monitors rejected the lineup 52.6% of the time. Next consider the lineup rejection rates of low self-monitors. When given biased lineup instructions, low self-monitors rejected the lineup 30.8% of the time. When given unbiased lineup instructions, they rejected the lineup 32% of the time, a difference of only 1.2%. Thus, high self-monitors are very sensitive to social information and are more prone to be adversely impacted by biased lineup instructions.

This example illustrates an important point for us to consider. One reason why estimator variables may be so important is not simply because they allow law enforcement to estimate the likely accuracy of witnesses. Rather, estimator variables may act to moderate the effects of the system variables that will be discussed in Chapter 4.

Police as Witnesses

It is sometimes believed that police officers are more accurate as witnesses than are civilian witnesses (Loftus, 1984). Police, after all, are professional witnesses. They spend a good deal of time testifying in court, and the nature of their job requires that they be observant. Consistent with this view, a couple of studies have found that police are better at recalling details of crimes than are laypeople (Christianson, Karlsson, & Persson, 1998; Clifford & Richards, 1977). However, even those studies have typically found better recall for peripheral details rather than central details about the perpetrator's appearance or manner of dress. Moreover, studies have generally failed to find evidence that police are significantly better at recognizing people in lineups or face recognition tasks than are laypeople (Christianson et al., 1998; Lindholm, Christianson, & Karlsson, 1997).

In a study conducted in Sweden, police personnel, police recruits, college students, and teachers watched two slide presentations (Christianson et al., 1998). One slide presentation depicted a stabbing. The second slide presentation showed the faces of nine men and nine women. Following these slide presentations, participants were shown a lineup and were asked to pick which person, if any, was the assailant from the stabbing. These results are shown in the left panel of Figure 3.9. Police did a little bit better than the laypeople, but the difference was not statistically reliable (i.e., the difference was not more than one would expect based on chance alone). Memory for the 18 previously studied faces was also tested. Participants were shown a series of faces, some old and some new. For each face, participants were to indicate which face they had previously studied. The results of this measure are shown in the right panel of Figure 3.9. Again, there was no significant difference between the four groups of participants.

In another study, Swedish police officers and Swedish college students viewed a film of a robbery in which a Swedish perpetrator and an immigrant perpetrator were shown (Lindholm, Christianson, & Karlsson, 1997). Following the video, participants were asked a series of questions and viewed target-present photo lineups. As in the previously mentioned study, there was not a statistically reliable difference between the performance of police and laypeople on the lineup task. Additionally, both

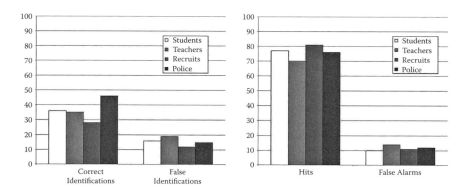

FIGURE 3.9 Comparison of performance between police officers, police recruits, and laypeople in a study by Christianson, Karlsson, and Persson (1998). No significant differences were found between the groups in terms of recognition accuracy. (*Source*: Based on data presented in Christianson, S. A., Karlsson, I., & Persson, L. G. W. (1998). Police personnel as eyewitnesses to a violent crime. *Legal and Criminological Psychology, 3*, 59–72.)

groups of participants were more accurate in recognizing the Swedish perpetrator than the immigrant perpetrator.

Both of the above studies used target-present lineups. In a different study, police recruits were shown a slide sequence of an automobile accident (Yuille, 1986). Following the viewing of the slide sequence, police recruits were shown a target-absent lineup. They were explicitly told that they had the option to reject the lineup. However, 51% of the police recruits ended up identifying one of the members of the lineup. Taken together, the evidence does not support the contention that police officers are substantially more accurate at eyewitness identification tasks than are laypeople.

☐ Characteristics of the Perpetrator

We next turn to characteristics of the perpetrator and the role this has on eyewitness identification accuracy.

Visual Distinctiveness

It is probably safe to say that some people are simply more recognizable than other people and should be easier for witnesses to pick out of a lineup or photospread. One factor that may contribute to this recognizability is how similar the person's appearance is to the appearance of other people. People who are very similar to other people in their appearance are low in their *visual distinctiveness*, whereas people who are not very similar to other people in their appearance are high in *visual distinctiveness*. There is a large body of research in memory generally showing that distinctive information is better remembered (Neath & Brown, 2007). In one study that examined distinctiveness and memory for faces, Light, Kayra-Stuart, and Hollander (1979) presented one group of participants with 100 pictures taken from a high school yearbook and asked them to rate the pictures with regard to how unusual looking they were. Another group of partici-pants was presented with a different set of 100 yearbook photos and was asked to do the same thing. After one day, the participants returned, and they were presented with the full set of 200 photographs. They were asked to indicate which of the photographs they had seen during the previous day. The correlation between correctly recognizing an old item and that item's rated unusualness was .37, indicating that participants were more likely to correctly recognize more distinctive faces than less distinctive faces. The correlation between falsely recognizing a new item and that item's rated unusualness was −.49, indicating that participants were less likely to falsely recognize distinctive faces than they were less distinctive faces. Similar effects occurred when participants were told ahead of time that their memories were going to be tested.

A number of other researchers have also found that unique or dis-tinctive-looking faces are better recognized (Bartlett, Hurry, & Thorley, 1984; Cohen & Car, 1975; Going & Read, 1974; Sheperd, Gibling, & Ellis, 1991; Valentine, 1991; Valentine & Bruce, 1986; Wickham, Morris, & Fritz, 2000; Winograd, 1981). It is useful to think about why this might be so. In Chapter 2, we introduced Valentine's *face space theory* (1991). The face space theory claims that faces are represented along a number of different dimensions. Dimensions can be things like length of face, width of face, size of eyes, youthfulness, or whatever. You can think about these dimen-sions as making up a kind of mental space. Figure 3.10 shows a simple example. It shows what face space might look like for the dimensions of face height and face width.

Consider the face labeled *A* in Figure 3.10. That face is pretty distinc-tive, because it is very narrow. There are not any other faces that are quite that narrow. The face labeled *A* is in a region of the face space that does not have many neighbors. If you saw that face, and later I asked you if you rec-ognized it, it would be easy for you to know you saw that particular face rather than another similar face. Now consider the face labeled *B*. That face is in a very dense region of face space. It has lots of neighbors very close to it. If you saw that face, and later on I asked you if you recognized it, it should be difficult for you to do so. It would be hard for you to know

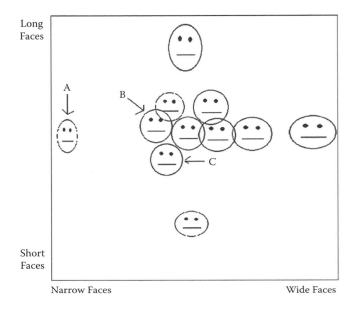

FIGURE 3.10 Illustration of Valentine's (1991) face-space theory using the dimensions of face height and face width.

for sure if you saw that exact face, or merely another face that was similar (i.e., from the same general region of the face space). Not only that, if you studied *B* and I tested you by showing you *C* (a face that you did not study but that is from the same region of face space), you might mistakenly identify it. As a result, less distinctive faces tend to produce fewer hits and more false alarms. Of course, in real life we evaluate faces on more than just two dimensions. But the same principle should apply.

An interesting implication of this way of thinking about things has to do with the effect of attractiveness on face recognition. According to one view, the attractiveness of a face is partly a matter of how close that face is to the prototypical face (Langlois & Roggman, 1990; but see Alley & Cunningham, 1991). If attractive faces are prototypical, they would tend to be clustered in the center of face space, the most densely packed region. This should make attractive faces more difficult to recognize. Some studies have found just that. In one study, Light, Hollander, and Kayra-Stuart (1981) had participants provide ratings of attractiveness, likeability, and distinctiveness of pictures from a high school yearbook. On a later test, recognition performance was poorer for the pictures of the more attractive individuals. Light et al. argued that this finding occurred because the pictures of attractive students were more similar to each other than the pictures of less attractive students. Using a smaller set of photographs,

Sarno and Alley (1997) found that more attractive faces were harder to recognize; however, this result was not statistically reliable.

More recently, Wickham and Morris (2003) failed to find a consistent effect of attractiveness on face recognition, although they did report increased false alarms for more attractive faces. Part of the reason for this inconsistent relationship could be that attractive faces may be attractive for more than one reason. Some faces may be considered attractive because they conform to the society's prototype. These faces will be represented in the center of the face space and will be low in distinctiveness. Other faces may appear attractive because they are distinctive in a particularly elegant or interesting way. In fact, Wickham and Morris (2003) reported that some faces rated as being attractive were very distinctive, whereas others were very typical. One consequence of this finding is that an attractive face may or may not be memorable, but particularly unattractive faces should be memorable, because they are necessarily different from the norm.

Appearance Change and Disguise

A perpetrator's appearance at the time of the crime may differ, sometimes subtly, sometimes dramatically, from their appearance in the lineup or photospread shown to witnesses. Perpetrators may even change their appearance purposefully or don a disguise in order to avoid being identified by witnesses. Research has shown that even slight changes in appearance may dramatically reduce recognition accuracy. In one set of studies, participants were shown a videotape of an armed robbery in which the perpetrator was either wearing a hat or not wearing a hat (Cutler, Penrod, & Maartens, 1987a, 1987b). The simple addition of a hat decreased recognition of the perpetrator by more than 10%. Context reinstatement manipulations can be used to decrease the effects of a perpetrator wearing a disguise but do not seem to entirely eliminate them (Cutler et al., 1987a).

Simple changes in the pose of a face can also influence face recognition. In one early study, Krouse (1981) presented police officers with 16 pictures of male faces. Half of the faces were shot at a full-face pose, and half were shot at a three-quarter pose (i.e., turned slightly to one side but not in full profile). Participants completed a four-alternative forced-choice (i.e., multiple-choice) test either immediately after viewing the 16 photographs or after a 2–3-day delay. Half of the target photographs on the test were shown in the same pose they had been shown in during the study session, and half were shown in the alternative pose. When tested immediately after presentation, participant accuracy was 74% for the photos when the test pose matched the study pose and only 50.08% when the study pose and test pose mismatched. The effect of pose was less after the 2–3-day delay with 59.5% accuracy when the study photos and test photos were matched in pose and 47.48% accuracy when the study photos and test photos did not match in pose.

These results provide part of the explanation for why eyewitness identification is so difficult. Relatively small changes in appearance from the time of the crime to the time of the identification can impact eyewitness identification accuracy. The general model of face recognition developed by Bruce and Young (1986) proposes that our face recognition system starts with viewpoint-dependent representations of individuals and then attempts to develop viewpoint-independent representations (see Chapter 2 for a discussion). The viewpoint-dependent representation is easy. It is just a description developed bottom up from the raw perceptual data. But the viewpoint-independent representation is more difficult. For such a representation to develop, one needs either repeated exposures to the individual from different angles and or in different situations (e.g., with or without hat, with or without facial hair, hair in a ponytail or not in a ponytail, etc.), or smart top-down guesses of what the person might look like in other situations. Many eyewitness situations involve limited exposure to the criminal's face, and thus provide little information to develop these viewpoint-invariant representations.

☐ Interactions Between Perpetrator Characteristics and Witness Characteristics

The final set of estimator variables involves interactions between characteristics of the target and characteristics of the witness. As a general matter, these variables are indicative of a *similar to self phenomenon*. The best known of these is the *own-race bias*, which we will turn to first.

Own-Race Bias

The own-race bias[4] is the finding that people show better recognition accuracy for members of their own race or ethnic group than they do for members of other racial or ethnic groups (for a review, see Brigham, Bennett, Meissner, & Mitchell, 2007). The difficulty of other-race identifications has been recognized for close to a century (Feingold, 1914) and is a robust and easy-to-replicate finding. Early studies of the other-race effect involved showing participants pictures of individuals of various races and then asking them to make recognition memory judgments for

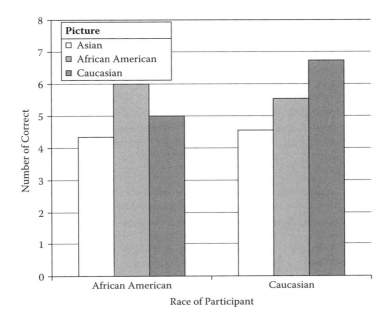

FIGURE 3.11   Recognition memory data from Chance, Goldstein, and McBride (1975). Caucasian participants were better at recognizing previously seen pictures of Caucasians, and African Americans were better at recognizing previously seen pictures of African Americans. (*Source*: Based on data presented in Chance, J., Goldstein, A. G., & McBride, L. (1975). Differential experience and recognition memory for faces. *Journal of Social Psychology, 97,* 243–253.)

both old and new pictures. For instance, Chance, Goldstein, and McBride (1975) showed African American and Caucasian students pictures of 10 African American male faces, 10 Caucasian male faces, and 10 Asian male faces. Figure 3.11 shows how the experiment turned out. Participants then were shown 40 pictures (10 old and 30 new) from each category and were asked to indicate which pictures had been previously shown. Caucasian participants performed best when presented with pictures of Caucasian men and did most poorly when presented with pictures of Asian men. By the same token, African American participants performed best when presented with pictures of African American men and did most poorly when presented with pictures of Asian men.

Dozens of studies like these have been conducted over the last several decades (Meissner & Brigham, 2001). Across studies it has been found that people are about 1.4 times more likely to correctly identify a member of their own race than a member of another race. False identifications are more than 1.5 times more common for other-race faces than for own-race faces. It has been suggested that as many as 48% of wrongful convictions are partially a consequence of the own-race bias (Scheck, Neufield, & Dwyer, 2001).

Although many studies of the own-race bias have used the face recognition paradigm, other studies have examined the effect in the context of more realistic eyewitness identification tasks. In one such study, Platz and Hosch (1988) had Caucasian, African American, and Hispanic confederates enter convenience stores and interact with the Caucasian, African American, and Hispanic clerks. The confederates engaged in scripted activities that the researchers thought would be memorable. For instance, in one script the confederates paid for a pack of cigarettes all in pennies. Two hours later, experimenters presented the store clerks with three different target-present photographic lineups. Each lineup had pictures of five individuals. Consistent with the own-race bias, the clerks were most accurate in identifying members of their own race. For instance, Caucasian clerks correctly identified the Caucasian confederate 53.2% of the time but correctly identified the African American confederate 40.4% of the time and the Hispanic confederate 34% of the time. The results were similar for the African American and Hispanic clerks.

Not only is there evidence that recognition memory is impaired for members of other races or ethnicities, but also there is evidence that the bias has a perceptual as well as a memorial basis. In a delayed match to sample task, Lindsay, Jack, and Christian (1991) presented Caucasian and African American participants with pictures of Caucasian and African American faces for 120 msec a piece. Three seconds following each presentation, participants were shown two pictures, side by side, and were asked to pick the picture they had seen. Caucasian participants showed an own-race bias, correctly recognizing more of the Caucasian pictures (86%) than African American pictures (75%). African American participants did not show an own-race bias, correctly recognizing 79% of the African American pictures and correctly recognizing 81% of the Caucasian pictures.

A number of different theories have been proposed to explain the own-race bias. One early proposal was that non-Caucasian faces show less variability in their facial features than do Caucasian faces, making them more difficult to recognize. This theory has not fared very well (e.g., Goldstein & Chance, 1978). For instance, if Caucasian faces were just more distinctive, one would predict that Caucasian faces would be easiest to remember, regardless of the participant's race or ethnicity. In point of fact, however, the own-race bias is just that, a bias to show better memory for members of one's own race. Caucasians remember Caucasian faces best. African Americans remember African American faces best. Asians remember Asian faces best. Additionally, Goldstein (1979a, 1979b) looked at data in which measurements of different facial features and configurations were compared for members of different racial and ethnic groups and found no evidence that there is any less variability in these measures for non-Caucasians faces than for Caucasian faces.

Of the remaining accounts of the own-race bias, one can see them as belonging to two broad categories. Social-functional accounts place the onus of the own-race bias in cultural and social experiences with members of other races and ethnic groups. The best known of these accounts are the contact hypothesis (Cross, Cross, & Daly, 1971) and the racial bias hypothesis (Brigham, 1983; Ferguson, Rhodes, Lee, & Sriram, 2001). There are also cognitive-perceptual explanations of the own-race bias. These can be thought of as accounts of the processing mechanisms that underlie the own-race bias. The accounts are not mutually exclusive. In fact, the cognitive-perceptual accounts may well serve as the mechanisms through which the social-functional accounts operate.

We start with the social-functional accounts. Perhaps the most intuitive account of the own-race bias is that a person's level of experience with members of racial or ethnic groups influences the ease with which people can recognize individual faces from those groups. Because most people have more experience with members of their own racial or ethnic group, the theory predicts that people should be better at own-race recognition. Wright, Boyd, and Tredoux (2003) examined the own-race bias in an interesting study that tested Caucasian participants from the United Kingdom, Caucasian participants from South Africa, and black students from South Africa. Participants studied 30 photographs (half black, half white) for 3 seconds a piece. They later received a recognition memory test consisting of 60 photographs, half old and half new. The researchers observed a robust own-race bias. Overall, white participants were more accurate in identifying white faces and black participants were more accurate in identifying black faces. Participants also completed a questionnaire assessing their experiences with members of other races. Amount of interracial contact was negatively correlated with the size of the own-race bias, but only for the black students. As Wright et al. (2003) pointed out, this may well have been due to a restriction of range for the white students. There was simply much more variability in the amount of contact black students had with white students than vice versa.

Other research consistent with the contact hypothesis comes from studies showing that the own-race bias can be decreased by providing participants with training that exposes them to other-race faces. For instance, Lavrakas, Buri, and Mayener (1976) tested the effects of training on the own-race bias in a group of Caucasian participants. Participants engaged in one of two category learning tasks based on Identi-Kit depictions of African American targets. In one version of the category learning task, participants were presented with Identi-Kit stimuli of African American individuals in which they had to learn a category based on the conjunction of two features. In the simple concept learning task, participants had to learn a category based on a single feature. Participants in a control task rated the Identi-Kit faces for attractiveness. All participants completed a pretest that occurred prior to any training, a posttest that occurred immediately after training, and a delayed posttest that occurred one week after the training session. Each test followed the same basic procedure. Participants first viewed 18 pictures of African American males for study. Following the study session, participants were shown 18 six-person lineups and were asked, for each lineup, to identify the member of the lineup who had been shown in the slides. Thus, on each test, scores ranged from 0 correct to 18 correct. Performance of participants who had engaged in the concept learning tasks improved after training from around 10 correct identifications on the pretest to nearly 12 correct identifications on the immediate posttest. Performance of participants in the control condition, by contrast, did not improve, remaining at around 10 correct on both the pretest and immediate posttest. This suggests that experience with members of other racial groups can increase facial recognition for members of those groups (for similar results with other training programs, see Elliott, Wills, & Goldstein, 1973; Goldstein & Chance, 1985).

Developmental studies have also been used to make the case for the contact hypothesis. For instance, Chance, Turner, and Goldstein (1982) found that face recognition improved steadily between the ages of 6 and 20 and that the size of the own-race bias also increased steadily with age. In more recent research, Sangrigoli, Pallier, Argenti, Ventureyra, and de Schonen (2005) tested Korean-born adults who had been adopted by Caucasian families between the ages of 1 and 9 years old, a group of Korean adults raised by Korean families, and a group of Caucasian adults. The experiment involved a match to sample task in which participants were presented with a face of an Asian individual or a Caucasian individual for a short time (120 msec or 250 msec) followed by a gray screen for one second. After the one-second interval had elapsed, participants were shown two pictures and were asked to indicate which one they had just seen. The standard own-race advantage was observed. Caucasian adults performed better with the Caucasian faces than the Asian faces, whereas Korean-born adults raised by Korean families performed better with the Asian faces than the Caucasian faces. The finding of most import, however, concerned the Korean-born adults raised by Caucasian families. Their results were much like those of the Caucasian adults. They recognized Caucasian faces better than they recognized Asian faces.

Other developmental research suggests that the own-race bias is mediated by very early perceptual experiences. In a fascinating study, Kelly et al. (2007) investigated the other-race effect in infants between the ages of 3 months and 9 months using a *habituation paradigm*. Habituation paradigms are a technique used by developmental researchers to investigate mental processes in preverbal children. The infants are presented with a stimulus repeatedly until they lose interest in the stimulus (as measured by looking time). This decrease in looking time is known as *habituation*. The stimulus is then changed slightly, and the researchers look at whether the child becomes interested again as measured by increased looking time. This increase in looking time is known as *dishabituation*. For instance, imagine a researcher presents a 3-month-old child a series of geometric shapes all in a particular shade of blue. The researcher does this for 20 trials or more until the infant starts to get bored and spends very little time looking at the stimulus. On the next trial, the researcher presents a geometric shape in a particular shade of green. If the infant once again becomes interested and increases the amount time she or he looks at the shape, it would show that the infant can tell the difference between blue and green.

Kelly et al. used this technique with 3-, 6-, and 9-month-old Middle Eastern infants. During the habituation phase, infants were repeatedly shown the same face of a particular individual of Middle Eastern, African, or Asian descent. After the children were habituated, they were shown a new picture. The picture either showed the exact same individual at a different camera angle or showed a new individual at that new camera angle. The new person was always of the same ethnicity as the photograph that the children had habituated to. When the pictures were of Middle Eastern children (just like the participants), children of all ages showed increased interest when presented with a new person. When the target face was Asian, 3-month-olds and 6-month-olds showed increased interest when the new individual was shown, but 9-month-olds did not. The 3-month-olds and 6-month-olds apparently recognized that they were looking at a new person, and hence they became interested in the new stimulus. The 9-month-olds acted as if they did not realize they were looking at a new person. When the target face was African, 3-month-olds showed increased interest when the new individual was shown, but 6-month-olds and 9-month-olds did not. This suggests that the 3-month-olds realized that the picture was of a different individual than the person they had been looking at but that the 6- and 9-month-olds did not. This is exciting research. It supports the notion that children become tuned by experience to better recognize own-race faces and that this occurs at 6–9 months of age. The own-race bias starts very early in childhood indeed.

Despite these findings, it is important to note that some research has failed to find evidence for the contact hypothesis. For instance, Jackiw, Arbuthnott, Pfeifer, Marcon, and Meissner (2008) compared identification accuracy of Caucasian and First Nation participants for Caucasian and First Nation targets. Participants were shown pictures of six individuals (either Caucasian or First Nation) for 3 seconds a piece. They then engaged in a 5-minute filler activity, after which they were shown 12 separate six-person photographic lineups. Half of the lineups were target-present lineups, and half of the lineups were target-absent lineups. Participants also completed the Social Experience Questionniare (SEQ) to measure degree of contact with First Nation individuals. Participants were more accurate in identifying members of their own group than they were in identifying members of the other group. Responses to the SEQ were not correlated with recognition of other-race faces, although there was a trend toward a correlation between SEQ scores and false alarms for other-race faces ($r = -.19$, $p = .08$). Thus, the effect of self-reported experience was small.

In another study, Slone, Brigham, and Meissner (2000) presented participants with yearbook photographs of 20 Caucasians and 20 African Americans for 3 seconds a piece for study. Participants were later shown 80 pictures (40 previously studied and 40 not previously studied) and were asked to indicate whether each picture was old or new. Participants also completed the SEQ. Results indicated that participants were more accurate in identifying members of their own race. However, experience with members of other races was not correlated with the size of the own-race bias.

What are we to make of these studies? Overall, the data are consistent with the hypothesis that the other-race effect is partly moderated by experience with members of other races. However, it may be that not all types of experience matter equally. For instance, some researchers have suggested that the own-race bias may crucially depend not merely on experience with members of other races, but also on close relationships with members of other races (Carroo, 1987). Other researchers have argued that it is the variability in experiences with members of other races that is most important. Malpass (1990) introduced the term *social utility variance* to describe this. His idea was that when our experiences with people belonging to different social categories are either uniformly positive or uniformly negative, we have no need to individuate the members of those groups. Group membership is sufficient to allow us to know how to respond. However, when our experiences with members of a social group are mixed, some good and some bad, it is important for us to treat the members of that group as individuals. Social group membership is no longer sufficient for us to make decisions about how to treat those group members. Unfortunately, tests of the social utility variance account have not tended to pan out (Slone et al., 2000). A more promising account may be that early experiences matter more than later experiences. It is well known that some perceptual abilities show *critical periods* in development (Columbo, 1982). Sangrigoli et al. (2005) have argued that other-race face recognition may also show a critical period in development. It is also important to note that questionnaire studies that assess amount of interracial contact may not be sufficient to produce reliable results because the effect of interracial contact may be heavily dose dependent and subject to restriction of range effects.

Another account of the own-race bias is the *racial attitudes* or *prejudice account*. According to this account, negative attitudes toward particular racial or ethnic groups lead to superficial processing of faces of members of those groups and poor performance. For instance, an early study by Seeleman (1940) found that Caucasian participants with negative attitudes toward African Americans recognized pictures of African Americans more poorly than less prejudiced participants. One recent study suggests that implicit attitudes may play a role (Walker & Hewstone, 2008). In this study, the size of the own-race effect in a perceptual task was found to be positively correlated with racial bias on the implicit association task. Moreover, Johnson (2006) recently demonstrated that simply invoking a positive emotional state in participants, either before or after studying photographs, can reduce or eliminate the own-race bias.

A recent take on the racial prejudice account of the own-race bias is provided by Hugenberg and Sacco's (2008) categorization–individuation model. The model is rooted in findings that people tend to see out-group members as more homogeneous and in-group members as more hetero-geneous. Applied to facial recognition, the model predicts that people tend to see members of their own racial group as individuals, but tend not to see members of other races as individuals. In one test of the theory (Shriver, Young, Hugenberg, & Bernstein, 2008), middle-class Caucasian participants were presented with pictures of Caucasian targets in contexts that suggested that they were either wealthy or poor. The participants showed better recognition memory for the targets presented in the wealth context than in the poverty context, suggesting that social class was suf-ficient to produce a finding analogous to the own-race bias. In another experiment the researchers produced an own-group bias in face recogni-tion based on the university the targets were said to be affiliated with (for related findings, see Bernstein, Young, and Hugenberg, 2007; Hugenberg, Miller, & Claypool, 2007). These findings indicate that it is not just experi-ence with members of other groups that produces the own-race bias but rather perceptions of group membership itself that may be of importance.

Given that the own-race effect is influenced by both experience with members of other races and social categorization, one can also ask ques-tions about the basic perceptual and cognitive mechanisms through which the effect occurs. One early attempt to understand the cognitive mechanisms underlying the own-race bias relied on the *depth of processing* account. Chance and Goldstein (1981) tested this idea by asking Caucasian participants to report on their first reaction to a series of pictures of Caucasian, Asian, and African American photographs. Judges later coded the transcripts for the depth of processing involved. Results indicated that participants engaged in deeper processing for same-race faces than for other-race faces. Other researchers have found that Caucasian and African American participants attend to different types of features when describing faces, leading to the hypothesis that the own-race bias occurs partly because the facial features people attend to are diagnostic for own-race faces but are less diagnostic for other-race faces (Ellis, Deregowski, & Shepherd, 1975; Shepherd & Deregowski, 1981).

Another account of the own-race bias is the *holistic processing account*. As discussed in Chapter 2, basic research in face perception suggests that face recognition relies on holistic processes (Richler, Gauthier, Wenger, & Palmeri, 2008). In particular, face recognition requires more than simply the recognition of individual features; it also requires accurate encoding of how those features are related to each other. This is known as *configural encoding*. Eyewitness researchers have argued that configural encoding depends on expertise, and as a result, configural encoding is better for same-race faces than for other-race faces (Rhodes, Brake, Taylor, & Tan, 1989). Rhodes et al. (1989) tested this hypothesis by making use of the inverted face paradigm. European and Chinese participants studied pictures of European and Chinese individuals. They were then presented with pairs of Chinese and pairs of European faces during a forced-choice recognition test. For each pair, the participant was to indicate which face they had seen. The test pairs were presented in either an upright orientation or an inverted orientation. The results supported the holistic processing explanation. Chinese participants showed a greater inversion effect for Chinese pictures than for European pictures, and Europeans showed a greater inversion effect for European pictures than for Chinese pictures, although this latter effect was only marginally significant.

Another paradigm we discussed previously was the composite face effect. Recall that in the composite face effect, participants view a composite face made up of the top part of one face and the bottom part of another face. They are then shown a new composite face and are asked to indicate if one half of the face (e.g., the top half) matches the previously seen face. When people are using holistic processing, this task is difficult because the fact that the face as a whole is a mismatch makes it harder to see that one half of the face (e.g., the top half) matches. Michel, Rossion, Han, Chung, and Caldara (2006) used this technique to see if holistic processing was crucial to the own-race bias. Participants were presented with Asian and Caucasian composite faces for 600 msec. After 300 msec they were shown a new composite face and had to indicate whether or not the top half of the face was the same. For half of the trials, the test stimuli were presented with the top and bottom halves of the faces misaligned. Misaligning the top and bottom halves of the faces in this way eliminates holistic processing, which should make it easier to concentrate just on the one half of the face. The results showed that Caucasian participants showed a greater composite face effect for own-race faces than for other-race faces, showing that the perception of own-race faces relies more on holistic processing.

In other recent research, the own-race bias was studied in split-brain patient J.W. (Turk, Handy, & Gazzaniga, 2005). It was found that the own-race bias occurred when the right hemisphere was tested, but that the own-race bias disappeared when the left hemisphere was tested. This is significant because the right hemisphere is specialized for the holistic processing of facial information, whereas the left hemisphere processes faces by decomposing them into individual features.

Another important processing account of the own-race bias is Levin's (2000) *race as a feature account*. Take the example of a Caucasian participant viewing slides of Caucasian and African American individuals. According to Levin's theory, for a Caucasian participant, the default value for race is Caucasian. Thus, when viewing another Caucasian individual, no feature is recorded for race. However, when viewing an African American individual, Caucasian participants will record race (i.e., Black) as a feature, which takes up part of their memory and leaves less capacity available in memory to encode other features. Levin (2000) tested this idea by making use of a procedure developed by Treisman and Souther (1985) in her tests of feature integration theory. Treisman and Souther (1985) distinguished between feature-present searches and feature-absent searches. In a feature-present search, participants are asked to identify an item that has a feature among a field of lures that do not have that feature. For instance, people might be asked to indicate when they see a Q in the following string:

OOOOOOOOOOOOOOOQOOOOOOOOOOOOOO

In a feature-absent search, the task is reversed. Participants are asked to identify a character that lacks a feature among a field of lures that have the feature. For instance, people might be asked to identify an O in the following string:

QQQQQQQQQQQQQQQOQQQQQQQQQQQQQQ

Treisman and Souther (1985) found that feature-present searches are easier and faster than feature-absent searches. In other words, it is easier to notice an item that contains a feature than to notice an item that lacks a feature. Levin's (2000) theory is that much as the Q has a feature that the O does not have, to a Caucasian witness, the memory representation of an African American has a feature (i.e., blackness) that is not present in the memory representation of another Caucasian (i.e., for a Caucasian participant, whiteness is not a feature, it is just assumed as a default value). Levin (2000) tested this idea by presenting pictures of a to-be-identified target (either Caucasian or African American) among a field of lures of the other race (i.e., if the target is Caucasian, the lures were African American; if the target was African American the lures were Caucasian). Analogous to Treisman and Souther's (1985) findings, Levin (2000) found that Caucasian participants were faster at identifying an African American face among a string of Caucasian faces than they were at identifying a Caucasian face among a string of African American faces. These results suggest that participants view their own racial or ethnic group as a default, and record an additional feature into memory for members of other races.

In addition to the effects that race has on recognition accuracy for faces, there is ample evidence that the other-race effect can influence a number of other forensically relevant situations. For instance, in an actual police investigation, the witness is shown a picture of the suspect as well as a number of foils. Foils can be selected either by matching the pictures to the suspect, or by matching the pictures to the description of the witness (see Chapter 4 for a discussion). Ideally, foils are chosen in such a way that if the perpetrator is not actually present in the lineup, then the witness should be just as likely to pick any individual foil as they are to pick the innocent suspect. This is the definition of a *fair lineup*. As we saw in Chapter 2, one way of testing the fairness of foil selection is to conduct a mock witness experiment. Participants who did not witness the crime (i.e., mock witnesses) are provided with witness descriptions of the perpetrator and are then shown the lineup. If they are more likely to pick the suspect than the other lineup members, then the lineup is not ideal in terms of fairness because it implies that the suspect resembles the witness descriptions more than the foils do. With regard to the other-race effect, Brigham and Ready (1985) found that unfair lineups are more likely to be created when the suspect and the police investigator who put together the lineup are of different races. Other forensically relevant outcome variables are also influenced by the match between the culprit's race and the witness's race. Dehon and Brédart (2001) presented Caucasian participants with pictures of white and black individuals and asked them to provide estimates of the age of the person depicted. They found that estimates of age were more accurate in the own-race condition than in the other-race condition. In other important work, Horry and Wright (2008) found that witnesses often mistakenly remember the context in which they encountered individuals of other races when compared to members of their own race.

The own-race bias continues to both fascinate and befuddle eyewitness researchers who have attempted to grapple with it. In the context of police practice, the most important finding is that other-race identifications are less reliable than are same-race identifications. Theoretical accounts of the own-race bias may, in the long run, help us ameliorate this problem or at least identify the witnesses who are most prone to falling prey to the effect.

Own-Age Bias

The own-race bias is extremely well known, among both eyewitness experts and students of psychology more generally. However, other similar biases have also been identified in the face recognition and eyewitness identification literatures. There is, for instance, evidence of an *own-age bias* in face recognition (Anastasi & Rhodes, 2006). Wiese, Schweinberger, and Hansen (2008) presented young adult and elderly participants with pictures of young adults and elderly adults. On a later old/new recognition test, young adults showed better recognition for young adult faces relative to elderly faces. The elderly participants did not show an own-age bias. In another study, younger (18–25 years old) and older (35–55 years old) participants viewed videotaped crimes in which the perpetrator's age varied from 21 to 51 years old. Younger participants were more accurate when the perpetrator was young, and older participants were more accurate when the perpetrator was older (although this latter finding was not statistically reliable). In another experiment, Anastasi and Rhodes (2006, Experiment 2) tested participants who were both young and elderly. The participants studied photographs of individuals who were young, middle aged, or elderly. Participants then took a recognition memory test that consisted of old pictures of previously studied individuals as well as new pictures depicting a person who had not been previously observed. Young adults did not demonstrate an own-age bias. However, elderly adults did show better recognition memory for individuals closer to their own age. The results of these and similar studies suggest that witnesses will be somewhat more accurate in recognizing perpetrators who are close to their own age, but that this effect is weaker and less consistent than is the other-race effect.

Similar biases occur in the recognition of children by adults. Kuefner, Cassia, Picozzi, and Briccolo (2008) presented college students with pictures of adults and newborns for one second per picture. Half a second after the presentation of each picture, participants were presented with two pictures and were asked which picture they had just seen. To examine the degree to which the faces were holistically processed, on some blocks the test photographs were presented upright, and on some blocks the test photographs were presented upside down. The results indicated that participants were better able to recognize adult faces than they were the faces of newborns. The typical face inversion effect was observed for pictures of adults, but no face inversion effect was observed for the pictures of newborns, suggesting that adult faces were processed holistically but faces of newborns were not processed holistically. When the experiment was repeated with pictures of 3–4-year-old children, recognition of upright adult faces were again superior to the recognition of upright children's faces. There was a face inversion effect for the pictures of both children and adults, but the face inversion effect was greatest for the adult photographs, suggesting that adult faces receive greater holistic processing than do children's faces. In a third experiment the researchers found that the own-age bias virtually disappeared when preschool teachers were tested rather than college undergraduates, suggesting that experience interacting with members of the particular age group can reduce the own-age bias.

Own-Gender Bias

There is also some evidence of an *own-gender bias* in studies of face recognition. One early study was conducted by Going and Read (1974). They presented male and female undergraduates with pictures of males and females that varied in distinctiveness. Distinctive faces were recognized better overall, but women were better at recognizing the female faces than the male faces, whereas men were equally good at recognizing both male and female faces. More recently, Lewin and Herlitz (2002) presented men and women with pictures of men and women. During one of the study blocks, the pictures included a full head shot including both internal facial features (i.e., eyes, nose, and mouth) and external facial features (i.e., hair, jewelry, etc.). During the other study block, only internal facial features were shown in the study pictures. There were two test blocks, one corresponding to each of the study blocks. On the test blocks, participants were presented with some previously studied faces and some new faces, and were asked to indicate if the face had been previously studied. As found by Going and Read (1974), women recognized female faces better than male faces, whereas there was no significant difference for men in terms of their recognition accuracy for male and female faces. Importantly, evidence of an own-gender bias for women occurred both when the stimuli were full head shots and when only internal facial features were shown. Most studies have found a greater own-gender bias among women than men. However, not all researchers have found such an asymmetry. In one study, Wright and Sladden (2003) found that their male participants remembered pictures of men better than those of women and that their female participants remember pictures of women better than those of men.

More forensically realistic studies of the own-gender bias have also been conducted, and they introduce some complications. In Shaw and Skolnick (1999), participants watched a videotape in which a person interrupted a lecture holding a book, a gun, or an unusual object. Later lineup performance indicated an own-gender bias, however, only when the target had been holding a book. In fact, in the condition where a weapon was present, or an unusual object was present, Shaw and Skolnick (1999) found a reversed own-gender effect. Shaw and Skolnick (1999) interpreted this finding as reflecting arousal differences between men and women.

What should we make of these findings? First, the finding of an own-gender bias has been replicated with sufficient regularity that it is fair to conclude that it is a real effect. Moreover, with only rare exceptions, the effect appears to be greater for female participants than for male participants. It may be that women are more interested in other women's appearance than men are interested in other men's appearance. However, this explanation is post hoc and has not been tested in any systematic manner.

☐ Concluding Remarks

In the present chapter, we have reviewed some of the variables that may impact the reliability of eyewitness identifications. The class of variables we have examined is that of estimator variables. That is, they are the sort of thing that police investigators have no control over, but that influence the accuracy of eyewitnesses. We distinguished four broad classes of estimator variables. Some estimator variables describe the witnessing situation. Some estimator variables describe the witness. Some estimator variables describe the perpetrator. And some estimator variables describe the interaction between witness and perpetrator. In all cases, we reviewed some of the representative findings and interpretations of the effects and tried to provide the reader with an idea of the reliability of the effect and the magnitude of the effect in terms of diagnosticity.

When Wells (1978) first created the distinction between system and estimator variables, his hope was not just to provide a taxonomic system, but rather to provide prescriptions for how the eyewitness testimony research community should prioritize applied research on eyewitness identification. In particular, Wells (1978) saw system variables as a potentially more fruitful avenue for researchers to follow. System variables, by definition, are variables under the control of law enforcement. To the extent that a system variable has an impact on eyewitness accuracy, it provides important information for law enforcement for how to minimize eyewitness errors to begin with. Indeed, it was the system variable approach that led to one of the biggest triumphs in applied psychology—the adoption of the Department of Justice guidelines (Technical Working Group, 1999).

The research reviewed in this chapter also demonstrates the importance of estimator variables for the legal system. Estimator variables can be useful in a number of different ways. They can help jurors evaluate the likely reliability of an eyewitness identification. They can also help police and prosecutors evaluate how strong of a case they have against a defendant. And in extreme cases, they can be valuable in determining whether evidence should be admissible at all. We also believe that it is time for a renewed emphasis on estimator variable research. Estimator variable research is important, because even when police use the very best practices in conducting interviews, lineups, and photospreads, there are simply some situations in which testimony is likely to be more reliable than others. Estimator variable research is our best hope to understand those variables and to help law enforcement and the triers of fact evaluate the reliability of the eyewitness.

☐ Endnotes

1. As noted previously, this conclusion assumes equal base rates.
2. If one assumes that a person's head is more rectangular than oval in shape, then the same logic holds. The number of pixels would be given by Area = Length × Width = 3.82 × 4.58 = 17.50. Thus, if the culprit is Sponge Bob Square Pants, the witness would have about 18 pixels to go on.
3. The outcome variable for these data was the number of correct identifications out of two possible. The authors analyzed the data using chi square tests and eliminated the oldest age group (11-year-olds) because the sample size was too small to achieve an expected value of at least five per cell. The clear trend in the data, however, appears to suggest a pretty stark improvement in performance on the test at age 11. The percent correct for 4-year-olds was 33.33%, for 5-year-olds was 42.00%, for 6-year-olds was 43.48%, for 7-year-olds was 47.83%, and for 11-year-olds was 85%.
4. The own-race bias has also been called the *other-race effect* and the *cross-race effect*. It has also been called the "own ethnicity bias" (Gross, 2009) in recognition of the fact that the effect occurs for ethnicity as well as race. We use the term *own-race bias* in this monograph because it is a broadly used term for the effect.

CHAPTER

System Variables

☐ *State of Tennessee v. Giovanni Marin*

On July 26, 2006, at approximately 10:00 p.m., Gabriel Marrufo was shot and killed in the banquet room of the Sunrise Hotel in Nashville, Tennessee. His brother, Juan Antonio Marrufo, and his sister, Claudia Marrufo, were both shot and wounded. When Detective Winter of the Nashville Police Department arrived at the scene, he found all three victims lying in a back hallway of the banquet room. The family had gathered at the hotel for the baptism of a cousin of the victims. During the festivities, five to seven Hispanic men, including Giovanni Marin, tried to enter the banquet room in order to join the party. Mr. Marrufo told them they were not welcome and asked them to leave. Shouting ensued, and Mr. Marrufo punched one of the interlopers in the face. Mr. Marin and his friends went to their car and then returned to the banquet room, two of them armed with guns. As they attempted to re-enter the party, someone shot Gabriel Marrufo twice and then fired several more times, striking Juan Antonio Marrufo and his sister, Claudia. They were both coming to the aid of their wounded brother. By the time the police arrived, the culprits had fled, and the Marrufo siblings were rushed to the hospital. Gabriel died shortly afterward, and Juan Antonio and Claudia were in critical condition.

On July 29, 2006, after Juan Antonio Marrufo had undergone several operations, Detective Winter interviewed him about the crime and asked him to try to identify the culprits from lineups. Before he came to the hospital, Detective Winter had constructed three photo lineups, each of which was composed of pictures of persons matching the general description of the culprits. A picture in one of the lineups was of Giovanni Marin.

Before he administered the lineups, Detective Winter informed Mr. Marrufo that he was going to be shown three photo lineups and that the

113

pictures of the culprits might or might not be in those lineups. He then instructed Mr. Marrufo as follows, reading from a set of instructions and interspersing his own comments as well:

Detective Winter: Okay. Tell you what I'm going to do—we like to give advice to people before they look at this so they know what to look for; so they know what to consider, okay? This won't take but a—but about another 5 minutes, if you've got it. Okay? You know how important this is 'cause obviously you're in a lot of pain. Uh, I'm going to read this to you, and you can just tell me if you understand or if you have any questions, okay?

Juan Antonio: Okay.

Detective Winter: All right. Are you ready? I've been advised that I'll be viewing several photographs of individuals for the purpose of attempting to identify the suspect in the criminal incident. Primarily, we're basically trying to identify the bad guys, okay? I understand that this is an important procedure which is designed to assure an accurate, reliable identification of the suspect, as well as to clear the innocent. Basically, if you see a guy here that you know who was there, but wasn't a shooter, say, "Hey, that guy was there but he wasn't the shooter. He's innocent," okay? I further understand that the following listed parameters apply to the procedure and these are the things I want you to under—keep in mind, okay? The subject in this display may not appear exactly as they did on the date of incident. Because features such as hairstyles, grooming, meaning facial hair and how they keep themselves, and body weight may be subject to change. That means in a couple of years you may be a little heavier than you are now. You might even grow a goatee or something like that. Make sense? Keep that in mind that the person—we didn't take the picture that I'm going to show you— we didn't take them on the day that you saw this guy, okay?

After looking at the lineups for several minutes, Juan Antonio identified Giovanni Marin as one of the people at the scene of the crime, but he was not sure whether Mr. Marin was the gunman. After Juan Antonio had made the identification, Detective Winter told him no less than five times that he was now their "star witness."

During the preliminary hearing on August 18, 2006, Juan Antonio identified Giovanni Marin in court as one of the assailants and indicated with great confidence that Mr. Marin was the person who shot his brother, his sister, and himself.

☐ System Variables

Wells (1978) coined the term "system variables" to refer to factors relevant to the accuracy and reliability of eyewitness testimony that are under the control of the police. Wells argued that social scientists could help improve the overall reliability of eyewitness identifications by studying these factors. Examples of system variables include the kinds of statements made to eyewitnesses prior to and after lineups; the types of instructions given to witnesses before identifications; the number of people in a lineup, and the way in which those people are presented; and the ways in which eyewitnesses are interviewed. Research on system variables has contributed to our understanding of the factors that influence identification accuracy and has led to applications affecting the way in which lineups are constructed and conducted. What follows is a summary of some of the system variables that have been studied, what the researchers have found regarding these variables, as well as the recommendations for collecting eyewitness evidence that have resulted from this research.

☐ System Variables: Pre-Identification

System variables can influence the accuracy of a witness's testimony from the very first contact the police have with the witness all the way to the time of trial. We begin our discussion of system variables by discussing factors that occur before the witness is shown a lineup. We then discuss the composition and administration of lineups and other identification procedures.

Misleading Postevent Information

Imagine that you are at a grocery store. You just had a long day at work, but you need to pick up a few things for dinner. You are tired. The store is crowded and busy, and the lines are long. As you approach the 20-items-or-less aisle, you notice a woman in front of you. She clearly has around 25 items in her basket. When she gets to the register, she takes out a gun and demands money from the cashier. You are in a state of shock as you watch the woman grab the money and run off. Your heart still racing, you ask the cashier if he is all right. When the police arrive, they first interview the cashier. You are standing close enough to hear the cashier describe the woman as a medium-build Caucasian female, with crooked teeth, black hair, and a serious attitude problem. When the police interview you, you provide a similar description. At one point during the interview, the investigator says, "The other witness says she was five foot six; is that about right?" You agree that that sounds close. You are at the grocery store for about 50 minutes. When you get home, your local news station has a story about the robbery. Apparently, the handgun the woman had used was a Glock automatic. When you go to bed that night, you have a difficult time getting the picture of this medium-build, 5'6" tall woman with crooked teeth, a Glock automatic, and a serious attitude problem out of your mind.

The above example illustrates a phenomenon known as *postevent information* (Loftus, 1979). Postevent information is information that an eyewitness encounters after an event that may later become incorporated into the witness's memory. Elizabeth Loftus and her colleagues (Loftus, 1979; Loftus, Miller, & Burns, 1978; Loftus & Greene, 1980) developed the *misleading postevent information* procedure in order to better understand the effect that postevent information has on memory. The experimental procedure Loftus developed involves three basic stages (see Figure 4.1).

1. Participants are exposed to an event. The event may be shown in the form of a slide show or video, or may be staged live. These events are meant to simulate the type of things a witness might see if they witnessed a crime or some other legally relevant event (e.g., a traffic accident).

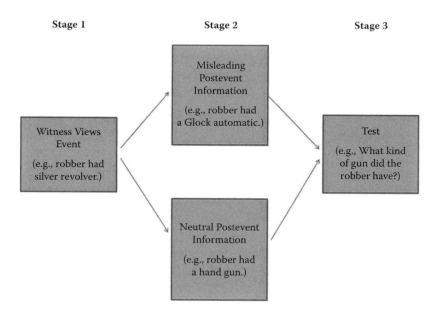

FIGURE 4.1 Illustration of the misleading postevent information paradigm.

2. After some time has passed, participants are presented with postevent information. For some participants the postevent information is misleading, whereas for other participants the postevent information is neutral. Postevent information can be presented in a number of different ways (e.g., an assumption embedded in a question, or a narrative description of the event).
3. Finally, the participant's memory is tested. The participant might be asked to describe the event or take a recognition memory test. In the real world, the witness might be asked to testify in court or to give a deposition.

The key finding from experiments using this procedure is that misleading postevent information can distort a witness's memory for the event. For instance, after you hear that the woman had a Glock automatic, you may develop a memory that you actually saw a Glock automatic, even if the woman actually had a revolver. The distortion of memory that occurs as a result of misleading postevent information is known as the *misinformation effect*.

To illustrate how postevent information is studied in the laboratory, consider a study by Loftus et al. (1978). The procedures used in this study are illustrated in Figure 4.2. In stage 1 of the procedure, participants were

	Postevent Information		
	Did another car pass the red Datsun while it was stopped at the stop sign?	Did another car pass the red Datsun while it was stopped at the yield sign?	Did another car pass the red Datsun while it was stopped at the intersection?
See Stop Sign	Consistent	Misleading	Neutral
See Yield Sign	Misleading	Consistent	Neutral

FIGURE 4.2   Illustration of the conditions in Loftus, Miller, and Burns (1978). (*Source*: Images of cars at traffic signs reprinted from Loftus, E. F., Miller, D. G., & Burns, H. J. (1978). Semantic integration of verbal information into a visual memory. *Journal of Experimental Psychology: Human Learning and Memory, 4*, 19–31.)

shown a short slide presentation involving an auto–pedestrian accident. For half of the participants, a key slide showed a car stopped at a *stop sign*. For the other half of the participants, the slide showed the car at a *yield sign*.

In the second stage of the procedure, participants were asked a series of questions. Embedded in one of the questions was a presupposition about the kind of traffic sign that was in the slides. Some participants were asked, "Did another car pass the red Datsun while it was stopped at the stop sign?" Other participants were asked, "Did another car pass the red Datsun while it was stopped at the yield sign?" Still other participants were asked, "Did another car pass the red Datsun while it was stopped at the intersection?" For participants who saw the slide showing a stop sign, the question that implied it was a yield sign was a *misleading question*, whereas the question that implied it was a stop sign was a *consistent question*. For participants who saw the slide showing a yield sign, the question that implied it was a stop sign was a *misleading question*, whereas the question that implied it was a yield sign was a *consistent question*. The question that asked about the car stopped at the "intersection" was a *neutral question* because it did not imply anything one way or the other about what kind of sign that was present.

During the third stage of the procedure, participants' memories were tested using a two-alternative forced-choice test. Participants were shown two slides, one that contained a stop sign and one that contained a yield sign, and they were asked which slide they had actually seen. Findings indicated that participants who had received the misleading information during stage 2 were substantially less accurate on this final memory test than were participants who received neutral or consistent information.

Loftus et al. (1978) showed that misleading information can cause witnesses to remember one detail when in fact they saw a different detail (e.g., a stop sign when they really saw a yield sign). Another way misleading information can change memory is by implanting entirely false details into a witness's memory report. For instance, in one study, participants saw a videotape of a car driving down a country road (Loftus, 1975). During stage 2 of the procedure, participants were asked a series of questions, including, "How fast was the white sports car going as it passed the barn on the country road?" Other participants were simply asked, "How fast was the white sports car going as it traveled along the country road?" In fact, there was no barn. In stage 3, close to 20% of participants who had been asked the misleading question indicated that they had seen the barn.

Misleading information can also produce subtle changes in memory along a continuous dimension. For instance, in Loftus (1977) participants saw a film in which a green car passed an accident scene. In stage 2, some participants were asked, "Did the blue car that drove past the accident have a ski rack on the roof?" (i.e., misleading question), whereas other participants were asked, "Did the car that drove past the accident have a ski rack on the roof?" (i.e., a neutral question). On the final test, participants were asked to pick out the color of the car. Participants who had been asked the misleading question often picked a bluish-green color, a color that was a compromise between the color they actually saw and the color implied by the question. These types of memory distortions are sometimes called *memory blends* (Belli, 1988; Metcalfe, 1990).

There have been a number of different theories offered for the misinformation effect. An early account offered by Loftus et al. (1978) was called *destructive updating.* According to this explanation, misleading information takes the place of the original memory, such that the original memory is no longer there. This is kind of like what would happen if you had a document on your computer and then you saved over it with another document with the same name. Other researchers proposed an *interference account* (Christiaansen & Ochalek, 1983). According to the interference account, misleading information interferes with the ability to retrieve the original information when taking the memory test. This is kind of like what would happen if you had a bunch of documents saved on your computer, and they all had very similar names. It might be hard for you to later find exactly the document you were looking for.

A third early explanation that was offered for the effect of misleading information proposed that misleading information influences only participants who would not have remembered the original event anyway (McCloskey & Zaragoza, 1985a). To understand this explanation, imagine what would happen if you tried to replicate the experiment involving the stop sign and the yield sign. Imagine that during stage one of the experiment, a particularly unmotivated group of participants fall asleep during the slide presentation that involved the car stopping at the stop sign or yield sign.[1] During stage 2, you ask the participants, "Did another car pass the red Datsun while it was stopped at the stop sign?" or "Did another car pass the red Datsun while it was stopped at the intersection?" The participants are then given a memory test where you ask them whether they saw a stop sign or a yield sign. How are these slacker participants likely to do on the test? If they are in the control condition, their only option will be to guess. They did not see the slides because they were asleep, and the postevent information did not say anything about the type of traffic sign. On average, these participants should be correct about half of the time. However, if these same participants were in the misleading information condition, the situation is different. They will not have a memory representation of the original event from stage 1. However, they might have a memory of the questions they were asked. They might reason as follows, "Well, I don't remember the slides. However, the experimenter asked me a question about a stop sign. So there must have been a stop sign." Because the postevent information is misleading (i.e., incorrect), these participants should do worse than chance. According to this explanation, misleading information has no effect on the original memory. Rather, it operates by influencing people who, for whatever reason, would not have remembered the original event in the first place.

These different explanations created a huge theoretical debate in the 1980s (Belli, 1989; Loftus & Hoffman, 1989; McCloskey & Zaragoza, 1985a, 1985b; Tversky & Tuchin, 1989; Zaragoza & McCloskey, 1989; Zaragoza, McCloskey, & Jamis, 1987). However, eventually, a picture emerged suggesting that misleading information can impair memory and that this probably occurs due to interference (Belli, 1989; Lindsay, 1990). At around the time these issues were being resolved, another important account of the effect of misleading postevent event information was being proposed. This explanation is based on the *source monitoring framework* proposed by Johnson and Raye (1981; see also Johnson, Hashtroudi, & Lindsay, 1993). The source monitoring framework has to do with how people distinguish between memories from different sources. For instance, it attempts to explain how people tell the difference between events that they experienced and events that they imagined or only heard about. According to the source monitoring framework, people make these decisions partly by examining qualitative details of their memories. For instance, a memory for an event that was actually experienced will include more perceptual detail than a memory for an event that was only imagined. A memory for an event that was only imagined might include more details about the thought processes used to create the mental image (i.e., cognitive operations) than would a memory for an event that was actually perceived.

Based on the source monitoring framework, Lindsay and Johnson (1989) proposed that misinformation effects can be thought of as a kind of *source misattribution error*. According to this theory, misleading information impairs memory when the participant becomes confused about the source of the memory (e.g., "Did I see this in the slides or hear about it in the question?") Consider the example of the grocery store robbery. If you actually were a witness to that robbery, you would form a memory representation of that event that would include visual details of what you saw, auditory details of what you heard, emotional content about how frightened you were, and cognitive details about what you were thinking. Later on, if you saw a news broadcast stating that the robber had a Glock automatic, that too would create a memory representation that you connect to the event. When you hear the news report, you might create a picture in your mind of the robber with a Glock automatic. The mental picture you create might also contain vivid visual details, especially if you have a good imagination. Later on, when you are asked what kind of gun the robber had, you might think you remember seeing a Glock automatic, when in fact you did not. That would be a source misattribution error.

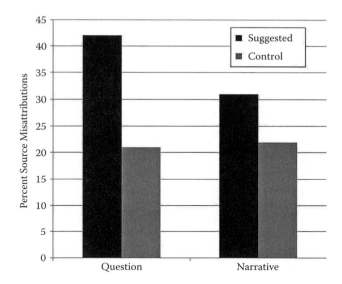

FIGURE 4.3 Percentage of source misattributions in Zaragoza and Lane (1994). (*Source*: Based on data presented in Zaragoza, M., & Lane, S. (1994). Source misattributions and the suggestibility of eyewitness memory. *Journal of Experimental Psychology: Learning, Memory, and Cognition, 20*, 934–945.)

In an early study, Zaragoza and Lane (1994) showed participants a set of slides that depicted an office theft. In stage 2, the participants read a postevent narrative describing the theft or answered postevent questions about the slides. The questions and the narrative mentioned some items that had been in the slides and some items that had not been in the slides. In stage 3, participants took a special test called a *source monitoring test*. For each item on the test, participants were asked to indicate whether the item occurred in the slides, in the postevent questions or narrative, in both, or in neither. Results of this experiment are reproduced in Figure 4.3. Participants were more likely to think they had actually seen items in the slides if they had been mentioned in the postevent information than if the items had not been mentioned. Thus source misattributions were occurring. This occurred both when the postevent information had been presented in a narrative format and when it had been presented in a question format. However, the size of the effect was much greater when the postevent information was presented in the form of a question.

In another study, Lindsay (1990) adapted Jacoby's (1991) process dissociation procedure (see Chapter 2) to show that participants sometimes misattribute the source of the misleading information. Participants in this study watched a slide presentation and then read a narrative that contained either misleading information or neutral information. When it came time for the final memory test, participants were told that the narrative mentioned some details that were not in the original slides. They were told that they were only to say "yes" to items that had actually been in the slides. Moreover, participants were given the following rule: (a) If an item is being asked about on the test, and (b) you can recall it from the narrative, then (c) it was *not* in the slides. Despite this warning, participants still committed a substantial number of source misattribution errors. These studies show that misleading information can become incorporated into memory, and that witnesses can come to believe that they really saw details that they actually only heard or read about.

A number of factors influence the likelihood that misleading information will have an impact on memory (Loftus, 2003). One variable that is important is the strength of the original memory. When memory traces for the target are weak, people are more susceptible to making mistakes about the target and are more likely to make source misattributions (Pezdek & Roe, 1995; Reyna & Titcomb, 1997). For example, Loftus et al. (1978) found more evidence of memory distortion when misleading information was introduced after a long delay, when the memory would likely be weak. In other research, Pezdek and Roe (1995) demonstrated that children are more susceptible to error when given misleading information about events that they experienced only once, compared to events that they were exposed to frequently.

Research also indicates that if the misleading information conforms to prior beliefs, it is more likely to be integrated into memory (Belli, 1988; Holst & Pezdek, 1992; Luna & Migueles, 2008; Smith & Studebaker, 1996). Because the scene of a car accident will typically contain broken glass, it is natural for us to recall broken glass at the scene of an accident, even if it was not there. In addition, it seems that when people attend to the discrepancies between the misleading information and features of the remembered events, they may be less susceptible to memory distortion (Tousignant, Hall, & Loftus, 1986). There is, however, some debate regarding this last point, because other researchers have found that merely alerting participants to the possibility of a discrepancy between remembered events and data received after the event is not enough to prevent distortion if the misleading data are highly accessible in memory (Eakin, Schreiber, & Sergent-Marshall, 2003).

Social factors have also been implicated in the misleading postevent information effect. One critical factor is the *expertise* of the source of the misleading information. *Expertise* refers to how knowledgeable a source of information is perceived as being (Pallak, Murroni, & Koch, 1983). Smith and Ellsworth (1987) examined the role of communicator expertise on the impact of postevent information. Participants viewed a videotaped bank robbery. They were then introduced to a person who they believed was another participant in the experiment, but who was actually a confederate working with the experimenters. Participants were told that the confederate either had never seen the film (i.e., novice source) or had seen the film several times (i.e., expert source). The confederate then acted as an interviewer and asked the participant a set of questions. For half of the participants, the interview included some misleading questions. For the other half of the participants, the confederate asked only neutral questions. Misleading information impaired memory, but only when the misleading information was provided by the expert source.

Social power and perceived authority can also increase the likelihood of memory distortion. Participants in one study listened to a recording that contained misleading postevent information and were asked to rate the speaker's power and social attractiveness based on the auditory stimuli (Vornik, Sharman, & Garry, 2003). Those who believed that the speaker was powerful or socially attractive were more susceptible to making mistakes due to misleading postevent information than were those who did not rate the speaker as highly in either power or social attractiveness. Similarly, Ceci, Ross, and Toglia (1987) found that susceptibility to misleading postevent data was reduced in children when another child, as opposed to an adult, provided the misleading descriptions. Lampinen and Smith (1995) found that preschoolers are more likely to accept misleading information presented by an adult described in neutral terms than an adult who was described as being "silly." These results show that even preschool-aged children are able to take into account the credibility of the source of the information.

Regardless of the cause of the effect, research consistently shows that misleading or suggestive information presented to witnesses after the fact can cause significant errors in their reports. These results suggest that it is important to limit witness contamination. Police should ask open-ended questions rather than leading questions whenever possible. They should segregate witnesses so that witnesses do not contaminate each other's memories. And witnesses should be advised to avoid media reports of the crime that might also contaminate their memories.

Co-Witness Effects

One of the most common ways for a witness to be exposed to postevent information is to hear the statements of another witness. These are called *co-witness effects*. Skagerberg and Wright (2008) found that in 88% of the cases they examined, there was more than one witness to the crime. In fact, on average there were about four witnesses to each event. In about 60% of these cases, witnesses reported discussing details of the crime with at least one other witness.

Co-witnesses can have powerful effects on eyewitness memory reports. For instance, Shaw, Garven, and Wood (1997) had participants watch a videotape of a bank robbery while seated next to a confederate who they believed was another participant. Following the videotape, the participant and the confederate were questioned together and they answered the questions out loud. On some trials, the participant answered the question first, and on other trials the confederate answered the question first. Half of the time, when the confederate answered first, he or she answered correctly; and half of the time, he or she answered incorrectly. When the participants went first or when the confederate went first and provided accurate information, participants were correct about 60% of the time. However, when the confederate answered first and provided false information, participants were correct only about one third of the time. The findings thus demonstrated that incorrect information obtained from another witness can seriously impair eyewitness accuracy.

Other research has found that co-witness information can exert particularly powerful effects on eyewitness memory. Paterson and Kemp (2006) showed participants a videotape of a simulated robbery. After a brief delay, participants were exposed to consistent and misleading postevent information. The postevent information was presented in one of four ways: (a) embedded in leading questions, (b) presented as part of a newspaper article, (c) indirectly in the form of written statements by other witnesses, or (4) during a discussion with a co-witness who had been trained to provide the postevent information during the course of conversation. One week later, participants returned to the laboratory and answered questions about the robbery. Mean percent correct in each of the conditions is reproduced in Figure 4.4. In the figure, the black bars show the percent correct on the final memory test, when no postevent information had been provided. The white bars show the percent correct on the final memory test, when misleading postevent information had been provided a week earlier. By comparing the white bars to the black bars, it is clear that misleading information decreased the participant's accuracy on the final memory test. However, the effect of misleading information was clearly greatest when it was presented by a co-witness. Given these results, it is quite clear that police should make every effort to segregate witnesses from each other and ask them not to talk with other witnesses. Additionally, police should avoid indirectly providing witnesses with information from other witnesses during the course of their interviews.

Cognitive Interview

Police officers and other officials interview eyewitnesses in order to gather as much relevant information as possible about the crime. The goal

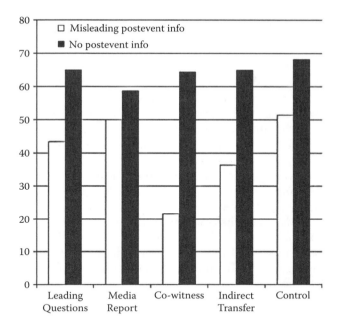

FIGURE 4.4   Results of Paterson and Kemp (2006) showing accuracy for different sources of misinformation. (*Source*: Based on data presented in Paterson, H. M., & Kemp, R. I. (2006). Comparing methods of encountering post-event information: The power of co-witness suggestion. *Applied Cognitive Psychology, 20,* 1083–1099.)

of such interviews is to obtain accurate, relevant facts without distorting the memories of witnesses. Because this is such an important part of the investigative process, researchers over the past two decades have worked to develop and refine a successful interviewing protocol for law enforcement. The *cognitive interview* is the protocol that has shown the best results (Fisher, McCauley, & Geiselman, 1994). The *cognitive interview* is divided into five sections: *introduction, open-ended narration, probing, review,* and *close.* The most important characteristic of the cognitive interview sequence is the wide-to-narrow progression of questions. In the *introduction,* interviewers establish good rapport with witnesses and tell them their expectations for the interview. This is followed by *open-ended narration.* At this stage the witness describes the relevant circumstances and events freely without being interrupted by the investigator. During this time the interviewer should be thinking of follow-up questions, but should refrain from asking them until after the open-ended narration has been completed. The follow-up questions should be designed to extract as much additional information from the witness's memory as possible.

Next, the interviewer reviews all of the information gathered and corrects any errors in the official account. At the close of the session, interviewers complete reporting information requirements that exist and encourage witnesses to contact them if further information becomes available.

The cognitive interview emerged out of basic theory and research in psychology. The technique takes into account three relevant psychological factors: memory/cognition, social dynamics, and communication (Fisher & Schreiber, 2005). Interviewers must understand the relevant aspects of these factors in order to acquire relevant, accurate information from the interview with little error.

Cognitive psychologists have developed a number of approaches that can be used to improve memory, and these techniques have been applied to the cognitive interview (Fisher et al., 1994). For instance, the *encoding specificity principle* states that memory will be best if the contextual cues available at retrieval match the cues that were available when the event was originally encoded (Tulving & Thomson, 1973). The cognitive interview takes advantage of this finding by encouraging the witness to mentally re-create the context of the original event. Such *context reinstatement* may also be facilitated by having witnesses return to the scene of the crime to be remembered.

Basic research in cognitive psychology also shows that working memory has a limited capacity (Baddeley & Hitch, 1975; see also Chapter 2). Because of this, an investigator conducting a cognitive interview asks open-ended questions, avoids interrupting witnesses, and encourages witnesses to close their eyes in order to limit distractions. Each of these practices allows witnesses to make the best use of their limited mental resources (Bekerian & Dennett, 1997).

Cognitive psychologists have shown that memory retrieval can be improved by using more than one retrieval pathway (e.g., Kazén & Solís-Macías, 1999). In the cognitive interview, investigators may ask witnesses to recall events from different perspectives (e.g., a bird's-eye view versus a person perspective). In the original version of the cognitive interview, witnesses were even asked to recall events in different orders (forward and backward). The cognitive interview encourages witness to say, "I don't know," rather than guessing, in order to protect witnesses from being exposed to other sources that may contribute to the creation of false memories. Finally, it is important for an investigator conducting a cognitive interview to recognize that each witness will have a unique perspective on the event. Because of this, investigators should tailor their questions to the individual witness rather than using a standardized checklist (Fisher, Geiselman, & Raymond, 1987).

The social dynamics at work in an interview can also affect the quality and quantity of data that are retrieved. The cognitive interview protocol directly addresses two major aspects of the social dynamics between the interviewer and the interviewee. The police investigator's official appearance can be intimidating and can act as barrier between the police officer and the witness, preventing the investigator from getting a complete report. To enhance the value of the data gathered from an interview, the interviewer must create a comfortable rapport with the witness. This takes considerable effort on the part of the interviewer, but it is a critical step that is frequently absent in interviews (Fisher et al., 1987). The second recommendation to improve the social dynamics in an interview is to encourage the active participation of the witness. An active witness gives longer, more detailed descriptions than a passive witness. Fisher and Schreiber (2005) propose several techniques to make witnesses more active: explicitly asking them to be more active, asking open-ended questions that are not interrupted, and balancing the power differential between the witness and the officer by explicitly indicating that the witness is an expert about the event to be remembered.

The final psychological factor addressed by the cognitive interview is communication. Though communication is present at all levels of interviewing, the cognitive interview specifically recommends free communication. In particular, the cognitive interview requires interviewers to explicitly communicate to witnesses what is expected of them during interviews. Though the time for an interview may be limited, insisting on brief responses to questions reduces the amount of useful information that is acquired and may also promote false statements by reducing witnesses' freedom to give detailed or nuanced answers (Fisher & Schreiber, 2005).

Despite more than two decades of demonstrated success both in the laboratory and in actual investigations, it is discouraging that the cognitive interview is not used much in the United States. One exception is the FBI's interview and interrogation training program, which closely follows the cognitive interview method (Fisher & Geiselman, 1992). The cognitive interview approach is used much more in Europe than in the United States, especially in the United Kingdom (George, 1991). One reason why the cognitive interview is not more widely used may simply be that it is more difficult to conduct than the standard police interview. For instance, a survey of British police noted that for a variety of reasons, with time constraints ranking high, the complete cognitive interview is often difficult to administer (Kebbell, Milne, & Wagstaff, 1999). One solution to this problem may involve the development of streamlined versions of the cognitive interview (Fisher & Schreiber, 2005). There has also been work on developing a self-administered interview in which the witness goes through a workbook, answering questions at his or her own pace (Gabbert, Hope, & Fisher, 2009). The workbook incorporates aspects of the cognitive interview (e.g., context reinstatement), and initial results indicate that it produces recall levels that are comparable to those of the cognitive interview.

The primary benefit of using the cognitive interview protocol in interviews is its ability to extract significantly more information while having an accuracy rate comparable to those of other protocols. Not only does the cognitive interview provide interviewers with a robust and reliable method by which to conduct interviews with normal adults, but also it has been shown to work effectively with other witnesses such as children, the elderly, and adults with learning disabilities (for a review, see Holliday, Brainerd, Reyna, & Humphries, 2009). Given the clear advantages in terms of amount of information extracted, police investigators should learn to use the cognitive interview and should use the technique whenever it is feasible to do so.

Hypnosis

When police are interviewing witnesses and trying to develop a suspect list, they sometimes make use of hypnosis in an attempt to help witnesses retrieve more information from memory. Most laypeople believe that hypnosis improves memory (Wagstaff, 1989). Moreover, jury simulation research suggests that jurors are more likely to believe testimony if hypnosis was used to retrieve the memory (Wagstaff, Vella, & Perfect, 1992; Wells, 1984). These findings are problematic, in that available evidence does not support the claim that hypnosis improves eyewitness accuracy.

A number of studies have examined the effectiveness of hypnosis in helping eyewitnesses retrieve details about crimes. In one early study, participants viewed a brief film showing a theft by a pickpocket (Sanders & Simmons, 1983). One week later, participants returned and viewed either a target-present or target-absent lineup. The target-present lineup included the pickpocket in position number 4. The target-absent lineup included a foil in position 4 who was wearing clothing that was similar to that worn by the actual culprit (i.e., clothing bias). Half of the participants were hypnotized. During the hypnotic induction, participants were told that they would be able to play back the event in their mind as if it were on a videotape, and that they would be able to rewind, fast-forward, or freeze-frame the event in their mind's eye. The other half of the participants was not hypnotized. The hypnotized participants were less accurate than were the participants in the control condition. This finding was largely driven by increased false recognition of the clothing-matched foil in the target-absent lineup. Hypnosis apparently increased the willingness of participants to rely on this cue, even though the actual faces did not match.

In another study, Yuille and McEwan (1985) tested participants who were moderately or highly hypnotizable based on a standardized test of hypnotic susceptibility. Participants viewed a videotaped bank robbery.

After a week, participants completed a simulated police interview and made a choice from a lineup. Some participants were hypnotized prior to being interviewed. Other participants were given relaxation instructions prior to being interviewed. A third group of participants completed the interview without doing either of those things. No significant difference was observed between the three groups.

Because hypnosis involves a heightened level of suggestibility, one concern has been that hypnotized witnesses may be more likely to be influenced by leading questions. For instance, Putnam (1979) asked participants in an eyewitness memory study a series of leading questions and found that hypnotized witnesses were more likely to be influenced by the leading questions than were non-participants. Thus, memory distortion may be more prevalent in hypnotized witnesses. Not only can hypnosis potentially lead to more errors, but also it tends to increase witness confidence in their errors. One consequence of these findings is that many courts will consider a witness who has undergone hypnosis to be tainted, and as a result will exclude the witness's testimony.

Taken together, these findings lead us to conclude that law enforcement should be leery of using hypnosis when interviewing witnesses. For one thing, any benefit that arises out of hypnosis probably comes from putting the witness in a relaxed and receptive state that is free of distractions. These characteristics of the interview can be more easily accomplished by using a quiet interview room and building rapport with the witness. The social communicative aspects of the cognitive interview are also designed to create a situation that will maximize recall and are to be preferred over forensic hypnosis.

Exposure to Mugshots

One approach that may be used to identify potential suspects is the use of mugbooks. Mugbooks are large collections of pictures (mugshots). One concern that has developed is that seeing a picture in a mugbook might increase the odds that that person will later be identified in an actual lineup. In *Simmons v. United States* (1968), the U.S. Supreme Court stated that multiple identification tests are detrimental to eyewitness accuracy.

Research has shown that exposing witnesses to mugshots can lead them to falsely identify someone at a later date. This has been called the *mugshot exposure effect* (Deffenbacher, Bornstein, & Penrod, 2006). In one study, Brown, Deffenbacher, and Sturgill (1977) had two groups of five confederates come into a classroom. The researchers told students to pay attention to these "criminals," because they would have to identify them later. A short time later, participants were shown 15 mugshots and asked to indicate if any of the mugshots were of one of the "criminals." The mugshots

TABLE 4.1 Percentage of Identifications in Lineups Following Exposure to Mugshots in Brown, Deffenbacher, and Sturgill (1977)

Criminals With Mugshots	Criminals Without Mugshots	Mugshot Only	Never Before Seen Foil
65%	51%	20%	8%

included the five original "criminals," five people who would later appear in a lineup, and five foils. One week later, participants were shown a series of lineups. Lineups included "criminals" who had been seen in the mugshots, "criminals" who had not been in the mugshots, people who had been in the mugshots but were not "criminals," and never-before-seen foils. When a person who was not one of the "criminals" had appeared in the mugshots, they were more than twice as likely to be falsely identified as a never-before-seen foil (see Table 4.1). Thus, exposure to the mugshots increased the chance of a false identification.

Mugshots can also decrease recognition of guilty culprits in later lineups. In a study by Gorenstien and Ellsworth (1980), experimenters had a person interrupt a class to inquire about a missing wallet. At the end of the class, half of the students remained to view 12 mugshots (culprit-absent) from which they were asked to identify the woman (culprit) who interrupted the class. The other half of the class served as the control group and did not view mugshots. Four to six days later, the participants attempted to make an identification of the "culprit" from a six-person culprit-present lineup. For those individuals who had viewed the mugshots earlier, the lineup included the individual they selected as well as the culprit. Those who viewed the mugshots were more likely to choose the person they had originally identified (44%) than the actual culprit (22%) or other foils. Gorenstein and Ellsworth (1980) proposed that once an eyewitness has chosen someone from an initial group of photographs, they are likely to choose that same person again in a later identification task. The witness may believe that if the person has been presented in the lineup a second time, then they must have been correct in their initial identification. This has become known as the *commitment effect* (Brigham & Cairns, 1988; Dysart, Lindsay, Hammond, & Dupuis, 2001; Goodsell, Neuschatz, & Gronlund, 2009; Schooler, Foster, & Loftus, 1988).

Brigham and Cairns (1988) demonstrated that the commitment effect occurs even when there is little or no external pressure from the lineup administrator. After viewing a videotape of a staged assault, one group of participants viewed 18 mugshots, whereas the other group saw none. During the mugshots task, some participants were asked to identify the culprit and were told that the culprit may or may not have been in the mugshot photographs (i.e., they were given unbiased instructions). The other participants were asked only to rate the attractiveness of the people in the photographs and were not asked to make an identification. The actual culprit was not in the mugshots shown to either group. Two days after viewing the mugbook, participants were asked to make an identification from a six-person photo lineup. If a person had identified someone from the mugshots, that mugshot picture was placed in the lineup along with the culprit. Participants demonstrated a strong commitment to their earlier selections even though the actual culprit was in the lineup.

So exposing a witness to mugshots can cause problems, but why does it cause problems? Some eyewitness scientists have proposed a *familiarity explanation*. According to this explanation, when witnesses are exposed to a mugshot of an individual, and then later are exposed to that same person in a lineup or photospread, the person's face will seem especially familiar. According to this view, the familiarity is caused by having seen the face before in the mugshots, and the witness misattributes that familiarity to having seen the person commit the crime. The familiarity explanation is an example of a source misattribution error, and the term *unconscious transference* has sometimes been used to describe the phenomenon. Other scientists have proposed a *commitment explanation* of the biasing effects of mugshots. According to this explanation, when witnesses are shown mugshots, they will sometimes select one of the members of the mugshots as the person they saw commit the crime. When the witness is later shown the same person in a lineup or photospread, they are more likely to pick him or her, not because of a heightened sense of familiarity, but rather to be consistent with a previous choice.

Memon et al. (2002) conducted research to try to unravel these two potential explanations. They had participants view a video of a mock crime. Some of the participants were exposed to 12 culprit-absent mugshots. One of these mugshots, the one who most resembled the culprit, was deemed the *familiar foil*. Participants in the control condition were not shown the mugshots. All participants were shown a culprit-absent lineup 2 days after viewing the video. The lineup consisted of five foils who had never been seen in the experiment and the familiar foil from the mugshots. Memon et al. analyzed the results by comparing those participants who made a selection from the mugshots, with those who saw the mugshots but did not make a selection, and those who did not see the mugshots at all. Participants who made a selection from the mugshots were significantly more likely to choose the familiar foil from the lineup (40%) than were those who did not make a selection from the lineup (16%) and those who were not exposed to the mugshots at all (13%). You might think that this result supports the commitment explanation, but that is not what the researchers concluded. In fact, the researchers pointed out that not everyone who selected someone from the mugshots selected the familiar foil. If one looks only at those participants who made a choice from the mugshots other than the familiar foil, those participants were still more likely to choose the familiar foil from the lineup (35%) than were those who did not make a selection from the lineup (16%) and those who were not exposed to the mugshots at all (13%). Clearly, commitment is not the explanation for this; the person they selected from the mugshots was not even in the lineup. In fact, if these participants were motivated to be consistent with their prior choice, they should have rejected the lineup.

Although Memon et al.'s results provide some evidence for a familiarity account, they do not rule out an important role for commitment. To see whether commitment is a factor, participants must be able to choose the person they selected from the mugbook in the lineup. Participants were precluded from doing this in the Memon et al. (2002) study unless they chose the critical foil.

Goodsell et al. (2009) tried to disentangle commitment effects and familiarity effects by conducting an experiment in such a way that each participant who chose from the target-absent mugshots would receive a subsequent lineup that contained his or her mugshot choice, a familiar foil (someone from the mugbook who was not chosen), and a picture of the actual culprit. This design provides a more valid test of the contributions of commitment because participants can choose their mugshot choice in the lineup. In contrast to Memon et al. (2002), Goodsell et al. found that participants who chose from the mugshots chose their mugshot choice more than 70% of the time even when the culprit was in the lineup. These results are consistent with the meta-analytic results of Deffenbacher et al. (2006), who found that commitment was a reliable contributor to the mugshot exposure effect. Thus, it appears that the effects of mugshot exposure are driven in part by commitment to a previously selected individual.

The research on mugshots supports two general conclusions. First, it appears that the effect of mugshot exposure on subsequent identification tasks can be strongly influenced by commitment. In fact, the effect of choosing from a mugbook is so powerful that people who choose incorrectly from a mugbook will stick with that choice even when the actual culprit is in a subsequent lineup (Goodsell et al., 2009). These results are consistent with the U.S. Supreme Court statement that viewing a mugshot may impair eyewitness identifications because the witness may remember the mugshot photo as opposed to the actual culprit (*Simmons v. United States*, 1968). The second general conclusion is that if a witness views a mugbook, the mugshot identification task should be used as the only identification procedure. Multiple identifications increase the risk of false identifications, especially when the conditions are not optimal for memory.

Having witnesses view a mugbook may best be viewed as an investigation tool in that it may provide police officers with new avenues to investigate rather than confirmation that the witness has identified the culprit. If mugshots can be used as an investigative tool, what is the best way to present the mugbook in order to get accurate and reliable information from the witness? It is clear that mugbooks are more than just large photo spreads. The major difference between the two procedures is the goal. The goal of a lineup is to identify the culprit. The goal of the mugbook task is to identify a potential suspect—a person who might or might not be the culprit but who resembles the culprit in important ways—who might later appear in a lineup. Given that the procedures are different, and that they have different goals, they warrant different methods to maximize their effectiveness.

One issue that has been considered is how the mugbook should be presented to witnesses. It has been suggested that with a lineup or photospread, the pictures should be shown one at a time (sequentially) rather than all at once (simultaneously) (see Neuschatz & Cutler, 2008). The rationale for this suggestion is that simultaneous lineups promote the strategy of looking at each photo and deciding which most closely matches the memory the witness has of the culprit. This is not a desirable strategy if the goal is correct identification of the culprit, because we want witnesses to pick the person who is the culprit, not the person in the lineup who looks most like the culprit. Picking the person who looks most like the culprit can lead to false identifications. With mugbooks, however, McAllister (2007) has argued that use of a relative judgment strategy—picking the person who looks most like the image of a suspect—may be less of an issue because witnesses usually know there will be another page to look at if they do not see a match on the current page. In fact, Stewart and McAllister (2001) found that sequential mugbook presentation led to significantly more false positives (i.e. identifying the wrong person) than did grouped mugbook presentation.

In addition to the way in which the mugbook is presented, its size is also important. Recent research suggests that the larger the mugbook, the more difficult it is for witnesses to correctly choose the culprit. However, in most of these studies the mugbook size and interference from similar pictures have been confounded. McAllister, Stewart, and Loveland (2003) investigated the role of similarity of the mugbook pictures to the culprit. *Similarity* was operationally defined by having 69 photos that were picked by a computer program for their similarity to the perpetrator as opposed to 69 randomly picked photographs. The results revealed that similarity had no effect on mugbook performance.

Another recent development is the use of dynamic mugbooks. Dynamic mugbooks are video or computerized mugbooks in which the depicted persons are presented walking and talking and not, as in static mugbooks, merely presented in still photos. McAllister and her colleagues (McAlllister, Bearden, Kohlmaier, & Warner, 1997) have shown that dynamic mugbooks increase identification accuracy relative to static mugbooks. More specifically, there were fewer false positives in the dynamic condition, and the correct identification rate of the culprit was the same in both conditions. This makes sense given that witnesses get more and richer information from the dynamic mugbook. Furthermore, McAllister, Blair, Cerone, and Laurent (2000) demonstrated that the most efficient way to show a dynamic mugbook is to allow the witness to look through the mugbook and choose the suspects about which he or she wants to see the dynamic information. This procedure cuts down on the amount of time taken to present a dynamic mugbook without sacrificing accuracy (i.e., fewer false positives without a reduction in hit rate).

Facial Composites

When police have a witness to a crime but do not yet have a specific suspect, they sometimes ask the witness to meet with a forensic artist, who then produces a rendering of the perpetrator based on the witness's description. This rendering can then be used in canvassing or can be shown to the general public in an attempt to generate leads. A number of different approaches have been utilized to produce these images. In some cases witnesses may provide a description to a skilled artist who then creates a sketch of the suspect based on the description. This process usually occurs iteratively, with the police sketch artist showing the witness an initial draft, and then revising the draft based on the witness's feedback (Taylor, 2001).

There are also systems that allow witnesses to pick various features from a large collection and then assemble those features into a composite image (i.e., *feature-based composite systems*). Early versions of this approach utilized features printed on clear transparencies, which were then assembled into an image of the perpetrator. For instance, the original version of Identi-kit provided the user with a choice of 130 hairlines, 102 eyes, 37 noses, 40 mouths, and 52 chins. The user selected the hairline that was the best match, the eyes that were the best match, the nose that was the best match, and so on, and these were assembled into a composite image. These systems were later replaced with computerized systems. You can see the interface for a computer-based version of Identi-kit in Figure 4.5. Other feature-based composite systems include Mac a Mug, FACES, and PhotoFit (for a review,see Frowd, Mcquiston-Surrett, Anandaciva, Ireland, & Hancock, 2007). The idea behind these systems is similar. The witness can select different features and assemble them into an image of the culprit's face.

With regard to the use of artist sketches and facial composites, there are two issues that eyewitness psychologists have evaluated. Some research has examined how well participants can recognize a target individual based on an artist sketch or facial composite. In this regard, early findings

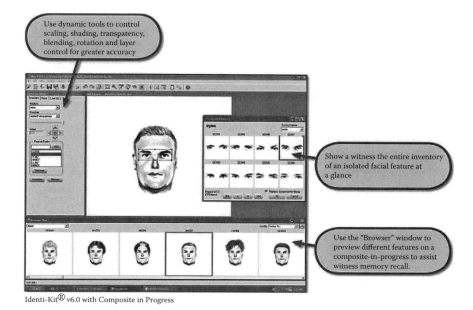

Use dynamic tools to control scaling, shading, transpatency, blending, rotation and layer control for greater accuracy

Show a witness the entire inventory of an isolated facial feature at a glance

Use the "Browser" window to preview different features on a composite-in-progress to assist witness memory recall.

Identi-Kit® v6.0 with Composite in Progress

FIGURE 4.5   Features available in Identikit. (*Source*: Provided courtesy of Paul Wright, President of Identi-Kit Solutions.)

were not especially favorable. For instance, Ellis, Shepherd, and Davies (1975) had witnesses use the Photofit system to create composites of six targets. A new group of participants was given the six composites and was asked to pick the targets from a set of 36 photographs. Recognition of the targets based on the composites was pretty low, only 12.5% (chance = 16.67%). Christie and Ellis (1981) found that participants who were merely given a verbal description of the targets are sometimes better able to identify them than are participants who had been shown facial composites. In other research, facial composites have been produced of well-known celebrities such as Brad Pitt or Jennifer Aniston and these composites have been shown to participants to see if they can name them. Some studies have found that participants recognize the celebrities less than 3% of the time (Wells & Hasel, 2007).

So that's not good. However, results like these tell only part of the story. The accuracy of a composite image likely depends on a number of factors including the skill and training of the person putting together the composite, the particular system being used, and how good of a memory the witness has of the perpetrator. For instance, some research has found that sketches produced by a trained artist tend to produce better matches than composites produced by commercially available composite systems (Frowd et al., 2005). Other research has shown that the interview technique matters as well. Frowd, Bruce, Smith, and Hancock (2008) combined a holistic cognitive interview with a feature-based composite image program. The researchers showed a video depicting characters from a well-known television program (i.e., *Eastenders*) to individuals who were unfamiliar with the show. Three to four hours later, the participants were interviewed by means of a cognitive interview and helped the experimenter create a composite image. Two types of cognitive interviews were used. The standard cognitive interview was conducted in the manner described earlier in this chapter in order to obtain descriptive information about the target individuals. In the holistic cognitive interview, interviewers also used the cognitive interview to obtain descriptive information about the target. However, after participants provided their description of the perpetrator, participants made holistic judgments about the perpetrator's facial appearance (e.g., intelligence, distinctiveness, and aggressiveness). Participants in both conditions then helped the experimenter produce composite images using a standard feature-based composite system (i.e., ProFit). Information from the cognitive interview was used to create an initial composite of the perpetrator. The participant was then asked to look at the composite and indicate how the composite should be changed so that it looked more like the perpetrator.

Once the composites were produced, they were shown to a new group of participants who were to name the individual. Participants were allowed to provide either the actor's name or the character's name on the show. Recognition of composites was poor when the composites were created using the standard cognitive interview (8.6% correct). However, for composites produced using the holistic cognitive interview, performance was dramatically better (41.2% correct). Note that these results suggest that focusing witnesses on holistic aspects of the perpetrator's face may greatly improve the accuracy of the composites that are produced using traditional feature-based composite systems. Another promising approach involves making use of composites produced by different witnesses and then morphing those composites together (Hasel & Wells, 2007; Valentine, Davis, Thorner, Solomon, & Gibson, 2010).

Composite systems that are based on holistic representations of the perpetrator's face have also been developed. For instance, in EvoFit, witnesses view a range of computer-generated faces and then select a small set that appears similar to their memory for the culprit (Frowd, Hancock, & Carson, 2004). The interface for the EvoFit program is shown in Figure 4.6.

The faces selected by the witness as being similar to the culprit are "bred together" to produce a new set of faces. By *bred together*, we mean that a computer algorithm is used to recombine features from faces that

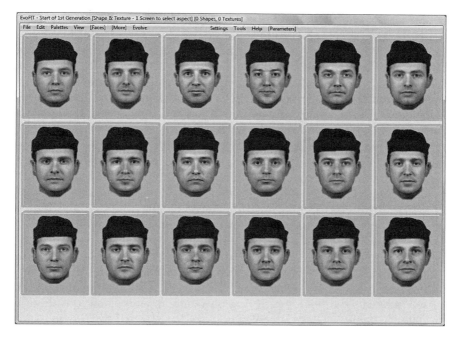

FIGURE 4.6   The interface used for EvoFit. (*Source*: Provided courtesy of Charlie Frowd, University of Central Lancashire.)

were initially selected by the witness in order to create a new set of faces. The witness goes through these new faces and picks the ones that most closely resemble their memory for the culprit. These faces are then "bred" together, and the process repeats itself. Note that, at each stage of the process, the witness is relying on holistic processing of whole faces in order to create the composite image. Research by Frowd et al. (2005) found that composites produced by EvoFit resulted in better recognition than composites produced using feature-based methods.

In addition to the accuracy of facial composites, there has been some concern that the process of building facial composites may interfere with the witness's ability to recognize the perpetrator at a later date. Wells, Charman, and Olson (2005) tested this possibility by asking some participants to help create facial composites of individuals they had seen. Other participants viewed the same individuals but were not asked to create facial composites. All participants were later shown target-present or target-absent lineups. Participants who had aided in the creation of facial composites showed poorer recognition in the target-present lineups. There was no effect for target-absent lineups. Although this finding raises some concerns, it may well be that the effects of composites on later recognition depend on the specific techniques used to produce the composites.

Taken together these results indicate that facial composites may not always be effective, but great strides are currently being made to improve the accuracy and utility of facial composite systems. A number of questions remain to be answered. For instance, Lampinen, Arnal, and Hicks (2009) have examined a phenomenon known as *prospective person memory*. Prospective person memory refers to the ability to recognize an individual you have been told to be on the lookout for (e.g., a wanted fugitive or a missing child). In field experiments examining prospective person memory, Lampinen et al. have provided students with photographs of targets with the instructions that the individuals may appear on campus at some point in the near future. Participants are told to contact the experimenters if they see the "wanted" individuals for a chance to win a substantial amount of prize money (e.g., up to $100). Research on prospective person memory has shown that, generally speaking, people are very poor at noticing individuals who they have been told to be on the lookout for, often hovering around 2–4%. This is true even if the target's current appearance very closely matches the photograph that participants were shown. Although no published studies have specifically looked at prospective person memory based on composite images, it stands to reason that if spontaneous recognition of a wanted person is poor with an exact photographic match, then even a very good composite may not always be effective.

☐ The Identification Procedure

Once witness reports have been obtained and a suspect has been identified, police will typically try to determine if the witness can identify the suspect. There are a number of different approaches that police can use. One distinction is between lineups and showups. A lineup is an identification procedure in which multiple individuals are shown to the witness and the witness is asked to indicate which person, if any, committed the crime. A showup is an identification procedure in which a single person is shown (i.e., the suspect) and the witness is asked whether this is the person who committed the crime. If police decide to conduct a lineup, they can either conduct the lineup live or present the witnesses with a group of photographs (i.e., a photoarray). Police also either can decide to display all of the members of the lineup at the same time, or can present the members of the lineup one at a time. In what follows, we describe some of the relevant choices that police can make and the potential consequences of those choices.

Composition of the Lineup

When police decide to conduct a lineup, one of the most important things they need to consider is the composition of the lineup—i.e., who is going to be in the lineup. A well-conducted police lineup is made up of one suspect and a number of foils. Recall that a suspect is a person who the police think may have committed the crime and a foil is a person in a lineup who the police know did not commit the crime. Foils are also sometimes called *fillers* or *distracters*. The purpose of a foil is to provide protection to an innocent suspect. In a fair police lineup, an innocent suspect is no more likely to be chosen than is one of the foils. That means that if an innocent suspect is placed in a fair six-person lineup, and the witness mistakenly picks someone, there is only one chance in six that the suspect will be chosen. In an unfair lineup, this procedural safeguard can be greatly limited, or in extreme cases entirely eliminated. For example, if the culprit was described as having a beard and only one person in the lineup has a beard, it will be much more likely that witnesses will pick that person, even if they have no memory of the culprit. It is necessary to avoid this kind of bias in order to construct a fair lineup.

The above suggests that proper selection of foils can provide an important procedural safeguard for innocent suspects and can greatly reduce the risk of a mistaken identification. An important question for police to consider is how best to select these foils (Wells, Rydell, & Seelau, 1993). There are two strategies that have been suggested for the selection of foils: match-to-similarity-of-suspect and match-to-description-of-culprit (Luus & Wells, 1991). The *match-to-similarity-of-suspect strategy* (i.e., match to suspect) involves the use of foils that resemble the suspect who is going to be in the lineup. The *match-to-description-of-culprit strategy* (i.e., match to description) involves picking foils that fit the witnesses' description of the culprit, without necessarily being concerned with how closely the foils match the suspect.

Survey research suggests that police usually use a match-to-suspect approach when constructing lineups (Wogalter, Malpass, & Berger, 1993). Luus and Wells (1991), however, argued that the match-to-description approach is actually the better strategy. The match-to-description strategy takes advantage of what Luus and Wells called *propitious heterogeneity* (i.e., favorable differences). In other words, a lineup should be constructed in such a way that an innocent suspect is no more likely to be chosen than one of the foils, but otherwise the lineup should preserve useful differences between the lineup members that might help the witness make a correct decision. In a lineup constructed by matching the foils to the description of the culprit, all members of the lineup will be equally good matches to the witness's description. The witness's memory of the perpetrator will include features that were in his or her description. The suspect will have these features, as will all the foils. The representation in the witness's memory will also include additional features that the witness failed to mention, or perhaps couldn't even put into words. If the suspect is innocent, there is no reason to believe that the suspect will match those additional features any better than will the foils. If the suspect is guilty, the suspect should be more likely to match these additional features than the foils, making it easier for the witness to correctly pick out the suspect.

The situation is different for the match-to-suspect approach. In this approach, the foils are selected based on their similarity to the suspect. The foils and the suspect will thus share a large number of features, not just features mentioned in the description, but also other features that were not mentioned in the description. Now, imagine that the suspect is guilty. There will be features in the witness's memory that were not mentioned in the description. These features are likely to match the suspect, but because the foils are chosen to look like the suspect, they are also likely to match the foils. As a result, the match-to-suspect approach may make the task of correctly selecting a guilty suspect needlessly difficult. In fact, guidelines published by the Department of Justice advise, "Consider that complete uniformity of features is not required. Avoid using fillers who so closely resemble the suspect that a person familiar with the suspect might find it difficult to distinguish the suspect from the fillers" (Technical Working Group, 1999, p. 29).

There are also reasons to believe that using the match-to-suspect approach may sometimes inflate mistaken identifications. Navon (1992) argued that suspects who are chosen with a match-to-suspect approach are likely to share more relevant features with culprits than foils do because, presumably, persons become suspects because of their similarity in appearance to actual culprits. Thus, if the witness chooses the person in the lineup who most resembles the culprit, he or she will choose the suspect. Thus, the match-to-similarity-of-suspect method can lead to a substantial number of false identifications or what has been referred to as the *backfire effect* by Clarke and Tunnicliff (1992). The match-to-description strategy does not suffer from the backfire effect because, when this method is followed, foils must match the relevant descriptions provided by the witness.

Early studies tended to support the view that the match-to-description approach produces better results. In one study, Wells et al. (1993) had participants witness a staged theft of a money box. Following the staged theft, participants were asked to provide a written description of the thief. The experimenter took the witness's description and then went to another room and constructed a six-person photospread. For some participants, the foils for the photospread were selected by selecting photos that were similar to the suspect (i.e., suspect matched). For other participants, the foils were selected by selecting photos that matched that particular witness's description of the culprit (i.e., description matched).[2] For half of the participants a target-present photospread was constructed, and for the other half a target-absent photospread was constructed.

The results of this study supported the view that selecting foils by matching them to the description of the witness produces better outcomes than selecting foils by matching them to the suspect. In particular, correct identifications in target-present lineups were more than three times higher when the description-matched approach was used than when the suspect-matched approach was use. The foil selection strategy had no influence whatsoever on the number of false identifications in target-absent lineups. Other researchers produced similar results (Juslin, Olsson, & Winman, 1996; Lindsay, Martin, & Webber, 1994).

More recent studies, however, have sometimes failed to find an advantage for description-matched lineups. For instance, Tunnicliff and Clark (2001, Experiment 1) had trained police officers create lineups using either a suspect-matched or description-matched strategy to select the foils. There was no significant advantage to using the description-matched approach. With both approaches, suspect identification rates were a bit over 50% in the target-present lineups. In target-absent lineups, there was no significant difference in false suspect identifications. In a second experiment, lineups were constructed by undergraduate students and the results were similar. Darling, Valentine, and Memon (2008) have also shown that description-matched lineups do not always produce better results than suspect-matched lineups.

So why do the later results not match up with the earlier results? To make sense of this, consider that the match-to-suspect strategy actually has a bit of ambiguity to it. The match-to-suspect approach simply says that foils should be selected based on their similarity to the suspect. But how similar is similar enough? At one extreme, you could imagine police picking foils that are so similar to the suspect that they are virtually indistinguishable from the suspect. Luus and Wells (1991) fancifully referred to these as "clone lineups." Clearly, a clone lineup would be a mistake, because even if the witness had a perfect memory for the culprit, the witness would be unable to distinguish the suspect from the foils. Talk about lack of propitious heterogeneity! At the other extreme, you could imagine police selecting foils who are only modestly similar to the suspect. This extreme would also be a mistake, because the foils would tend not to match even the description of the suspect, and the suspect would stand out like a sore thumb.

With this in mind, the conflicting results make more sense. In Wells et al. (1993), when experimenters constructed suspect matched lineups, they were told to pick the five foils that were "most similar" to the suspect. Thus, there was probably a very high degree of similarity between the foils and the suspect. This may have made it difficult for witnesses to identify guilty suspects from target-present lineups. In the work by Tunnicliff and Clark (2001), the instructions merely indicated that the line-ups should be constructed by selecting foils that are similar to the suspect, without specifying exactly how similar the foils should be to the suspect. In other words, the police (Experiment 1) and students (Experiment 2) who constructed the lineups were given discretion when determining how similar the foils should be to the suspect. Thus, a less extreme degree of similarity may have been used, making it easier for witnesses to correctly select guilty suspects. These results suggest that police may be able to, when left to their own devices, use an appropriate degree of similarity when constructing suspect-matched lineups.

There may also be times when a match-to-suspect strategy is unavoidable. Lindsay, Martin, and Webber (1994) noted that the match-to-description-of-culprit strategy is less effective when the description of the culprit is limited or vague (e.g., "white male"). They studied three types of line-ups: match-to-similarity-of-suspect, match-to-description-of-culprit, and biased match-to-description-of-culprit. In the biased condition, the foils were chosen so that they matched the features mentioned in the witness's description of the culprit, but were otherwise very different in appearance from the culprit. For example, if hair color was not mentioned in the witness' description of the culprit and all the foils have a hair color that differs from that of the suspect, then the lineup is biased. In this biased condition, Lindsay et al. (1994) found that there were more false identifications of the suspect than in the other two conditions. It appears, therefore, that some combination of both strategies is desirable. That is, match-to-description-of-culprit is the best strategy as long as the foils selected match the witness' description of the culprit and also match the appearance of the culprit on salient characteristics such as race, hair color, or presence or absence of facial hair. Lindsay et al. (1994) suggested that, in order to get more complete descriptions of the culprit, free recall of the descriptions should be augmented with some probing questions about the general appearance of the culprit.

Sequential Versus Simultaneous Lineups

In Chapter 2 we discussed the distinction, originally made by Wells (1984), between absolute and relative judgment strategies. An absolute judgment strategy is one in which each lineup member is evaluated against a fixed criterion to determine whether that person is the culprit. These judgments are made independently of the other members of the lineup. In relative judgments, by contrast, a witness will compare and contrast members of the lineup, selecting that member who is the best match to the witness's memory, relative to all the other members of the lineup. Wells points out that there will always be *some* member of the lineup who best matches memory. As a consequence, relative judgment strategies are more prone to error.

A number of methods have been used in an attempt to discourage relative judgment strategies. One early approach was called a *blank lineup* (Wells, 1984). In a blank lineup procedure, the witness is shown two lineups, without being told in advance that there will be two lineups. The first lineup is made up entirely of foils. If a witness is prone to making relative judgments, then it is likely that the witness will pick a foil from this lineup. The police are then able to conclude that this witness tends to make relative judgments and is likely to be unreliable. If the witness rejects this lineup, it suggests that the witness is using an absolute judgment strategy, and is likely a reliable witness. The witness is then shown a second lineup. This lineup is made up of a suspect and a set of foils. Research indicates that blank lineups can substantially decrease the rate of false identifications (Wells, 1984).

Lindsey and Wells (1985) took the idea of a blank lineup a step further. They reasoned that if there was an advantage in presenting two six-person lineups, then why not present three four-person lineups, four three-person lineups, etc? Taken to the extreme, why not present 12 one-person lineups? Each presentation of a foil would be like presenting a blank lineup of size 1. Moreover, because the lineup members are presented one at a time, it would be impossible for witnesses to compare and contrast the lineup members. It would force the witness to use an absolute judgment strategy. This mode of presentation has been called a *sequential lineup*. The traditional approach of presenting all lineup members at the same time is called a *simultaneous lineup*.

Early research suggested that sequential lineups produced better outcomes than simultaneous lineups. In one study, Lindsay and Wells (1985) staged a crime for participants. Participants were seated in an experiment room, and the experimenter left the room for a few minutes. During this time period, a confederate entered the room, searched through several drawers, and then left with a calculator. When the experimenter returned, the participants were told that they had just witnessed a simulated crime. They were asked to make an identification from a sequential or simultaneous lineup. Half of the participants viewed a target-present lineup, and half viewed a target-absent lineup. The results are reproduced in Figure 4.7.

In the target-present lineups, there was not a significant difference between the sequential and simultaneous lineups. In the target-absent lineups, there were substantially fewer mistaken identifications in the sequential lineup than in the simultaneous lineup. Recall from Chapter 2 that diagnosticity is the ratio of correct identifications of guilty suspects

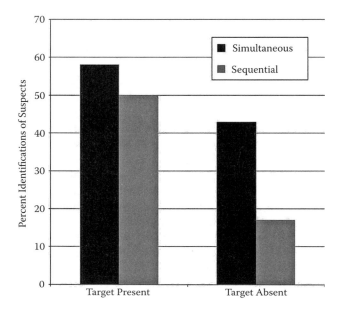

FIGURE 4.7 Percentage of times the suspect was identified in simultaneous and sequential lineups in the study by Lindsay and Wells (1985). (*Source*: Based on data presented in Lindsay, R. C. L., & Wells, G. L. (1985). Improving eyewitness identification from lineups: Simultaneous versus sequential lineup presentations. *Journal of Applied Psychology, 70*, 556–564.)

to mistaken identifications of innocent suspects. In the sequential lineup the diagnosticity was 3.06, whereas in the simultaneous lineup it was a measly 1.36. Other research suggested that sequential lineups were especially helpful when the lineup was biased (Lindsay et al., 1991).

A number of other studies have been conducted comparing simultaneous and sequential lineups. Steblay, Dysart, Fulero, and Lindsay (2001) conducted a meta-analysis on 23 studies, 9 published and 14 unpublished. Overall, participants were more accurate when shown sequential lineups than when shown simultaneous lineups. With regard to target-present lineups, simultaneous lineups resulted in more correct identifications (50% vs. 35%) and fewer lineup rejections (26% vs. 46%). With regard to target-absent lineups, false identifications of innocent suspects were more common in simultaneous lineups than sequential lineups (51% vs. 28%). Thus, Steblay et al.'s (2001) meta-analysis concluded that sequential lineups decrease both correct and incorrect identifications of suspects.

There has been some debate about exactly how to interpret these results. One possibility is that, just as Lindsay and Wells (1985) originally proposed, sequential lineups operate by decreasing the use of relative judgment strategies. In simultaneous lineups, witnesses can use both relative and absolute judgment strategies. In a target-absent lineup, use of a relative judgment strategy should result in more false identifications. In the target-present lineup, use of a relative judgment strategy will usually result in the correct choice of a guilty suspect, who will presumably be a better choice than any of the foils. If participants are precluded from using a relative judgment strategy by means of a sequential lineup, fewer false identifications will be made in the target-absent lineup and fewer correct identifications will be made in the target-present lineup. If relative judgments are the more dominant strategy in target-absent lineups, then one would expect that sequential lineups would reduce both true and false identifications, but would have a bigger effect on false identifications.

Other researchers, however, have proposed an alternative account. This account can be thought of in terms of signal detection theory, which we outlined in the previous chapter. Recall that according to signal detection theory, lineup members can be thought of as differing in familiarity, with familiarity being normally distributed. Participants set a response criterion to decide whether or not to choose a particular lineup member. According to this theory, you can explain the difference between sequential and simultaneous lineups by assuming that participants set a more stringent criterion when they are presented with a sequential lineup. This would reduce both correct and false identifications. Moreover, when memory is good (i.e., larger values of d′), setting a more stringent criterion should decrease mistaken identifications more than correct identifications.

Kneller, Memon, and Stevenage (2001) provided some data consistent with the decision process (i.e., relative vs. absolute) account. Participants watched a videotaped crime. Following the crime, they were presented with either a simultaneous or sequential lineup. Half of the participants were presented with a target-present lineup, and half were presented with a target-absent lineup. Following the lineup, participants were asked how they made their decision. They were given the choice among a number of options, some of which indicated an absolute decision process (e.g., "His face just 'popped out' at me") and others indicating a relative decision process (e.g., "I compared the photographs to each other in order to narrow down the choices").

Simultaneous lineups resulted in somewhat more correct identifications in target-present lineups (61.1% vs. 50%), but substantially more incorrect choices in target-absent lineups (61.1% vs. 22.2%). When they examined the self-reported reasons for making their choices, participants who had been shown a simultaneous lineup were much more likely to indicate that they used a relative judgment strategy than were participants who had been shown a sequential judgment lineup (50% vs. 2.8%).

Moreover, in both types of lineups, accurate witnesses were more likely to report having used an absolute judgment strategy than were inaccurate witnesses (41.7% vs. 20.8%). These results have been replicated using computer-administrated lineups for both simultaneous and sequential lineups (MacLin, Zimmerman, & Malpass 2005).

Other researchers have argued that a signal detection account provides a better explanation of the difference between sequential and simultaneous lineups (Meissner, Tredoux, Parker, & MacLin, 2005). Specifically, they argued that the decreases in the false identification rate in sequential lineups, as opposed to simultaneous lineups, occur because witnesses are less willing to choose when presented with sequential lineups. One reason may be that in a sequential lineup, even if a lineup member provides a good match to memory, the witness may fear that there might be another member of the lineup that provides an even better match. Moreover, Carlson, Gronlund, and Clark (2010) have argued that the advantage shown by sequential lineups primarily occurs when the composition of the lineup is biased. They compared sequential and simultaneous lineups that differed in terms of *functional size* (see Chapter 2 for a description of functional size). In a series of three experiments, Carlson et al. (2010) found the sequential lineup advantage (i.e., fewer false alarms without a decrease in correct identifications) only when the lineups had low functional size. By contrast, when the lineups had high or intermediate functional size, there is no difference in the false alarm rate for simultaneous and sequential lineups. Thus, sequential lineups appear to provide protection to innocent suspects when police use biased lineups.

The finding that sequential lineups can decrease both accurate identifications from target-present lineups and mistaken identifications from target-absent lineups is, perhaps, not too surprising. Nor is it necessarily a rap against the sequential lineup. Imagine the following scenario: A witness views a crime under poor lighting conditions and from a long way away. The witness is shown a lineup, and because the witness wants to be helpful, the witness makes a choice from the lineup. Presumably that witness's judgment would not be especially valid given the witnessing conditions we just described. If the witness was shown a target-absent lineup, the witness will make a false identification. If the witness was shown a target-present lineup, about one sixth of the time the witness will make a correct suspect identification (i.e., "Even a broken clock is right twice a day"). Now anything that decreases the chances that the witness will make an identification under these circumstances should decrease false identifications and should decrease correct identifications. From the point of view of doing justice, the decrease in correct identifications would not be a bad thing, because the correct identification was not based on the witness's recollection.

Debate about the pros and cons of sequential versus simultaneous line-ups continues. This debate focuses on both the theoretical mechanism that can be used to explain the effect, as well as the recommendations that are most appropriate for law enforcement. Although debate continues as to the optimum way of presenting a lineup, both approaches can result in fair lineups with good diagnosticity. To some extent the strengths of the approaches depend a great deal on other circumstances surround-ing the identification, including the strength of the underlying memory representation, as well as good sound practices in creating the lineup and instructing the witness.

Showups

After police come up with a suspect, they do not always conduct a full lineup. Sometimes they show the suspect to the witness without using any foils at all. This procedure is called a *showup*. Somewhere between 30% and 70% of all identification procedures conducted by police offi-cers are showups (Dysart & Lindsay, 2007a; Flowe, Ebbesen, Burke, & Chivabunditt, 2001). Showups are widely regarded as a suggestive inter-viewing practice (Lindsay, Pozzulo, Craig, Lee & Corber, 1997; Technical Working Group, 1999; Yarmey, Yarmey & Yarmey, 1994, 1996). In a survey of eyewitness experts, 74% agreed to the statement "The use of a one-per-son showup instead of a full lineup increased the risk of misidentifica-tion" (Kassin, Tubb, Hosch, & Memon, 2001). Guidelines published by the U.S. Department of Justice indicate that showups are "inherently sugges-tive" (Technical Working Group, 1999). Those same guidelines imply that showups should be reserved for exigent circumstances, when there is not enough time to construct a fair lineup.[3]

There are two potential problems with showups. The first problem is that showups are thought to be suggestive. Witnesses who are presented with a showup are likely to conclude, "The police would not be showing me this person unless investigators already believed that the person was guilty." Because of this, if the suspect looks similar to the perpetrator, the witness is likely to draw the conclusion that the suspect must be guilty. The second problem with showups is that they lack procedural safeguards in case the witness makes a mistake. In a fair target-absent lineup, if a witness makes a mistake, they are more likely to falsely iden-tify a foil than they are an innocent suspect. In a target-absent showup, if a witness makes a mistake, the result is a mistaken identification of the person the police suspect of the crime—there is nobody else for the witness to pick.

A number of research studies have been conducted by psychologists to compare lineups and showups. In a typical study, participants see

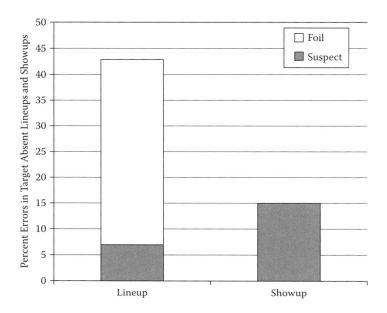

FIGURE 4.8 A comparison of errors in target-absent lineups and show-ups. Estimate of false suspect identifications assumes a fair six-person lineup. (*Source* of data: Steblay, N., Dysart, J., Fulero, S., & Lindsay, R. C. L. (2003). Eyewitness accuracy rates in police showup and lineup presentations: A meta-analytic comparison. *Law and Human Behavior, 27,* 523–540.)

an event (e.g., a videotaped crime) and then are presented with either a showup or a lineup. Both target-present and target-absent showups and lineups are typically examined. A meta-analytic review of these studies by Steblay, Dysart, Fulero, and Lindsay (2003) found that there was little difference between lineups and showups in terms of accurate identifications in the target-present situation (M = 47% showups; M = 45% lineups). For target-absent identifications, the overall error rate for showups was 15% and the overall error rate for lineups was 43%.

Keep in mind that target-absent lineups and target-absent showups differ in terms of the types of errors that are possible. These different types of mistakes are displayed in Figure 4.8. In a target-absent lineup, there are two types of errors that are possible: selecting an innocent suspect and selecting an innocent foil. Selecting an innocent suspect is a *dangerous error,* because it may lead to criminal charges being filed against the suspect. Selecting a foil is a *harmless error* because the foil is known to be innocent. Nobody is going to jail. In a fair target-absent lineup, the probability of selecting the suspect is no greater than the probability of selecting one of the foils (see Chapter 2). Thus, in a fair six-person target-absent lineup, the probability of selecting the suspect should be one sixth of the overall error rate (sometimes called the *choosing rate*). Steblay et al. (2003) reported that the overall error rate in target-absent lineups was 43%. Given those findings, the chance of mistakenly selecting the suspect in fair target-absent lineups was estimated to be 7.167% (i.e., 43%/6).

The situation in a target-absent showup is different. There is only one person that the witness can identify in a showup, namely, the suspect. Therefore, all the errors in target-absent showups are *dangerous errors*. The mistaken suspect identification rate for showups in the Steblay et al. (2003) meta-analysis was 15%, roughly double the rate for lineups. If you are an innocent person, your chance of being mistakenly identified in a showup is roughly double your chance of being mistakenly identified in a fair six-person lineup.

Why should this be the case? To answer this question, it is useful to consider the following analogy. Imagine some nefarious researchers strap you to a chair and hook you up to some electrodes capable of delivering horrendously painful but harmless electric shocks. You spin a wheel that has numbers between one and 100. If the wheel lands on a number that is greater than 85, you get zapped. This is analogous to the situation where an innocent person is in a showup. There is a 15% chance that you will experience a bad outcome.

Now consider this alternative. The researchers strap you and five other people to chairs and hook each of you up to electrodes that can deliver painful electric shocks. Behind each person there is a wheel numbered from one to 100. All the wheels are spun simultaneously. If only one person's wheel lands on a number over 85, that person gets zapped. If more than one person's wheel lands on a number over 85, then whoever's number is largest gets zapped (if there's a tie, the shock is delivered randomly to the people who tied). This situation is roughly analogous to an innocent person who is in a six-person lineup.

Which scenario would you rather be in? If you think about it for a minute, you will quickly conclude that you are better off in the situation that is analogous to a lineup. When only you are hooked up to the device, there is a 15% chance that you will get zapped. No "ifs," "ands," or "buts" about it. When six people are hooked up to the device, and each person's wheel is spun, the probability that *someone* will get shocked is higher than 15%. You have a 15% chance that your wheel will land on a number over 85, but even if your wheel does not land that high, there is a good chance that one of your compatriots' wheels will land on a number that is higher than 85. You can get the probability that *someone* is going to get shocked using the following equation:

$$p \text{ (someone gets shocked)} = \sum_{i=0}^{n-1} \left[1 - p \right]^{i} p$$

The p in the equation stands for the probability that any given person's wheel lands on a number greater than 85 and n is the total number of people in the scenario. In the current example, p would equal .15 (15%) and n would equal 6. If you plug in the numbers, you would end up with about a 62% chance that *someone* will get zapped.

Even though the chance that *someone* is going to get zapped is higher than 15%, the chance that *you personally* will get zapped is less than 15%. Think about why that is. Imagine you spin the wheel and it lands on 89. If you are the only person up there, you are going to get shocked for sure. But if there are other people up there with you, it is possible that one of their wheels will land on a number that is even higher (e.g., 93). So, you might not get shocked even though your wheel landed on a number over 85. The probability that *you* personally will get shocked in this scenario is given by

$$p \text{ (YOU get a shock)} = \frac{1}{n} * \sum_{i=0}^{n-1} \left[1 - p \right)^{i} p$$

This equation follows from the fact that it is a fair process (everyone has an equal chance of getting zapped). So the probability that you will get zapped is 1/nth the probability that someone will get zapped. In the above scenario, the probability that you would get zapped is about 10%, compared to 15% if you were the only person in the experiment, a sizeable decrease in your risk.

You can see how this same reasoning could apply to lineups and showups. If you are in an innocent person in a showup and you kind of look like the culprit, there is a good chance that the witness will pick you. However, if you are in a lineup, even if you kind of look like the culprit, there is a good chance that one of the foils will look even more like the culprit. In that case, the witness is likely to pick that foil and you will not be picked. We are not claiming that this analogy perfectly matches how people make choices in lineups. It is clearly an oversimplification and in fact may understate the advantage of lineups over showups. For instance, the analogy suggests that witnesses are exclusively making use of absolute judgment strategies, which is probably not true. It is possible that witnesses sometimes use relative judgment strategies. It also may not be the case that the degree of familiarity needed to make a selection is identical in lineups and showups (i.e., the p in the equation). It would certainly be possible to tweak the analogy to incorporate those elements (e.g., you get zapped if your wheel lands on a number that is highest and that is at least five higher than the next closest person). However, the analogy does demonstrate why we should not be surprised that the overall choosing rate in target-absent lineups is higher than in target-absent showups. *It almost has to be.* Furthermore, it demonstrates why the probability of falsely identifying an innocent suspect in a fair lineup should be lower than in a showup.

It is also noteworthy that when we took the 15% error rate from Steblay et al.'s (2003) meta-analysis and inserted it into the above equations, we ended up with an overall predicted error rate for target-absent lineups of around 60% and a predicted false suspect identification rate of around 10%. In fact, as we saw previously, the observed error rate is actually somewhat lower. This finding is consistent with the notion that showups are suggestive. A reasonable interpretation would be that the response criterion that is set in a showup is somewhat more liberal than it is in a lineup.

There is also another way of thinking about the relative dangers of lineups and showups. Recall that a fair lineup is one in which an innocent suspect is no more likely to be chosen than any of the individual foils. Steblay et al. (2003) found that an innocent suspect has a 15% chance of being chosen from a target-absent showup. To produce a false suspect identification rate of 15% from a fair six-person target-absent lineup, there would have to be an overall choosing rate of 90% (i.e., 6 × 15%). The actual choosing rate is less than half of that. Not only that, if the overall choosing rate for target-absent showups is 15%, then a fair target-absent lineup of size 7 will *in principle* always produce a lower suspect identification rate than a target-absent showup (i.e., 100% ÷ 7 < 15%). All of this leads to the clear conclusion that lineups will decrease the false identification rate relative to showups, as long as the following conditions are met: (a) The lineup is a fair lineup, (b) there are a sufficient number of foils, and (c) the response criterion witnesses use in lineups is at least as conservative as in a showup.

It goes without saying that an unfair lineup will not offer the same level of protection as a fair lineup. But, of course, nobody is suggesting that police should use unfair lineups rather than showups. Rather, what makes sense is for police to utilize fair lineups with a functional size of six or greater. However, even a slightly unfair lineup probably provides more protection than a showup. Given that the overall error rate in lineups was 43% in Steblay et al. (2003), the functional size of the lineups would have to be less than three (2.87) to produce a false suspect identification rate of 15% (i.e., approximately one third of the errors would have to be suspect identifications and two thirds would have to be foil identifications). So, even a slightly unfair lineup is likely to offer more protection to innocent suspects than would a showup.

The suggestive nature of showups can be exacerbated by a number of conditions. One issue that is of particular concern for showups is clothing bias. Clothing bias occurs when the clothing worn by a suspect at the time of the identification is similar to the clothing of the culprit described by the witness. Clothing bias can produce mistaken identifications in lineups (Lindsay, Wallbridge, & Drennan, 1987), but it provides an even bigger problem in showups (Dysart & Lindsay, 2007a). Showups are generally conducted with suspects who are found in close proximity to the crime scene and who match the general description given by the eyewitness. Much of the information contained in an eyewitness description is about what the culprit was wearing (Lindsay, Nosworthy, Martin, & Martynuck, 1994; Lindsay, Wallbridge, & Drenna, 1987). As evidence for the potential effect of clothing bias in showups, take the case of *State of Georgia v. TB.*[2] The victims were held at gunpoint at 10:00 p.m. outside a restaurant during a botched carjacking. The victims and a witness described the culprit as wearing a blue hooded-sweatshirt with the word FUBU printed across the chest and dark jeans. The culprit also had a bandanna covering his face and had the hood of his sweatshirt pulled down over his forehead. In the early morning hours, TB[3] was apprehended in the area of the crime because he was wearing a hooded FUBU sweatshirt, jeans, and had a bandanna tied to his pants. The police conducted a showup, and all of the victims identified him as the culprit. One victim said that it was him because they remembered the emblem on the sweatshirt.

It is not known whether TB would have been identified if he had been wearing different clothing at the time he was apprehended, but the culprit had his hood pulled tightly over his head and wore a bandanna covering the lower half of his face. Consequently, TB's clothing played a crucial role in his identification. Is clothing bias particularly problematic for showups? A study by Dysart, Lindsay, and Dupuis (2006) examined this question. They had the target (culprit) wear either typical clothing (a blue button-down shirt) or atypical clothing (a white Harley Davidson T-shirt). They found no difference in accurate identifications in either condition, but false alarms were increased in the atypical clothing condition. Witnesses were more likely to falsely identify an innocent suspect when the suspect was wearing the same atypical clothing as the target. Clothing bias had no effect when the target was wearing typical clothing.

Taken together, the research findings suggest that showups are likely to be a dangerous technique. However, laboratory findings may understate the danger. Showups conducted in the laboratory are generally executed under ideal conditions, and the best recommended procedures are generally followed. For instance, in every study reviewed in the Steblay et al. (2003) meta-analysis, unbiased lineup instructions were used. This is not always the case in the real world. For example, an experienced detective from Savannah, Georgia, told a Georgia public defender that although the Savannah police use admonition forms before all lineups, it is not standard practice to inform witnesses at showup identifications that the suspect may not be the culprit (Todd Martin, Georgia public defender, personal communication). Moreover, the social pressures inherent in actual criminal cases may be much greater than in laboratory settings. In laboratory experiments, participants undoubtedly know that some of the targets are "guilty" and some are "innocent." This is especially likely to be true in showup conditions, because to a student participant showups are likely to seem analogous to true-false tests and lineups are likely to seem analogous to multiple-choice tests. In an actual police identification procedure, the presumption on the part of the witness is likely to be "The police would not be showing me this individual unless they had reason to think he or she was guilty." This may make showups an especially dangerous procedure.

Instruction Bias

Another factor that can have a large impact on eyewitness accuracy is the instructions police give to witnesses prior to the lineup (Brewer, Weber, & Semmler, 2005; Clarke, 2005; Malpass & Devine, 1981; Steblay, 1997; Wells & Olson, 2003). Imagine again that you had witnessed a robbery at a grocery store. At some point during the course of the investigation, the police may identify someone that they think committed the crime (i.e., the suspect). The police may then contact you to see if you can identify the person. Imagine what it would be like to be a witness in that situation. Presumably you would want to help the police. You would want to get this dangerous grocery store robber off the streets. You may also be thinking that the police would not be calling you down to the police station to make an identification if they did not have good reason to think they had the robber in custody. Thus, going into the lineup, you may be predisposed to believe that one of the people in the lineup is probably guilty.

Proper lineup instructions are the key to overcoming these sorts of assumptions that witnesses make. Prior to viewing a lineup, witnesses should be told that the actual perpetrator may or may not be in the lineup, and that it is just as important to clear innocent suspects as it is to select guilty suspects (Technical Working Group, 1999). Failure to provide admonishments such as these is known as *instruction bias*. In their seminal article, Malpass and Devine (1981) examined the effect of biased and unbiased lineup instructions on identifications in target-present and target-absent lineups. They found that in the case of target-present lineups, accurate identifications were not significantly affected by instructions (75% accuracy with biased instructions vs. 83% accuracy with unbiased instructions). By contrast, false identifications from target-absent lineups were more than twice as high in the biased-instructions condition (78%) as in the unbiased-instructions condition (33%).

This pattern of results was confirmed in a meta-analysis conducted by Steblay (1997). Pooling data from 18 different studies, she found that mistaken identifications of innocent suspects can be reduced by 42% by providing unbiased instructions. The flip side of this is that providing biased instructions close to doubles the chances of a false identification. Steblay (1997) also found that unbiased lineup instructions reduce false identifications without substantially reducing correct identifications (although see Clark, 2005, for another view).

It has also been suggested that law enforcement should provide instructions that the appearance of the perpetrator in the lineup may be different from the perpetrator's appearance at the time of the crime (Technical Working Group, 1999). This has been called the *appearance change* instruction (Charman & Wells, 2007). The logic of this instruction seems clear. A guilty suspect in a lineup or photospread may not look *exactly* the way he or she looked at the time of the crime. It seems reasonable that police would want to alert witnesses to this fact. However, in a test of the appearance change instruction, Charman and Wells (2007) found that the instruction does not appear to increase correct identifications from target-present lineups. What's worse, the instructions appear to increase false identifications of innocent suspects and foils. Thus, despite the recommendations of the Technical Working Group (1999), this research suggests that investigators should not mention that the perpetrator's appearance might have changed.

The results of all of these studies show that police investigators need to be circumspect in what they say to witnesses. They should not say anything that implies that they have the guilty person in custody. In fact, there is no excuse for police not to warn witnesses that the perpetrator may or may not be present in the lineup. Failure to provide such a warning can close to double the chance of a false identification of an innocent suspect.

Administration Bias and Double-Blind Lineups

There is a famous story that has been told in countless psychology classes about a horse known as Clever Hans (Pfungst, 1911). Hans's owner, Wilhelm von Osten, was convinced that his horse was a genius and had amazing communication and reasoning abilities. He believed that Hans could do mathematics, solve puzzles, answer questions about times and dates, and perform all sorts of other wondrous abilities. Nowadays the horse would have been featured on *Letterman's Pet Tricks*. But Letterman wasn't around yet, so instead Von Osten took Hans all over Germany staging events that showcased his horse's impressive abilities (see Figure 4.9).

FIGURE 4.9. Clever Hans. (*Source*: Original figures from Krall, K. (1912). *Denkende Tiere*. Leipzig, Germany: Engelmann. Obtained from WikiCommons at http://commons.wikimedia.org/wiki/File:Krall_Zarif_lernt_buchstabieren.jpg and http://commons.wikimedia.org/wiki/File:CleverHans.jpg.)

Admission was free. Herr von Osten would read out a problem such as "3+2" and Hans would provide an answer, stamping his foot five times. He would read another problem such as "5–1" and Hans would stomp his foot four times and so on. You can imagine how amazed people would be to see such a thing. You could imagine how excited von Osten must have been to have a horse like that.

Some people were skeptical. They suspected fraud. So a commission of researchers was formed to investigate von Osten's claims. The job of examining the horse fell to a research psychologist by the name of Oskar Pfungst. Pfungst tested Hans in a number of different ways. He had people other than von Osten ask the questions. He had Hans try to answer the questions while wearing blinders. He had people ask the questions who did not know the answer in advance. Pfungst quickly ruled out fraud. Herr von Osten was not making any money off of the horse because he did not charge admission. In addition, it did not seem to matter who asked the horse the questions, or even whether von Osten was present. Hans still got the answers right.

However, Pfungst made some additional findings that helped shed light on what was going on. It turned out that if the person asking the question knew the answer in advance, Hans tended to get the answer right. However, if the person asking the questions did not know the answer in advance, Hans could no longer answer the question. Moreover, if the horse could not see the person who was asking the questions, he was not able to get the answers right. Pfungst concluded that the horse had learned to read the body language of the questioner, and it did not matter who the questioner was.

The Clever Hans experiments are classic because they illustrates how a questioner can inadvertently influence the responses of her or his test subject without really meaning to. Von Osten really believed that his horse could do these tasks. He was not cuing the horse on purpose. Rather, the horse was picking up on subtle cues as to what the right answer was. In poker vernacular, the horse was reading von Osten's tells. Hans really was clever, but he was not clever in arithmetic, he was clever in being able to read people.

It stands to reason that if horses are smart enough to pick up on these types of subtle cues, that people can pick up on these types of cues as well. We know, for instance, that researchers can inadvertently cue their research participants to act in ways that confirm the researcher's hypothesis (Rosenthal, 1966). Because of this, researchers whenever possible, set up experiments so that they are blind as to what conditions particular participants are in. That way, the experimenter cannot inadvertently influence the response of the participant. Such experiments are called double-blind. Double-blind experiments are just a common sense precaution to prevent researchers from inadvertently influencing their participants.

Wells and Olson (2003) noted that police officers conducting a lineup are in a similar situation. The police investigator has a hypothesis. The hypothesis is that the suspect is the person who committed the crime. To test this hypothesis, the investigator conducts an experiment. The experiment is a lineup. The suspect is shown to the witness along with a number of foils. The foils serve as the control condition. If the witness picks the suspect, the investigator's hypothesis is confirmed. If the witness rejects the lineup or selects one of the foils, the investigator's hypothesis is disconfirmed. Here's where the problem arises. It is usually the investigating officer who creates and administers the lineup. The investigating officer knows who the suspect is. It stands to reason, then, that just as an experimenter may inadvertently tip their participants how to respond, the investigator may inadvertently tip the witness as to who the suspect is. Nobody is saying that police do this on purpose. Rather, the concern is that the witness might consciously or unconsciously pick up on the police investigator's tells (Wells, 1993; Wells & Luus, 1990).

Consider the case of *Florida v. Stephens*. Mr. Jonathon Stephens and several others were arrested for an armed robbery that occurred on July 2, 2005. Two days after the robbery, police put together several photospread lineups for the victim to view. Before showing the lineup to the victim, the police officer conducting the interview instructed the witness that the culprit may or may not be in the lineup. Here is a transcript of the audio tape of the identification:

Detective: Yeah. Today's 7-7-05. Okay. I'm going to show you another one [lineup] up here and see if you recognize anybody in that one.
Victim: No. [She is unable to make an identification.]
Detective: Look at them close. Nobody there? Okay. Okay.
Victim: They all have [inaudible].
Detective: Well, some of them were wearing skullcaps, weren't they?
Victim: Yeah. They both were, but I saw the guy's dreads coming through.
Detective: Okay. Could you tell how many people were in the [getaway] car?
Victim: There [Inaudible].
Detective: Okay.
Victim: [Inaudible] here so…
Detective: Right. But there had to have been at least three [perpetrators] since the two got into the back seat and somebody drove away, right?
Victim: Yes
Detective: Okay.
Victim: The guy that had the gun—
Detective: Uh-huh.
Victim: he—Chris [the second victim] had the gun pointed at his head said that he had tiny dreads, but he was basically like this one

[suspect in photo-array]. So Chris got a better look at him than I did.

Detective: Okay.

Victim: Chris said that he saw his dreads popping out the cap.

Detective: Okay. But that one looks familiar to you?

Victim: That one kind of, yeah.

Detective: Okay. All right. Let the statement reflect that the victim has pointed to black male Jonathan Stephens, for a possible person with the gun. Okay. Would you please sign and date under his name, under his photo?

This transcript clearly shows that the detective exerted significant influence on a witness who was having difficulty making an identification. Yet, when she testified at the pretrial hearing months later, the victim stated that she was certain about the identity of the culprit and that she never had any doubts about the accuracy of her identification.

The lineup administrator's influence does not always have to be as blatant as in the Stephens case to influence the eyewitness's memory (Wells, 1993). In a study by Phillips, McAuliff, Kovera, and Cutler (1999), participants were tested in pairs, with one member of the pair acting as the witness and the other acting as the lineup administrator. The witnesses saw a staged event in which two confederates entered a classroom and took out some audiovisual equipment. Several days after this event, the lineup administrator presented the witness with two lineups. For one lineup, the administrator was told in advance who the suspect was. This is called a *single-blind lineup*. In a single-blind lineup, the witness does not know in advance who the suspect is, but the lineup administrator does. For the other lineup, the administrator was not told who the suspect was. This is called a *double-blind lineup*. In a double-blind lineup, neither the witness nor the lineup administrator knows in advance who the suspect is. False identifications of the suspect were more common in the single-blind lineup than the double-blind lineup, suggesting that the lineup administrator was inadvertently cuing the witness how to respond. However, this effect only occurred for sequential lineups rather than simultaneous lineups. In another study, Haw and Fisher (2004) varied the amount of contact that the lineup administrator had with the witness during the identification. They found that the witness was less likely to make a decision that conformed to the lineup administrator's expectations if the amount of contact between the two parties was limited (the administrator was present but did not speak). This was true whether or not the lineup was simultaneous or sequential, and whether or not the target was present or absent from the lineup.

In some cases, there may be more than one witness to the same event. This presents additional complications. Information that an investigator learns from one witness may contaminate the identification of another witness. For instance, if the first witness picks lineup member C, the lineup administrator may come to think that C is the culprit. When the next witness is asked to make an identification, the lineup administrator may inadvertently influence that witness. Douglas, Smith, and Fraser-Hill (2005) had participants acting as lineup administrators conduct the same target-absent lineup twice, first with a confederate and then with an actual participant. The authors were interested in determining whether the lineup administrator's knowledge of the confederate's selection would influence the selection of the second witness. The results revealed that even if the confederate witness selected a suspect with low confidence, the lineup administrator was likely to influence the participant to select the same person. Furthermore, even though the participant's selection was influenced, the influence was so subtle that independent observers could not detect it when watching the identification.

These studies provide strong evidence that lineup administrators can inadvertently influence witnesses' selections from lineup. As a consequence, there are a number of initiatives pushing for the use of double-blind lineups by police (Innocence Project, 2010). We think these initiatives make a good deal of sense. Although police investigators are somewhat resistant to the use of double-blind procedures (Lampinen, Judges, & Odegard, 2002), their use provides an additional safeguard to innocent suspects and at no cost when it comes to identifying guilty suspects.

Multiple Lineups

A witness may at times be exposed to more than one lineup involving the same suspect. Imagine you witnessed the grocery store robbery described earlier in the chapter. The police call you in for a lineup and show you six individuals, matching the general description of the perpetrator. You are not able to make an identification based on this lineup. Some time later, the police develop additional information about the case. They show you a new lineup. The new lineup has the same suspect as the previous lineup, but entirely new foils. How are you likely to respond? There are two things to consider. Because you saw the suspect in the previous lineup, she is likely to seem familiar to you on the subsequent lineup. This is likely to increase the probability of a false identification. Additionally, you may well realize that there is only one person who is the same in the two lineups. This will make it obvious to you who the suspect is, and may lead you to pick the suspect.

Hinz and Pezdek (2001) investigated the effects of exposure to multiple lineups. In their study, participants viewed one target photograph for 60 seconds. A week later participants viewed a target-absent lineup and were asked to make an identification. Two days later participants viewed a six-person lineup that was either target present or target absent and either contained a previously seen foil (i.e., familiar foil–present condition) from the previous identification procedure (2 days before) or did not contain a previously seen foil (i.e., familiar foil–absent condition). All other slots in the lineup were filled with new foils. The presence of the familiar foil resulted in a lower correct identification of the target in target-present lineups, indicating that exposure to an innocent person can cause an eyewitness to misidentify the target in a later identification.

Pezdek and Blandon-Gitlin (2005) followed up by investigating conditions that would most likely lead to memory errors when multiple-identification tests were employed. They argued that memory impairment is most likely to occur when memories are acquired under conditions that promote poor memory and less likely when the encoding conditions promote good memory. In three experiments, Pezdek and Blandon-Gitlin (2005) showed that multiple identifications caused the most impairment when the encoding conditions were not conducive to good recognition memory. More specifically, the conditions included cross-race identification (Experiment 1), long retention interval (Experiment 2), and short exposure time (Experiment 3). The disturbing part of these findings is that crimes usually occur under conditions that are not conducive to good recognition memory (i.e. stressful, low illumination, short exposure times, long retention intervals, and so forth). Thus, those factors that make multiple identifications risky procedures are likely to be present during crimes.

Multiple identification procedures can also lead to mistaken eyewitness identification. Consider the recent case of Michael Green, who was accused of sexual assault in Houston, Texas, and sentenced to 75 years in prison (see Chapter 1). Green was initially shown to the victim using a live showup procedure shortly after her attack. She failed to identify him. One week later, Green was shown to the witness again, this time in a photographic lineup. This time she picked him. The witness was then shown a live lineup that included Green. She picked him again. Based on her identification, Green spent 27 years in prison before being exonerated based on newly tested DNA evidence. Although it is impossible to know for sure in any individual case, it is likely that the procedure of having the same witness make multiple identification attempts of the same suspect contributed to Green's wrongful conviction. There are two reasons for this. First, if one assumes that witnesses want to cooperate with the police, multiple identification attempts make it obvious to the witness who the police believe the suspect is. Thus, witnesses may resolve any uncertainties they have in favor of selecting the person the police have identified as the suspect. Second, viewing the same person multiple times may increase the familiarity of that person's face and may lead to a mistaken identification based on this heightened sense of familiarity.

In a recent study, Steblay, Tix, and Benson (under review) examined the effect of multiple lineups on mistaken identifications. Participants in the study watched a 30-second video depicting a purse snatching. Following the videotape, participants were shown a six-person photographic lineup, either with a guilty suspect, a designated innocent suspect, or six foils (no designated innocent suspect or control). For half of the participants a simultaneous lineup was presented and for the other half of the participants a sequential lineup was presented. Following this initial lineup, participants were scheduled for a follow-up session 2 weeks later. In the follow-up session, participants were shown a new lineup. The suspect was repeated in these lineups, but all foils were new. That is, participants saw either the same guilty suspect that was in the original lineup (i.e., guilty common denominator) or the same designated innocent suspect (innocent suspect common denominator), or the new lineup did not include any of the original lineup members and all six members of the lineup were novel (i.e., no common denominator). Repeatedly presenting the same innocent suspect in a simultaneous lineup increased mistaken suspect identifications from 36% to 52%. Diagnosticity for the second lineup was only 1.25(!). The presence of a common denominator had no significant effect in the sequential lineup (increase mistaken identifications of the innocent common denominator from 7% to 10%).

There is also an additional problem with utilizing multiple lineups involving the same suspect. It ignores the fact that a nonidentification provides diagnostic information about whether or not the suspect is guilty (Wells & Lindsay, 1980). It is like conducting an experiment that disconfirms your hypothesis, and then repeating the experiment until one gets the results you want. Consequently, exposing a witness to multiple lineups with the same suspect is problematic and should be avoided if at all possible.

☐ Guidelines and Suggestions

In this chapter, we reviewed a number of the most important system variables that have been identified by eyewitness psychologists. The great strength of the system variable approach is that system variables provide proactive steps that law enforcement can take in order to improve eyewitness accuracy. During the first decade of the 21st century, great strides have occurred in actually implementing the system variable approach by developing guidelines for police to use when interviewing witnesses or showing witnesses lineups or photo arrays.

In 1998, the Executive Committee of the American Psychology-Law Society developed a set of good practice guidelines for the collection of identification evidence (Wells, Small, et al., 1998). These guidelines were published in the journal *Law and Human Behavior*, and are typically referred to as the APLS whitepaper on eyewitness identification. Shortly thereafter, the U.S. Department of Justice (DOJ), under the direction of Attorney General Janet Reno, commissioned the Technical Working Group for Eyewitness Memory to develop guidelines for collecting eyewitness identification evidence.[4] The working group consisted of 34 people from the fields of law enforcement, law, and psychology.[5] The working group was convened to create a set of guidelines that are supported both by social scientific research and by practical experience. An exhaustive review of both sets of guidelines is beyond the scope of this chapter. For the purpose of this review, we will focus on the guidelines developed by the Executive Committee of the American Psychology-Law Society (Wells et al., 1998).

The first recommendation is concerned with who conducts a lineup. It is common practice for the arresting officer to prepare and conduct the lineup. This is problematic because the psychological research unequivocally demonstrates that a lineup administrator who knows the identity of the suspect can intentionally or unintentionally influence the decision process of the eyewitness (Douglas, Smith, & Fraser-Hill, 2005; Haw & Fisher, 2004; Phillips et al., 1999; Wells & Olson, 2003). To protect against the influence of lineup administrators, it is suggested that the lineup administrator be blind to the identity of the suspect.

To this suggestion, we would add two things. First, based on the research of Haw and Fisher (2004), the amount of interaction between the lineup administrator and the witness should be held to a minimum. Second, the lineup administrator should not present the same lineup to separate witnesses. Being privy to the choice made by one eyewitness can undermine the protection afforded by having administrators blind to the identity of the suspect, because an official's knowledge about one witness' choice can influence the choice made from another lineup conducted by the same official (Douglas, Smith, & Fraser-Hill, 2005).

Given the potential problems of having the lineup administrator aware of the identity of suspects, we suggest automated lineup identification procedures (MacLin, Meissner, & Zimmerman, 2005). The person who programs the lineup for each individual witness should be kept blind as to identity of the suspect. With computer-assisted lineups, there can be no influence of the lineup administrator because the lineups are administered entirely by means of computer. Additionally, it makes a good deal of sense to videotape the identification procedure (Kassin, 1998). This is especially true if the person conducting the lineup knows the identity of the suspect. Videotaping the identification procedure would allow the trier of fact, perhaps with the aid of an expert witness, to evaluate whether subtle cues may have influenced the witness' selection.

The second guideline is that the witness should be explicitly informed that the culprit may not be in the lineup. Simply warning the witness that the culprit may not be in the lineup reduces the number of false identifications from target-absent lineups substantially, while having a minimal effect on the rate of correct identifications from target-present lineups (Malpass & Devine, 1981; Steblay, 1997).

The third guideline is that the suspect should not stand out in the lineup based on the witness's description of the culprit. Simply put, if the witness describes the culprit as having red hair, then the suspect should not be the only person in the lineup with red hair. To the extent that the foils are selected based on the match-description-of-the culprit strategy, this guideline is not violated. This does not mean that all persons in the lineup must be a clone of the witness's description. The technical working group also discourages the use of one person showups. Their rationale for this suggestion is twofold. First, one-person lineups, such as showups, clearly violate this third guideline as the suspect will stand out because there is no one else in the lineup. Second, there is no way of knowing whether the person has made an error because there are no foils in the lineup.

The fourth guideline is that a confidence statement should be taken immediately after the eyewitness makes an identification and prior to any feedback from the lineup administrator. Confidence is quite malleable and can change based on a variety of social factors, as we will show in the next chapter. One such factor is feedback from the administrator after the identification has been made. Wells and Bradfield (1998) compellingly demonstrated that confirming postidentification feedback can dramatically affect the witness's confidence about a lineup identification. The confidence statement serves two protective functions. First, as Wells and Bradfield (1998) demonstrated, the confidence statement made before postidentification feedback counteracts confidence inflation that may occur as result of feedback. Second, if a confidence statement is taken at the time of the identification it can be entered into the court record. Therefore, the witness's confidence at the trial can be compared to the confidence reported at the time of the identification. We will have more to say about the malleability of confidence in the following chapter.

There were also two procedures that the committee fell short of formally recommending, but rather included as *suggestions*: using sequential lineups and videotaping the entire identification process. Sequential lineups lead to fewer false identifications and appear to have somewhat less of an effect on accurate identifications (Lindsey & Wells, 1985; Maclin, Zimmerman, & Malpass, 2005; Steblay et al., 2001). The suggestion to videotape the entire procedure makes sense because it provides a record of what occurred during the identification. This may even the playing field for the defense by providing defendants with evidence relevant to the fairness of identification procedures (see Kassin, 1998).

Many states have started implementing these reforms in order to ensure fair and unbiased lineup identification procedures (Innocence Project, 2010). In New Jersey and North Carolina, for example, police departments and prosecutors are now required to conduct sequential lineups. Similarly, Santa Ana, California, and several counties in Minnesota have opted for sequential lineups. In Clinton, Iowa, an arresting officer who works a case is not allowed in the room during identification procedures relevant to that case. In New Mexico, there are reminders on the photos used for photospread identification that the lineup administrator is to inform the witness that the culprit may not be in the lineup. Many cities, including New York and Seattle, have started using computerized programs to present photo arrays. Jurisdictions in Chicago, Wisconsin, and Minnesota have commissioned panels to start investigating identification procedures in order to reduce false identifications.

These developments are promising. Police and eyewitness researchers all too often encounter each other only when they meet on opposite sides of the courtroom, with the researcher acting as a defense expert disputing the validity of the eyewitness evidence. These new developments provide an opportunity for police and eyewitness experts to work together, using science to limit the number of false identifications and to maintain or even increase the number of correct identifications.

☐ Endnotes

1. We originally proposed this thought experiment in Lampinen, Neuschatz, and Payne (1998).
2. There was also a third condition meant to illustrate the effects of foil selection bias. In these lineups, the foils were systematically chosen to mismatch the description of the perpetrator given by the witness. This biased lineup condition approximately quadrupled the chances of a false identification in the target-absent lineups.
3. Initials are used in cases that are still ongoing in order to protect the innocent.
4. The Department of Justice Guidelines read in part, "When circumstances require the prompt display of a single suspect to a witness, the inherent suggestiveness of the encounter can be minimized through the use of procedural safeguards." The phrase "When circumstances require …" suggests that lineups are the preferred method and that showups should be reserved for situations where there is not enough time to construct a lineup.

5. Although the working group included researchers, a majority of the working group was actually made up of prosecutors and law enforcement personnel, which should make the recommendations especially palatable to police investigators.

CHAPTER

Indicia of Reliability

☐ Overview

In the previous chapters we talked about some of the most important variables that can influence the accuracy of eyewitness identification. In Chapter 3, we reviewed estimator variables—those variables that police have no control over that can influence eyewitness accuracy. In Chapter 4, we reviewed system variables—those variables that police have control over that can influence eyewitness accuracy. An important point about both types of variables is that they are best understood as being causal antecedents of eyewitness accuracy. For example, poor lighting *causes* eyewitness identification to suffer. Giving biased lineup instructions *causes* false identifications to increase.

The variables we are going to talk about next are variables that may serve to indicate that an eyewitness is accurate or inaccurate. However these variables are not best seen as the *cause* of that accuracy or inaccuracy. Rather, they provide an indicium of reliability that may be used by the legal system to judge the likely accuracy of the eyewitness. These variables have often been classified as *estimator variables*, and strictly speaking they match the conventional definition of that term. However, we believe it is useful to make a distinction between these variables and the estimator variables we discussed in Chapter 3. The distinction we are making is between variables that *cause* eyewitnesses to be accurate or inaccurate and those variables that may provide an *indication* that the witness is accurate or inaccurate, even though they are not the cause of that accuracy or inaccuracy. To give an analogy, spotted skin provides an indicium of having measles, but the spots do not cause the measles.

A number of different *indicia of reliability* have been examined by eyewitness researchers. These include things like how confident the eyewitness is, the accuracy of the witness's memory for other details of the crime, how quickly the witness makes a choice, and the witness's self-reported decision strategy. Each of these indicators provides some diagnostic information about how accurate the witness is. But just like clinical indicators of disease (e.g., spots for measles), the indicia of eyewitness reliability are imperfect and sometimes even misleading (e.g., not everyone with spots has measles). Combined with the estimator variables and system variables discussed in the previous chapters, the indicia may provide additional information that can be useful for determining how much trust to place in the witness's account.

☐ Eyewitness Confidence

Imagine you are on a jury. The crime involves a robbery of a woman who was hiking in Yellowstone. The woman is in her early 30s and is dressed professionally as she sits on the witness stand. The woman takes an oath to tell the truth, the whole truth, and nothing but the truth. She testifies that, on the day the crime occurred, she had been hiking through Yellowstone. As she got back to the campground, she approached her car, where she was confronted by a stranger who pulled out a hunting knife with apparent ill intent. He demanded her backpack. He demanded money. He took her cell phone and car keys. He then ran off. The witness testifies that the entire incident lasted approximately one minute and that she got a very good look at her attacker's face. Police were dispatched to the scene, and the woman provided a description of the event and described her attacker's appearance and manner. The witness testifies that a week following the robbery she was called in to the police station, where she positively identified the suspect from a six-person photo lineup. The prosecutor asks if that person is in the courtroom today, and she points to the defendant as the person who attacked her. The prosecutor asks her if she's sure, and she says, "I'm absolutely certain—not a doubt in my mind."

If you were on this jury, how would you evaluate the witness? If you are like most people, you would probably take into account the witness's demeanor, the witnessing conditions at the time of the crime, and the witness's confidence. In fact, jury simulation studies have shown that the single biggest predictor of how credible jurors find a witness is the witness's stated confidence (Cutler, Penrod, & Dexter, 1990; Fox & Walters, 1986; Lindsay, Wells, & Rumpel, 1981; Wells, Lindsay, & Ferguson, 1979). In one recent study, Brewer and Burke (2002) had mock jurors listen to an audiotape of a mock trial in which a defendant was charged with armed robbery. During the course of the trial, participants heard both direct and cross-examination of an eyewitness who had identified the defendant as the person who committed the robbery. For half of the mock jurors, the witness made a number of inconsistent statements during her testimony. For the other half of the mock jurors, the witness did not make the inconsistent statements. In addition to manipulating the consistency of the testimony provided by the witness, the researchers also varied how confident the witness appeared. In some trial simulations the witness answered in such a way that she appeared low in confidence, and in other trial simulations the witness answered in such a way that she appeared high in confidence. Witness confidence was manipulated by varying how much the witness hesitated when she answered questions (e.g., "'Ahh ... it would have been about 3 seconds' versus 'About 3 seconds'") and by varying the use of verbal hedges (e.g., "'I am reasonably sure' versus 'I am absolutely sure'") (Brewer & Burke, 2002, p. 357). Brewer and Burke asked participants to indicate how probable they believed it was, based on the evidence presented, that the defendant was guilty of the crime. Results indicated that when the witness was confident, mock jurors rated the probability the defendant was guilty as being much higher (M = 57.50%) than when the witness was less confident (M = 32.50%). By contrast, participants rated the probability of guilt as being only slightly higher when the testimony was consistent (M = 49.46%) than when it was inconsistent (M = 40.92%). In fact, when the witness was confident, there was hardly any difference between the consistent (M = 61.36%) and inconsistent conditions (M = 56.64%). The result suggests that a witness who contradicts herself will continue to be viewed as credible by jurors as long as she expresses high levels of confidence.

Not only do jurors often use eyewitness confidence as an indicium of accuracy, but also the use of confidence in this way is endorsed by the court system in the United States and other countries. In the United States, the legal precedent of *Neil v. Biggers* (discussed in Chapter 3) advised that, in assessing the credibility of an eyewitness identification, one should consider the level of subjective confidence of the witness. The use of confidence as an indicator of reliability was later reaffirmed in *Manson v. Braithwaite* (1977). Survey research in both the United States and other countries indicates that judges tend to place a great deal of weight on how confident an eyewitness is in making an identification (Magnussen et al., 2008; Rapus-Benton, Ross, McDonnell, Thomas, & Bradshaw, 2006). Similar results have been found in surveys of police officers and attorneys (Brigham & Wolfskeil, 1983; Deffenbacher & Loftus, 1982; Noon & Hollin, 1987).

Theoretical Accounts of Confidence and Accuracy

Is confidence a good predictor of accuracy? One way of addressing this question is to consider what the psychological theories outlined in Chapter 2 would predict. To take one example, consider the predictions of a theory like signal detection theory. According to signal detection theory, items presented on a memory test (lineup) vary in terms of the subjective sense of familiarity they produce in the participant (witness). On average, items that were previously encountered should be experienced with a greater subjective sense of familiarity. Participants decide if an item is old or new by comparing its familiarity to a criterion. If the familiarity is above that criterion, the item is called *old*. If the familiarity is below that criterion, the item is called *new*. So how does confidence fit into this scheme? Signal detection theory claims that when a participant is asked to make confidence judgments, they simply set a number of additional response criteria for every confidence point on the confidence scale (see Figure 5.1). Confidence is simply an external marker of this internal sense of familiarity. Because old items are more familiar on average than are new items, the proportion of old items at very high levels of familiarity (and thus in the confident old range) will tend to outnumber the proportion of new items at very high levels of familiarity. This leads to the predictions that confidence should be correlated with accuracy and that the correlation between confidence and accuracy should be greatest when memory is relatively strong (i.e., large values of d′).

To give a sense of the relationship between confidence and accuracy expected based on signal detection theory, we generated some hypothetical data assuming the situation shown in Figure 5.1. For the example, we set d′ equal to 1. Recall that d′ indicates how much more familiar, on

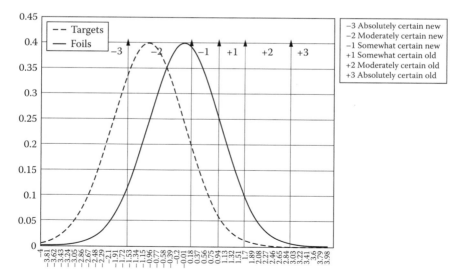

FIGURE 5.1   Signal detection account of how confidence judgments are made. This graph assumes a six-point confidence scale.

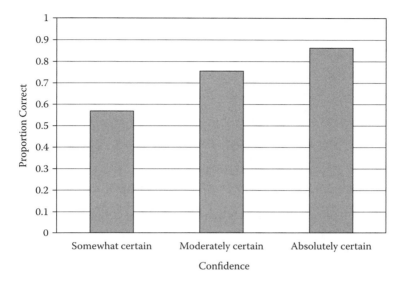

FIGURE 5.2   Simulated accuracy and confidence data for an old/new recognition test based on assumptions of signal detection theory. We simulated this by randomly generating 2,000 data points based on assumptions of signal detection theory, assuming d′ = 1 and using 2.96, 1.68, .96, .19, and −1.57 as the response criteria corresponding to different confidence values.

average, old items are than new items. We set up confidence boundaries as shown in Figure 5.1. We then randomly generated data for 1,000 old items and 1,000 new items based on those hypothetical assumptions. As can be seen in Figure 5.2, confidence in these simulated data appeared to be a pretty good indicium of accuracy. At the confidence level of 1, accuracy on an old/new recognition test was around 57%, which is just above chance. At the confidence level of 2, accuracy was a little over 75%. And at the confidence level of 3, accuracy was more than 85%. So under these theoretical assumptions, confidence was a good, but not perfect, predictor of accuracy.

The situation is a little more complicated in an actual lineup, however, because participants are not just responding with old/new judgments. Rather they are making a choice among several lineup members. Not only that, but in a real lineup, witnesses are also free to reject the lineup altogether. Given this more complex situation, the decision rule witnesses are using becomes very important. One way of thinking about that situation is to apply the insights from the WITNESS model (Clark, 2003) we talked about in Chapter 2. In that model, the probability of choosing the suspect is based on both absolute judgments (how similar is the suspect to the representation of the culprit stored in memory?) and relative judgments (how much more similar is the suspect to the representation of the culprit than the next closest lineup member is to the representation of the culprit?). This absolute and relative judgment information is combined to produce an overall goodness of match, which presumably impacts not just lineup choice but also confidence.

Dual process models (see Chapter 2) also provide a way of understanding the relationship between confidence and accuracy. These models assume two qualitatively distinct ways of making recognition memory judgments (Brainerd & Reyna, 2002; Diana, Reder, Arndt, & Park, 2006; Jacoby, 1991; Joordens & Hockley, 2000; Lampinen, Watkins, & Odegard, 2006; Mandler, 1980; Yonelinas, 1994). These are usually referred to as recollection and familiarity. *Recollection* is thought to involve the conscious re-experiencing of the target event. *Familiarity* is thought to involve a decontextualized feeling that the item had previously been experienced. Recollection is sometimes described as a high-threshold, all-or-none process and is typically associated with very high levels of confidence (Yonelinas, 2001). Familiarity is usually described as a graded process. It varies along a continuum and thus can be associated with varying levels of confidence. Although false recollection (sometimes called *phantom recollection*) does occur (Brainerd, Payne, Wright, & Reyna, 2003; Brainerd, Reyna, Wright, & Mojardin, 2001; Lampinen, Odegard, Blackshear, & Toglia, 2005; Lampinen et al., 2006; Stahl & Klauer, 2009), it has typically been found that recollection is less error prone than familiarity (e.g., Rajaram, 1993). Because recollection tends to involve high levels of confidence, a natural conclusion to draw would be that high confidence judgments, on average, should also be more accurate.

The Confidence–Accuracy Correlation

The opinions of laypeople and members of the legal community, then, appear to agree that confidence should be a good predictor of the accuracy of a witness. People tend to believe that, everything else being equal, a more confident witness is probably also a more accurate witness. Not only that, but also there are good theoretical reasons to believe that confidence and accuracy should be at least somewhat related. What has research found on this topic? Over the past quarter of a century, there have been a large number of studies in which participants made choices from lineups and also provided information about how confident they were. The initial conclusions drawn from this research were that confidence and accuracy were related, but that the relationship tended to be weak. For instance, one early review of the literature reported average correlations between accuracy and confidence of .07, and another reported an average correlation of

.25 (Bothwell, Deffenbacher, & Brigham, 1987; Wells & Murray, 1984). Note that a correlation of zero would have indicated no relationship between accuracy and confidence and a correlation of 1 would have indicated a perfect relationship between accuracy and confidence. Findings like these led most eyewitness researchers to draw the conclusion that the relationship between accuracy and confidence was weak at best, and that jurors, judges, police, and lawyers place too much reliance on the expressed confidence of a witness (Wells, Olson, & Charman, 2002).

A number of early theoretical accounts were developed in an attempt to explain these findings. For instance, Deffenbacher (1980) developed the *optimality hypothesis* in an attempt to account for when accuracy and confidence would be related and when accuracy and confidence would not be related. According to the optimality hypothesis, the accuracy confidence correlation will be weak when overall witnessing conditions are poor, and will be stronger when overall witnessing conditions are good. One way of thinking about this is that when witnessing conditions are very poor, people will be guessing much more than they would if witnessing conditions were good. Such witnesses will probably indicate relatively low levels of confidence, but some of those guesses will nevertheless be accurate by chance alone. Indeed, when witnessing conditions are poor, lucky guesses may be the predominant form of accurate responses. Thus confidence will not be a very reliable indicator of accuracy. Consistent with the optimality hypothesis, Bothwell, Deffenbacher, and Brigham (1987) found that in situations where the perpetrator was visible for a longer period of time, the correlation between accuracy and confidence was stronger.

There are also other reasons why the relationship between accuracy and confidence may not always be strong. In an insightful analysis, Leippe (1980) pointed out there are a number of factors that may influence witness accuracy without necessarily influencing witness confidence and there are a number of factors that may influence witness confidence without influencing witness accuracy. With regard to the first set of factors, Leippe (1980) argued that factors such as the seriousness of the crime, the duration of the event, and the effects of postevent information may change accuracy without changing confidence very much. With regard to the second group of factors, Leippe (1980) argued that witnesses may assess their confidence partly by assessing how subjectively strong their memories are, but that confidence can also be influenced by a number of factors that are arguably unrelated to accuracy. For instance, factors like biased testing instructions (see Chapter 4) may imply that the perpetrator is in the lineup. This may provide witnesses with a false sense of certainty, that if they pick the best match to their memory, then they have likely picked the culprit. Because these factors can influence confidence independently of accuracy, it is possible to have highly confident witnesses who are not particularly accurate.

Another interesting suggestion about the confidence–accuracy relationship was provided by Kassin (1985). Kassin's account was based on Bem's (1972) self-perception theory, which holds that we may not always have privileged knowledge of our own internal mental states. Rather, Bem argued that we learn about our own mental states in much the same way that other people learn about our mental states: by observing our actions. If this theory is correct, then assessing our own confidence in an identification task should be difficult. We do not typically view ourselves as we are making a judgment. This should be doubly difficult if we have to indicate retrospectively how confident we were when we made a judgment. For instance, several months later, at time of trial, if we are asked how confident we were when we picked the person from the lineup, all we may have to go on is the fact that we picked the suspect. We may reason, "I would not have picked the suspect if I was not confident; therefore, I must have been confident."

To test the self-perception account, Kassin (1985) showed participants a mock crime and then asked them to make an identification from a photospread. Participants indicated their confidence immediately, after a 5-minute delay, or after a 5-minute delay that included viewing their identification on videotape. According to self-perception theory, this last condition (retrospective self-awareness) should lead to the strongest relationship between accuracy and confidence. Consistent with this prediction, the correlation between confidence and accuracy in the retrospective self-awareness condition was .84, a very strong correlation. The correlation between confidence and accuracy in all the other conditions was less than .20. The result of Kassin's research suggests that part of the reason confidence is not always a great predictor of accuracy is because we often do not have privileged access to our own internal mental states.

For many years, the results of studies like the ones reported above led eyewitness researchers to conclude that the relationship between accuracy and confidence was weak at best. The practical implication that was drawn from these studies was that the legal system was mistaken to place much trust in the confidence of eyewitnesses. However, in recent years there have been a number of important critiques of this generalization. One important distinction, suggested by Brigham (1988), was between the accuracy–confidence correlation when calculated among all participants versus the accuracy–confidence correlation when calculated only among those who actually made an identification (i.e., *choosers*). As Brigham pointed out, the accuracy–confidence relationship is important because jurors make use of eyewitness confidence in order to assess the accuracy of the witness's identification. However, jurors typically only see witnesses who actually made a choice. As a consequence, it is only the relationship between confidence and accuracy among those witnesses who made an

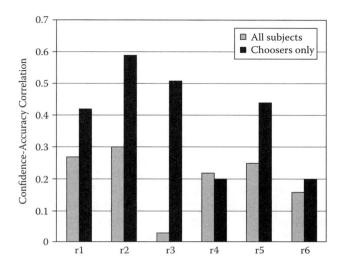

FIGURE 5.3   The size of the accuracy–confidence correlation in six different data sets. The lowercase *r* is the symbol for correlation and can
vary between –1 and +1. The closer the absolute value of *r* is to 1, the
stronger the relationship between accuracy and confidence. The figure
compares cases where the correlation is calculated using all the data
with cases where the correlation is computed, looking only at those
participants who choose someone from the lineup. In almost every
case, the correlation is much stronger when looking only at "choosers."
(*Source*: Brigham, J. (1988). Is witness confidence helpful in judging
eyewitness accuracy? *Practical Aspects of Memory: Current Research
and Issues: Vol. 1. Memory in everyday life* (pp. 77–82). Oxford: John
Wiley & Sons.)

identification that may be most relevant. Brigham went back to data from
five different studies that included a total of six accuracy–confidence correlations calculated on the entire sample, and he recalculated the correlations based only on the participants who actually made an identification.
As can be seen in Figure 5.3, in almost every case, the correlation was
stronger, usually substantially stronger, when only the "choosers" were
considered. In fact, the average size of the correlation when all participants were included was .205, but when only choosers were included the
average size of the correlation jumped to .393. Similar results have been
found by other researchers (e.g., Sporer, 1993).

   Another important critique of the claim that the accuracy–confidence
correlation is weak came from work by Lindsay, Nilsen, and Read (2000).
The critique begins by noting that the size of a correlation depends on the
amount of variability in the things being measured. To give an analogy,

suppose you wanted to establish that alcohol intoxication is associated with decreased driving performance. To examine this issue, you decide to conduct a study in which you measure the reaction time of participants in a driving task. Imagine that the participants all have the same body weight and each drinks a six pack of home-brewed beer (Neuschatz Nectar IPA).[1] You measure the blood alcohol of your participants and calculate the correlation between blood alcohol and reaction time on the driving test. If you were to actually conduct this study, you might well find that the correlation between blood alcohol and driving ability, as observed in this study, is very weak. Statisticians refer to the problem as a *restriction of range*. Because all the participants have the same body weight and all drank the same amount of alcohol, their blood alcohol content would probably be very close to identical. Because of this, any variation in reaction time would probably be due to other factors. As a consequence, the size of the correlation would be small (see Figure 5.4a). It would, of course, be a deadly mistake to conclude from such a study that blood alcohol content is unrelated to driving ability. Rather, what one would really want to do is look at participants whose blood alcohol content varies widely, from very low to very high, to see what effect that variable has on driving (see Figure 5.4b for an illustration). If you were to do so, you would undoubtedly find that high levels of blood alcohol result in slower reaction times. Drinking and driving don't mix. The principle that this example illustrates is that when you evaluate the relationship between any two variables, you should do so over a wide range of conditions, similar to what will occur in the settings you want to generalize to.

Lindsay et al. (2000) made a similar argument with regard to eyewitness research. In particular, they pointed out that in most studies of the accuracy–confidence relationship, all the participants in the study view the event under tightly controlled witnessing conditions. The problem with this, according to Lindsay et al. (2000), is that in real life, witnesses view crimes under a variety of different witnessing conditions. Given the variability that occurs in the real world, the authors argued, the confidence–accuracy relationship might actually be a lot stronger than the previous research studies have shown. Indeed, when Lindsay and colleagues systematically allowed witnessing conditions to vary, they found that the size of the accuracy–confidence correlation grew much stronger.

From the above, it appears clear that the size of the confidence–accuracy correlation often reported in the eyewitness literature may be unrepresentative of the confidence–accuracy correlation in actual police investigations. On the one hand, jurors typically are called upon to assess the likely accuracy not of all potential witnesses, but only of those witnesses who actually end up picking someone from a lineup. Thus, the relevant measure is not the overall confidence–accuracy correlation, but

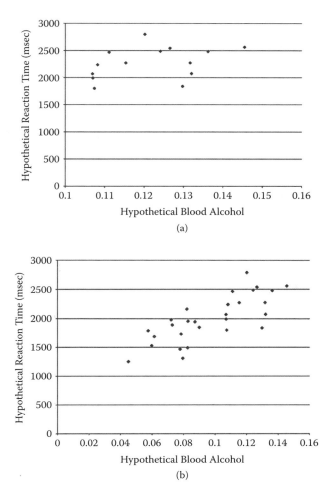

FIGURE 5.4 Hypothetical example illustrating the effect of restriction of range. In the graph labeled (a), only a limited range of blood alcohol values is tested (i.e., a restricted range), and it appears as if there is no relationship between blood alcohol and reaction time. In the graph labeled (b), a larger range of blood alcohol volumes is tested, and there is a clear correlation between blood alcohol and reaction times.

the confidence–accuracy correlation among choosers (i.e., the witnesses who make a choice from the lineup). Moreover, when assessing the likely accuracy of a witness, we need to consider the full range of likely witnessing conditions. Failing to do so may understate the confidence–accuracy correlation due to a restriction of range.

Calibration of Confidence and Accuracy

More recently, there has been an even more fundamental critique of the claim that confidence and accuracy are only weakly related. The problem, according to these researchers, is that calculating the correlation between accuracy and confidence is not the appropriate statistical technique for this situation (Juslin, Olsson, & Winman, 1996). To see why, it is useful to consider what is meant by the concept of a correlation. In the standard case, a correlation indicates the degree of linear relationship between two variables. For instance, if we were to actually conduct a study of the effects of blood alcohol levels on reaction time, we could look at the degree to which as blood alcohol rises reaction times also rise. If that relationship can be represented perfectly with a straight line, we would have a perfect linear correlation between the two variables (see Figure 5.5a). If most of the points come close to a straight line, we would have a strong, but not perfect, correlation (see Figure 5.5b). If few of the points came close to falling on a straight line, the correlation would be weak (see Figure 5.5c). If the points just appear to be scattered about higgledy-piggledy, the correlation would be close to zero (see Figure 5.5d).

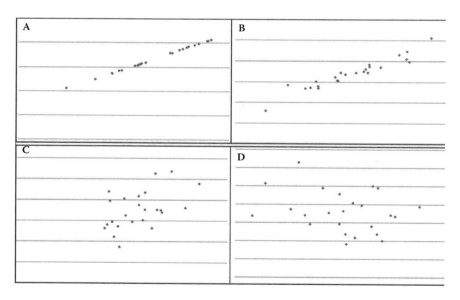

FIGURE 5.5 Hypothetical examples illustrating correlations differing in strength. (A) Illustrates a very strong correlation between two variables. (B) Illustrates a case where the correlation is somewhat weaker. In (C), the correlation is very weak. In (D), there is almost no correlation between the two variables.

When researchers calculate a correlation between confidence and accuracy, they are typically using a numerical scale that indicates multiple confidence levels (e.g., 1, 2, 3, 4, 5, or 6) as the measure of confidence and a dichotomous scale (e.g., 1 or 0) to represent accuracy. A measure called a *point biserial correlation* is then calculated. The problem is that it is generally not possible to fit a straight line if the one scale has the points 1, 2, 3, 4, 5, and 6, and the other scale is either a 1 or a 0. Rather, by its very nature, the relationship between individual accuracy scores and individual confidence scores necessarily diverges from a straight line (Juslin et al., 1996).

For this reason, it has recently been argued that a better measure of the confidence–accuracy relationship is the *calibration* of confidence and accuracy (Brewer, Keast, & Rishworth, 2002; Brewer & Wells, 2006; Juslin et al., 1996). The calibration of the relationship between confidence and accuracy concerns how accurate a witness is when he or she indicates that there is a 50%, 60%, 70%, or the like probability that he or she is accurate. For instance, if witnesses were perfectly calibrated, then witnesses who indicate that they are 80% certain would be correct 8 out of 10 times. Experiments examining the calibration of accuracy and confidence typically involve testing large numbers of participants. Each participant acts as an eyewitness and views an event. The participant is then presented with a lineup task. After making a choice or rejecting the lineup, the witness is asked to indicate the probability that the choice is correct, usually in percentage terms (e.g., "There's a 60% chance I am correct").

How well calibrated witnesses are can then be examined by means of *calibration curves*, such as the hypothetical calibration curve shown in Figure 5.6. On the x-axis, you see the probabilities assigned by witnesses to their judgments. For instance, the point on the x-axis that says 20% represents all the participants who said they were 20% sure their answer was correct. The point on the x-axis that says 50% represents all the participants who said that they were 50% sure that their answer was correct. The y-axis on a calibration curve indicates the actual percent of correct judgments made by each of those groups of participants. In Figure 5.6, the dashed line illustrates the relationship between confidence and accuracy if witnesses were perfectly calibrated. The solid line in Figure 5.6 is hypothetical data that might be generated in an eyewitness experiment. Note that data points that fall above the dashed line represent witnesses who are *underconfident*. For instance, in the hypothetical data, witnesses who indicated that they were 20% confident were actually correct 30% of the time. Data points that fall below the dashed line represent witnesses who are *overconfident*. For instance, the witnesses in this hypothetical case who said they were 90% confident were actually correct only 80% of the time.

In addition to providing a graphical representation of the degree of calibration between accuracy and confidence, there is also a numerical

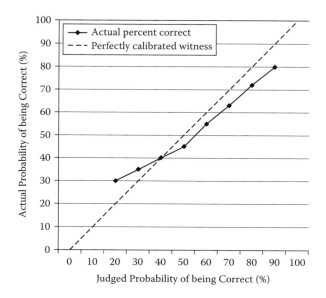

FIGURE 5.6   Hypothetical example illustrating how calibration curves are constructed. The x-axis shows participants' judgments of how likely they think it is that their answers are correct. The y-axis shows the actual accuracy of witnesses. The dashed line shows what the calibration curve should look like if witnesses were perfectly calibrated. The solid line shows data from a hypothetical experiment. When the solid line is above the dashed line, it indicates that witnesses are underconfident. When the solid line is below the dashed line, it indicates that witnesses are overconfident.

measure called *the calibration statistic*, or *C statistic* or *C* for short. The formula used to calculate the C statistic is as follows:

$$C = \frac{1}{n}\sum_{j=1}^{J} n_j (c_j - a_j)^2$$

In this equation, n refers to the total number of identifications made in the study. The total number of confidence categories is represented by the letter J. The number of identifications made in each category is represented by n_j. The confidence assigned to each category is represented by c_j, and the actual percent correct in that category is given by a_j. To see how to apply the formula, imagine you collected the data shown in Table 5.1. To calculate the C statistic, you would take the following steps:

TABLE 5.1 Example Illustrating How to Calculate Calibration Based on Hypothetical Data

Stated Confidence (c_j)	Actual Accuracy (a_j)	Number of Witnesses (n_j)	c_j-a_j	$(c_j-a_j)^2$	$n_j(c_j-a_j)^2$
20	30	100	−10	100	10,000
30	35	100	−5	25	2,500
40	40	150	0	0	0
50	45	150	5	25	3,750
60	55	100	5	25	2,500
70	63	200	7	49	9,800
80	72	100	8	64	6,400
90	80	100	10	100	10,000
				Sum =	44,950
				Total n =	1,000
				C =	44.95
				Square root of C =	6.70

- First, for each confidence category subtract the actual percent correct from the stated confidence and square the difference. In the example, participants who said they were 20% confident were actually accurate 30% of the time. Twenty minus 30 is −10, and −10 squared is 100.
- Second, multiply this squared difference by the number of observations in this confidence category. In Table 5.1 you can see that there are a total of 100 witnesses who said they were 20% confident. So one would multiply the squared difference from step 1 by the number of participants ($100 \times 100 = 10,000$).
- This is repeated for each of the confidence categories, and then the results for each category are added up. When we add this up, the number we get is 44,950.
- The sum from step 4 is then divided by the total number of identifications made. In this case, there were 1,000, so C = 44,950 / 1,000 = 44.95

Note that if calibration were perfect, then C should equal zero, because for each category the difference between the stated confidence and the actual accuracy would be zero. Second, when C is large, it indicates that the witnesses are not very good at predicting their accuracy. What C is giving you is an average of sorts (a weighted average). It indicates the averaged squared difference between the stated confidence and the actual accuracy. When witnesses in this hypothetical example predict how accurate they are, the square of how much their prediction is off by is around 45. The measure is a very close analogy to the measure of variance offered in statistics, and it is not unreasonable to take the value of C and take its square root to get a better impression of the typical error in calibration. In this case, the square root of 44.95 would be 6.7. So an interpretation would be that if a witness tells you he or she is X% certain, it is likely that the true probability that he or she is accurate is about 7% to either side of that value (remember, though, this is a hypothetical example for illustration only).

A second measure of calibration is often calculated as well. This is the over- and underconfidence statistic (O/U). The equation for this is the same as for the C statistic, only the differences are not squared.

$$OU = \frac{1}{n}\sum_{j=1}^{J} n_j (c_j - a_j)$$

Because the differences are not squared, the equation can produce either negative or positive values. The calculation of this statistic is shown in Table 5.2. If the OU statistic ends up being positive, it means that witnesses tended to be overconfident. Their stated confidence tended to be greater than their actual accuracy. If the OU statistic ends up being negative, it means that witnesses tended to be underconfident. Their stated confidence tended to be less than their actual accuracy. Keep in mind that the OU index could be zero and witnesses could still be poorly calibrated.

The above examples were just hypothetical examples and were used simply for illustration. How do actual participants do in studies of the

TABLE 5.2 Example Illustrating How to Calculate Over- or Underconfidence (O/U) Based on Hypothetical Data

Stated Confidence (c_j)	Actual Accuracy (a_j)	Number of Witnesses (n_j)	$c_j - a_j$	$n_j(c_j - a_j)$
20	30	100	−10	−1,000
30	35	100	−5	−500
40	40	150	0	0
50	45	150	5	750
60	55	100	5	500
70	63	200	7	1,400
80	72	100	8	800
90	80	100	10	1,000
			Sum =	2,950
			Total n =	1,000
			O/U =	2.95

Note: Positive value of O/U indicates that witnesses are, on average, overconfident.

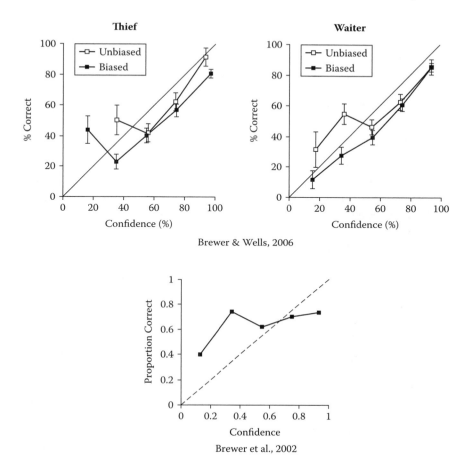

FIGURE 5.7   Actual calibration curves. In these studies, participants appear to be overconfident at the high end of the confidence scale and underconfident at the lower ends of the confidence scale. (*Source*: Reprinted from Brewer, N., & Wells, G. (2006). The confidence-accuracy relationship in eyewitness identification: Effects of lineup instructions, foil similarity, and target-absent base rates. *Journal of Experimental Psychology: Applied, 12*, 11–30.)

calibration of accuracy and confidence? The best studies that have examined these questions have been conducted by Neil Brewer and colleagues (e.g., Brewer et al., 2002; Brewer & Wells, 2006). Figure 5.7 shows calibration curves from two of Brewer's studies.

The first thing to note about these studies is that confidence and accuracy seem to be related. It is fair to say that, on average, witnesses who are more confident also tend to be more accurate. However, the calibration of the witnesses is far from perfect. In particular, at low confidence levels participants tend to be somewhat underconfident and at high confidence levels participants tend to be somewhat overconfident. For instance, witnesses who indicate that they are 95% confident are often accurate around 80% of the time or less.

A number of factors have been found that affect how well calibrated confidence and accuracy are. In particular, Brewer et al. (2002) used two instructional manipulations in an attempt to improve witness calibration. In one manipulation, called *reflection*, witnesses were asked a series of questions about their experiences at the time of the witnessed event and at the time of the lineup. These questions focused on both external factors such as how long the perpetrator was visible and internal factors, like how easy the identification seemed. The other manipulation, labeled *disconfirmation*, asked participants to indicate reasons why they might have picked the wrong person out of the lineup.

In the control condition, calibration was poor. Participants appeared to be underconfident at the lower confidence levels and overconfident at higher confidence levels. Both reflection and disconfirmation instructions improved overall levels of calibration. The disconfirmation instructions decreased the amount of overconfidence that occurred at high confidence levels, but did not decrease the problem of underconfidence at lower confidence levels. This makes sense. The disconfirmation manipulation seems designed to weaken confidence levels. On the other hand, the reflection strategy appeared to both limit overconfidence at high confidence levels and to limit underconfidence at the lower confidence levels.

In another study, Brewer and Wells (2006) examined how confidence was related to the diagnosticity of a lineup choice. Recall from Chapter 2 that diagnosticity is the ratio of correct identifications of suspects to incorrect identifications of suspects. For instance, a diagnosticity of 10 would indicate that when a witness identifies a suspect, it is 10 times more likely that the suspect is guilty than that the suspect is innocent.[2] Figure 5.8 shows the relationship between confidence and diagnosticity in Brewer and Wells's study. It is difficult to look at the relationship without being impressed. Consider the participants who indicated that they were 90–100% confident in their lineup choice. The ratio of correct identifications to false identifications in those participants was more than 30 to 1. Compare that to participants who indicated that they were 50–60% confident. The ratio of correct identifications to false identifications for those participants was around 5 to 1.

Clearly a diagnosticity ratio of 30 to 1 is impressive. The authors, however, advise caution in interpreting these results. First, it is noteworthy that this study used an eight-person lineup. Because diagnosticity is the ratio of correct suspect identifications to incorrect suspect identifications,

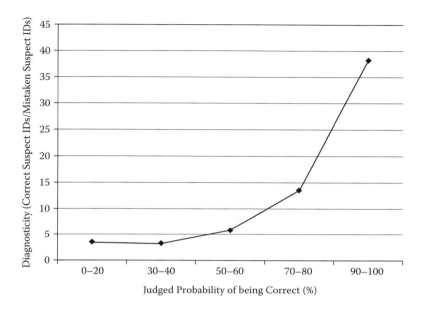

FIGURE 5.8 Relationship between confidence and diagnosticity in Brewer and Wells (2006). Confidence was measured as the judged probability of being correct. Diagnosticity is the probability of a correct identification in a target-present lineup divided by the probability of a false identification of the suspect in a target-absent lineup. (*Source*: Based on data presented in Brewer, N., & Wells, G. (2006). The confidence–accuracy relationship in eyewitness identification: Effects of lineup instructions, foil similarity, and target-absent base rates. *Journal of Experimental Psychology: Applied, 12,* 11–30.)

theoretically, using a lineup with a large functional size should increase diagnosticity because false identification of foils will be the predominant error in the target-absent lineup. Second, Brewer and Wells (2006) point out that the data were collected under close to ideal conditions, with few external pressures that might inflate confidence judgments. Later we discuss in more detail, research showing that confidence is malleable and can be distorted by external factors.

Conclusions

What do we make of the accuracy–confidence relationship? The overall lesson of the past 3 decades of research on eyewitness identification is that broad generalizations (i.e., eyewitnesses are unreliable) are misleading. However, we have learned some important lessons about the relationship between witness confidence and accuracy. Under ideal circumstances, witness confidence may be a useful, but far from perfect, predictor of accuracy. However, this positive conclusion is limited in two regards. Witnesses are often overconfident, especially at the high ends of the confidence scale. As a result, a witness who indicates that he or she is absolutely certain of his or her identification may be correct around 80% of the time. Additionally, as we will see shortly, confidence can be quite malleable, and this malleability can lead to high levels of confidence without correspondingly high levels of accuracy (see Wells et al., 2002). All of these considerations suggest that caution should be applied in evaluating eyewitness confidence. This is readily apparent if one looks at the DNA exoneration cases (Scheck, Neufeld, & Dwyer, 2000). Many of those cases involved highly confident witnesses who were nevertheless mistaken.

Witness Demeanor

The above discussion focuses on the witness's stated confidence and the witness's accuracy. Another potential indicium of the reliability of a witness concerns the ability of members of the jury to judge witness accuracy based on viewing the witness's demeanor. Lindsay, Wells, and Rumpel (1981) used a three-part procedure to examine how well people can judge witness accuracy based on viewing the witness's testimony. In part 1 of the procedure, participants saw a staged theft of a calculator. Participants were then shown a six-person lineup and were asked to make an identification from the lineup. In part 2 of the procedure, witnesses who had made an identification were cross-examined as they would be in court. These cross-examinations were videotaped. In the third part of the procedure, a new group of participants were shown videotapes of these cross-examinations and were asked to pick which witnesses were accurate and which witnesses were inaccurate. Results indicated that participants were unable to distinguish between accurate and inaccurate witnesses. These results suggest that merely viewing a witness who has undergone cross-examination may not be sufficient to allow jurors to judge the accuracy of the witness.

Memory for Other Details

Another factor specifically mentioned in *Neil v. Biggers* (1972) concerns the accuracy of the witness's prior description. The basic premise of this aspect of the decision is that if people are accurate at recalling details of the perpetrator's appearance or other aspects of the crime, then they should also be accurate in their lineup identification. This view has a good deal of intuitive appeal. In one study, Bell and Loftus (1989) compared mock jury decisions in cases where the witness recalled seemingly trivial details with cases where they did not recall these details. Witnesses were seen as being more credible when they could recall more details, even if they were superfluous (see also Bell & Loftus, 1985, 1988).

Although the view that recall of person and event details should be related to recognition of the perpetrator in the lineup, basic memory research suggests that this relationship may not always hold. Indeed, among memory researchers an important distinction is made between tasks that involve recall and tasks that involve recognition (Loftus & Loftus, 1976). Recall tasks require the participant to generate information (e.g., "Tell me what the robber looked like"), whereas recognition tasks require the participant merely to pick items that were previously pre-sented (e.g., "Is this a picture of the robber?"). It is well known among memory researchers that recall and recognition are not always strongly related (Adlam, Malloy, Mishkin, & Vargha-Khadem, 2009; Balota & Neely, 1980; Bastin et al., 2004; Karlsen & Snodgrass, 2004; Kintsch, 1968; Tulving & Wiseman, 1975). In a recent meta-analysis, Meissner, Sporer, and Susa (2008) examined studies that had compared eyewitness identifi-cation with the quality and quantity of the description given. They found that the relationship between these variables was typically weak. Across studies, the correlation between description accuracy and recognition accuracy was only .14 (recall that a perfect correlation would be 1.00 and a lack of any relationship at all would be indicated by a correlation of 0.00). Moreover, when the authors examined details of the studies they were reviewing, they found that the correlation between description accuracy and recognition accuracy was greatest for artificial laboratory simulations and lowest for more naturalistic experiments. The correlation was also lower in studies that used a longer delay between the description and recognition portions of the experiment.

Quantity of descriptive information generated was an even worse pre-dictor of recognition accuracy, resulting in a mean correlation across stud-ies of −.04. The negative correlation indicates that witnesses who included more details in their descriptions tended to be slightly less accurate in their identification decisions (although this negative correlation was not statistically significant). This review of the literature suggests that, con-trary to U.S. Supreme Court opinions, the degree of match between a witness's description of a perpetrator and the person chosen from the lineup may not be a very useful indicium of reliability.

Response Time

As an alternative to some of the above indicia of reliability, Sporer (1992) suggested that the speed with which a witness makes an identification might be a useful index of how accurate the witness is likely to be. Sporer argued that decision time was a useful index because, unlike confidence, recollection, and observations of demeanor, choice time can, at least in principle, be objectively measured. This can be done by videotaping the identification procedure, or the police detective can even use a stopwatch to time the witness. There are good reasons for thinking that decision time ought to be related to accuracy. Theories of recognition memory (i.e., Ratcliff & Starns, 2009) view recognition judgments as involving the accumulation of evidence for and against a particular choice until sufficient evidence is collected to make a decision. When there is a lot of evidence in favor of a particular choice, and little evidence against that choice, the process of accumulating evidence will proceed quickly, resulting in fast accurate responses. Additionally, Dunning and Stern (1994) have argued that accurate witnesses tend to rely on automatic decision processes, whereas inaccurate witnesses tend to utilize a time-consuming process of elimination (see section on self-reported strategy use for more details on this view).

Sporer (1992) tested the proposition that response time could be used as an index of accuracy in a lineup identification task. Participants thought they were taking part in a perception experiment. As the experimental procedures were being explained, a target individual entered the room and insisted that the projector being used by the experimenter was needed by another professor. This resulted in a verbal confrontation between the confederate and the experimenter, who refused to give up the projector. The whole incident lasted about 20 seconds. One week later, participants returned to the laboratory, where they provided verbal descriptions of the target and were presented with a seven-person target-present or target-absent simultaneous lineup. The results supported the view that decision time could be used to predict accuracy. In particular, looking at only those participants who made a choice out of the lineup (i.e., choosers), the correlation between decision time and accuracy was −.43 (pretty strong for a point biserial correlation). Participants who choose someone from the lineup but who took a long time to make their choice were less likely to be accurate than were participants who made their choice quickly. Witnesses who identified someone quickly were also more confident in their identifications and provided more detailed descriptions of the target. In later research, Sporer (1993) examined decision times in both simultaneous and sequential lineups. Once again, when looking at people who made choices from the lineup, accurate witnesses were faster in making their choices (M = 3.61 seconds per lineup member) than were inaccurate witnesses

(M = 8.06 seconds per lineup member). Decision time was a useful predictor in both simultaneous and sequential lineups. Note that response time is a good indicium of accuracy for witnesses who make choices from lineups, but does not appear to be a good indicium of accuracy for witnesses who reject lineups (Dunning & Stern, 1994)

A short time later Dunning and Stern (1994) reported similar findings. In their study, participants were shown a videotape of a man stealing money from a purse. Following the videotape, participants answered a series of questions that took about 5–10 minutes. Participants were then asked to make a choice from a five-person lineup. Response times were recorded across three separate experiments. Results indicated that accurate witnesses tended to make choices more quickly than inaccurate witnesses. Across the experiments, accurate witnesses picked someone in an average of 38.4 seconds. Inaccurate witnesses picked someone in an average of 63.9 seconds. Notice that these response times are quite long. The reason for this is that in addition to making a choice, participants were also verbalizing all of their thoughts as they were making their decisions.

In another experiment examining the relationship between response time and accuracy, Smith, Lindsay, and Pryke (2000) showed participants a videotape of a criminal stealing money from a woman's purse. Participants were then asked to view either a target-present or target-absent lineup. Across participants, these lineups varied in quality with some lineups being biased and some unbiased. The experimenter noted how long it took the participant to make a decision, either using a watch or a digital clock that was on the wall. Time to make a decision was negatively correlated with accuracy ($r = -.38$). Witnesses who made a decision in fewer than 15 seconds were correct 69.4% of the time. Witnesses who took between 16 and 30 seconds were correct 42.6% of the time. Witnesses who took more than 30 seconds were correct only 17.6% of the time.

If faster witnesses are more accurate witnesses, is there an ideal speed that discriminates accurate from inaccurate witnesses? Dunning and Perretta (2002) suggested a 10–12-second rule that claimed that accurate witnesses tend to make decisions in about 10 seconds or so. In their studies, they performed a *time boundary analysis* to try to determine what the optimal response time was for eyewitness identification. A time boundary analysis is a statistical analysis in which accuracy prior to a particular time boundary is compared to accuracy following that time boundary. For instance, imagine that the time boundary one is interested in is 5 seconds. In a time boundary analysis, one would compare accuracy for witnesses who responded within 5 seconds with the accuracy of witnesses who responded in more than 5 seconds. This analysis is then repeated across a range of time boundaries (e.g., 6 seconds, 7 seconds, 8 seconds … 60 seconds). The analysis then finds the time boundary that produces the largest accuracy difference. Across four studies, Dunning and Perretta found that the time boundary that produced the largest difference tended to be about 10–12 seconds.

It is important to note what this finding means. It does not mean that witnesses who take more than 12 seconds are necessarily inaccurate. Indeed, Dunning and Perretta (2002) found no time boundary where witness accuracy fell to chance. Rather, what the time boundary analysis tells us is that the largest change in accuracy occurs when one compares witnesses who respond in 12 seconds or less with witnesses who respond in more than 12 seconds. In fact, Dunning and Perretta reported data showing that witnesses who made an identification in 10 seconds or less had an average accuracy of around 87%. When witnesses took between 11 and 20 seconds to make an identification, accuracy dropped to around 52%. For witnesses who took 21–30 seconds to make an identification, accuracy was around 51%. And for witnesses who took 31–40 seconds, accuracy dropped to around 40%. Dunning and Perretta (2002) argued that the main reason why fast decisions tend to be more accurate is because they reflect relatively automatic absolute judgment strategies, whereas slower decisions reflect more strategic relative judgment strategies. Because automatic judgments are, by definition, quite rapid, Dunning and Perretta proposed that the 10–12-second time boundary should be relatively stable across situations.

Not all eyewitness experts agree that there is anything magical about the 10–12 seconds rule. In particular, Weber et al. (2004) have argued that, although faster responses tend to be more accurate than slower responses, the optimal response time for identifying accurate eyewitness identifications can vary considerably depending upon conditions. In particular, Brewer et al. suggested that sometimes accurate responses occur due to automatic processes that occur with relatively little attention, but that other times accurate responses may require a time consuming search throughout the entire photoarray. In these situations, the optimum time boundary would depend on a number of factors, including the size of the lineup, how similar the foils are to the target, the placement of the suspect in the lineup, how degraded the witnesses' memories are, and so on.

To examine the generalizability of the 10–12 seconds rule, Weber et al. reanalyzed results from four of their previous experiments. The four studies that were reanalyzed were quite variable. They differed in terms of stimuli used, retention interval, and one study included children as participants. All data was reanalyzed just as in Dunning and Perretta's (2002) research by making use of a time boundary analysis. Consistent with prior research, all four of the data sets showed that accurate identifications tended to be made more quickly than inaccurate identifications. Across the experiments, the mean time for accurate witnesses to make an identification was 19.18 seconds, whereas the mean time for inaccurate witnesses to make an identification was 24.92 seconds. However, when the time boundary analyses were conducted, they did not support the 10–12 seconds rule. Indeed, across the data sets the optimal time boundary was quite variable, ranging from around 5 seconds to about 24 seconds.

The above studies suggest that both confidence and response speed can provide useful indicia of accuracy. However, these studies have primarily relied on laboratory identification tasks. Recently, Sauerland and Sporer (2009) examined the utility of confidence and response speed in evaluating eyewitness accuracy in a naturalistic setting. Participants were approached on the street by a confederate who asked for directions. After the confederate left, participants were approached by an experimenter. The experimenter showed them either a target-present or target-absent lineup. The experimenter recorded the amount of time taken to make the decision and also asked participants to indicate their confidence using a 100-point scale. The results indicated that both response time and confidence were very helpful in distinguishing between accurate and inaccurate witnesses and that they were even better predictors when used in combination.

Taken together the results of all these experiments support three conclusions. First, accurate identifications tend to be made more quickly than inaccurate identifications, suggesting that time taken to make an identification is likely to be a useful indicium of eyewitness reliability. Second, accurate rejections of lineups do not appear to be related to response time. Last, although faster witnesses tend to be more accurate, there is no magic line (10–12 seconds) that can be used to distinguish accurate from inaccurate witnesses.

Self-Reported Strategy Use

As we discussed in Chapter 2, Wells (1984) proposed an important theory of how witnesses make decisions when presented with lineups. According to Wells's account, there are two basic strategies that witnesses use when presented with a lineup. One strategy is called an *absolute judgment strategy*. Absolute judgment strategies involve examining each member of the lineup and determining whether that lineup member is the perpetrator, without reference to the other members of the lineup. The other strategy is called a *relative judgment strategy*. Relative judgment strategies involve comparing and contrasting members of the lineup in order to pick the best choice. According to Wells, relative judgment strategies tend to be error prone. The reason for this is that in a target-absent lineup, there will always be some member of the lineup who is the best match to the witness's memory. It is this basic idea that underlies the use of the sequential lineup as we saw in Chapter 4.

Dunning and Stern (1994) took this basic idea and tested whether people's self-reported strategy use could provide a useful indicium of reliability. Participants in the study were shown a videotape that included a scene in which a man stole money out of a woman's purse. Following the videotape, the participants answered a series of questions and were then shown a five-person target-present lineup. Participants chose someone from the lineup or indicated that the perpetrator was not present in the lineup. Subsequent to the identification (or lack thereof), the participants indicated how confident they were in their judgment. Participants were also asked how they made their choice from the lineup. Choices (and people could choose more than one) included some items that focused on absolute judgment strategies. These included, "I just recognized him, I cannot explain why" and "His face just 'popped out' at me." Other choices focused on relative judgment strategies. These included "I compared the photos to each other to narrow the choices," "I first eliminated the ones definitely not him, then chose among the rest," and "He was the closest person to what I remember, but not exact." As an additional measure of the use of absolute versus relative judgment strategies, Dunning and Stern asked people the degree to which the other lineup members influenced their choice. If one is using an absolute judgment strategy, then the other lineup members should not influence the choice. If one is using a relative judgment strategy, then by definition the other lineup members are influencing the choice.

Dunning and Stern (1994) reported four experiments in which they used this basic procedure. They compared witnesses who made accurate identifications with those who made inaccurate identifications in terms of the number of times they indicated they used an absolute versus a relative judgment strategy in reaching their decision. Figure 5.9 shows the overall results from the four experiments. As can be seen, absolute judgment strategies were more likely to be used by accurate witnesses than by inaccurate witnesses. On the other hand, relative judgment strategies were more likely to be used by inaccurate witnesses than by accurate witnesses.

☐ Malleability of Confidence and Other Indicia of Reliability

Based on what we have discussed thus far, one might reach the conclusion that there are a number of indicia of reliability that can be of great help to the jury in judging the likely accuracy of a witness. These indicia are by no means perfect (e.g., witnesses tend to be overconfident), but they

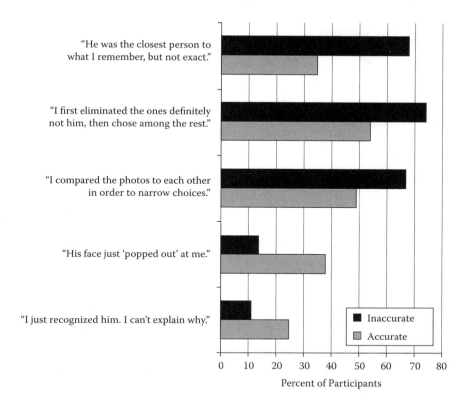

FIGURE 5.9   Self-reported use of absolute versus relative judgment strategies reported by Dunning and Stern (1994). (*Source*: Based on data presented in Dunning, D., & Stern, L. B. (1994). Distinguishing accurate from inaccurate eyewitness identifications via inquiries about decision processes. *Journal of Personality and Social Psychology, 67*, 818–835.)

somewhat track accuracy. Unfortunately, the cases where confidence and other indicia of reliability are most helpful tend to be fairly idealized situations. Nowhere is this more apparent than in research demonstrating that confidence and other indicia of reliability can be highly malleable.

By *confidence malleability*, we mean that outside influences can alter a witness's statement of confidence. In particular, witnesses who receive feedback that their choices were correct not only report higher levels of confidence but also report that they had a better view, paid more attention, and are more willing to testify than witness who receive no feedback (Lampinen et al., 2007; Neuschatz et al., 2007; Quinlivan, Wells, & Neuschatz, 2010; Wells & Bradfield, 1998). Throughout this section, we discuss several types of feedback that can inflate eyewitness confidence.

Co-Witness Effects

As we discussed in Chapter 4, when there is more than one witness to the same crime, witnesses may be exposed to information about what another witness said. If a witness finds out that another person identified the same person that she or he did, this can serve to reinforce the witness's judgment, and increase her or his confidence. In one study, participants viewed a staged theft, and then made individual lineup identifications from target-absent photospreads (Luus & Wells, 1994). Participants were subsequently given false information regarding their co-witnesses' identification (e.g., the other witness had "also identified her"). Participants who were told that they selected the same person as the other witness ended up being more confident than participants in a no-feedback control group. This was true even if the experimenter later told the participant that the feedback was mistaken—that actually the other witness had chosen someone else or that the experimenter was not sure who the other witness had chosen. Note that the participants were not explicitly told whether their identifications were correct. The experimenter simply told the participants that they had made the same choice as the co-witness they were partnered with.

In an interesting twist, participants in Luus and Wells's (1994) experiment were interviewed by confederates posing as campus police officers, and the interview was videotaped. These videos were shown to mock jurors, who were asked to rate how accurate they thought each witness was. When mock jurors saw witnesses who had been told that they had chosen the same person as the other witness, they rated the witnesses as being more accurate and believable than the no-feedback controls. Thus, knowledge that another witness made the same choice not only increased witnesses' confidence in their identifications but also made their testimony more believable to jurors.

Information about co-witnesses can influence confidence in both target-present and target-absent lineups. For instance, Semmler, Brewer, and Wells (2004) showed participants a videotape of a crime. Following the videotape, participants were presented with either a target-present or target-absent lineup. After they made their decision, a screen popped up on the computer telling them that 87 participants had been in the experiment to date and 84 of them made the same decision as the participant. Rated confidence following this feedback increased for both target-present and target-absent lineups, relative to a no-feedback control.

Other researchers have confirmed the above findings and extended the results to other kinds of judgments. For instance, Skagerberg (2007) presented participants with a short video of a man stealing a cell phone. Witnesses were tested in pairs and shown target-absent photo lineups. Following their identification decisions, participants were asked to tell each other who they picked. In some cases the individuals chose the same person from the lineup (i.e., confirming feedback), and in other cases the individuals chose different people from the lineup (i.e., disconfirming feedback). Following this feedback, participants filled out questionnaires asking them to indicate their level of certainty as well as a number of other specific questions about their experiences as witnesses. Relative to witnesses who received disconfirming feedback, witnesses who received confirming feedback from their co-witness were more confident in their identifications, estimated that they made their identification more quickly, had lower estimates of the difficulty of making an identification, indicated that in general they had good memories, and indicated that they had a clear image of the suspect in their mind. Thus, not only does feedback from co-witnesses influence the subjective sense of certainty, but also it can impact the witness's memory for other indicia of reliability.

Knowledge of Self-Incriminating Statements

Knowledge of other kinds of incriminating information can also lead to confidence inflation. In particular, if witnesses become aware that the person they identified made self-incriminating statements, it can result in an inflated sense of retrospective confidence on the part of the witness. This was demonstrated in a recent study by Hasel and Kassin (2009). Participants viewed a staged theft of a laptop from an experiment room. Participants were then told that the theft had actually been staged as part of a study on criminal investigations. The experimenter indicated that he did not know who had actually stolen the laptop and that he was being evaluated to see whether he would be able to solve the "crime." The experimenter then showed the participants a six-person target-absent lineup, and asked them to identify "which person, if any, stole the laptop today." Immediately after the lineup, participants indicated how confident they were. Two days later, participants who had made an identification were told that the suspect they identified had confessed, that the suspect they identified had denied involvement, that a different suspect had confessed, or that all suspects had denied involvement. After receiving this information, participants rated their retrospective confidence in the identification they had previously made. Hearing that the suspect they identified confessed led to large increases in retrospective certainty. Hearing that the suspect denied involvement, that all suspects denied involvement, or that somebody else had confessed led to substantial decreases in confidence.

Postidentification Feedback

Some studies have examined the impact of feedback provided directly by the lineup administrator. This has been referred to as *postidentification feedback*. For instance, after an identification is made, a lineup administrator may tell a witness, "Good job!" or "Yup, that's our guy." Feedback from lineup administrators may be especially problematic. A lineup administrator is an authority figure, and it is not surprising that witnesses may assume that a lineup administrator has special access to information (e.g., fingerprints or ballistics) that makes her or him a reliable source of information. Thus, if a lineup administrator tells a witness, "Good job—you identified the suspect," this may have a big impact on the witness's subsequent confidence.

In one study, Wells and Bradfield (1998) had participants watch a clip from a security camera video and attempt to identify the culprit from a target-absent lineup. Following their identifications, some participants were told that they had selected the suspect (i.e., confirming feedback), others were told they had selected the wrong suspect (i.e., disconfirming feedback), and others were given no feedback. Participants who were given confirming feedback not only were more confident about their selections but also indicated that they had paid more attention to the perpetrator, had a clearer view of the incident, had a clearer image of the culprit's face in their memory, and were more willing to testify than participants who were not given feedback.

The effect of postidentification feedback is extremely robust and reliable (see Bradfield and Steblay, 2006, meta-analysis). The effects have been demonstrated using a wide variety of dependent measures, have been found to persist over a one-week retention interval (Neuschatz et al., 2005), and have been observed in witnesses of varying ages (Hafstad, Memon, & Logie, 2004; Neuschatz et al., 2005; Quinlivan et al., 2010). What makes the postidentification feedback so problematic is that the effects are not restricted to confidence. Postidentification feedback also distorts witnesses' reports of many other relevant factors such as how good their view was when the event occurred, how much attention they paid during the event, and numerous other factors relevant to the quality of their evidence.

Think of the potential harm this can cause in the criminal justice system. As we have seen, jurors are especially willing to accept eyewitness identification testimony when an eyewitness is confident about the identification (e.g., Cutler, Penrod, & Dexter, 1990; Fox & Walters, 1986; Luus & Wells, 1994; Wells, Ferguson, & Lindsay, 1981). Thus any defendant, guilty or innocent, who is identified in court by a confident witness is more likely to face prison time. Now consider the data from Quinlivan, Wells, and Neuschatz (2010). Participants made identifications from target-absent lineups and were given either confirming feedback or no

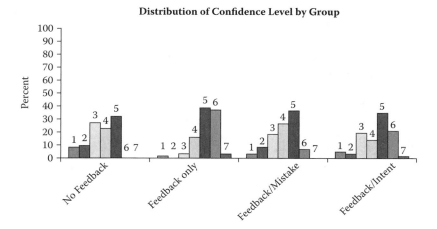

FIGURE 5.10 Confidence as a function of confirming feedback from Quinlivan, Wells, and Neuschatz (2010). (*Source*: Based on research published by Quinlivan, D. S., Wells, G. L., & Neuschatz, J. S. (2010). Is manipulative intent necessary to mitigate the eyewitness post-identification feedback effect? *Law and human behavior, 34*, 186–197.)

feedback. Following the feedback, participants indicated their confidence using a 7-point scale. The results are shown in Figure 5.10. Not a single participant in the no-feedback condition reported a certainty level above 5. However, *feedback-only* participants reported a high certainty level—6 or 7—40% of the time. It is not unreasonable to think that a good proportion of those defendants would have been convicted. These effects are even more worrisome given that there are no legal prohibitions that we know of against police or lineup administrators giving confirming feedback in most jurisdictions.

The harmful effects of postidentification feedback have been demonstrated in real-world settings (Wright & Skagerberg, 2007). Wright and Skagerberg asked real eyewitnesses questions about how certain they were in their testimony. After choosing from an identity parade—a video lineup—eyewitnesses were asked questions about their identifications before and after receiving feedback from the police about the accuracy of their selections. As in laboratory studies, witnesses who were told they picked correctly showed confidence inflation and witnesses who were told that they picked incorrectly demonstrated lower confidence than people who were given confirming feedback.

To help explain the postidentification feedback findings, Wells and Bradfield (1998) suggested an *accessibility–inference* account. As in Kassin's (1985) retrospective self-awareness account, they argued that witnesses typically don't have privileged access to what their mental state was at the time of the identification. When a witness is asked about his or her confidence at the time of the identification, or how good of a view he or she had, the witness cannot simply retrieve that information from memory. Rather, witnesses are likely to use memory for other information, such as the feedback they received, in order to infer the answers to these sorts of questions. For instance, a witness might infer that because she was told that she made a correct identification, she must have had a good view, paid close attention, and been confident at the time of the identification. Wells and Bradfield (1998, Experiment 2) tested the accessibility–inference account by having participants give confidence ratings before receiving feedback and then again after receiving feedback. They argued that this procedure would force participants to think about certainty, view, and other factors, and store this information in memory. As predicted, the feedback effect was reduced in those participants who received the confidence question prior to the feedback. Wells and Bradfield referred to this as the "confidence prophylactic effect."

Unfortunately, this effect may be short-lived. Quinlivan et al. (2009) and Neuschatz et al. (2007) found that the confidence prophylactic effect works immediately but not after a one-week retention interval. Quinlivan et al. (2009) demonstrated that there is differential forgetting of memory traces, so that after a week retention interval the feedback is remembered but the confidence statement is forgotten. This problem is likely to be exacerbated in forensic settings because there is usually a substantial amount of time that passes between when an identification is made and when testimony is given at trial.

The effect of postidentification feedback occurs because the person providing the feedback (e.g., police officer) is a trusted authority figure. Lampinen et al. (2007) examined whether the postidentification feedback effect could be reduced if participants were led to believe that the source of the feedback was unreliable. To examine this issue, participants were shown the videotape of the rooftop bomber that had previously been used in research by Wells, Olson, and Charman (2003). After viewing the video, participants were presented with either a target-absent lineup or a target-present lineup on a computer monitor. Participants indicated which lineup member they believed had been on the rooftop by pressing one of the number keys on the computer. Following this response, the computer paused momentarily, then provided confirming feedback, disconfirming feedback, or no feedback. The feedback was randomly generated regardless of the participant's actual choice. Subsequent to the feedback, participants completed a postidentification survey with questions about confidence, viewing conditions, and so on. Prior to completing the survey, half of the participants were told to ignore any feedback they received, because the feedback had been randomly generated by the computer. The other half of the participants were told nothing about the reliability of the feedback. Participants who were told nothing about the reliability of the feedback showed the typical postidentification feedback effect. Participants who received confirming feedback were more confident that their answers were correct than participants who received no feedback or disconfirming feedback. However, feedback had no effect on confidence for participants who were told that the feedback had been randomly generated.

Lampinen et al.'s experiments demonstrated that telling participants that the feedback they received was unreliable can greatly reduce the effect of postidentification feedback. Merely telling people to ignore the feedback and rely on their own memories did nothing to ameliorate the effect of postidentification feedback (Lampinen et al., 2007, Experiments 3 and 4). Consistent with this view, Neuschatz et al. (2007) examined whether inducing suspicion about the lineup administrator's motives would weaken the postidentification feedback effect.[3] Inducing suspicion has been found to reduce biases in other psycholegal contexts, such as the impact of prejudicial pretrial publicity and inadmissible evidence on jury decision making (Fein, Hilton, & Miller, 1990). Neuschatz et al. (2007) tested this idea by having participants view a video and complete a lineup identification task from a target-absent photo lineup. After making an identification, some participants were given confirming postidentification feedback, whereas others were given no feedback regarding their lineup choices. Either immediately or after a one-week retention interval, participants were taken to another room by a different experimenter. Some participants who received feedback were given reasons to entertain suspicion regarding the motives of the lineup administrator (e.g., "Did the first experimenter tell you that you chose the right person from the lineup? She is telling everybody that, and it can't possibly be true, can it?"). Subsequently, participants answered a questionnaire regarding their identifications. Neuschatz et al. found that inducing suspicion eliminated the effects of the feedback. The authors hypothesized that making the participants suspicious of the motives of the lineup administrator led the participants to question the validity of the feedback and to adjust their ratings of their confidence in their identifications.

There are at least two possible reasons why suspicion might reduce the postidentification feedback effect. One possibility is that when participants become suspicious, they may ignore the feedback provided by the administrator and may be more apt to rely on their own memories while answering questions. One might call this a *suspicious perceiver hypothesis*. Alternatively, suspicion may induce a reactance-like process. Reactance is a motivational state that occurs when an individual perceives that a personal freedom or entitlement may become unavailable due to a threat (Brehm, 1966). In the case of suspicion, participants may feel that they were manipulated by the experimenter and attempt to regain their freedom by revising their initial rating in the opposite direction of the experimenter who deceived them (i.e. lower ratings of confidence, view, attention, and so forth). The difference between the two accounts is that reactance does not really involve the witness relying on their own memory. Rather, it simply involves a kneejerk reaction. The witness does the opposite of what they think the interviewer is trying to get them to do.

The suspicion manipulation employed by Neuschatz et al. (2007) had two components. One was the suggestion that the feedback was not necessarily correct. In this case, the second experimenter said this to participants: "Were you told that you selected the correct person in the lineup? She [the lineup administrator] is telling everyone that. I know for a fact … not everyone is correct." The second component was a suggestion that the lineup administrator intentionally and willfully tried to influence the witnesses' answers by inducing a false belief. For example, participants were told, "She is trying to make the DA happy," or, "They are trying to prove the accuracy of eyewitness identifications." When participants are told they are being intentionally manipulated into believing that they are correct in order to make them appear to be accurate, both hypotheses predict a reduction in the postidentification feedback effect. However, when no manipulative intent is implied, as in cases where participants were told that the experimenter just made a mistake, then the reactance hypothesis does not predict a reduction in the confidence inflation. By contrast, the suspicious perceiver hypothesis implies that there will be a reduction in the effect in such cases because witnesses still have reason to doubt the ground truth of what the lineup administrator told them.

Quinlivan, Wells, and Neuschatz, (2010) tested these competing hypotheses by varying the apparent manipulative intent of the lineup administrator. In their manipulative intent condition, participants were told that the lineup administrator had lied to them about the accuracy of their identifications. In the mistake condition, the feedback was discredited without implying a manipulative intent on the part of the feedback provider. In this case, participants were told that the experimenter read instructions from the wrong condition and unintentionally gave false feedback about the accuracy of the participants' identifications. The results revealed that manipulative intent was not necessary for the suspicion to reduce the confidence-inflating effects of postidentification feedback.

So what can be done about the effects of postidentification feedback? A defense attorney could simply raise suspicion in the mind of a witness. However, this is not as easy as it sounds. It is rarely the case that the identification procedures are recorded. Therefore, it is generally impossible to know whether feedback was given. Second, it is unclear whether the witness will believe a defense attorney who tells them the police made inaccurate statements. Lineup administrators are police investigators, and for the most part, police investigators are seen by the public as being trustworthy sources of information. Attorneys might also ask witnesses whether or not feedback influenced their judgments. Unfortunately, research indicates that witnesses are unable to accurately report whether they were influenced (Charman & Wells, 2008).

Another solution might be to alert jurors of the potentially biasing effects of postidentification feedback. In a direct test of the effects of admonishments about postidentification feedback on jurors' judgments, Douglas, Neuschatz, Imrick, and Wilkerson (2010) investigated the effect of postidentification feedback on mock jurors. Participants watched interviews of eyewitnesses who had been given confirming feedback, disconfirming feedback, or no feedback. After watching the videos, mock jurors evaluated the witnesses on several testimony relevant issues (e.g., confidence, view, and attention). Witnesses who received confirming postidentification feedback were evaluated as more accurate and more confident. In Experiment 2, similar effects were obtained even though some mock jurors heard instructions about how feedback distorts witness memories. Taken together, these studies support researchers' claims that prefeedback judgments should be recorded and preserved for use at trial (e.g., Kassin, 1998; Wells & Bradfield, 1998) and that double-blind lineup administration procedures should be routinely implemented (e.g., Douglass, Smith, & Fraser-Thill, 2005; Haw & Fisher, 2004).

Administrator Bias

In Chapter 4 we reviewed how lineup administrators' expectations can influence the choices made by a witness. Recall that if a lineup administrator knows who the suspect is, the administrator may unintentionally cue the witness to pick the suspect. Not only can administrator expectations influence lineup choices, but also they can influence the witness's subsequent confidence. This makes a good deal of sense. If you are a lineup administrator and you know that the suspect is in position D of the photoarray, it might be difficult for you not to show some satisfaction on your face or through your body language or even verbally, if the witness picks D.

This effect was demonstrated in a study by Garrioch and Brimacombe (2001). In the study, participants arrived in pairs, and one was assigned the role of lineup administrator, whereas the other was assigned to the role of witness to the crime. While the witness watched the videotaped crime, the lineup administrator was told which person in the lineup was the perpetrator but was also instructed to keep this information from the witness. In fact, the perpetrator was not in the lineup—it was a target-absent lineup. After the witness watched the video, the witness and the lineup administrator were reunited for the identification task. The results were significant: Witnesses were more likely to choose the person who the lineup administrator believed to be the culprit. They were also more confident about their selections than witnesses who made selections that differed from the lineup administrator's expectations. When asked if the lineup administrator had any influence on their decision, witnesses indicated that the administrator did not in any way influence their choice.

Malleability of Confidence

The results reviewed in this section show that confidence and other indicia of reliability can be distorted in a number of different ways. Combating this problem requires taking systematic steps to keep witnesses from being influenced by outside sources. This includes (a) not letting them hear about other evidence in the case, (b) obtaining an explicit statement of confidence from them prior to providing them with any feedback, and (c) using double-blind administration procedures (see Chapter 4) so the lineup administrator does not inadvertently influence the witness's choice or subsequent confidence in that choice.

☐ Indicia of Reliability

The results reported in the present chapter provide evidence that there are a number of indicia of reliability that can help legal professionals judge the likely accuracy of eyewitnesses. Used cautiously, these variables can be of some help in evaluating eyewitness testimony. It is important to keep in mind, however, a number of factors that may limit the utility of these variables. First, most of the variables included in this chapter are based on subjective first-person reports. These reports undoubtedly correlate with underlying memory processes, but can also be influenced by pre-event and postevent factors. As already mentioned, one of these factors is feedback given by law enforcement subsequent to the identification. This feedback can inflate confidence, change memory for decision processes, and alter the witness's perception of their decision time and witnessing conditions (Wells & Bradfield, 1998). Feedback of this sort can be given directly by law enforcement (i.e., "You've identified the correct suspect") or in the form of co-witness effects (i.e., "I picked out number 3 too") (Luus & Wells, 1994). These sources of contamination can seriously undercut the utility of the indicia of reliability that have been covered in this chapter. Second, although confident witnesses tend to be more accurate than less confident witnesses, and fast witnesses tend to be more accurate than slower witnesses, the relationships between these variables are far from perfect. Indeed, witnesses may be relatively poorly calibrated in terms of assessing confidence, and research suggests that overconfidence is pretty common among witnesses (Brewer et al., 2002). Indeed, the results we reviewed showed that when witnesses select the highest confidence level, they tend to be accurate about 80% of the time. That is lower than near ideal witnessing conditions. When comparing conflicting stories from two witnesses, it is possible that one witness may be overconfident and the other witness maybe underconfident. Indeed, DNA exoneration cases teach us that even highly confident witnesses can sometimes be mistaken (Scheck, Neufeld, & Dwyer, 2000). Thus, although the indicia of reliability described in this chapter can be useful, one should use them with these potential limitations in mind.

☐ Endnotes

1. Recipe available from the authors upon request.
2. Assuming that the base rate of guilty suspects is 50%.
3. Suspicion has been formally defined as the orientation in which the perceiver maintains the possibility that multiple causes may be influencing the actor's behavior and that the actor may be hiding something that might change the meaning of that behavior (Fein, Hilton, & Miller, 1990).

CHAPTER

Field Studies of Eyewitness Identification

□ *United States v. Mark Gilliam*

On March 23, 2006, at around 10:00 p.m. in Morristown, Tennessee, an armed robber walked into a Pizza Plus Restaurant and motioned to the manager to be quiet by putting his finger to his mouth and pointing his gun at her. The manager was ordered to go to the cash register and put the money on the counter. The manager complied and put around $450 on the counter. The manager described the culprit as wearing black sweatpants, a black sweatshirt, and a bandanna that covered his face from the bridge of his nose to the top of his shirt collar.

Several days later the manager was brought to the police station and asked to describe the culprit so the police sketch artist could develop a composite (see Chapter 4). The sketch was drawn with a bandanna covering the lower half of the face. The lead detective on the case told the victim that he thought he recognized that caricature in the sketch. A few days later, the victim was again called down to the police station and this time was asked to look at a photospread lineup. The detective told her to look at the lineup and to indicate which of the people in the lineup was not the perpetrator. After 15–20 minutes the victim was able to exclude all the photographs except for the persons in positions 1 and 4. The photograph in position 1 was Mark Gilliam. Following a little deliberation, the detective collected the two remaining photographs and used a black sharpie to color in a bandanna over the two remaining faces. After the pictures were altered, the victim identified Mark Gilliam as her assailant.

Gilliam eventually confessed to the armed robbery charge as well as some other charges in order to avoid being classified as an *armed career criminal.* Under the Armed Career Criminal Act, an *armed career criminal* is defined as anyone who has three prior convictions for a violent felony or drug offense. The charge of armed career criminal carries a mandatory additional 15-year sentence served consecutively after all other sentences are completed with no eligibility for parole. Without the plea bargain Mark Gilliam would have met the prerequisite conditions to be an armed career criminal. The federal judge in this case would only accept the plea bargain if Gilliam admitted to the victim that he was the one who robbed the pizza parlor. Although Gilliam agreed to confess to the robbery, he maintained that he did not commit this crime but would obey the judge's conditions in order to procure the best deal with the least amount of jail time for himself.

Only Mark Gilliam will ever know if he really robbed the pizza parlor. It is true that, during the trial, he confessed to other crimes that he did not adamantly deny after the fact. Based on our previous review of the literature, there are factors present in this particular case that could affect eyewitness accuracy such as the disguise worn by the culprit (Cutler & Penrod, 1988; Cutler, Penrod, & Martens, 1987a, 1987b), the weapon (Pickel, 2007), and the probability of a high stress level for the witness (Deffenbacher, 1981). With regard to lineup identification, factors such as verbal overshadowing (Schooler et al., 1986), biased lineup instruction (Levett & Kovera, 2008), multiple identification attempts (Hinz & Pezdek, 2001), and the lineup administrator knowing the identity of the suspect in the lineup (Phillips et al., 1999) could also influence the accuracy of the identification.

Most of the findings that are relevant to Gilliam's case, and that we have reviewed throughout this book, were initially demonstrated in laboratory settings. Studies of eyewitness memory typically involve undergraduate students who knew they were participants in psychology experiments. Some commentators have wondered whether the findings from laboratory research can be generalized to real-world cases (Konecni & Ebbesen, 1986; McCloskey, Egeth, & McKenna, 1986; Yuille, 1993).

There are several ways of addressing the issue of whether laboratory studies can be generalized to real-world crimes. First, although laboratory eyewitness studies are certainly not identical to actually witnessing a crime, they are designed to tap psychological mechanisms (e.g., memory, attention, and social influence) that are present in real-world situations. It would be odd to think that there is one set of psychological mechanisms that is present in laboratory settings and another set of psychological mechanisms that is present in the *real world.* The degree to which different psychological constructs are present in the laboratory and real-world settings may differ, but the general operation of these constructs is likely to be similar. Consider a variable like psychological stress. In laboratory studies it has typically been found that increased levels of stress lead to poorer eyewitness identification (see Chapter 3).

Although it certainly is the case that we can never duplicate the degree of stress in the laboratory that may occur in some crimes, there is no reason to think that in the real world stress improves memory, whereas in the laboratory stress impairs memory.

A second approach to address this issue is to ask, "How do the real-world eyewitness scenarios differ from the particular laboratory study we are examining?" The answer to that question can provide a set of variables that differ between the two settings. Those variables themselves can then be systematically manipulated (in laboratory settings) to see if they matter. For instance, in the mid-1980s there was a renewed interest in the suggestibility of child witnesses, brought on partly by a series of high-profile child sexual abuse cases. A good deal of research demonstrated that preschool-aged children are oftentimes more suggestible than are older children and adults (for a review, see Ceci & Bruck, 1995). Rudy and Goodman (1991) pointed out that one difference between these studies and the real-world application of these studies was that in the real-world application, the child was often a victim of abuse, not merely an observer of what was happening. Based on a solid theoretical rationale, Rudy and Goodman reasoned that being an active participant in an event is likely to have different memorial consequences than being a passive observer. To test this hypothesis, they conducted a clever study in which children either observed a game of Simon Says or actually played the game. They found that children who merely observed the game were more likely to be influenced by misleading questions than were children who actually took part in the game. This approach to the question of generalizability of laboratory research is powerful, because it identifies key differences between naturalistic settings and laboratory settings and actually tests whether those differences make a difference.

Another important method for testing the generalizability of laboratory research is to move the research into the field (Yuille, 1993). In a field study, eyewitness researchers collect data on actual eyewitness identification attempts and try to draw conclusions based on that data about the variables that influence eyewitness accuracy. The advantage of field research is that the results quite clearly are about real eyewitnesses making identifications in actual forensic settings. The disadvantage of field research is the lack of experimental control. Clearly the best approach to understanding the factors that influence eyewitness accuracy is to use both laboratory and field research as sources of converging evidence.

In an alarming number of the cases that have been overturned due to DNA evidence, mistaken eyewitness identifications have played a key role (see www.innocenceproject.org). The psychological community has published volumes of laboratory research on why this would be the case (Neuschatz & Cutler, 2008). Unfortunately there are only a handful of field studies of eyewitness identification, partly because the studies are so difficult to carry out. Increasingly, psychologists are being called upon to testify as expert witnesses in cases involving disputed eyewitness identification evidence. The lack of field research has been employed as an argument to exclude this expert testimony. The rationale is that laboratory studies are so dissimilar to actual crimes that the laboratory research is not meaningful for jurors when they consider the facts. We believe this reasoning is flawed. However, to the extent that eyewitness identification experts are excluded, issues that may influence the reliability of identification may be overlooked or ignored, which may adversely affect the falsely accused and lead to more wrongful convictions. Clearly field studies can help provide a response to these objections.

To this point, there have been nine major field studies conducted on eyewitness memory (Behrman & Davey, 2001; Behrman & Richards, 2005; Klobuchar, Steblay, & Caligiuri, 2006; Mecklenburg, Malpass, & Ebbesen, 2006; Pike, Brace, & Kynan, 2002; Slater, 1994;[1] Tollestrup, Turtle, & Yuille, 1994; Valentine, Pickering, & Darling; 2003; Wright & McDaid, 1996). As can be seen, many of the field studies have only recently been published. The plan of this chapter is to review the field studies in chronological order. More specifically, for each study we will review the methodology, list the major results of the study, and indicate how the results compare to findings from the laboratory research. In the penultimate section we consider all the studies collectively and ascertain whether the laboratory research is consistent with the data from the field, as well as draw conclusions about the findings from these studies. In the final section we will discuss future research and challenges for researchers conducting field studies.

Comparisons between field studies and laboratory studies are fraught with many problems. We will discuss some of these issues later in the chapter. However one of the chief difficulties is that in the laboratory you know if the witnesses are correct, whereas in the field you do not. Field studies typically deal with this issue by treating suspect identifications as a proxy for accurate identifications and foil identifications as a proxy for inaccurate identifications. This approach is clearly imperfect. It is true that foil identifications are known false identifications, and thus provide an indication of how often witnesses will select an innocent lineup member. However, suspect identifications are not always accurate. Rather, suspect identifications are a mixture of correct identifications of guilty suspects and false identifications of innocent suspects.

There is also one other important point to consider when examining field studies of eyewitness identifications. Field studies depend on an examination of police records in order to determine relevant case characteristics, suspect identifications, foil identifications, and so on. The accuracy of these studies depends in part on the accuracy and systematicity of the police records. Wells (2006) pointed out that police records may not always be detailed or accurate enough to draw valid conclusions. To give one example, when a photospread is conducted and the witness chooses a foil, the investigator may identify this as a foil identification or may simply document it as a failure to identify the suspect (see also Tollestrup, Turtle, & Yuille, 1994). This variability may well lead to an underestimate of the number of false identifications in field studies. Field researchers thus are dealing with impoverished information, and they need to be aware of these limitations. With these limitations in mind, we next turn to the results of existing field studies of eyewitness identification.

□ Tollestrup, Turtle, and Yuille (1994)

Methodology

Tollestrup et al. (1994) conducted an archival study using the files from the Royal Canadian Mounted Police in the Vancouver Suburbs. The cases were taken from 1987 to 1989. The records included 119 robberies and 66 fraud cases. The researchers recorded descriptive information from each crime file such as date, time of day, number of eyewitnesses, perpetrators, and weapon presence. In addition they also garnered, from the police reports, information about the relationship between those involved (witness vs. victim, or friend vs. stranger), eyewitness descriptions, use of mugshots, as well as type of identification (live lineup, photospread lineup, or showup) and the outcome of the lineup.

Results

Tollestrup et al. analyzed the number and type of descriptors used to describe the culprits. The details in the descriptions were categorized as physical (e.g., height, weight, and hair color) or clothing. Each descriptor was assigned a point. Witnesses and victims provided more physical than clothing descriptors. All eyewitnesses displayed the same pattern with regard to accuracy. As compared to the police reports, witnesses tended to provide higher estimates of age and lower estimates of height and weight than was actually true for the suspect.

Overall, there were 170 identification attempts, and over 90% were photospread lineups. Tollestrup et al. created three categories of evidence strength: no evidence, some evidence implicating suspect, and a confession. The confession was considered the strongest category of evidence. The suspect identification rate was lowest in cases in which there was no evidence (17.5%). When there was a confession, the suspect identification rate rose to 47%, and when there was some implicating evidence the suspect identification rate was 41.9%.

One of the strongest patterns to emerge was the negative effect of time on the suspect identification rate. That is the suspect identification rate for robberies when the identification procedure was less than one day after the crime was 71.43%. By contrast, if the retention interval between the crime and the identification was 7–34 days or 34 or more days, then suspect identification rate dropped to 33.33% and 14.29% respectively. With respect to presence of a weapon, a very small number of the crimes in the data set actually included a weapon ($n = 77$). Only 30.61% of identification attempts made when a weapon was present at the crime resulted in a suspect identification, whereas the suspect identification rate was 73.33% when there was no weapon present. Furthermore eyewitnesses to crimes with weapons involved provided more details then eyewitnesses to crimes in which there was no weapon present.

Comparison With Laboratory Results

The result that suspect identification decreases after a retention interval from the time of the crime to the time of the identification is consistent with scientific research (Dysart & Lindsay, 2007b). In their meta-analysis Shapiro and Penrod (1986) examined the effect of delay on facial recognition. Shapiro and Penrod found a negative effect of delay on both accurate and false identifications, with the average delay being just over 4 days. Cutler, Penrod, O'Rourke, and Martens (1986), in the context of an eyewitness identification study, found a significant effect of delay as participants were more likely to make positive target identifications and less likely to make false identifications after a delay of 7 days between the event and the identification as opposed to 28 days.

With regard to weapon presence, the result of fewer suspect identifications when a weapon was present is also consistent with the weapon focus effect. Steblay (1992) meta-analyzed 19 empirical studies of the weapon focus effect. Of the 19 studies she examined, six demonstrated a significant weapon focus effect, whereas 13 found null results. When the results of these studies were combined, the weapon focus effect for identification accuracy was significant but relatively small in magnitude. The weapon focus effect was larger among studies which used more ecologically valid research designs.

It is important to note that an inherent problem with field studies is that predictor variables tended to be confounded with one another. In the present study, weaponless crimes tended to be associated with identification attempts which occurred after a shorter delay. Moreover, presence of a weapon is also related to the type of crime (i.e., fraud versus robbery). This confounding of predictors makes interpretation difficult.

☐ Wright and McDaid (1996)

Methodology

This study was conducted in the greater London area in 1992. All identifications took place at one of two specialty suites or at one of the police stations in London. Specialty suites were created in several London areas because it is hard to find foils that match the description of the culprit. In theory the suites are supposed to minimize these problems by having a list of the innocent volunteers who are willing to serve in the live lineups. This study is different from the prior study in that the researchers collected the data as the identifications were being conducted, as opposed to collecting the information from files that already existed. There were a total of 1,561 witnesses and 616 suspects.

Results

Overall 611 witnesses or 39.1% of the sample picked the suspect from the lineup. Almost 20% of the witnesses picked a foil and 41% refused to choose from the lineup. In addition, the race of the suspect and length of time between the event and the lineup significantly affected choosing rates. When the suspect was white, witnesses were less likely to choose anyone out of the lineup, and as the delay between the event and the lineup increased, witnesses were more likely to make a foil identification.

Comparison With Laboratory Results

The retention interval results are consistent with both Tollestrup et al. (1994) and the laboratory research (Shapiro & Penrod, 1986). Length of delay significantly and negatively affected suspect identification rates. The results regarding the race of the suspect are more difficult to interpret within the existing cross-race identification literature. The major difficulty is that the race of the witnesses is not reported. Thus, it is unclear if the race of the suspect interacted with the race of the witness because both race of the witnesses and suspect are needed to evaluate cross-race identification. At the very least, it is clear that race had a major influence on the suspect identification rate.

☐ Behrman and Davey (2001)

Methodology

In this archival study, Behrman and Davey analyzed files from the Sacramento City Police Department as well as crimes committed in neighboring northern California counties. There were a total of 271 cases analyzed that consisted of 349 crimes of which the vast majority were armed robbery. The crimes were committed between 1987 and 1998. There were a total of 689 identifications that included 258 field showups, 289 photographic lineups, 58 live lineups, and 18 photo showups. The data were analyzed for race of victim, race of criminal, presence of a weapon, and whether a victim or a witness made the identification. For the purposes of the analyses, the cases were broken into three categories based on the strength of the evidence reported in the police files. Cases that included extrinsic incriminating evidence were divided into two categories: those with substantial probative value (SPV) and those with minimal probative value (MPV). Examples of substantial probative value might include a confession or the culprit being caught on a surveillance tape, whereas examples of minimum probative value would be anonymously provided information or information from an unreliable source such as a jailhouse informant or accomplice. The third strength of evidence category was no extrinsic evidence (NEE). The NEE category refers to cases in which there is no reliable evidence linking the suspect to the crime. Finally, the data were coded as to whether the victim or witness identified the suspect or a foil.

Results

Behrman and Davey (2001) reported that a little under half of the identifications resulted in suspect identifications. The delay from the time that the crime occurred and the time that the identification was administered was a significant factor in suspect identification rates, and this was especially true when the extrinsic evidence had substantial probative value (SPV). More specifically, in the SPV condition suspect identifications were approximately 64% if they occurred within 0–7 days of the crime, but dropped to 33% if the identification occurred 8 or more days after the crime.

With regard to cross-race identification, the overall suspect identification rate in cross-race identification cases was 45%, which was significantly lower than the same race identification rate (60%). This difference was significant in the MPV and NEE conditions but not in the SPV condition. There was no significant effect of the presence of a weapon on suspect identification. The suspect identification rate was 48% and 51% for crimes with a weapon and without a weapon respectively. There was also no difference in the suspect identification rates for victims versus witness. The suspect identification rate for live lineups was 50%, which is very similar to the suspect identification rate for photospread lineups (48%).

The overall suspect identification rate for field showups was 76%. This rate rose to 91% for showups that were conducted within a day of the crime. The showup suspect identification rate (76%) was significantly higher than the identification rate for field showups that occurred with 0–7 days of the crime. The identification rate for showups was not significantly influenced by race or weapon focus. It is noteworthy that in a showup, the only possible choice is the suspect. So all identifications in showups are suspect identifications. It is therefore not clear if the higher suspect identification rate in showups reflect greater levels of accurate suspect identifications or greater levels of false suspect identifications.

Comparison With Laboratory Results

The results regarding cross-race identification are consistent with the scientific literature. That is, it has been consistently found that eyewitnesses are less accurate when they have to identify someone from a different race (Brigham, Bennett, Meissner, & Mitchell, 2007). For example, in their meta-analysis Meissner and Brigham (2001) found that eyewitnesses were 1.4 times more likely to correctly identify members of their own race than members of other races, and they were 1.56 times more likely to falsely identify members of other races than members of their own race. This meta-analysis included 31 separate studies involving 91 separate experimental tests of own versus same-race identifications. The studies included in the meta-analysis involved over 5,000 participants. These results are clearly consistent with those of Behrman and Davey, who found more same race suspect identifications in the MPV and NEE conditions. However, cross-race and own-race identification rates were similar in the SPV condition. It may be that an overwhelming amount of evidence in the SPV conditions trumps other factors like cross-race identification.

Similarly, with respect to retention interval, the results are consistent with both the scientific literature (Cutler et al., 1986; Dysart & Lindsay, 2007b; Shapiro & Penrod, 1986) as well as with the Tollestrup et al. (1994) study. Furthermore, in the Behrman and Davey study, this relationship was apparent regardless of the amount of evidence, but it was especially strong when the evidence was strongest. Behrman and Davey found no effect of weapon presence on suspect identification rates. This was true regardless of the strength of the evidence. However, recall that in laboratory studies, the weapon focus effect tends to be weak and to have a larger effect on detail accuracy than identification accuracy (see Chapter 3 for a discussion).

Results for showups are consistent with laboratory research. Generally speaking, laboratory studies have found higher suspect identification rates in showups than in lineups, with the difference being primarily attributable to greater false suspect identifications of suspects in showups than in lineups.

☐ Pike, Brace, and Kynan (2002)

Methodology

Pike et al. (2002) collected data from three different sources: police force data, identification surveys, and police interviews. The police force data consisted of examining an existing archival identification database from eight different English police forces. The database included outcome data on 18,475 identification procedures. The identification archive also consisted of detailed surveys of the identification procedures from nine English police forces. Included in this data set were characteristics of the witnesses and perpetrators as well as the nature of the offense. The interviews were composed of 50 in-depth interviews with police officers who worked in identification suites and criminal investigation departments in 14 police departments.

Results

Pike et al. (2002) reported that 52% of the identification procedures were canceled before they ever occurred. Of the identification procedures that occurred, 49% resulted in suspect identification, which means that only 23% of the identification procedures that were arranged resulted in suspect identifications. There were no data provided on whether the remaining 51% resulted in foil identification or no choice. Pike and colleagues also provided data on the suspect identification by type of crime. Robbery and burglary resulted in the lowest rate of suspect identifications. The authors reported that violence, threat of violence, or presence of a weapon were associated with more suspect identifications, although it is unclear whether these were accurate or inaccurate identifications.

One factor that was related to identification outcome was age of the witness. Child witnesses and elderly witnesses made fewer suspect identifications than young adults. Specifically, the identification rate for witnesses who were younger than 18 years old was 46%. Witnesses 60 years of age or older identified the suspect 29% of the time. By contrast, the corresponding suspect identification rate for 17–21-year-olds and 22–29-year-olds were 58% and 54%, respectively.

The interview and survey data revealed several interesting procedural problems. Officers reported that conducting live identifications is a logistical nightmare because it requires all relevant parties to be at the same place at the same time and that they all be separated from each other once they arrive on location. This latter point makes sense because it would be unwise for the suspect and the witness to be in the same room before the identification, as this could potentially cause bias in the lineup and jeopardize the fairness of the lineup. Many officers reported that delays were a frequent problem with live lineups and that these delays sometimes would have serious consequences for the outcome of the identification. The survey revealed the average time between the request for the identification procedure and the lineup actually occurring was around 10 weeks. The officers acknowledge that some of the delays were due to administrative problems such as finding suitable foils. However, the officers also felt the defense attorneys deliberately delayed the procedure as a way of affecting the outcome of the identification procedure.

Comparison With Laboratory Results

The finding that older adults made fewer suspect identifications is consistent with laboratory research. There is a large and growing literature that demonstrates that elderly eyewitnesses are more likely than younger witnesses to make identification errors after viewing an event (Searcy et al., 1999, 2000, 2001). In fact, recent laboratory research has shown that elderly adults make 25–50% more errors on identification tasks than younger adults (Searcy et al., 1999, 2000), and these errors tend to be exacerbated as the retention interval increases (Searcy et al., 2001). These findings suggest that internal memory records are already weak when elderly participants make lineup identifications immediately after the event, which signals greater difficulty with the passage of time as memory traces fade progressively with delay (see Chapter 3 for more details).

If one assumes that suspect identifications are a good proxy for accuracy, then the finding that violence, threat of violence, or presence of a weapon were associated with more suspect identifications is at odds with current scientific data on stress and weapon focus. With regard to stress, a meta-analysis conducted by Deffenbacher et al. (2004), examined 27 separate tests of the impact of stress on identification accuracy. Across all studies of identification accuracy, stress significantly and negatively affected the likelihood of correct identification ($h = -.52$, corresponding to correct identification rates of .19 in the high-stress conditions and .34 in the low-stress conditions). However, suspect identifications may not be a good proxy for accuracy in this case. It may be that higher stress crimes led to higher choosing rates and thus more suspect identifications. Pike et al. found that the presence of a weapon did not affect suspect identification rate. This finding is consistent with the typically weak effect of weapon presence on identification found in laboratory studies.

☐ Valentine, Pickering, and Darling (2003)

Methodology

Valentine et al. (2003) collected data from four identification suites that served the greater London area from January 2000 to September 2000. There were a total of 664 witnesses and 323 lineups. Investigating officers provided the following data for the witness: age, race, gender, relationship (witness, friend, bystander, or victim), approximate time the witness had to view the culprit during the crime, view, lighting quality, the distance from the suspect, and whether or not the suspect had a gun. For the suspect, the police gathered data on age, race, gender, height, build, type of crime, and the number of days from the crime to the lineup identification. Officers recorded the following details about the lineup: outcome of the lineup (suspect identification, foil identification, or no choice), the speed with which the identification decision was made (fast, average, or slow), and the difficulty involved in creating the lineup.

Results

Valentine et al. (2003) broke down their data into witnesses who knew the suspect ($n = 56$) versus those who did not ($n = 584$). Witnesses who were familiar with the suspect, not surprisingly, identified the suspect 73% of the time. These witnesses made foil identification 5% of the time and elected not to choose from the lineup 21% of the time. The rate of suspect identification was 41% when the witness did not know the suspect and the foil identification rate 21%. The no-choice rate was 39% for these stranger identifications.

Valentine et al. also analyzed a number of variables that effect a witness's view of the crime (i.e., duration of viewing the culprit, lighting quality, view, and distance). Witnesses who had more than a minute to view the culprit were more likely to make suspect identifications as opposed to witnesses who viewed the culprit for less than a minute. Poor lighting conditions and obstructed view were associated with fewer suspect identifications (although these findings were not statistically significant in the regression analysis). Distance was not significantly related to suspect or foil identification rates, although this may be because the comparison made involved a dichotomous comparison between witnesses who were closer than 2 meters and those who were further than 2 meters. It may be that this breakdown may not have been the optimal comparison.

There were 584 witnesses and 295 lineups for which weapon presence data were available. Overall there were 238 witnesses who reported seeing a weapon during the crime and 346 who did not see a weapon. The presence of a weapon had no significant effect on suspect identification, foil identification, or the no-choice rate. The type of weapon (knife, gun, or other) also had no significant effect on identification rates. The effect of cross-race identification fell in the predicted direction as there were more suspect identifications in the same race as opposed to different race conditions. More specifically, the suspect identification rate was 45.1% when the witnesses and the suspect were of the same race, as opposed to 37.4% when the witnesses and suspect were from different races. Race of the suspect and witness did not affect the percentage of foils identified.

Comparison With Laboratory Results

The results of exposure time are consistent with both the memory and the eyewitness literature. Exposure duration is often associated with more identifications (Davies, Ellis, & Shepherd, 1977; MacLin, MacLin, & Malpass, 2001; Shapiro & Penrod , 1986), although as we saw, increased duration can also lead to more false identifications under some circumstances (see Chapter 2). Both lighting conditions and view were also associated with decreased suspect identifications, a finding consistent with laboratory studies. The fact that there were no significant effects of presence of a weapon on suspect or foil identification is consistent with the laboratory findings. As we saw in Chapter 3, laboratory studies of the weapon focus effect have tended to produce only weak effects when the dependent variable is the accuracy of the identification.

As noted above, the researchers failed to observe a significant effect of distance; however, this finding likely reflects the way distance was operationalized. The researchers compared identifications made by witnesses who were less than 2 meters from the perpetrator at the time of the crime with identifications made by witnesses who were more than 2 meters from the perpetrator at the time of the crime. This way of breaking down distance may not have been optimal for observing an effect of distance (see Chapter 3).

☐ Behrman and Richards (2005)

Methodology

In this study, Behrman and Richards employed the same archival database used in Behrman and Davey (2001) from the Sacramento City Police Department. For this study, there were a total of 183 cases analyzed for 219 crimes. Once again, the vast majority were armed robbery (n = 163). There were a total of 689 identifications that included 424 photographic lineups and 37 live lineups. For the data analyses, the cases were broken into the same three categories used in Behrman and Davey (2001). Cases were divided into three categories: those with substantial probative value (SPV), those with minimal probative value (MPV), and those with no extrinsic evidence (NEE). Finally, the data were coded as to whether the victim or witness identified the suspect or foil. All of the lineups were single-suspect lineups, and photographic lineups included six photos. Live lineups contained either five or six people.

Results

A total of 238 witnesses or 52% made suspect identifications and 15% identified a foil as the perpetrator. The authors also investigated how well witness confidence discriminated witnesses who chose the suspect from witnesses who chose a foil from the lineup. In order to analyze this issue, confidence statements from both groups were broken down into three categories that translated into high, medium, and low confidence based on the degree of confidence expressed in the witness's statements. For example, if the witness said they were absolutely certain that it was the perpetrator, their statement would go in the highest confidence category. If the witness said that it kind of looks like the culprit, then their statement would be classified in the category representing the least amount of confidence.

The verbal confidence statement did in fact distinguish witnesses who chose a suspect versus those who chose a foil. More specifically, witnesses who were classified in the highest confidence category were more likely to choose the suspect, and witnesses who expressed less confidence were significantly less likely to choose the suspect. This pattern was particularly pronounced when there was at least some extrinsic evidence (i.e., SPV and MPV categories) in the case. In addition to confidence, participants who did not use a process of elimination strategy were more likely to choose the suspect as opposed to a foil.

Comparison With Laboratory Results

The confidence data are broadly consistent with prior research. As we saw in Chapter 5, witness confidence is far from a perfect predictor of accuracy. Indeed, calibration studies show that witnesses tend to be overconfident, meaning that a witness who indicates that he or she is 100% confident might be right 80% of the time, even under very good witnessing conditions. However, the calibration studies also show that, on average, confident witnesses are more accurate than less confident witnesses. This empirical generalization is consistent with Behrman and Richards's (2005) findings.

There is also another possible interpretation of Behrman and Richards's (2005) findings with regard to confidence. The identification procedures used by the investigators in these cases were not double blind. As we saw previously, when an investigator knows who the suspect is, he or she may give verbal or nonverbal cues that indicate to the witness whether or not they chose the suspect. These subtle cues can serve as postidentification feedback, and we know that postidentification feedback can result in an increase in expressed levels of confidence (Wells & Bradfield, 1998). Thus, it might be that the confidence results obtained by Behrman and Richards reflect the following scenario: (a) When a witness picks a foil, the investigator provides feedback indicating that the choice was not the suspect, and the witness confidence declines; whereas (b) when a witness picks a suspect, the investigator provides feedback indicating that the choice was the suspect, and the witness confidence increases. Given the large corpus of research showing the effects of postidentification feedback, this seems like a plausible account of the findings.

The result that faster lineup selections were associated with more suspect identifications and fewer foil identifications accords nicely with the experimental research (Brewer, Weber, & Semmler, 2007; Dunning & Stern, 1994). Witnesses who choose quickly tend to be more accurate (i.e., more suspect identifications and fewer foil identifications) relative to witnesses who take longer to choose from the lineup (Dunning & Stern,

1994; Smith, Lindsay, Pryke, & Dysart, 2001; Sporer, 1993, 1994). However, the actual time boundary for what discriminates accurate from inaccurate witnesses is still up for debate. Dunning and Perretta (2002) found that 10–12 seconds might be the time stamp that discriminates accurate from inaccurate witnesses. More recently, Weber, Brewer, Wells, Semmler, and Keast (2004) argued that boundary might extend out to as far as 29 seconds. In addition, the fact that a process of elimination strategy led to fewer suspect identifications is consistent with the theory behind lineup choosing. Wells and colleagues (see Wells, 1993) have long argued that relative judgment strategies lead to more errors.

☐ Klobuchar, Steblay, and Caligiuri (2006)

Methodology

The study was conducted in Hennepin County, Minnesota. The four cities that were included were Minneapolis, Bloomington, Minnetonka, and New Hope. Overall the data comprised 280 lineups from 117 cases with 206 eyewitnesses. All of the lineups were double-blind sequential lineups. The instructions used in every lineup were unbiased, meaning that the witness was informed either in written form or verbally that the culprit may or may not be in the lineup. The data were collected directly from the police officers' reports. The officers conducting the lineups were instructed to include in their reports information regarding lineup structure and administration, crime type, identification choice, speed of identification, and statements regarding certainty. For each lineup, lineup administrators were required to use different photos for all new suspects, witnesses were to be interviewed privately, unbiased instructions were used, identifications were to be followed up with a statement regarding certainty of the choice, photos were shown one at a time, witnesses were to look through all photos regardless of whether or not they had chosen a suspect, witnesses were allowed to look through the photos more than once, and the officer conducting the lineup was unaware who the suspect was. The procedures varied a little between cities, but these are the basic protocols followed by all lineup administrators in participating precincts.

Results

It is important to note that Klobuchar et al., (2006) did not use a control group—a simultaneous lineup with biased instructions or a sequential lineup with biased instructions—so that all the comparisons they made were with the extant psychological literature on simultaneous and sequential lineups. The suspect identification rate was 54% in the Hennepin County (HC), which is similar to the target identification rate found in the laboratory with simultaneous target-present studies (50%) but higher than the target identification rate from sequential target-present lineup studies (35%). The foil identification was much higher in the laboratory studies than in the HC study. The percentage of foil identifications was 8% in HC as opposed to 24% for simultaneous target-present laboratory studies and 19% for sequential laboratory studies.

With regard to allowing participants to repeatedly see the photos as noted by Klobuchar et al. (2006), this is different from the typical laboratory study. The typical laboratory procedure is only to let witnesses go through the lineup photos one time as opposed to allowing as many viewings as they want. This could make the sequential lineup into what Klobuchar et al. (2006) referred to as a de facto simultaneous lineup, which might eliminate the advantage of sequential lineups. Repeated viewing of the photos did lead to significantly more foil identifications. When the suspect was a stranger and the witness was allowed to view the photos more than once, the foil identification increased to 29%, as opposed to 3% when the suspect was a stranger and the witness only viewed the photos one time. As expected, suspect identifications were much higher when the suspect was someone the witness already knew (90%) as opposed to being a stranger. The number of witnesses not willing to select from the lineup was much higher when the suspect was a stranger (53%) as opposed to someone the witness knew (6%). Unfortunately, only 15% of the officers included confidence statements in their reports. The low reporting made it very difficult to interpret the confidence data for a variety of reasons, chief among them being that the researchers do not know what other factors were different about the way in which the lineups were conducted by officers who obtained confidence statements relative to those who did not.

Comparison With Laboratory Results

The data are broadly consistent with the data on simultaneous lineups from the Steblay et al. (2001) meta-analysis. The suspect identification rate in HC (54%) is similar to the 50% accuracy rate for target-present simultaneous lineups. The foil identification rate is lower in HC data than in the meta-analysis. However, when we compare HC results with sequential lineups, the data are less consistent. The HC suspect identification rate is much higher than the target identification rate for sequential target-present lineups (50% vs. 35% respectively). The benefit of sequential lineups is that they are supposed to reduce false identifications from target-absent lineups without reducing correct target identifications. In the HC data, there was a lower foil identification rate (8%) than either simultaneous (24%) or sequential (19%) laboratory data. If we accept suspect identifications as a proxy for accurate identifications in the HC data, which is admittedly a big stretch, then it is indeed the case that sequential lineups lead to similar correct identifications as compared with simultaneous lineups and fewer false identifications. Exactly what sequential lineups are predicted to do was found in Steblay et al. (2001).

☐ Mecklenburg, Malpass, and Ebbesen (2006)

Methodology

Mecklenburg et al. (2006) collected data from three cities in Illinois: Chicago, Joliet, and Evanston. The police in each city were asked to collect data in two ways: sequential double-blind lineups and simultaneous lineups. Each jurisdiction was asked to assign individual lineups to either lineup procedure on their own as long as they satisfied three criteria. First, the assignment had to be random and not predetermined. The case officer could not make the decision. Second, the officer involved in the studies would have to administer both simultaneous and sequential lineups. Third, the assignment had to be random with respect to the type of crime committed. This was done so that crime type would not be a confounding variable. Mecklenburg et al. also had the officers collect data on foil identification, no choice, and suspect identifications for both sequential and simultaneous lineups. In addition, the authors also examined factors known to affect eyewitness identification, such as delay between the crime and the lineup, cross-race identification, stranger versus known suspect, duration of the crime, age of the witness, and multiple perpetrators.

All identifications conformed to the following protocols. Witnesses were explicitly told that they did not have to choose from the lineup, that the culprit may or may not be in the lineup, and that they should not assume that the police officer knew the identity of the suspect. For sequential lineups, witnesses were given additional instructions informing them that they had to make a decision on each photograph shown, that they would see the remaining pictures even if they chose a suspect, and they were told that they could have the opportunity to see the photographs again.

The reporting forms for the officers were standardized to ensure that all the data were collected precisely. The first form required information regarding date, case number, type of crime, district where the crime occurred, type of lineup, and whether the identification was a live physical lineup or a photospread lineup. This form also required the lineup administrator to supply the witness' age, suspect's age, race, whether the suspect had changed his appearance since the crime, and whether the crime contained multiple offenders. The second form required the officer to collect the data regarding the lineup identification, such as whether the witness chose the suspect, chose the foil, or made no choice.

Results

Overall there were 548 stranger identifications and 71 identifications of known suspects. Of the 548 stranger identifications, there were 319 simultaneous lineups and 229 sequential double-blind lineups. The results revealed that simultaneous lineups led to more suspect identifications (59.9%) and fewer foil identifications (2.8%) than double-blind sequential lineups in which the suspect identification rate and foil identification rate were 45% and 9.2% respectively.

The authors also analyzed identification rates for photospread lineups conducted inside the police station and those conducted outside the police station for both simultaneous and double-blind sequential lineups. The results showed that foil identifications were higher for the sequential procedure regardless of where the lineup was conducted. However, the rate of foil identifications increased for both procedures when they were conducted in the field as opposed to the police station.

The researchers also investigated cross-race identification in both lineup procedures. For procedures when the suspect and the witness were from different races, the suspect identification rate was significantly higher in simultaneous lineups as opposed to the sequential double-blind procedure, but there was no significant difference in foil identification rates. In same-race lineups, the suspect identification rate was the same for both lineups but the foil identification rate was higher in sequential lineups (12.6%) than in simultaneous lineups (2.0%).

Those witnesses who viewed the sequential lineup more than one time made fewer suspect identifications, slightly more foil identifications, and fewer no picks when compared to witnesses viewing simultaneous lineups. Overall, there were no significant differences between identifications made by victims and by bystanders. In simultaneous lineups, victims were more likely than bystanders to identify the suspect. The suspect identification rate for sequential procedures did not vary with regard to whether the person making the identification was a victim or a bystander. Finally, there was no significant effect of delay, age of victim, violence, or weapon presence on identification rates.

Comparison With Laboratory Results

The interpretations of the results from the Mecklenburg et al. (2006) are very controversial and have generated a great deal of debate in scientific literature—so much so that there have been no less than 16 commentaries on the field study, including a special issue of *Law and Human Behavior*. The results that have drawn the most attention are the low rate of foil identifications in the simultaneous nonblind conditions relative to the sequential double-blind condition. This finding is at odds with not just laboratory findings but also previous field studies. As we have seen, foil identification rates in field studies where simultaneous lineups have been examined are typically around 20%. Thus a finding of a foil identification rate of 2.8% appears anomalous. Given the amount of attention that the Mecklenburg et al. (2006) study has received, we felt it was important to briefly review the major criticism outlined in some of the commentaries. This will also serve as a segue into the final section of this chapter.

The major criticisms of the field study were twofold. First, almost all commentators pointed out that there was a major confound which jeopardizes the conclusions that can be drawn from the data. That is that lineup administrators were only blind to the identity of the suspects in the sequential lineup condition and were aware of the identity of suspect in the simultaneous lineup. That's a big confound! Wells (2008) argued that this confound makes interpretation of the results impossible; as it is unclear whether the results are due to the lineup procedure or administrator influence. Wells (2008) goes on to argue that nonblind simultaneous lineups would lead to experimenter expectancy effects. These expectancy effects should in turn cause less foil identifications in those conditions in which the lineup administrator was aware of the identity of the suspect. This is exactly the result that was found in the field study for only the simultaneous lineup, which was not conducted in a double-blind manner.

The second criticism can be termed the overreliance on foil choosing as a substitute for lineup effectiveness. In field studies it is impossible, in most cases, to know if the suspect is in fact the culprit, but foil identifications are known errors. So even if the researchers do not know if a correct decision is made, foil identifications can be compared for each lineup technique to provide a known-error rate. This strategy can indeed produce valuable data, if and only if the conditions in the experiment are equal or the same on all factors other than the lineup technique. The problem that arises in the Mecklenburg et al. (2006) study stems from the above mentioned confound of the simultaneous conditions being nonblind and the sequential conditions being double blind. This confound stacks the deck in favor of fewer foil identifications in the nonblind conditions. In Mecklenburg et al. (2006), the simultaneous lineups were never conducted in a double-blind fashion. This is why meaningful comparisons between the two lineup procedures in this study—simultaneous and sequential lineups—are very problematic. Thus, it is impossible to make comparisons with the laboratory research.

☐ Overall Patterns From the Field Studies

Collectively, the results of field investigations are, for the most part, consistent with findings from laboratory studies in terms of the overall pattern of the results. One clear finding was the negative effect of retention interval on suspect identifications. Three of the four studies that included retention interval as a variable found that as the time between the crime and the identification increased, the likelihood that the suspect would be identified decreased. Similarly, the effects of race were also consistent with what would be expected from the laboratory research. The scientific literature is clear that identifying people from different races decreases target identifications and increases foil identifications (Meissner & Brigham, 2001; Neuschatz & Cutler, 2008). Consistent with this, Behrman and Davey (2001) and Valentine, Pickering, and Darling (2005) both found that suspect identifications were reduced when the suspect and the witness were from a different race as opposed to the suspect identification rate when the witness and the victim were from the same race. Two other studies that examined race of suspect did provide enough information to evaluate whether a cross-race effect was present in the data. Wright and McDaid (1996) reported that the suspect identification rate was higher when the suspect was African American as opposed to Caucasian. However, they do not report the race of the witness, so it is impossible to know if this effect is a cross-race effect or whether some other factor is causing the effect. Mecklenburg et al. (2006) reported that when the suspect and the witness were from different races, the suspect identification rate was significantly higher in simultaneous lineups as opposed to a sequential double-blind procedure. Foil identification rates were statistically the same in both lineup procedures regardless of race. In lineups in which the victim and the witness were from the same race, the suspect identification rate was the same for both lineups, but the foil identification rate was higher in sequential lineups than in simultaneous lineups. It is unclear what the results from this study mean in terms of the cross-race effect because the authors do not report the effect of cross-race conditions either within each lineup type or overall. Taken together, the results of these studies are consistent with the findings expected if there was a cross-race bias.

Four of the field studies examined the effect of weapon focus on suspect identification. In only one of these studies (Tollestrup et al., 1994) was a significant association found between the presence of a weapon and lower suspect identification rates. These findings are consistent with laboratory studies, which typically find only weak effects of weapon presence on identification rates. Indeed, in her meta-analysis of the weapon focus literature, Steblay (1992) found that in only six out of 19 cases (32%) was there a significant effect of weapon presence on identification accuracy. That finding is in relatively good agreement with the 25% of field studies that found an effect.

The findings are also broadly consistent with laboratory research and theory on viewing conditions (see Chapter 3). Valentine et al. (2005) found that witnesses who had a longer time to view the perpetrator were significantly more likely to identify the suspect. Note that viewing time in laboratory studies has been associated with more correct suspect identifications, and can also at times be associated with more false suspect identifications. Valentine et al. also found a pattern of results consistent with an effect where poor lighting conditions and obstructed view were associated with fewer suspect identifications. Although these effects were not significant in the regression analyses, the pattern of the results matches the predictions of laboratory studies and the lack of a significant effect may simply reflect a lack of sufficient statistical power. Valentine et al. failed to find an effect of distance, but that may reflect the particular cutoff they used for the comparison. They broke the data into two groups: cases where the witness was less than 2 meters away and cases where the witness was more than 2 meters away. A cutoff of 2 meters may not be ideal for finding an effect of distance, given the research we discussed in Chapter 3.

There were also two studies comparing simultaneous versus sequential lineups, Klobuchar et al. (2006) and Mecklenburg et al., (2006), which arrived at different conclusions. Both studies are fraught with problems that make interpretations difficult. Klobuchar et al. did not have a control group and compared their findings to the Steblay et al. (2001) meta-analysis. The aforementioned confound in the Mecklenburg et al. (2006) study will not be restated here, but suffice it to say that the confound between the simultaneous and sequential lineups makes interpretation impossible (see the special in *Law Human Behavior* volume). Thus, we can't really tell from this study if the oft-cited advantage of sequential lineups occurs in the real world.

Behrman and Richards (2005) found that faster identifications resulted in more suspect identifications relative to identifications that took longer. The laboratory findings are consistent with this result, as it has been repeatedly shown that faster identifications are associated with higher hit rates relative to accuracy with slower identification latencies (Dunning & Perretta, 2002; Weber et al., 2004). There is still debate over the precise time boundary that distinguishes accurate and inaccurate identifications (Weber et al., 2004).

Behrman and Richards (2005) also found an association between confidence and suspect identifications. This finding is broadly consistent with results showing that confident witnesses are on average more accurate than less confident witnesses. The research reviewed in Chapter 5 indicates an association between confidence and accuracy, but also demonstrates that witnesses are imperfectly calibrated. In particular, witness overconfidence is common at the high end of the confidence scale, such that witnesses who indicate that they are absolutely confident may actually be correct around 80% of the time. In that chapter, we also reviewed evidence showing that witness confidence is malleable. Indeed, the association between confidence and suspect identification in field studies might reflect a dynamic in which suspect identifications are followed by feedback, which subsequently inflates confidence.

Pike et al. (2002) found an age effect for suspect identification, which is consistent with scientific research (LaVoie, Mertz, & Richmond, 2007). More specifically, Pike et al. found that there were more suspect identifications when the witnesses were younger (age range 22–29) than when the witnesses were older (60 and up). As reviewed in Chapter 3, there is good evidence that older witnesses are sometimes less accurate than are younger witnesses.

An interesting additional issue deals with effect of a stranger versus nonstranger suspects. In Klobuchar et al. (2006) and Valentine et al. (2005), the researchers looked at the effect of knowing the suspect prior to the crime. When the suspect was not a stranger, the suspect identification rate was significantly higher than when the suspect was a stranger. This may seem like a commonsense finding, but there are some important points that follow from this result. First, we are not aware of any laboratory research that compares stranger versus nonstranger identifications. We surmise that laboratory research would probably match the field studies in that there would most likely be more accurate identification rates (more hits and fewer misses) when the witness is familiar with the culprit. Second, this issue often arises in court and experts are asked to give opinion on the reliability of nonstranger identifications. The field studies provide important information and justification to inform this testimony.

☐ Problems, Challenges, and Future Directions

There are several challenges associated with conducting field research, many of which were outlined by Ross and Malpass in their 2008 commentary on the Mecklenburg et al. (2006) field study. In this section, we will outline the challenges and indicate ways in which they may be dealt within future studies. Finally, we will make some recommendation for future research.

Probably the biggest challenge with conducting field research is that it is nearly impossible, unless there is a confession or some physical evidence, to know what is referred to as *ground truth*. In another words, it is a rare occasion when the police are 100% positive that the suspect actually is the culprit. In the laboratory, this is not a problem because the experimenter has created the video or staged the event, so the experimenter always knows the identity of the culprit. This allows the experimenter to determine when participant witnesses make correct identifications and when the participant witnesses fail to identify the culprit when the culprit is actually in the lineup. Although throughout this chapter we have treated suspect identification as a proxy for culprit identifications, this is certainly a false assumption as evidenced by the numerous DNA exonerations in which the major evidence in the original case was eyewitness identification (see www.innocenceproject.org).

Moreover, the proportion of suspect identifications that are culprit identifications are likely to be influenced by the very predictor variables that are of interest to the researchers. There are two ways in which this confounding can occur. First, as we reviewed throughout this book, particular predictor variables may influence the diagnosticity identification. Diagnosticity is the ratio of correct to false suspect identifications. To the extent that diagnosticity is high, suspect identifications will be a relatively good proxy for culprit identifications. To the extent that diagnosticity is low, suspect identifications will be a relatively poor proxy for culprit identifications. Indeed, under conditions where one would predict poor diagosticity, it would be dangerous to equate suspect identifications with culprit identifications.

The second way in which an independent variable might influence the proportion of suspect identifications that are culprit identifications is if the variable is related to the base rate of guilt. For instance, under good lighting conditions a witness might be able to give a fuller description than under poor lighting conditions. The fuller description might make it easier for the police to identify a suspect who has a good chance of being guilty. Thus the base rate of being guilty may end up being higher under good lighting conditions.

How do you get meaningful data if you do not know if witnesses are correct? Furthermore, how do you compare the results from the field to the laboratory findings where these data are available? We would argue that there are two solutions, and both have been done to some extent in the field studies. First, you can break down each case in terms of the amount of probative evidence that points to the suspect being the culprit as was done by Behrman and colleagues (Behrman & Davey, 2001;

Behrman & Richards, 2005). This does not get to the "ground truth," but it gets a lot closer than just relying on suspect identifications. The second recommendation is to use foil identification as a measure of lineup identification inaccuracy. Foil identifications are known errors so you can be confident that the witness has made a false identification. However, for foil identification to provide meaningful data, great care has to be taken to ensure that the lineups are properly constructed and as many factors as possible are held constant across the conditions that are being compared. For instance, if the lineup is suggestive, in either administration or composition, then the rate of foil identifications will be misleading.

For instance, imagine a field experiment in which one police department uses fairly constructed lineups (large functional size) and another police department uses lineups that are very unfairly constructed (small functional size). The department that uses the unfair lineups will tend to have fewer foil identifications (because the foils do not match the description of the suspect very well in an unfair lineup) and more suspect identifications (because the lineups will make it obvious to the witness who the suspect is). Obviously, it would be a mistake to conclude from such a result that low functional size lineups are the way to go.

Another large challenge faced by field researchers is protocol noncompliance. Researchers spend an enormous amount of time working out the details and protocols of the study to ensure that the data are collected in a nonbiased format. To the extent that these protocols are not followed, it makes interpretation of the data difficult at best because it adds in an enormous amount of systematic error. In both the Illinois study (Meckelburg et al., 2006) and the HC study (Klobuchar et al., 2006), police officer noncompliance was a big issue. In the Illinois study and the HC study, the protocols stipulated that officers were to gather and report confidence statements. Officers only did so 62% and 15% of the time in the Illinois and HC studies, respectively. As suggested by Ross and Malpass (2008), field studies will need to require some sort of compliance monitoring in the future to ensure that all parties involved in the study follow protocols.

In addition, researchers conducting field research on lineup identification and eyewitness memory will have to retain copies of the lineups. As suggested by both Wells (2008) and Ross and Malpass (2008), the quality of a lineup is an important issue with regard to identification accuracy (Lindsay & Wells, 1980; McQuiston & Malpass, 2002; Tredoux, 2002). Biased lineups are ones in which the suspect stands out based on the description of the witness. The benchmark of an unbiased lineup is one in which all the members of the lineup are chosen equally often by participants who were given a description of the culprit but never saw the event. The only way to assess lineup quality is to actually have the lineups and the witness's descriptions of the culprit. In the future, researchers will need to retain the actual lineups to assess their quality and fairness.

What are the future directions? It is our opinion that these initial field studies are very important first steps in moving the research from the laboratory to the field. We also echo the sentiment of many commentators who have suggested that field research is desperately needed if the policy changes on how eyewitness identifications are conducted is the goal (Ross & Malpass, 2008; Schacter et al., 2008; Wells, 2008). It is our hope that future research will be able to utilize the lessons learned in these studies to implement and conduct well-designed field studies.

☐ Endnote

1. The report written by Slater was published by the Home Office in London. We were unable to obtain a copy and do not discuss it further.

CHAPTER

Expert Testimony

☐ *State of Arkansas vs. Jessie Lloyd Misskelley, Jr., State of Arkansas vs. Charles James Baldwin and Damien Wayne Echols*

In 1993, three 8-year-old boys were found mutilated and murdered in a woodsy area in West Memphis, Arkansas. The police had very few leads due to the lack of physical evidence. It is remarkable that, with the mutilation of three young boys, there was almost no blood at the crime scene. The police narrowed their focus to three teenage boys as suspects: Damien Echols, Jason Baldwin, and Jessie Misskelley Jr. The major break in the case came when the police interrogated Misskelley, who is mentally disabled. The interrogation lasted for 12 hours and occurred without counsel or parental consent. At the end of the marathon session, Misskelley confessed to the crime and implicated Echols and Baldwin. Although there was no murder weapon and almost no physical evidence, the prosecution and the local media portrayed the teenage boys as depraved devil worshippers because of their preference for black clothes and heavy metal music.

In the first trial, *State of Arkansas v. Jessie Misskelley Jr.*, the primary evidence was Jessie's confession, which was grossly inconsistent with the facts of the case. In fact, during the confession Jessie gave the wrong time of day for the murder. The initial time given was a time when the victims were known to have been in school. During the course of the interview, through suggestive questioning, Jessie's story changed, making it better fit the facts of the case. Specifically, Jessie changed his confession regarding the time of the murder and the way in which it was carried out. To combat this confession, the defense sought to introduce the testimony of an expert witness, Dr. Richard Ofshe. Ofshe is an expert on the topic of coerced confessions. The crux of Ofshe's testimony was to be about the coercive and suggestive nature of the interview. The presiding judge, Judge Burnett, did not allow Ofshe to testify about whether the confession was voluntary or involuntary. Burnett's opinion was based on the fact that he had already ruled that the confession was voluntary, so in the judge's view, there was no need for Ofshe to testify about the voluntariness of the confession. Thus, the defense was not allowed to make an argument that was crucial to their strategy: Jessie Misskelley was coerced into confessing to a crime that he did not commit through suggestive and misleading questions.

In the second trial, *State of Arkansas v. Echols and Baldwin*, the prosecution argued that Echols and Baldwin killed the boys as part of a satanic ritual. Misskelley's confession was not admitted into trial because he refused to testify against the defendants. The jury never heard his confession. As previously stated, there was no other physical evidence linking the boys to the murder. In order to bolster their argument that the motive for the murder was Satanism, the prosecution brought in an expert on the occult. The expert, Dr. Dale Griffis, received his doctorate from Columbia Pacific University. Under cross-examination, Griffis could not name a single class that he took in order to get his degree, nor could he name a single occult case that he had worked on. Furthermore, he had never published in a peer-reviewed academic journal or outlet. Judge Burnett allowed him as an expert, a decision that has been upheld by the Arkansas Supreme Court. Additionally, there were no restrictions placed on his testimony. Griffis testified that the crime was linked to "occultism" because it occurred around May 5, a date close to two satanic holidays. In reality, Griffis's testimony was factually inaccurate on a number of issues related to the occult (see www.wmp3.org).

In these cases there were two experts, Griffis for the prosecution and Ofshe for the defense. The prosecution expert, Dr. Dale Griffis, was allowed freedom to testify on many issues regardless of the following facts: He could not name any classes taken to obtain his degree, his degree was obtained from an unaccredited and currently closed university, he had never published in a peer-reviewed journal, and he could not provide details of any cases he had previously worked. The expert for the defense, Dr. Richard Ofshe, had testified in 25 separate cases by the time of the trial, had published in numerous peer-reviewed academic journals, and holds an academic position at a prestigious university. However, he was limited in what he was allowed to testify about despite his impeccable credentials. Is there something wrong with this picture?

☐ Who Is an Expert?

In the previous chapters we discussed the errors that can be made by eyewitnesses and many of the factors that can influence eyewitness identification accuracy. There are different ways the legal system can make use of that research. At the front end, police can use the system variables we discussed in order to reduce the incidence of false identifications in the first place. Prosecutors can use knowledge of estimator variables, system variables, and indicia of reliability to judge the likely reliability of witnesses before deciding if their case is strong enough to go to trial. But sometimes a case will go to trial despite problems with the identification evidence. When this occurs, the defense may decide to hire an expert witness in order to educate the jury about case specific variables that might have an impact on the reliability of the identification. An expert witness is a person who is qualified by "knowledge, skill, experience, training, or education" to provide testimony regarding "scientific, technical, or other specialized knowledge" (Federal Rules of Evidence, rule 702). Eyewitness experts who testify in court are usually college professors with training in cognitive and social psychology, who teach courses and conduct research on issues related to eyewitness identification.

☐ The Frye Standard

Since the early part of the 20th century, federal and state courts have attempted to establish standards of reliability regarding scientific evidence and the admission of expert testimony. The goal of having a legal standard is to keep "junk science" out of the courtroom. One standard that was applied at both the federal and state levels for nearly a century was known as the *Frye standard*. It was established in 1923 in the case of *Frye vs. the United States*. James Alphonzo Frye was accused of second-degree murder. An expert hired by the defense gave Frye a polygraph test based on changes in systolic blood pressure and concluded that Mr. Frye was not being deceptive in his answers. The defense wanted to have this expert testify about the results of the polygraph. The prosecution objected, and the objection was sustained. Mr. Frye was convicted of second-degree murder. After the conviction, the case was appealed to the Federal Circuit Court in Washington, D.C., on the grounds that the judge in the original trial had made the wrong decision in not allowing the expert testimony. The Circuit Court ruled against Mr. Frye, providing the following justification:

Just when a scientific principle or discovery crosses the line between the experimental and demonstrable stages is difficult to define. Somewhere in this twilight zone the evidential force of the principle must be recognized, and while courts will go a long way in admitting expert testimony deduced from a well-recognized scientific principle or discovery, the thing from which the deduction is made must be sufficiently established to have gained general acceptance in the particular field in which it belongs. (*Frye v. U.S.*, 293 F. 1013 [D.C. Cir 1923])

The Frye decision was extremely influential, becoming the guiding precedent for years when courts ruled on the admissibility of expert testimony. Under the Frye standard, expert testimony is admissible as long as what the expert is going to testify about is "generally accepted" in the particular field of expertise. The Frye standard had plenty of proponents and opponents (Faigman & Monahan, 2005). One advantage of the Frye standard is that it puts judgments of scientific reliability into the hands of the people who are in the best position to make that judgment. Lawyers are not scientists. Judges are not scientists. The Frye standard does not require judges to have any specific scientific training or sophistication. The courts take advantage of the collective wisdom of the relevant community of scholars in deciding what expert testimony is and is not reliable. Furthermore, "general acceptance" takes some time to develop, so that the courts have some protection against novel findings that are not replicated.

On the other hand, critics of the Frye standard argued that the "general acceptance" standard is ambiguous. For example, are the standards for general acceptance the same in all fields, and does general acceptance mean the same thing in the scientific and legal communities? It may also be difficult, at times, to determine what the "relevant" scientific community is. In addition, they argue that Frye may be restrictive, in that innovative discoveries that are material to the facts of a particular case can be excluded if they have not yet been generally accepted because the research, while reliable, is still in its nascent stage. In 1993, the court abandoned the Frye standard in favor of Daubert.

☐ The Daubert Standard

In *Daubert v. Merrell Dow Pharmaceuticals, Inc.* (1993), the mothers of Jason Daubert and Eric Schuller claimed that their children were born with severe limb reduction birth defects because of a drug they were given while pregnant. The drug, Benedictin, is manufactured by Merrell Dow Pharmaceuticals and is commonly given to pregnant women to alleviate nausea. In their defense, Merrell Dow had an expert witness testify that no support for a causal link between the drug and birth defects could be evidenced. More than 30 published studies were reviewed and provided as support for this testimony. The Daubert's lawyer had eight expert witnesses who were going to testify that Benedictin could in fact cause birth defects. In support of this claim, they planned to use analyses of animal studies and a reanalysis of previously published studies. However, Dow argued that the evidence was inadmissible and the district court agreed, stating that expert testimony is only admissible if it is generally accepted by the relevant scientific community. The court held that expert testimony based solely on nonepidemiological studies could not establish a causal link between the drug and birth defects. Furthermore, the court ruled that the reanalyses of the epidemiological studies were not admissible because they had not been peer-reviewed or published and therefore did not meet the general acceptance criteria.

In response to this, the plaintiffs appealed arguing that the Frye standard was not the correct standard to use. They argued that since the time of the Frye decision, the Congress had enacted the Federal Rules of Evidence. Section VII of the Federal Rules of Evidence specifically covers the introduction of expert and opinion testimony. So the plaintiffs argued that the standards for admission of expert testimony in the Federal Rules of Evidence superseded the standards enunciated by the Frye standard. The Federal Rules of Evidence were created by an explicit act of Congress, whereas the Frye standard was created in case law. Rule 702 states,

> If scientific, technical, or other specialized knowledge will assist the trier of fact to understand the evidence or to determine a fact in issue, a witness qualified as an expert by knowledge, skill, experience, training, or education, may testify thereto in the form of an opinion or otherwise. (Federal Rules of Evidence, 2009, as amended)

Like all evidence introduced at trial, expert evidence must relate to the issues of a given case in order to be admitted (Rule 702). However, even if evidence is relevant, it can still be excluded if it would prejudice or mislead the jury, as would be the case if the evidence were unreliable (Kovera, Russano, & McAuliff, 2002).

The plaintiffs argued that the Federal Rules of Evidence do not require that there be general consensus about the issues the expert is testifying about, merely that the testimony be sufficiently reliable to assist the jury in fairly deciding the case. To clarify the confusion, the U.S. Supreme Court granted *certiorari*. The Supreme Court agreed with the plaintiff, finding that the Federal Rules of Evidence, not Frye, govern the admissibility of expert testimony. The responsibility of determining the reliability of expert evidence was placed entirely in the hands of federal trial court judges. The role of the judge was to act as a gatekeeper.

The decision in *Daubert* provided a list of criteria lower court judges could use to determine the admissibility of expert testimony. Under these rules, judges are to admit only relevant and reliable testimony, and they must assess the scientific validity of the methods and techniques used by the expert (Tamarelli, 1994; Walker & Monahan, 1996). Although there was no specific checklist for determining reliability, four factors were listed that trial court judges should consider when making decisions about reliability of evidence. First, they need to determine whether or not the expert's theory or technique is falsifiable and if they used proper methods of hypothesis testing. Second, they must consider the error rate of the technique and the standards of operation for the technique. Third, they should consider whether the theory or technique has been peer reviewed or published. Finally, they should consider the degree to which the theory or technique is generally accepted (Kovera, Russano, & McAuliff, 2002).

The court understood that even new evidence, which was unpublished and therefore potentially unreliable, could enter the courtroom despite screening by a judge. With this possibility in mind, the court ruled that traditional safeguards used to attack unreliable evidence should remain in place. These safeguards include cross-examination, introduction of opposing evidence, instruction on the standard of proof, and the judges' ability to grant summary judgment or to direct a judgment. In Frye, the burden of assessing reliability was left to the relevant scientific community. However, under Daubert, judges can consider general acceptance, but general acceptance is not the only criteria they are to consider. Rather, the judge's role is to consider, as a whole, whether the testimony is sufficiently reliable to be of assistance to the trier of fact. Trial judges are granted broad discretion in making these decisions (*General Electric v. Joiner*, 1997). Recently, the Supreme Court clarified the scope of Daubert by deciding that the ruling extended to all expert evidence, not just scientific evidence (*Kumho v. Carmichael*, 1999).

☐ Is Expert Testimony Needed?

Is there a need for expert witnesses on issues related to eyewitness memory? We believe so. There are at least six very compelling reasons to allow psychological expert testimony on eyewitness memory:

- The Innocence Project, an organization dedicated to overturning wrongful convictions, lists eyewitness identification as the primary evidence in close to three quarters of the DNA exoneration cases they have catalogued (www.innocenceproject.org). There are currently more than 250 exonerations listed, but the Innocence Project only investigates cases in which DNA evidence exists and is intact. Therefore, the DNA exoneration cases uncovered by the Innocence Project likely represent just the tip of the wrongful conviction iceberg. Given the way that random sampling occurs, there is statistical certainty that many more cases of wrongful conviction due to faulty eyewitness evidence exist in which there is no DNA evidence.

- Second, judges and attorneys see expert witnesses as useful for the jury under many circumstances (Safer & Wise, 2004). These are the people in the best position to evaluate expert testimony because they deal with it on a regular basis.
- Third, although much of the research on eyewitness evidence may seem like common knowledge, it is not the case that lay people are aware of the factors and procedures that affect the reliability of an eyewitness. Survey research indicates that potential jurors and judges do not understand basic memory processes especially as related to eyewitnesses (Schemechel et al., 2006).
- Fourth, laboratory research has shown that participant jurors are insensitive to the factors that affect eyewitness memory and show an overreliance on factors that are not always strongly predictive of accuracy (Leippe & Eisenstadt, 2007; Wells & Quinlivan, 2009).
- Fifth, the Biggers and Bradwaithe criteria which are used to instruct jurors on how to judge the veracity and reliability of eyewitness testimony are misleading and may cause the jurors to rely on factors that are poor indicators of eyewitness accuracy (Wells & Quinlivan, 2009).
- Sixth, there is an overreliance on eyewitness memory. For example, take the case of Payne Boyd. Boyd was tried three times for murder and spent over a year in jail. At his trial, 55 witnesses were called. Of these witness, 31 were confident that he was not the murderer, eight identified him, and 16 were unsure if he was the murderer. The fact that Boyd was convicted underscores how persuasive eyewitness testimony can be, even in the face of other contradictory evidence.

All of these reasons suggest an important role for eyewitness experts in the court system.

☐ Experts

A list of variables examined in eyewitness recall and identification is presented in Table 7.1 (Column 1), followed by the percentage of experts in

TABLE 7.1 List of System and Estimator Variables with Expert and Judges and Attorney Agreement Regarding the Reliability of the Variable

Variable	Expert Agreement*	Judge Agreement	Major Results
Weapon focus	87%	64%	Lower ID and description accuracy when weapon is present.
Disguise	NA	45%	Lower ID accuracy with disguises and physical transformations.
Expectations	92%	95%	Expectations can lead to memory to be in line with expectation if it is not accurate.
Misleading postevent information	94%	84%	Lowers witness accuracy.
Retention interval	83%	31%	Longer retention intervals (> week) lead to less accurate identifications.
Confidence malleability	95%	90%	Witness confidence is affected by social factors unrelated to accuracy.
Confidence accuracy	87%	33%	Related, but calibration is imperfect and witnesses tend toward overconfidence at higher confidence levels.
Double-blind lineups	NA	64%	Increases lineup identification accuracy.
Lineup presentations	81%	19%	Sequential lineups lower false IDs.
Mugshot exposure	95%	74%	Exposure to mug shots lowers identification accuracy.

* This column represents the percentage of experts that agree that research on the variable is reliable and the percentage that would be willing to testify on these factors. Those variables that do not have percentages in expert agreement column were not included in the Kassin et al. (2001) survey.

the field that agree that phenomena are reliable (Column 2), percentage of judges who agree with the statement (Column 3), agreement by a lay sample (Column 4), and descriptions of their general effects (Column 5). The original survey data was collected by Kassin and colleagues (2001), who surveyed 64 eyewitness researchers who had authored published research on eyewitness memory. The experts were questioned regarding their opinions about the extent to which the factors listed are reliable enough to testify about in court.

Our purpose in including this information is to provide another index of the extent to which the findings are generally accepted in the scientific community and compare to that of potential jurors and judges. This is very important for the present chapter for two reasons. First, one criterion for allowing the testimony of an expert is whether the phenomena have been generally accepted in the field. This is true under both the *Frye* and *Daubert* standards. This table gives an index of what phenomena or factors the experts think have been generally accepted. It is important to note the breadth of factors that have been studied and generally accepted by the experts as affecting eyewitness memory. Second, as will be discussed later in the chapter, one of the reasons expert testimony may be excluded is that information that the expert would provide is thought to be common knowledge and the average juror can be expected to know this information without the aid of an expert. The table speaks to that issue by allowing comparisons between expert and lay opinion on relevant factors.

☐ Gatekeepers

Since early 1920, courts have been very concerned with allowing experts to testify on what is considered poor science or what is known as "junk science." "Junk science" or "pseudoscience" may be defined as claims that are portrayed as being scientific, but that are not accurate or reliable because the data from which the conclusion was drawn are flawed or the reasoning applied to the data is logically invalid (Lilienfeld, Lynn, & Lohr, 2003). As mentioned earlier, the standard for allowing expert testimony was, until recently, "general acceptance" in the particular field. The *Daubert* decision changed this standard such that scientific evidence now must be relevant and reliable to be admissible. Relevance requires the information to be related to material evidence in the case. Reliability requires that the method of collecting data conform to the scientific method. General acceptance is one method of evaluating the reliability of evidence, under *Daubert*, but not the only method.

One important aspect of *Daubert* is that it makes judges the gatekeepers of what is good science—science that adheres to the scientific method— and what is "junk science." It is reasonable to ask whether judges are in the best position to evaluate the reliability of scientific evidence. Psychologists have examined this issue in three ways: Judges have been presented with experimental vignettes and have been asked to judge the reliability of the experiments, judges have been asked to complete surveys that assess their knowledge on scientific findings, and finally there is a research literature on complex decision making of novices, or people not trained in the scientific method. The bulk of this evidence leads to the conclusion that judges are not prepared to handle this task.

There has been very little published work on how judges evaluate the reliability of scientific experiments. The majority of this work has been done by Kovera and colleagues (Kovera & McAuliff, 2000; Kovera, McAuliff, & Hebert, 1999). Kovera and McAuliff had judges in Florida read a short summary of a hostile work environment case that included expert testimony that the plaintiff's lawyer intended to admit during the trial. The expert was to testify about the psychological factors that increase the likelihood of sexual harassment with particular reference to a study conducted by the expert. The trial summaries were manipulated such that there were four versions of the experiment, three with methodological flaws and one sound experiment. The methodological flaws were a confound, a missing control group, and experimenter bias due to the confederate knowing the hypothesis and conditions of the experiment. After reading the trials, judges answered a series of questions regarding the expert evidence and the scientific method employed by the expert. If judges are competent gatekeepers, then their assessments of the research should vary with the methodological errors presented. In reality, they did not. Judges' ratings of the quality of the research were the same regardless of the methodological errors.

In a similar vein, Wingate and Thorton (2004) examined the decisions of federal judges to admit expert testimony in a hypothetical case involving testimony by an industrial organizational psychologist. In a mail survey, judges were presented with a summary of a case where a 55-year-old plaintiff alleged that he was wrongfully and illegally terminated due to his age. There were four different versions of the expert testimony that varied with regard to the source of the information on which the expert drew his conclusions. The different versions consisted of the expert basing his conclusions on (a) only personal experience, (b) personal experience and one unpublished empirical study, (c) personal experience and a published empirical study, and (d) personal experience and a published meta-analysis. After reading the trial summary, judges answered a series of questions regarding the reliability of the expert's conclusion and the likelihood that the expert would be allowed to testify. For the most part, the willingness to admit the expert was not affected by the quality of the information on which the expert based his conclusion. (The only significant effect was that judges were more likely to admit the testimony in the personal experience + meta-analysis as opposed to the personal experience alone condition.) Interestingly, when asked which *Daubert* criteria impacted their admissibility ratings, judges indicated that only the general acceptance criteria influenced their decisions.

These two studies came to the same conclusion. Judges are not very good at evaluating the quality of scientific evidence. Maybe these findings are not surprising, given that judges generally do not receive much formal training in the scientific method. Additionally, the research on complex decision making indicates that persons without formal training are not good at making complex statistical decisions. For example, Nisbett (1993) has demonstrated that laypersons are insensitive to factors that differentiate valid and flawed research, such as failing to understand the necessity of a control group (see Jepson, Krantz, & Nisbett, 1983). Furthermore, lay-persons also have difficulty understanding that larger samples are more representative of the population than smaller samples and that larger samples produce results that are more reliable. If we assume that judges are like laypersons in terms of their amount of training and knowledge of the scientific method, then perhaps it is not surprising that they have diffi-culty differentiating reliable from flawed research. After all, it is a difficult task even for people who are trained in the scientific method.

In addition to asking judges to evaluate reliable and flawed research, psychologists have also surveyed judges regarding their knowledge and beliefs about the factors that affect the reliability of eyewitness memory (Wise & Safer, 2003, 2004). In their survey, Wise and Safer (2004) asked 160 judges to answer questions regarding their knowledge of basic findings in eyewitness memory. More specifically, they were asked to indicate their agreement with 14 statements about factors that have been studied by eye-witness scientists. These statements were similar to those evaluated by Kassin et al. (2001), such that comparisons could be made between experts in the field of eyewitness memory and the judges. Columns 2 and 3 of Table 7.1 display the relevant percentage of agreement for the psychologi-cal experts and the judges respectively.

As can be seen in Table 7.1, the judges' ratings were in line with experts on almost every statement. The majority of judges either agreed or strongly agreed with the experts in the field on seven of 11 questions relating to findings from the psychological research on eyewitness memory. More specifically, the majority of judges agreed with the experts on issues relat-ing to the effect of attitudes and expectations on memory, effects of poste-vent information, procedures for conducting lineups, memory for minor details, confidence malleability, mugshot-induced bias, and weapon focus. There were a few notable deviations from the experts' opinions (i.e., confidence, lineup presentation, and the forgetting curve), but overall the judges were quite knowledgeable in their understanding of the eyewit-ness research.

In addition to the survey results, Wise and Safer (2004) also asked judges to indicate how many jurors they thought would agree with a sub-set of the statements. This is an important question because, as Wise and Safer pointed out, one of the most frequently used arguments to prohibit an eyewitness expert testimony is that the information that the expert will present is common knowledge and jurors will not benefit from being exposed to it (also see *United States v. Hall*, 1999). (We will return to this point later in the section on challenges to expert testimony.) Interestingly, judges indicated that they thought jurors would not be aware of the fac-tors that affect eyewitness memory. More specifically, only 36% of judges thought that the jurors would correctly answer the statement regarding confidence malleability (i.e., an eyewitness's confidence can be influenced by factors that are unrelated to identification accuracy). More importantly, 64% of judges disagreed with the statement that "Jurors know how most eyewitness factors affect identification accuracy." Thus, judges' beliefs about juror knowledge are inconsistent with the rationale that the information that is proffered by eyewitness experts is a matter of common sense or common knowledge.

How do judges measure up as "gatekeepers" as mandated under *Daubert*? The evidence appears to be mixed. In terms of their knowledge of eyewitness memory, they appear to be pretty knowledgeable. They understand most of the major effects that have been examined by eyewitness researchers. When judges are asked to evaluate the reliability of scientific evidence, the picture gets much grimmer. According to the research (Kovera & McAuliff, 2003; Wingate & Thorton, 2004), judges are unable to identify relatively obvious and simple methodological flaws. However, judges do indicate that they need more training on scientific reasoning (Wise & Safer, 2004), and there are data that suggest that people given brief training in methodological reasoning are better able to apply this training to real world problems (Fong, Krantz, & Nisbett, 1986). As of now it seems that although judges may understand the basic phenomena and procedures regarding eyewitness memory, they are presently ill equipped to make sophisticated evaluations of scientific research. This may be why judges indicated that they employed the general acceptance criteria of *Daubert* to exclusion of the other criteria in the study by Wingate and Thorton (2004). This may be the criteria that they understand and are most competent and comfortable applying and evaluating. General acceptance also has the advantage of showing deference to the subject area experts in deciding what is and is not reliable.

☐ Jurors' Knowledge

Along with surveying judges and attorneys, psychologists have also evaluated the knowledge of potential jurors about factors affecting the reliability of eyewitness memory (Deffenbacher & Loftus, 1982; Durham & Dane, 1999; Kassin & Barndollar, 1992; Schmechel, O'Toole, Easterly, & Loftus, 2006). All these studies arrive at a similar conclusion: Jurors, unlike judges, know very little about the many factors that affect eyewitness memory. First, we review the results from the Schemechel et al. (2006) survey because it is the most recently published of the studies. We follow this with a brief summary of the findings from older studies. Because most of the surveys come to the same conclusion, we see no reason to cover each in great detail.

Schemechel et al. (2006), with the help of Public Defender Services, conducted a survey with approximately 1,000 jurors from the District of Columbia. The survey consisted of approximately 20 questions regarding jurors' beliefs about memory in general, as well as some specific questions about the factors that affect the reliability of eyewitness memory. The results indicated that jurors have a very limited understanding of memory in general, as more than 52% of the respondents indicated that remembering a traumatic event was like a video recording in that one could recall details as they were imprinted on the brain. Similarly, 46% of the sample thought that a witness' testimony consisted of a video recording that she can see in her mind. Furthermore, 66% of the sample thought the statement that "I never forget a face" applied to them to some degree, and 77% thought that the statement "I have excellent memory" applied either very well or fairly well to them. The latter two results demonstrate that jurors overestimate their memory abilities.

With regard to eyewitness memory, jurors were at odds with the consensus of the experts. More specifically, almost 40% of the sample thought that violence would make memory for the event more reliable. In addition, 40% of the sample thought that confidence is a reliable indicator of accuracy and 48% of the sample thought that cross-race and own-race identifications were equally reliable. Respondents also showed very little sensitivity to the effect of lineup procedures. For instance, 51% of the respondents thought the lineup would be more reliable if the witness was not warned that the culprit may not be in the lineup and only 55% thought that the officer conducting the lineup should not know the identity of the suspect.

The results from some older surveys are consistent with the findings of Schmechel et al. (2006). Deffenbacher and Loftus (1982) found that the majority of potential jurors they surveyed answered a number of questions regarding variables that affect eyewitness memory in a manner that diverged from the consensus of the experts. For example, over half of the respondents answered incorrectly pertaining to cross-race identification and the confidence–accuracy relationship. Kassin and Barndollar (1992) compared the responses of students and nonstudents to the responses given by experts in the field (Kassin et al., 1989). Kassin and Barndollar reported that students and nonstudents had incorrect knowledge about many issues that the majority of psychological experts agreed were reliable enough to testify about in court. Some of the factors in question concerned the confidence–accuracy relationship, lineup instructions, exposure time, the forgetting curve, and cross-race identification. Similarly, Yarmey and Jones (1983) surveyed law students, legal professionals, and community members, and found that the respondents did not understand the relationship between confidence and accuracy. They also showed little sensitivity to issues such as mugshot bias. Based on the research, it is clear that, unlike judges, laypersons and students have a very limited knowledge of the factors that affect eyewitness memory, and in some instances have false beliefs about eyewitness memory.

Not only are jurors unknowledgeable about factors that influence eyewitness accuracy, there is also evidence that jurors show a general pattern of overreliance on eyewitness identification evidence. In one study, Loftus (1974) presented mock jurors with a simulated trial involving a defendant accused of a robbery. There were three versions of the trial. In one version, there was no eyewitness identification evidence presented. In a second condition, reliable eyewitness identification evidence was presented. In a third condition, eyewitness identification evidence was presented by a witness who had 20/400 vision and was thus legally blind. Without the identification evidence, only 18% of the mock jurors voted to convict. When identification evidence was presented from a reliable witness, the conviction rate was 72%. When identification evidence was presented from a witness who was legally blind, the conviction rate was 68%. The study demonstrates that jurors have a tendency to rely on eyewitness identification evidence even when it should not be relied on.

These findings are of legal significance when it comes to the admissibility of expert testimony regarding eyewitness identification. For expert testimony to be admissible, it must be reliable, relevant, and of assistance to the trier of fact (e.g., jury members). As noted above, judges tend to exclude expert testimony if they believe that the members of the jury are already likely to know about the factors the expert is testifying about. Telling jurors something they already know is not likely to help them decide the case. The above research demonstrates that on a large number of issues, jurors would be assisted by accurate and reliable expert testimony.

☐ Challenges to Experts

Although it is clear that eyewitness identification can be unreliable, some judges are still reluctant to allow eyewitness experts to testify about factors that affect the reliability of eyewitness memory. As recently as 2007, the Supreme Court of Tennessee reversed the conviction of Arthur Copeland. The basis of the appeal was that the circuit court had denied Copeland the services of a psychological expert on eyewitness identification (*State of Tennessee v. Copeland*). Based on the decision by the Tennessee Supreme Court, the lower courts in Tennessee have started allowing experts in eyewitness identification to testify.

With the maturing scientific data on eyewitness memory and recent court decisions, more and more psychological experts on eyewitness testimony are likely to testify. As a result, opposing counsel will undoubtedly attempt to prevent these experts from testifying. The major objections to expert testimony can be classified into four categories: (a) The information that experts would testify on is common knowledge and is thus unlikely to be of assistance to the trier of fact; (b) the testimony is too general to assist the trier of fact; (c) the evidence given by the expert is too prejudicial; and (d) the scientific basis of the research is not well enough established to assist the jury. This is by no means intended to be an exhaustive list. Rather, it is merely the objections that we have most frequently come across in our readings and work as expert witnesses.

According to O'Hagan (1993) one of the most common challenges to allowing eyewitness experts is that the information that they are going to testify about is common knowledge. For example, in *United States v. Hudson* (1989), the defendants were accused of entering a credit union with the intent of committing burglary. The major evidence against the defendants was an eyewitness identification. The defense tried to introduce expert testimony on issues related to the reliability of eyewitness memory such as stress and cross-race identification (issues that we know laypersons do not understand from survey data; Schemechel et al., 2006). The defense was denied its expert, and on appeal the Seventh Circuit upheld the lower court's decision to exclude the expert. The rationale the court gave was that the expert would not aid the jury in their decision because the jury is already aware of the information to be proffered by the expert (see O'Hagan, 1993, for more information regarding the case).

In some respects it is certainly true that some of the information about memory and eyewitness identification is simply common sense. For example, it is reasonable to expect that jurors would realize that it is harder to identify someone in the dark than when the crime takes place in an area where there is good illumination. At another level, however, jurors may not be fully aware of the degree to which these variables influence identification accuracy or the specific dose–response relationship between the variables. For many variables, eyewitness experts can provide useful information about the degree of impairment to be expected under different circumstances.

There are other variables and procedures that dramatically affect eyewitness memory that are counterintuitive, and jurors (Schemechel et al., 2006) as well as judges (Safer & Wise, 2003) do not understand their effects. A good example is the confidence–accuracy relationship. It seems intuitive that eyewitnesses that are more confident would be more accurate. However, as we saw in Chapter 5, the relationship between confidence and accuracy is complex and can be influenced by a wide range of factors. Under some circumstances, confidence and accuracy may be well calibrated, but under other circumstances they may not be. Eyewitness experts can assist the court by helping jurors understand the full complexity of this relationship. Jurors show the same lack of understanding of procedural issues that affect the reliability of the lineup identification such as double-blind lineup administration and the benefit of informing the witness that the culprit may not be present in the lineup (Schemechel et al., 2006).

Another argument against the use of eyewitness experts is that, under Rule 702, the testimony is too vague to assist the trier of fact. According to this argument, even though eyewitness experts testify about factors that affect eyewitness testimony that are relevant to the case, the information is still too vague because the experts do not offer opinions as to the accuracy of the identification. A good example cited by O'Hagan (1993) occurred in *United States v. Poole* (1986), where the Ninth Circuit affirmed the trial court's decision to exclude the eyewitness expert based on the fact that the testimony was not specifically about factors in the case. According to O'Hagan (1993), the expert would have likely testified about such factors as weapon focus, stress, reliability of the lineup procedures, and the effect of expectancy on memory for the event. The court ruled that because the expert would not have offered opinion as to the reliability of the eyewitness, the testimony of the expert would not have been helpful. O'Hagan (1993) stated that this reasoning, that an expert's opinion is helpful only in the form of an opinion, is in direct contrast to the Advisor Committee's Note under Rule 702, which explicitly states that expert testimony need not be in the form of an opinion in order to assist the jury. Furthermore, the note goes on to say that an expert may give testimony regarding scientific factors that are relevant to the case, allowing the jurors or the attorneys to draw their own inferences about how those factors apply to the specific case in front of them.

In addition, it would be irresponsible for experts to offer opinions on the accuracy of an eyewitness, because the expert was not there to witness the event and could have no idea if the witness is correct. The best an expert can do is report on the factors that would help or hinder eyewitness identification that may or may not have been present during the crime. If the Ninth Circuit decision is adhered to, it would, in effect, eliminate all expert testimony on identification evidence because experts should never offer opinions as to the accuracy of the eyewitness. The expert should only recite the relevant scientific findings that can affect eyewitness testimony as they apply to the fact pattern in the case.

Experts have also been excluded because it was deemed that their testimony would be too prejudicial (see *United States v. Fosher*, 1979). The rationale behind this objection is that the jury would be so overcome by the expert testimony that the jurors would not consider any other evidence in the case. It is hard to see how testimony from an eyewitness expert could be this persuasive. However, it is important to note that the implication of this position is that neither the prosecution nor the defense can offer any type of scientific evidence, as the same reasoning would apply. This position effectively eliminates all scientific experts from taking the witness stand.

Another commonly used rationale for disqualifying experts in eyewitness testimony is that the research is not sufficiently reliable and valid to be applied to real world settings. Under either the *Frye* or *Daubert* standard, the results from the psychology literature are both reliable and valid. First, Kassin et al. (2001) surveyed experts in the field regarding phenomena that are reliable enough to testify about in court. As you can see in Table 7.1, the factors that eyewitness experts are most likely to testify on (e.g., cross-race identification, weapon focus, stress, etc.) have a very high percentage of agreement from experts in the field. Furthermore, in 1999, the American Psychology and Law Society published a white paper on the best practice for conducting lineup and photospread identifications that has been endorsed by the society (Wells et al., 1999). Thus, it is fair to say the findings surpass the "general acceptance" under the strictest criteria. Additionally, all of the factors listed in the table have had volumes of research published in the particular area. Therefore, we are not talking about one published paper. We are talking about effects that have been replicated multiple times, often with thousands of participants using a wide range of procedures. It is also fair to say that this amount of independent replication would indicate the results are both valid and reliable.

The final common argument is that the scientific data do not generalize to real-world situations. There are two pieces of evidence that are inconsistent with this argument. It is true that the majority of studies conducted in psychology are done with college students in laboratory settings. This is a good thing, because it gives the scientist control over the variables that are relevant to the situation. Indeed, as Wells (1993) pointed out, studies that have compared students and nonstudents have rarely found differences. In addition, field studies on eyewitness memory have generally found results consistent with laboratory studies (see Chapter 6). Furthermore, in studies in which more lifelike situations have been simulated, the results have typically confirmed the results from other laboratory studies. For example, as mentioned in Chapter 3, the Morgan et al. (2004) study with active military personnel demonstrated that those who were exposed to stressful interrogation which included a physical altercation had worse identification accuracy then those who were in the low-stress, no-physical-altercation condition. The results from this study are consistent with the results found on stress in the laboratory. Taken together, the evidence indicates the laboratory findings do indeed generalize to real world situations as well as nonstudent populations.

In conclusion, the objections to expert eyewitness testimony seem to be at odds with the current literature. Jurors, as evidenced by their survey responses, are not familiar with the factors that affect eyewitness memory (see Schenechel et al., 2006). In other words, the information provided by an eyewitness expert is not common knowledge, and it is not reasonable to expect jurors to be aware of these issues. In addition, the scientific studies related to eyewitness testimony have certainly been generally accepted in the field. This is clearly evidenced by the majority of agreement among the experts on many factors from the Kassin et al. (2001) survey that are listed in Table 7.1. Finally, the scientific study of these factors involves many independently published experiments that have included thousands of participants, and when these factors are tested in more real-life situations, the results are consistent with the laboratory findings. Thus, experimental results on which an expert on eyewitness testimony would testify about are valid, reliable, and generalize to the real world.

☐ Procedural Safeguards

As mentioned earlier, eyewitness testimony is often the only evidence in a trial. It is clear from numerous sources that confident eyewitnesses are extremely persuasive even if they are not always accurate (see Wells & Quinlavin, 2009). These factors suggest that jurors may at times be exposed to eyewitness testimony that is not entirely accurate, and given the persuasiveness of this testimony, jurors may make decisions that are in error. To protect against the effect of unreliable eyewitness evidence, attorneys have several procedural safeguards: judicial instructions, cross-examination, opening and closing statements, exclusion, and expert testimony. The question is how effective these safeguards are.

Judicial Instructions

One way of educating jurors about the factors that influence eyewitness accuracy would be for judges to include admonishments when they instruct the jury. The judge, after all, is the ultimate authority figure in the courtroom and is likely to be seen as impartial and unbiased. Despite these considerations, judicial admonishments may not be an effective remedy for the problem of mistaken eyewitness identifications. First, mock jury studies have typically found that judicial instructions generally have only limited effects on jury decision making. For example, in a meta-analysis on inadmissible evidence, Steblay, Hosch, Cullhane, and McWehty (2006) examined the impact of judicial admonishments on juror verdicts. They found that verdicts did not vary with judicial instructions. There is no reason to assume the judicial instructions would be more effective when the instructions were about the reliability of eyewitness evidence.

Second, it stands to reason that in order for jurors to effectively use the judicial instructions they must first understand the instructions. Without a thorough understanding, it is impossible for jurors to comply with and correctly apply the instructions. Unfortunately, the psychological literature suggests that jurors have difficulty understanding the instructions given by judges (Ogloff & Rose, 2005; Reifman, Glick, & Ellsworth, 1992). For example, Ogloff (1998) examined the comprehension of judicial instructions with more than 500 jury-eligible participants. In this study, participants watched a 2.5-hour simulated video trial and mock jurors deliberated in groups. The videotaped trial included lengthy judicial instructions that were similar to what is typically used in real trials. The results revealed that mock jurors had very little comprehension of the judicial instructions. For example, when jurors were asked how sure one must be that the accused is guilty under the reasonable doubt standard, the majority of people responded 100% sure. Obviously this is an unreasonably high standard given the legal definition of reasonable doubt, which indicates there can still be some doubt that the accused committed the crime but the doubt must not exceed a reasonable person's opinion that the defendant is guilty. Furthermore, not only do jurors have trouble understanding the judicial instructions, but also the remedies that have been devised to increase juror understanding such as note taking and giving jurors written copies of the instructions do not seem to improve juror comprehension or application of the instructions (see Ogloff & Rose, 2005).

However, some innovations, such as the use of flow charts, have led to improved jury comprehension. The flow charts contain the legal issues that need to be addressed by the jury and the order in which they can be handled. Using a mock jury paradigm, Semmler and Brewer (2002) found that allowing jury members to refer to flow charts increases comprehension and application of judicial instructions relative to participants who were not exposed to flow charts. However, results about the use of flow charts are not always positive. For instance, Ogloff (1989) did not find that flow chart use increased juror comprehension of judicial instructions. Ogloff suggested that participants may not have referred to the flow chart often enough, so that his null result could be due to the ineffective use of the flow chart as opposed to the flow chart itself.

Cross-Examination

The empirical data on cross-examination suggest that it is not an effective method to counter unreliable eyewitness testimony (see Leippe 1995). A number of studies have exposed participant witnesses to cross-examination to determine whether these witnesses are perceived as less reliable by jurors after being cross-examined (Berman, Narby,

& Cutler, 1995; Turtle & Wells, 1988). Although witness confidence can be shaken, cross-examination does not make jurors more sensitive to the factors that affect the reliability of the testimony (Lindsay, Wells, & O'Connor, 1989). Furthermore, when witnesses are coached, which they almost always are, cross-examination does not even reduce their confidence (Spanos, Quigley, Gywnn, Glatt, & Perloni, 1991).

According to Leippe (1995), cross-examination as a method of countering unreliable eyewitness testimony falls short of its goal for two main reasons. Leippe argued that, generally, the goal of cross-examination is to attack the credibility of the witness rather than to bring out the factors and procedures that draw into question the accuracy of the testimony. This strategy leads to a focus on factors that are less diagnostic, such as witness demeanor and trivial inconsistencies (Berman et al., 1995). Second, Leippe argued that even if the lawyer tries to bring more diagnostic factors to light during cross-examination, there is no guarantee that they are actually knowledgeable enough on the issues to be effective. Although the survey data suggest that attorneys know many of the issues related to eyewitness testimony (Wise, Pawlenko, Meyer, & Safer, 2007), being aware of the factors and being able to effectively cross-examine a witness on them may be two different things

Opening and Closing Arguments

Attorneys can also try to educate jurors about factors that can influence eyewitness accuracy during opening and closing arguments. As far as we know, there has been no direct research of the effect of opening and closing arguments as procedural safeguards for jury decision making with eyewitness evidence. However, there is evidence from the literature that leads to the conclusion that it will not be an effective way to educate the jury. The rationale behind this safeguard presupposes that lawyers will have the knowledge regarding the factors and procedures that affect the reliability of eyewitness testimony. Furthermore, they also need to be able to point out when research is unreliable and why it is unreliable. Unfortunately, the survey and experimental data do not give confidence that lawyers will be effective at doing either.

Wise et al. (2007) surveyed defense attorneys' knowledge regarding the factors and procedures affecting eyewitness testimony. More than 1,100 attorneys responded to the survey, which consisted of 18 questions about variables and procedures that affect eyewitness testimony. When compared to the response of experts to the survey (Kassin et al., 2001), the majority of attorneys agreed that stress impairs eyewitness accuracy, eyewitness perceptions of memory may be affected by expectations, eyewitness memory often contains information from the event and information received after the event, confidence is not always a good indicator of accuracy, and the presence of a weapon can impair eyewitness identification to mention. The attorneys were less knowledgeable about the questions addressing the effect of simultaneous and sequential lineups, as well as general questions about memory such as when memory loss is the most rapid. In general, these results suggest defense attorneys know a great deal about factors influencing eyewitness identification accuracy. However, their response to the questionnaire may reflect a general distrust of eyewitness memory as opposed to any real substantive knowledge of these factors and procedures (see Lindsay, et al., 1990; Wise et al., 2007). It is also unclear if having this knowledge will translate into attorneys being able to educate jurors about the factors that affect eyewitness memory.

Can attorneys evaluate flawed research? To answer this question, Kovera and McAuliff (2002) sent attorneys surveys containing the same case scenarios about a hostile work environment as the aforementioned study conducted with the judges (Kovera & McAuliff, 2000). Again, the internal validity of the study reported by the expert was manipulated so that there were four methodological variations: a valid study, a study missing a control group, a study that employed a nonblind confederate, and a study that contained a confound. Attorneys showed no ability to discriminate valid from flawed research. More specifically, the attorneys' judgments of the reliability of the study did not vary as a function of the methodological variations.

Exclusion

Another safeguard is to simply not let eyewitnesses testify when there is no other corroborating evidence. No jurisdiction in the country has adopted this standard. However, judges frequently have a Daubert hearing to determine if the evidence of the expert is reliable and if the evidence will help the jury. On rare occasions, judges can decide to exclude an expert because the accuracy of the identification is not in doubt. For example, if the culprit is described as having green hair and there are pictures of the culprit with green hair, the judge may decide that so few people have green hair that the accuracy of the identification is not in doubt and that there is no reason to have an expert testify about the factors that influence eyewitness identification.

Expert Testimony

One of the more promising safeguards to protect against mistaken eyewitness identification is expert testimony on the psychology of eyewitness identification. Expert testimony has been defined as "the delivery to a jury by a qualified research psychologist of information about research and theory" (Leippe, 1995, p. 910). Mock jury research has shown that expert testimony about eyewitness accuracy can impact jury decision making. In one early study, Loftus (1980) presented mock jurors with a short written summary of a trial in which eyewitness identification evidence was pivotal. For half of the participants, the trial summary included expert testimony concerning factors that can impair eyewitness accuracy (i.e., cross-race identification, stress, and intoxication). Expert testimony substantially reduced judgments of guilt. In a more elaborate trial simulation, Hosch, Beck, and McIntyre (1980) produced similar results. Community residents and college students viewed a mock trial either live (community members) or through videotape (college students). Half of the mock jurors saw expert testimony concerning eyewitness identifications including direct and cross-examination of the expert. The other half of the mock jurors saw the trial without seeing the expert testimony or the cross-examination of the expert. Following the trial, participants were impaneled in six-person juries and were asked to deliberate. The results indicated that mock jurors who saw the expert testimony rated eyewitness identification evidence as being less reliable than mock jurors who did not see expert testimony. Not only that, transcripts of deliberations indicated that mock jurors who had heard the expert testimony spent considerably more time discussing issues related to the eyewitness identification than did mock jurors who did not see the expert testimony. Thus, expert testimony appeared to have a positive impact on the process by which the impaneled juries made decisions.

When expert testimony impacts jury decision making, there are two ways that this can occur (Cutler, Penrod, & Dexter, 1989). On one hand, expert testimony could make jurors more sensitive to the factors that influence eyewitness accuracy. On the other hand, expert testimony might simply make jurors more skeptical with regard to eyewitness evidence generally. To examine these issues, some researchers have created mock trials in which the presence or absence of expert testimony is crossed with the presence or absence of problems with the witnessing conditions (e.g., poor vs. good lighting), police procedures (e.g., biased vs. unbiased lineups), or other evidence in the case (e.g., degree to which there is corroborating evidence).

Consider the predicted outcomes based on the two explanations (Figure 7.1). If expert testimony makes jurors more sensitive (Panel A), then expert testimony should produce no effect when witnessing conditions are good and the police used proper procedures (or the expert testimony might even help the prosecution). However, when witnessing conditions are poor or the police used improper procedures, expert testimony should reduce guilty verdicts. If expert testimony simply makes jurors more skeptical (Panel B), then expert testimony should reduce guilty verdicts when

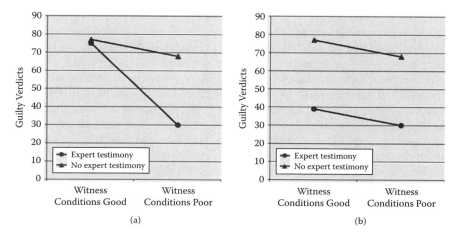

FIGURE 7.1   Possible effects of expert testimony. According to the increased sensitivity account, expert testimony will have its largest effect when witnessing conditions are poor (a). If expert testimony just makes jurors more skeptical, then expert testimony should decrease guilty verdicts both when witnessing conditions are poor and when they are good (b).

witnessing conditions are poor and the police use improper procedures, but it should also reduce guilty verdicts when witnessing conditions are good and police use proper procedures.

A number of studies have supported the view that expert testimony can make jurors more sensitive to the factors that influence eyewitness accuracy (Cutler, Penrod, & Dexter, 1989; Devenport et al., 2002; Geiselman et al., 2002). For instance, in Cutler, Penrod, and Dexter (1989) participants watched a videotaped trial of a defendant accused of armed robbery. Among the evidence presented by the prosecution was a positive identification of the defendant by the robbery victim. For half the participants the witnessing conditions were described as being poor (e.g., disguise worn, long retention interval, etc.), and for half the participants the witnessing conditions were described as being good (e.g., no disguise worn, short retention interval). In addition, for half of the participants the trial included expert testimony, and for half the participants the trial did not include expert testimony. The results supported the view that the expert testimony made jurors more sensitive. Witnessing conditions had a larger effect on jurors who heard expert testimony than on jurors who did not hear the expert testimony. The results did not support an increase in skepticism as a result of expert testimony.

Other researchers have found results consistent with the increased skepticism account (Fox & Walters, 1986; Leippe, Eisenstadt, Rauch, &

Seib, 2004; Wells, Lindsay, & Tousignant, 1980). For example, Leippe et al. (2004) had participants read a murder transcript in which an eyewitness expert either did or did not testify for the defense. The expert testimony either preceded or followed the testimony and the judge's instructions either reminded or did not remind the jurors about the expert's testimony. In addition, the strength of the prosecution's case was manipulated by varying the amount of corroborating evidence. Consistent with the skepticism account, the impact of expert testimony did not vary as a function of case strength. However, this effect was limited to conditions in which the eyewitness evidence was made especially prominent (i.e., expert testimony following the eyewitness evidence with a reminder from the judge).

What are we to think of these results? The findings suggest that expert testimony on eyewitness issues can, under some circumstances, make jurors more sensitive to the factors that impact eyewitness accuracy. This is clearly a beneficial outcome. Expert testimony can also increase juror skepticism with regards to eyewitness testimony. In evaluating studies that produce a skepticism effect, an important point to consider is that studies of expert testimony that include very good witnessing conditions and very good police procedures are unrealistic in that expert testimony is rarely going to occur in such cases. Indeed, as we saw, for expert testimony to be admitted it typically has to be specifically relevant to the facts of the case. Thus, expert testimony is only likely to occur in cases where (a) there is some sort of problem with the identification evidence, and (b) jurors are unlikely to have a full appreciation of the impact of the problem.

It is also important to keep in mind that studies have shown that expert testimony not only can impact decisions reached by jurors, but also can improve the process by which juries make decisions during deliberations (Hosch et al., 1980; Loftus, 1980). Of all the safeguards mentioned, expert testimony shows the most promise as it appears to be the most effective at mitigating the effects of eyewitness identifications.

☐ Conclusions

The first six chapters of this book focused on variables that impacted eyewitness identification. In this chapter, we have been dealing with an issue of what to do about errors in eyewitness identification. One answer, of course, is to prevent those errors in the first place by implementing proper police procedures, and screening out witnesses who are likely to be unreliable. However, sometimes a witness of questionable reliability may be introduced at trial, and it may be necessary to educate the jury about why that witness may be unreliable. Expert testimony on eyewitness issues can have a beneficent effect under those circumstances.

CHAPTER

Conclusions and Thoughts

Ten years ago; On a cool dark night; There was someone killed 'neath the town hall light; There were few at the scene and they all did agree; That the man who ran looked a lot like me.

—Wilkin and Dill, "Long Black Veil"

In concluding this volume, we will assess how the courts evaluate the reliability of eyewitness identification evidence. The goal of this section is to outline the reliability of the test of accurate identification evidence as defined by the Supreme Court in *Neil v. Biggers* (1972) and *Manson v. Braithwaite* (1977). After reviewing these criteria, we will evaluate these factors in order to determine if they can achieve the purpose they were created to accomplish—preventing the admission of suggestive eyewitness procedures and unreliable eyewitness evidence in court. Wells and Quinlivan (2009) have already started this important work, and we will summarize and expand on their findings.

Before the 1970s the courts, based on *Stovall v. Deno* (1967), had a per se exclusion policy regarding admissibility of suggestive eyewitness identification evidence. Any suggestive identification procedure or unreliable eyewitness evidence was excluded from trial. The problem of the per se exclusion approach became apparent in cases in which there was evidence corroborating the accuracy of the identification even when there were problems with the manner in which the eyewitness evidence was collected.

The per se exclusion policy was done away with in favor of a two-pronged test of reliability (*Neil v. Biggers*, 1972; *Manson v. Braithwaite*, 1977). The first prong evaluated the suggestiveness of the identification procedure. If the identification procedure was determined to be fair, then the reliability test was complete and the evidence or witness was admitted at the trial. The second prong was initiated only if the identification procedures were suggestive. In the second prong, the court attempts to ascertain whether the identification is accurate in spite of any biased procedures that were employed to collect the evidence. For example, a police officer may influence an eyewitness during the lineup procedure, but because the witness was the neighbor of the defendant for 20 years, the court might recognize that the identification is still likely to be accurate and allow the testimony. Under the per se exclusion rule, this evidence would have been excluded regardless of the witness's relationship with the defendant.

☐ First Prong: Lineup Suggestiveness or Bias

A biased lineup is defined as lineup in which people who did not witness the event choose the suspect or perpetrator at a rate that is greater than $1/n$ where n is the number of suspects in the lineup (see Chapter 2). Three major factors that bias lineups are prelineup instructions, lineup administrator influence, and the composition of the lineup.

Lineup Instructions

As mentioned in Chapter 4, there has been a considerable amount of research devoted to designing fair and unbiased lineup instructions. Witnesses are most likely already biased or predisposed to want to choose someone out of the lineup before even seeing the lineup. They may feel that they would only be asked to make an identification if the police had the suspect in custody, or, in some cases, they might be explicitly told that the suspect is in custody. Either way, the expectation that the culprit is in the lineup will increase the likelihood that a witness will make an identification (Quinlivan et al., under review).

Instructing the witness that the culprit may or may not be in the lineup (unbiased instructions) reduces this bias (see Chapter 4). In her meta-analysis, Steblay (1997) demonstrated that false identifications of innocent suspects from target-absent lineups were significantly reduced when the witness is warned that the culprit may not be in the lineup. Unbiased lineup instructions did not, however, cause a reduction in accurate identifications in target-present lineups.

Lineup Procedures

It is well understood, in the field of social psychology, that investigators can influence performance by inadvertently communicating expectations to the test takers (Rosenthal, 1967, 1976, 2002). The same is true for lineup administrators. Lineup administrators can intentionally or unintentionally convey the suspect's identity to the eyewitness, if the lineup administrator knows the identity of the suspect (a "single-blind" lineup), and therefore influence the identification decision. In "double-blind" lineups, the lineup administrator does not know the identity of the suspect and therefore cannot give any cues to the suspect's identity. Double-blind lineups reduce the number of false identifications from target-absent lineups (Haw & Fisher, 2004; Phillips et al., 1999).

Lineup Members

The foils selected to be in the lineup can have a large influence on the fairness of the lineup. Imagine a situation in which the witness described the culprit as having a tattoo on his face. Further imagine that the only person in the lineup with a tattoo on his face is an innocent suspect. Most people would agree that this is an unfair lineup. This problem could be avoided if all lineup members matched the description given by the witness—in the present example, if they all had tattoos on their faces or they all had a patch covering the tattoo. The match-to-description approach protects against the witness deducing the identity of the suspect based merely on the description of the perpetrator (Clark & Tunnicliff, 1992; Luus & Wells, 1991). Deduction, like guessing, is not the preferred method of making a positive identification. The match-to-description strategy ensures all lineup members possess those unique features described by the witness; therefore, the culprit cannot be identified merely on the basis of the description. Furthermore, Clark and Tunnicliff (1992) demonstrated that using a match-to-appearance strategy to choose lineup members can result in what the authors referred to as a "backfire effect." In short, a backfire effect refers to the fact that an innocent suspect in a target-absent lineup will on average be a closer match to the culprit than the other foils. Thus, the suspect is more likely to be identified.

To the extent that due to any of these factors—lineup administrator influence, single-blind lineups, and foils that do not match the description given by the witness—the lineup could be biased, the second prong would be initiated. The second prong allows the court to assess the reliability of the identification in spite of any suggestive procedures that have occurred.

☐ Second Prong: Five Factors

The Supreme Court has endorsed five factors for jurors to use in evaluating the reliability of eyewitness testimony. These five factors are (a) opportunity to view, (b) attention, (c) description, (d) time to identification, and (e) certainty. The notion is that if a witness had ample opportunity to view the culprit, paid attention to the culprit as the crime was occurring, gave an accurate description of the culprit, and was confident that they had identified the correct person as the culprit, then the jurors can trust that the eyewitness is accurate in their identification.

All five factors suggested in Manson and Biggers can improve memory, and it is silly to argue that having the resources to pay close attention or having a good view of the event would impair memory performance. As suggested by Wells and Quinlivan (2009), however, these factors (i.e., opportunity to view, attention, description, time to identification, and certainty) are sometimes only weakly related to eyewitness accuracy. Just because someone paid close attention and had a good view of an event does not guarantee accurate memory performance. If these criteria are only slightly correlated with memory performance, then they can be misleading as indices of identification accuracy, and therefore can mislead jurors (see Chapter 5).

Postidentification feedback creates a situation where confidence, view, and attention are not correlated with identification accuracy. *Postidentification feedback* refers to any statement made to the witness by the lineup administrator regarding the accuracy of the lineup selection. In the original study, Wells and Bradfield (1998) had participants watch a video clip from a security camera and make an identification from a culprit-absent lineup. Following the identification, some of the participants were erroneously told that they had made an accurate selection ("Good, you identified the culprit"), whereas others were given no feedback. Participants who were given confirming postidentification feedback reported that they paid more attention to the perpetrator, were more certain in their identification, and had a clearer view of the perpetrator compared to participants that were not given feedback. Keep in mind that the lineup was culprit-absent, so all identifications were wrong. Confirming feedback increased participants' self-ratings on the variables that jurors are instructed to use as indicators of eyewitness accuracy: confidence, view, and attention. Confirming feedback made the witness feel and appear to be a more reliable eyewitness, even when their identifications were false. In situations like this one, if jurors were to rely on the witness confidence, opportunity to view, and amount of attention paid to crime, then jurors would wrongfully conclude that the witness was accurate. These conclusions were confirmed by Douglas et al. (2010), who

videotaped interrogations of participants who were or were not given confirming postidentification feedback and showed the tapes to mock jurors.
The mock jurors rated the witnesses who received confirming feedback as
more accurate and indicated that they were more likely to convict based
on their testimony relative to the testimony of no feedback witnesses.

One of the Biggers criteria not mentioned in the postidentification feedback study is description accuracy. Description accuracy can be broken
down into two parts: quantity and quality, or amount and accuracy. It has
intuitive appeal that a witness who provides a complete detailed description of the culprit (e.g., the witness might give this description: "The
culprit was 6'2", 205 pounds, Caucasian, thinning black hair, white goatee, medium build, and beady green eyes. He carried a green knapsack
that was held together by binder clips and he rode a bike.") will make a
more accurate witness than one that provides a less complete description.
Unfortunately, the amount of information in witness descriptions is also
only weakly correlated with identification accuracy (Grass & Sporer, 1991;
Pigott & Brigham, 1985). However, mock jurors more readily believe eyewitnesses are reliable when descriptions of the culprit are more detailed
(Lieppe, Manion, & Romanczyk, 1992; Miessner, Spoore, & Schooler, 2007).

As is the case with quantity of descriptors, there is only a weak correlation between quality of descriptors and identification accuracy. In studies
in which participants have been forced to generate elaborate descriptions
of faces, there is still no positive correlation between description accuracy
and identification accuracy (Meissner, Brigham, & Kelly 2001). In fact, it
has been shown in some studies that forcing participants to derive elaborate descriptors may cause the participants to come up with descriptions
of features that are inaccurate, which in turn may impair subsequent
recognition accuracy. Although accuracy of descriptors is not strongly
related with identification accuracy, inaccurate descriptors are predictive
of subsequent identification errors (Finger & Pezdek, 1991; Meissner, 2002;
Meissner et al., 2001).

One situation where description accuracy is moderately correlated with
identification accuracy is when the face in question is easy to describe.
Wells (1985) showed participants multiple faces and tested their ability to
both recognize and identify the faces. He found that faces that were more
distinct were easier to describe and identify. The correlation, however,
between description accuracy and identification accuracy for nondistinct
faces was only modest.

Confidence

In addition to what was already mentioned we are going to elaborate on
confidence because it is one of, if not the most, persuasive factor to jurors

when it comes to eyewitness testimony (Cutler, Penrod, & Dexter, 1990). It seems reasonable to assume that confidence and accuracy would be strongly correlated. Those witnesses who are accurate know they are correct and in turn are highly confident in their selections. In fact, survey research on actual jurors and laypersons confirms that the majority of people hold this belief (see Chapter 5). Eyewitness confidence, however, is moderated by many factors that are not related to memory, such as the aforementioned postidentification feedback effect. Confirming postidentification feedback creates a situation in which witnesses who are inaccurate report being very confident in their identifications. In this situation the correlation between confidence and accuracy is nearly zero. None of the identifications are correct, so high confidence is not correlated with accuracy.

Many researchers have studied the confidence–accuracy relationship and have generally arrived at the same conclusion. Sporer and colleagues (1995), for example, meta-analyzed 30 separate tests of the correlation between confidence and eyewitness identification accuracy with data from over 4,000 mock witnesses and concluded that the relationship was, under the best of circumstances, moderate in magnitude. The best of circumstances are high illumination, no stress, clear view, no distractions, and so forth. All of these factors should make it easier to remember the event but still only provide a modest accuracy–confidence correlation.

Deffenbacher (1980), in a similar account, offered the "optimality hypothesis" to explain the weak confidence–accuracy correlation. Optimal viewing conditions, according to this hypothesis, improve both accuracy and the relation between confidence and accuracy. Witnesses, under optimal conditions, should give more accurate metacognitive judgments. The optimality hypothesis has received some experimental support (Deffenbacher, 1980; Shapiro & Penrod, 1986; Sporer et al., 1995), but this support is not universally obtained (Penrod & Cutler, 1995).

The best explanation, we believe, is that although eyewitnesses are somewhat sensitive to the accuracy of their identifications, their expressions of confidence are influenced by cognitive, personality, and social factors that are independent of identification accuracy. Any factor that influences confidence independent of accuracy will attenuate the relation between confidence and accuracy.

☐ Conclusion

In summary the factors endorsed by the Supreme Court in the second prong of *Manson* (*Manson v. Braithwaite*, 1977) to evaluate the reliability of eyewitnesses will be misleading when those factors are weakly or not at all correlated with accuracy. All five factors are mediated by social and cognitive variables that influence the witness's perception independent of accuracy. It is possible that confirming postidentification feedback and other variables can make witnesses feel and appear to be more reliable even when they are inaccurate (see Douglas et al., 2010). This is particularly disconcerting in the case of confidence, because it is considered the single most persuasive factor by jurors (Cutler et al.). The danger with using the five factors of second prong of Manson is they can be misleading as to the reliability of eyewitness evidence and mislead jurors to make the wrong decision.

There is no magic bullet that will fix the problem of faulty eyewitness identification. The best alternative, we believe, is twofold. First, organizations like the Innocence Project must continue to help exonerate inmates who have been wrongly convicted. These exonerations generally grab the attention of the national media, which in turn raises public awareness. Second, social scientists must continue to conduct psycho-legal research with special emphasis on designing experiments that have more external validity. The research, in addition, must continue to try to influence policy and law makers so that change can be systemic.

Philosophical Afterword

Memory and Reasonable Belief

☐ Introduction

Philosophy is the attempt to formulate and give reasons for general theories about what exists or is real (*metaphysics*), the nature and extent of knowledge (*epistemology*), what makes something worth doing or having (*value theory*), and the difference between correct and incorrect arguments (*logic*). Memory is implicated in a range of philosophical problems including problems in metaphysics (how much of our identity depends upon our ability to recall our past?), in value theory (do we have a moral obligation to remember atrocities?), and in epistemology (is memory somehow a source of knowledge or is it merely the capacity to store knowledge acquired by other means?).

Because the topic of this book is eyewitness identification and testimony, the focus of this chapter will be a philosophical problem about memory and knowledge or reasonable belief that we call *the paradox of absent evidence*. An examination of this problem will provide some conceptual tools for understanding the implications of empirical results about memory, and will illustrate some connections between memory research in philosophy and in psychology. The main goal is to introduce representative theories of reasonable belief and to briefly scout their strengths and weaknesses as they apply to memory.

☐ The Paradox of Absent Evidence

Memory is constituted by a range of psychological capacities, processes, and procedures for the mental storage, retention, and activation of skills and data. Some memory—*nondeclarative, or nonpropositional, memory*—is not *of* or *about* anything and therefore lacks representational content. Memory of previously acquired skills is habit or procedural memory, *know-how*. Some nondeclarative memory has uninterpreted, raw content: the sound of the hook to "Be My Baby," what Ingrid Bergman looked like in *Casablanca*, and so on. Representational (declarative) memory uses representational data (Latin for "things that are given": concepts, propositions, mental images, and so on) by means of which we think *of* or *about* the things that we recollect, in the broadest sense of "things." We are concerned with memory that has *propositional content*, roughly what psychologists call *declarative memory*.

Representational memory is distinguished by the fact that its contents are *of* or *about* things, events, or states of affairs. Representational memory includes not only our grasp of concepts (semantic memory) and beliefs that are not indexed to our own experiences (my memory that James Buchanan was president) but also the episodic memories we have of or about things and states of affairs that are essentially indexed to our own past awareness (my recollection that I saw the Kansas City Royals win the 1985 World Series on television).

Propositional memory is the foundation for a stable system of beliefs. It is essential to our self-conception and may even be a necessary condition for thinking at all (Kurtzman, 1983). It is characteristic of the assumptions that inform the institutions and practices in which inquiry plays a role that memory can provide us with *knowledge* and *reasonable beliefs*. Our system of justice, to take an example that is central to the research discussed in this book, depends upon the assumption that eyewitnesses can present *evidence* in their testimony that is based on their memory-based *knowledge* about persons and events they have experienced.

The paradox of absent evidence challenges the assumption that propositional memory provides us with a significant amount of knowledge and reasonable belief. For although it seems that we know quite a bit by means of memory, it also seems that we recollect almost no evidence for most of the propositions that we recollect. I now seem to remember that James Buchanan was president, but I seem to remember none of the evidence that I had when I acquired this belief. Did I read it in a book? Who wrote it? Did a teacher tell me? Which one? Nothing comes to mind. I also seem to remember that I crashed my parents' orange Mercury when I was 2 years old after having accidentally disengaged the parking brake, but the images that accompany this memory are both indistinct and, alas, false (as

I learned when I returned to the scene of the accident years later). Finally, it also seems that an essential feature of having knowledge—knowledge is a special kind of reasonable belief—is having evidence for what one knows or, more generally, reasonably believes.[1] These three assumptions constitute a *paradox* because although they are individually plausible, they cannot all be true.

The following argument poses the problem clearly and concisely by showing that the conjunction of two of our assumptions entails that the third is false:

1. A person S reasonably believes a proposition P, only if S has good evidence that P is true.
2. Persons lack good evidence for almost all of the propositions that they recollect.
3. ∴ Almost none of our recollections is a reasonable belief.

The premises—(1) and (2)—are individually plausible, as we have seen. Furthermore, if (1) and (2) were true, then (3) would have to be true. Yet (3) expresses a counterintuitive and apparently intolerable skepticism about memory.

To solve this problem without embracing skepticism, we must either reject the assumption expressed by premise (1), that we must have evidence for what we reasonably believe, or the assumption expressed by premise (2), that we lack evidence for most of the propositions that we recollect.

In this chapter we shall investigate some issues in the epistemology of memory by considering the strengths and weaknesses of several proposed solutions to this paradox. In particular, we shall consider theories about memory knowledge that reject (1) and others that reject (2). First, we clarify some terms that will play important roles in our investigation.

☐ Terms

We use *proposition* and *statement* interchangeably for thought content that has, or that *could* have, one of the classic *truth values*: *true* or *false*. Propositions are related to the declarative sentences that are used to express them, but cannot be identified with sentences. A useful criterion by which to identify propositions would be that a sentence expresses a proposition if, and only if, it makes *grammatical* sense to ask whether that sentence is true (or whether it is false). Thus, "Lincoln was the 14th president" expresses a (false) proposition because it makes grammatical sense to ask, "Is it true that Lincoln was the 14th president?" On the other hand, "Do you know the way to San Jose?" does not express a proposition, at least not in our language. "Is it true or false that 'Do you know the way to San Jose?'" is ungrammatical.

Unfortunately this proposed criterion, though useful, is not generally correct. For one thing, rhetorical questions and rhetorical imperatives—such as "Who doesn't know the way to San Jose?" or "Don't tell me that Obama hasn't kept his promises!"—do not satisfy the criterion but can express propositions. For another, the criterion does not tell us what proposition is expressed by a sentence. The same declarative sentence can express different propositions on different occasions. For example, the sentence "I exist" expresses a different proposition when I say it than the proposition it expresses when you say it. We need not resolve these and related thorny issues. It will suffice for our purposes to say that propositions are the sorts of contents that can have the classical truth values *true* and *false*, or that they are the sorts of things that can be the contents of sentences or beliefs that purport to represent states of affairs.

We use *evidence* to abbreviate *propositional evidence*—evidence for the truth of a proposition. By *propositional evidence* for a proposition P, we mean a proposition or set of propositions E that, if true, would be positively relevant to the truth of P. So, for example, if E entails P or if the truth of E would increase the likelihood that P is true, then E is evidence for P. We shall say that a person S has *good evidence* for a proposition P if S has evidence for P and, given all of the evidence at S's disposal, the evidence that P is true is better than the evidence that P is false.

The word *remember* and its cognates are *success terms*. To say that persons *remember* something is to ascribe a kind of success to them. If someone remembers a proposition and does not merely *seem* to remember it, that person has succeeded at something. What kind of success? In our view, *remember* ascribes *doxastic* (=involving belief), *factive* (=involving truth), and weak *evidential* success. Let us elaborate. *Remember* expresses doxastic success because S *remembers that* P implies that S *believes that* P, at least at the time of the remembering. *Remember* expresses *factive* success because if S *remembers that* P, then P is true. Finally, remembering involves a kind of weak *evidential* success because if S remembers that P, then, at some point, S had good evidence for P. We leave it open, however, that a person might never before have believed a proposition that they now remember—perhaps they only now form the belief in light of other remembered data—and that persons can remember propositions for which they no longer have good evidence. We also leave it open whether the *contents* of memories—the propositions that one remembers—were ever represented by the person prior to the activation of the memory beliefs in which they figure (Hacking, 1998, pp. 249–250).

We need a term that refers to the activation of a belief by memory but that does not imply factive or evidential success. We use the word *recollect* for this purpose. In particular, we use *recollect* and its cognates to describe cases in which a person forms a belief in a proposition by means of memory without implying that the belief is *true* and without implying that it was ever *supported by good evidence* for the person who recollects it. Recollections, in short, are *ostensible* cases of remembering.

We use *memory belief* to refer to any beliefs formed by means of the psychological capacities, procedures, and processes of memory and not to refer to beliefs that are *about memory* itself. So, in our terminology, the paradox of absent evidence purports to show that almost none of the beliefs that we form by means of memory are cases of reasonable belief. The paradox is not merely a problem for reasonable belief *about memory*, but also a problem about having any reasonable beliefs that are activated by memory.

There is an important distinction between the *accuracy* of a given memory belief and the *reliability* of the system by means of which a memory belief is activated. This distinction is analogous to the distinction between getting a hit in a single trip to the plate in baseball (which is analogous to *accuracy*) and a batting *average* (which is analogous to *reliability*). A memory belief is *accurate* if, and only if, the believed proposition is true. By contrast, the capacities, processes, and procedures that constitute our system of memory are *reliable* to the extent, and just to the extent, that they *tend* to produce true memory beliefs. The *reliability* of a person's memory is, so to speak, that person's cognitive "batting average" with respect to memory: the ratio of true memory beliefs to total memory beliefs formed by that person's memory processes or procedures. Just as a poor batter can hit a home run in a given trip to the plate, a true memory belief can result from a highly unreliable memory system. Just as an excellent batter can strike out, a false memory belief can result when a highly reliable memory system activates a false belief. Mighty Casey struck out in his most famous appearance at the plate. One complication here is that memory per se may not be the source of the falsehood of false memory beliefs. Some false memory beliefs are false because, for example, of perceptual errors made at the time a belief was first formed. We shall ignore this complication.

The empirical results that we have been most concerned with in this book are about conditions that significantly affect the reliability of our system for forming eyewitness memory beliefs. These results are not directly concerned with whether any given memory belief is accurate or not, although one way in which psychologists study reliability is by studying cases in which they know that memory beliefs are false (by using "target-absent" lineups, for example). We have been especially interested in exploring various cognitive "blind spots" that are built into our system for forming, storing, and retrieving memory beliefs. Such "blind spots" affect the reliability of our memory systems by either preventing us from forming true beliefs or, worse, promoting the formation of false memory beliefs. We have seen, for example, how factors such as cross-race identification, head covering, and postidentification feedback affect the reliability of the procedures we use in making eyewitness identifications on the basis of memory.

Finally, we use the expression *reasonable belief* to express an *epistemic* and not a *pragmatic* value. Thus a memory belief is reasonable, in our sense, just in case it is permissible, virtuous, or otherwise good to believe it *given the goal of holding as many true and as few false beliefs as possible* on topics that are important to us. Whether or not holding a memory belief benefits us or harms us in pursuit of other goals we have is a separate, pragmatic issue. We leave it open whether the epistemic value of an epistemically reasonable belief is a function of the evidence that is available for the believed proposition or whether, for example, a belief can be epistemically reasonable if it is produced and sustained in the right sort of way, whether or not forming a belief in that way involves having evidence for it.

☐ Accounts That Reject Premise (2)

Because premise (1) is essential to a widely shared, plausible, and traditional account of knowledge—the view that knowledge is (at least) true belief for which a person has good evidence—we begin by considering the possibility that (2) is false. In particular, we begin with accounts according to which, preliminary appearances to the contrary, we do have evidence for much of what we recollect. We shall consider four accounts that reject (2): the *diachronic theory, evidentialist foundationalism*, the *two-factor theory*, and *evidentialist coherentism*. These theories all assume what we call *evidentialism*, the view that knowledge and reasonable belief require that we have evidence for what we know and reasonably believe.[2] As we shall see, although there are strengths to each of these views, each also suffers from significant problems in accounting for reasonable memory beliefs.

The Diachronic Theory

The *diachronic theory*, as we call it (it is typically called the *preservation theory*), holds that knowledge requires evidence but that we do have evidence for much of what we recollect. According to the diachronic theory, the evidence that can support memory beliefs is the very same nonmemory evidence, if any, that previously supported the propositions that we now recollect, typically at the time those beliefs were formed. So, for example, if I came to believe that you were wearing a red vest at the Christmas party on the basis of the sensory experiences that I had when I saw you at the party, those same experiences provide evidence for my present recollection that you were wearing a red vest at the Christmas party, even if I have now forgotten the experiences that provided that evidence. According to the diachronic theory, forgotten evidence provides evidential support for beliefs across time.

Sidney Shoemaker (1967) argued for a version of the diachronic theory in this argument for the existence of memory knowledge:

> [I]f beliefs can, indeed must, be retained for some period of time, the same must be true of knowledge. At any rate, this will be so if … a person's belief can be well grounded (well enough grounded to qualify it for being knowledge if it is true) by virtue of its having been so grounded in the past—and certainly we do not require, in our ordinary use of the word "knowledge," that a person must constantly be acquiring new grounds for a belief, if his retention of it is to be the retention of knowledge. But if there is retained knowledge, then there is memory knowledge. (P. 274)

Shoemaker's argument is about knowledge, not reasonable belief, but it applies to memory knowledge because it is about the conditions for having reasonable belief, and knowledge is a special case of reasonable belief. His argument can, therefore, be generalized as follows:

1. Beliefs persist over time.
2. Many of our present beliefs were reasonable in the past because they were well-supported by nonmemory evidence that we had in the past.
3. Having reasonable beliefs does not require that we acquire new evidence for what we reasonably believe.
4. If having reasonable beliefs does not require that we obtain new evidence for what we reasonably believe, then evidence that supports a belief at one time can support it at later times.
5. ∴ Many memory beliefs can be well supported by (past) evidence, whether or not that evidence is remembered.

The diachronic theory—so called by us because of its distinctive hypothesis regarding evidential support-at-a-distance, and because the standard name of *preservation theory* can wrongly suggests that it is the evidence that is preserved—would account for how we can have supporting evidence for present memory beliefs even when we have forgotten that evidence. According to the diachronic theory, because we do not need new evidence for beliefs that were reasonable in the past, memory beliefs can be supported by evidence that we have forgotten.

A problem for the diachronic theory is that it implies that two persons who form the same belief on the basis of the same evidence will, in the absence of new evidence, have the same amount of evidential support for the belief that they had to begin with. For example, suppose that two persons, $S1$ and $S2$, form the belief P at the same time and on the basis of the same good evidence E. Suppose, further, that $S1$ retains the belief P but forgets E. $S2$, by contrast, retains both the belief P and the belief E and, furthermore, that $S2$ frequently notes the evidential connection between E and P. If the diachronic theory is correct, then both $S1$ and $S2$ have the same amount of evidential support for P because the diachronic theory implies that E supports P over time. This is incorrect, however, because $S2$'s belief is much better supported by evidence than is $S1$'s belief. The diachronic theory is incompatible with the fact that evidence for memory beliefs decays over time as original evidence is forgotten.

Where, then, has Shoemaker's argument gone wrong? It contains a subtle confusion about the sense in which having reasonable beliefs does not require that we acquire new evidence for those beliefs. In particular, premise (4) is false given the interpretation that is required to establish the diachronic theory. On one interpretation, (4) says that "if having reasonable beliefs does not require that we obtain new evidence over time, then propositions that are positively relevant to the truth of P are always positively relevant to the truth of P." This is true, but does not support the diachronic theory because it says nothing about whether having evidential support for a proposition requires having *present access* to evidence for P. Shoemaker's argument requires that (4) be interpreted to say that *if having reasonable beliefs does not require that we obtain new evidence over time, then any evidence that a person ever has for a proposition P supports P for that person at later times, **whether or not S is aware of that evidence**.* This assumption is false, as our example shows. So premise (4) is false on the interpretation needed to establish the diachronic theory. It is not true that evidence that a person has for a proposition always supports that person's belief in the proposition.

Evidentialist Foundationalism

According to a *foundationalist* epistemology, a person's reasonable beliefs comprise a properly structured edifice of beliefs with a base, or foundation, of beliefs that have a reasonability that does not come from the evidence provided by *other beliefs*. Foundationalists, therefore, hold that there are two kinds of reasonable beliefs: beliefs that are reasonable because other reasonable beliefs provide evidence for them (*nonbasic beliefs*), and beliefs that are reasonable independently of any evidence provided by other beliefs (*foundational* or *basic beliefs*). So, because circles and infinite sequences of reasons cannot provide evidence for beliefs, nonbasic beliefs are reasonable only if they stand in the right sort of relationship to basic beliefs. A key question for foundationalists, therefore, is "What makes basic beliefs reasonable?" An important question for the epistemology of memory is "How can a foundationalist epistemology respond to the paradox of absent evidence?" If my original evidence for *P* was *E*, how can I reasonably believe *P* when I have forgotten *E*?

Evidentialist foundationalism holds that basic beliefs, like all reasonable beliefs, must be supported by evidence. What makes basic beliefs *basic* is that the evidence that supports them is not provided by other *beliefs*. Some evidentialist foundationalists think, for example, that present mental states that are not beliefs—features of our present sensory experiences, for example—provide evidence for basic beliefs. So, for example, my belief that *there is something red in front of me* might be supported by my basic belief that *I am now having an experience of red*, which is, in turn, supported by my present non-belief sensory experience of *having an appearance of red*.

Memory beliefs are reasonable, then, provided that they are either basic or stand in the right kind of relationship to basic beliefs. Evidentialist foundationalists must show that reasonable memory beliefs are reasonable because of their relationship to presently accessible evidence that is provided by other beliefs or that they are ultimately made reasonable by nondoxastic states of affairs. What kind of presently accessible evidence is available when we have forgotten the original evidence we had for our memory beliefs?

One strategy for evidentialist foundationalists is to claim that memory beliefs—my belief that *James Buchanan was president*, for example—are nonbasic beliefs that can be supported by basic beliefs about *what one seems to remember*. Basic beliefs about what one seems to remember, in turn, can be supported by nondoxastic states of *seeming to remember*. Such states are not beliefs but can provide evidence for beliefs. They might, for example, be mental images acquired in the past that typically accompany recollections and that presently serve as evidence for beliefs about what we seem to remember. According to this approach, *seeming to remember* provide evidence for *beliefs about what one seems to remember* that, in turn, are evidence for memory beliefs. So, for example, my nonbelief state of *seeming to recollect Buchanan being president* provides evidence for a belief about my present mental state—that *I seem to remember that Buchanan was president*—which, in turn, provides evidence for my memory belief that *Buchanan was president*. Having lost track of the evidence that supported this belief for me in the past, I now have evidence for it in the form of my present experience of seeming to remember it.

This approach to memory knowledge is described by Pollock and Cruz (1999):

> [I]f we are to accommodate memory within foundationalism, memory must provide us with beliefs about what we "seem to remember" and then we infer the truth of what are ordinarily regarded as memory beliefs from these apparent memories. The viability of such an account turns in part on whether there is such a psychological state of "seeming to remember" that is analogous to being appeared to in some way or other. (P. 48)

This view holds that "seemings to remember" are not beliefs but can provide evidence for basic beliefs about what one seems to remember, which, in turn, provide evidence for ordinary memory beliefs.

There is a major problem for this theory, however. If it were true, we would have too much evidence for memory beliefs, because the theory implies that we have evidence for virtually *every* belief that is activated by memory. This can be shown by considering two sorts of cases: cases in which we recollect beliefs that were not supported by evidence when we formed them and cases in which we have both recollections and the original evidence for our memory beliefs.

The foundationalist theory under consideration implies that we can acquire evidence for memory beliefs that have never been supported by any other evidence. Suppose that at time $t1$ a person S formed the belief P without any evidence for P and, indeed, despite the fact that S was aware of strong evidence D against P. At a later time $t2$, S has forgotten the defeating evidence D but reactivates the belief P and seems to remember it. According to the version of evidentialist foundationalism under consideration, S's previously unsupported, defeated belief P is now supported by evidence *merely because S has recollected it*. Furthermore, if it is reasonable to believe a proposition for which one has undefeated evidence, the theory implies that S's unreasonable belief P has become reasonable merely by having been recollected. Neither of these consequences of the theory is true (Huemer, 1999). To avoid these conclusions, we must reject the view that nondoxastic seemings to remember provide evidence for memory beliefs.

By parity of reasoning, the theory also implies that mere recollection enables us to add to the evidence that we have had for our beliefs merely by recollecting them. For suppose that at time $t1$ a person $S1$ is aware of conclusive evidence E for a proposition P—suppose that S has a demonstration of a mathematical theorem P—and that S believes P on the basis of E. At a later time $t2$, S not only recollects P on the basis of the experience of seeming to remember P, S also clearly remembers the conclusive evidence E for P. This version of evidentialist foundationalism implies that, at $t2$, S has *more* evidence for P than S had at $t1$. For at $t1$ S's evidence for P consisted only of E whereas, according to this theory, S's evidence for P at $t2$ consists of both E and R. In this case, too, the theory implies that we can increase the evidence that we have for propositions merely by recollecting them.

Because we are driven to this conclusion by the assumption that seemings to remember and beliefs about them can provide evidence for memory beliefs, we must reject this assumption. Seemings to remember and beliefs about seemings to remember do not provide evidence for memory beliefs. So we must reject the version of evidentialist foundationalism under consideration and its proposed solution to the paradox of absent evidence.[3]

The Two-Factor Theory

Michael Huemer has a theory of reasonable memory belief that is designed to avoid the weaknesses of both the diachronic theory (that only nonmemory evidence that was available at the time a belief was formed can support it when it becomes a memory belief) and of evidentialist foundationalism (that seeming memories are nonbelief mental states that provide evidence for memory beliefs). Huemer's theory, however, also attempts to retain key elements of each theory in order to maintain that most present memories are supported by good evidence. According to the two-factor theory, memory beliefs are reasonable if, and only if, they were acquired on the basis of good evidence and have remained supported by good presently available evidence, including the evidence provided by seeming memories. Unfortunately, the theory fails because it is incompatible with the view that only presently available evidence is relevant to the evidential support that persons have for their beliefs.

Huemer proposes the two-factor theory as an account of what is called *justification*, but we avoid this technical term. The trouble with the word *justification* is that it is used to refer to importantly different things. In one of its senses, *justification* expresses a normative (that is, *value*) property of beliefs such that beliefs with the property are such that it is *permissible*, *intellectually virtuous*, or otherwise epistemically *good* for a person to hold them. In another sense, *justification* refers to the *reasons*—in particular to the *evidence*—that a person has for a belief.[4] If we suppose, as some do, that only propositions for which one has adequate evidence are good to believe (*weak evidentialism*), then these two senses of *justification* are linked. For if this connection obtains, then a belief that is justified in the good-to-believe sense must be a belief for which one has evidence, hence must have justification in the second sense. Because, as we shall see, it is contested whether weak evidentialism[5] is correct, we use *reasonable* and its cognates instead of *justified* to refer to beliefs that it is epistemically good to hold, and we use *evidence*, not *justification*, when we mean evidence.

Like the diachronic theory, Huemer's theory requires that reasonable memory beliefs be *acquired* on the basis of good presently available evidence. Like evidentialist foundationalism, it requires that reasonable memory beliefs be *retained* on the basis of good presently available evidence. Finally, the theory holds that seeming memories can be evidence for memory beliefs under the appropriate conditions. Under normal circumstances, nonmemory and memory evidence are individually necessary but only jointly sufficient for reasonable memory beliefs. For, according to the two-factor theory, a memory belief is reasonable if, and only if, "one had an adequate justification for adopting it at some point, and thenceforward one was justified in retaining it" (Huemer, 1999, p. 351).[6] Under normal conditions, nonmemory evidence provides support for adopting a belief and memory evidence—including the evidence provided by seeming memories—provides support for retaining the belief as a memory belief. So, to state Huemer's theory in our terms, a person S's memory belief P is reasonable if, and only if, S had evidence sufficient to make *acquiring* the belief P reasonable (*the acquisition condition*) and, at every subsequent time, S has evidence sufficient to make it reasonable to *retain* the belief P (*the retention condition*). An important consequence of Huemer's theory, therefore, is that memory beliefs are reasonable only if they are supported by good evidence that is presently available.

Huemer argues that evidentialist foundationalism is false because seeming memories are not normally sufficient for reasonable belief. If they were, then beliefs that are otherwise unreasonable would be reasonable merely in virtue of being held. Our argument against evidentialist foundationalism is adapted from Huemer's, yet we take the most powerful version of the argument to be about *good evidence*, not *reasonability*. Our conclusion is not, like Huemer's, that seeming memories do not make memory beliefs *reasonable*, it is that seeming memories do not provide *good evidence* for memory beliefs. For if seeming memories did provide good evidence for memory beliefs, then we would have good evidence for any recollection simply by having it. It makes no difference whether or not having the evidence provided by seeming memories is sufficient for reasonable belief. We claim, therefore, that evidentialist foundationalism is false because seeming memories do not provide good evidence for present memory beliefs whether or not seeming memories are sufficient for reasonable belief. Huemer claims that seeming memories do provide evidence for memory beliefs but that this evidence is not *normally* sufficient to make memory beliefs reasonable (there is an important exception, as we shall see). Because it is a crucial part of Huemer's theory that seeming memories can provide good evidence for present memory beliefs, his view is incompatible with ours. Where does he go wrong?

The answer is to be found by considering Huemer's main objection to the diachronic theory. Huemer rejects the diachronic theory on the grounds that it fails to recognize the contribution that the evidence provided by *seeming memories* can make to the reasonability of memory beliefs. Huemer argues that because it does not recognize that seeming memories can provide evidence for memory beliefs, the diachronic theory cannot solve the *two-Mikes problem.*[7] Mike1 is a normal person who lives in the actual world and who has memory beliefs including, say, the belief that *"Mugsy robbed me yesterday."* Mike1 formed this belief yesterday on the basis of then-present but now-faded sensory experiences and has subsequently maintained it on the basis of present seeming memories. Mike2's world is presently identical to Mike1's in every respect. So Mike2 is like Mike1 in every present respect, hence Mike2 also believes that "Mugsy robbed me yesterday" and also maintains this belief because of his present seeming memories. Huemer commits himself to the view that under these conditions, (a) Mike1's belief about Mugsy is reasonable; (b) if Mike1's belief about Mugsy is reasonable, then Mike2's belief is reasonable; and (c) Mike1 and Mike2 have *the same degree and kind of evidence for their beliefs* about Mugsy (Huemer, 1999, p. 350). The diachronic theory is false because it does not imply these things.

For suppose that although Mike1 lives in the actual world, Mike2 lives in a world that was created only 5 minutes ago, with all of the present features of Mike1's world in place, including recollections and seeming memories. Mike1 *remembers* that "Mugsy robbed me yesterday," whereas Mike2 only recollects this because it did not happen. The diachronic theory—according to which memory beliefs can be supported only by nonmemory evidence available in the past—implies that Mike1's belief is reasonable because Mike1 had the appropriate nonmemory evidence when he first formed the belief about Mugsy. Mike2's belief, however, is not reasonable according to the diachronic theory because there was no past nonmemory evidence that ever supported Mike2's belief that "Mugsy robbed me yesterday." The only potentially relevant cognitive resources available to Mike2 are his present recollections and seeming memories about Mugsy. According to the diachronic theory, however, such recollections and seeming memories are not evidence for memory beliefs. So, because Mike2 did not exist yesterday, almost *none* of his memory beliefs are reasonable because almost none of his memory beliefs were acquired on the basis of past nonmemory evidence. Huemer concludes that because the diachronic theory implies that Mike2's memory belief about Mugsy is not reasonable and that Mike1 and Mike2 do not have the same degree and kind of evidence for their beliefs, the diachronic theory is false.

A problem for Huemer's argument against the diachronic theory is that it seems to be incompatible with Huemer's own two-factor theory. For the two-factor theory also seems to imply that Mike1's belief is reasonable but that Mike2's belief is not. Because Mike2 did not acquire his belief that *Mugsy robbed me yesterday* in the way that Mike1 did—Mike2 began his existence with the ostensible memory that *Mugsy robbed me yesterday* built in and never had non-memory evidence for this belief—it seems that Mike2 does not satisfy the acquisition condition that the two-factor theory requires. What is more, Huemer argued that seeming memories are not generally sufficient to make memory beliefs reasonable, contrary to the defining thesis of evidentialist foundationalism. So even if Mike2 did somehow satisfy the acquisition condition, it seems that Huemer's theory implies that his evidence would be insufficient to make his memory belief reasonable.

To solve these problems, Huemer needs to make it plausible that Mike2 *does* satisfy the acquisition condition and that Mike2's seeming memories *suffice* to make his memory belief reasonable. To do this, Huemer (1999) made the assertion (we shall call it *Huemer's posit*) that "coming to believe something by seeming to remember it (in the absence of defeaters that one is aware of) is an epistemically rational way of *acquiring* the belief" (p. 351, our emphasis). So although under ordinary circumstances the evidence provided by the state of seeming to remember P is not sufficient to make believing P reasonable, seeming to remember P can satisfy the acquisition condition and make believing P reasonable *if it occurs at the very time the belief is formed.* Under these special conditions, seeming memories provide evidence that is sufficient for the reasonability of memory beliefs because they enable memory beliefs to satisfy *both* the acquisition condition and, in the fullness of time, the retention condition.

Huemer's theory fails, however, because it is incompatible with the view that is needed to solve the two-Mikes problem: that only presently available evidence can support a belief. Suppose that a person S comes to reasonably believe that "John has seen *Full Metal Jacket*" on the basis of nonmemory evidence but that S's evidence for this is misleading because it is false that John has seen *Full Metal Jacket*. Later S hears, from an equally credible source, that John has *not* seen *Full Metal Jacket*. In light of the counterbalanced evidence for the proposition in question, S suspends judgment on the matter and stops believing that John has seen *Full Metal Jacket*. A significant amount of time passes, after which S again forms the belief that John has seen *Full Metal Jacket* and seems to remember it.[8] The two-factor theory, including Huemer's posit, implies that S's belief is reasonable, because seeming memories are sufficient to make beliefs reasonable if they occur at the time the belief is formed. This is a mistake. For, as this example shows, the two-factor theory together with Huemer's posit incorrectly implies that *any* belief that is given up and subsequently reacquired will be reasonable if only we seem to remember it. An obvious extension of this argument in light of our objection to evidentialist foundationalism shows that, under similar conditions, seeming memories can boost the evidence we have for propositions for which we have good present evidence.

Huemer's posit is relevant to cases involving eyewitness identification. As we have seen, it is not uncommon for persons to form new false beliefs while at the same time seeming to remember that they are true. Under a range of different kinds of circumstances, for example, eyewitnesses can come to form new false memory beliefs in the presence of seeming memories, for example that "person number 4 in the lineup is the person who assaulted me." These beliefs would be supported by enough evidence to make them reasonable, if Huemer's posit were true. The two-factor theory thus has a significant epistemic blind spot: It opens the door to lots of ostensibly reasonable false beliefs and thus tends to reduce the reliability of processes or procedures of belief formation that conform to it. To avoid this blind spot, we should reject the two-factor theory.

The deep problem with the two-factor theory is brought into focus by the two-Mikes problem. For there is only one way to solve the two-Mikes problem that implies that Mike1 and Mike2 have the same kind and degree of evidence for the relevant memory belief: One must hold that only presently available evidence can provide support for memory beliefs. If past evidence were relevant, then Mike2 would not have the same kind and degree of evidence that Mike1 has. This leads Huemer to make his posit, which, unfortunately, makes his theory vulnerable to our fatal counterexample. Our response to the two-Mikes problem is to agree that Mike1 and Mike2 have the same kind and degree of evidence because *neither* has good evidence.

An alternative approach that Huemer might take is to reject his implicit assumption that good beliefs require the support of presently available evidence. On this view, he might agree that the two-factor theory does not imply that we have significant evidence for most of our memory beliefs but that reasonable belief does not require evidential support. This suggestion, if developed, would make Huemer's theory a response to the paradox of absent evidence that rejects premise (1). Although we shall not try to develop such a theory here, we think this approach to reasonable memory belief, and to reasonable belief generally, is promising.

Evidentialist Coherentism

Evidentialist (also known as *positive*) coherentism is characterized by a negative thesis and a positive thesis. The negative thesis is that no belief is basic: Beliefs are reasonable only by means of the evidential support they acquire from other beliefs, and no beliefs play a special role in making other beliefs reasonable. The positive thesis is that beliefs in a system confer reasonability on a given belief only to the extent that the system as a whole is *coherent*. So a belief is reasonable for a person at a time just in case it is supported by other beliefs in a coherent system of beliefs that the person holds at that time. Coherence, in turn, is explained in various ways, all of which amount to a view according to which coherence is *consistency* plus *something else*: explanatory integration, mutual support, or some such thing. Harman (1986) put the point with characteristic simplicity, saying only that "[coherence] includes not only consistency, but also a network of relations among one's beliefs, especially relations of implication and explanation" (p. 32). Although, in our view, evidentialist coherentism is the most promising evidentialist account of reasonable memory beliefs, it faces substantial problems. For it seems that evidential coherence is not a necessary condition for reasonable memory belief.

Richard Feldman objected to a general coherence theory of reasonable belief on the grounds that coherence is insensitive to factors other than relationships between beliefs that are relevant to reasonability. For suppose that at some time t while he is playing a hockey game, Sidney Crosby has a set of experiences, a set of nonbelief mental images, and a set of beliefs. Suppose further that at that time Crosby's beliefs are maximally coherent according to some favored theory about the nature of coherence. According to a coherence theory of reasonable belief, Crosby's beliefs are fully rational because they are maximally coherent. Now suppose that *you* have a vivid imagination that is so powerful that *at this very moment* you are able to believe all and only the propositions that Crosby believes at t. If the coherence theory of reasonable belief is true, it would follow that your present beliefs are fully reasonable because, by hypothesis, they are the same beliefs that Sidney Crosby holds at t and therefore are maximally coherent and hence fully reasonable. But your beliefs would not be reasonable because they would be completely isolated from epistemically relevant states of affairs that obtain in your present situation including the states of affairs that are constituted by your present sensory experiences. Your present experiences are those of a person reading a chapter on the philosophy of memory and not of a professional ice hockey player in the middle of a game. So, no matter how it is spelled out, coherence is not sufficient for reasonable belief for the reasonability of beliefs is never just a matter of the relationships among beliefs. To be reasonable, beliefs require relevant relations to non-belief states of affairs. Such factors such as the character of one's experience or the provenance of one's beliefs must play a role in explaining their reasonability. (See Feldman's 2003 "Magic Feldman" case, pp. 68–69.)

Perhaps a more limited version of a coherence theory can explain reasonable memory beliefs, however. For even if factors other than belief are required for the reasonability of perceptual beliefs—"The puck is on my stick right now!"—it is not as obvious that factors other than belief play a role in making memory beliefs reasonable. To see this, imagine a person S who is just like you right now with the very same present sense experiences and beliefs, including memory beliefs. Suppose, further, that all of your beliefs and therefore all of S's beliefs are maximally coherent. The only difference between you and S is that S has none of the nonbelief mental states that happen to accompany your memory beliefs. In particular, S has no nonbelief states of seeming to remember P when S recollects P, and S has no mental images accompanying S's recollections. S may, of course, have beliefs to the effect that some of S's beliefs are memory beliefs, but these beliefs are not accompanied by any nonbelief experiences that might be described as "seemings to remember." S is, in short, just like you except for lacking the nonbelief experiences and images that happen to accompany your memory beliefs.

What shall we say about the reasonability of S's memory beliefs? We do not find it obvious that S's memories are unreasonable because they lack the evidential support that may be provided by nonbelief mental states such as seemings to remember and the imagery associated with memories. So although coherence does not provide a sufficient condition for the reasonability of any belief, perhaps the coherence of memory beliefs with a system of beliefs that is otherwise reasonable is a sufficient condition for the reasonability of memory beliefs.

The problem is that coherence does not provide a *necessary condition* for the reasonability of memory beliefs. For if, as seems correct, our belief-forming procedures provide us with different *kinds* of reasons for belief and most of these kinds of reasons for belief are fallible—a reason R for a proposition P is fallible if, and only if, it is logically possible that R *is true* but P *is false*—then it is possible that a person has a good reason to believe a proposition and another good reason to believe a proposition that is logically incompatible with it. For suppose that one recollects P and has a battery of supporting memory beliefs for P but that one has counterbalancing evidence—beliefs about present sensory experience, beliefs about the testimony of authorities, for example—to the effect that Q is true, although P and Q cannot both be true. One seems to remember that "Mugsy was my assailant," but the testimony of authorities and other witnesses indicates that "Itchy was my assailant." We find it likely that under such conditions, both P and Q can be fully reasonable for a person, even though P and Q are not consistent with one another (Foley, 1979). Yet if coherence requires consistency, it is not the case that one's beliefs plus P and one's beliefs plus a proposition inconsistent with P are both coherent. If so, then being supported by beliefs that are part of a coherent system of beliefs is not a necessary condition for the reasonability of memory belief, and a coherence theory of reasonable memory belief fails.

We began this section in search of an account of reasonable memory belief that implies that, appearances to the contrary, we do have sufficient evidence for most of what we recollect. We have, however, found significant problems with each of the accounts of reasonable memory belief that we have surveyed. Perhaps we have been looking in the wrong places. For perhaps the paradox of absent evidence is right to claim that we lack good evidence for most of what we recollect but wrong to suppose that reasonable beliefs require the support of evidence. In light of this possibility, we turn now to a consideration of some accounts of reasonable memory belief that attempt to resolve the paradox of absent evidence by rejecting premise (1). According to each of these theories, having evidence for one's memory beliefs is not required in order for a memory belief to be reasonable.

☐ Accounts That Reject Premise (1)

Some philosophers hold that the account of reasonable belief expressed by premise (2) is overly intellectual. According to this approach, evidentialist accounts of reasonable belief take as stereotypical the special kinds of beliefs about which inquirers have rational discussions and debates. Most of our beliefs, however, are not acquired on the basis of explicit reasons and are not normally the subjects of rational discussion. I now recollect that "I had a salad for dinner yesterday." This belief seems to be as reasonable as it is uninteresting. Debate or discussion about it would be unprofitable, and my inability to recall any specific evidence for it does not give me a reason to doubt that it is true, let alone to think that my belief in it is not fully reasonable. Even beliefs that we do acquire on the basis of reasons are such that we forget the evidence we had for them rather quickly. Such lost evidence is a problem for the reasonability of memory, however, only if reasonable beliefs must be supported by evidence. In this section we shall consider the strengths and weaknesses of two accounts of reasonable belief that do not require presently available evidence: reliabilism and a nonevidentialist coherence theory. According to reliabilism, the reasonability of beliefs is a function of the reliability of the belief-forming procedures or mechanisms that produce them. According to nonevidentialist coherentism, the beliefs we happen to have are reasonable just because they are ours and so do not require support. New beliefs are rational to the extent that they improve the coherence of one's system of beliefs.

Reliabilism

Reliabilism is the view that whether or not it is reasonable—permissible, virtuous, or otherwise good—to hold a belief is a function of the *reliability* of the process or procedure that produced it. Forming beliefs by having evidence for them may or may not be reliable but, according to reliabilism, having reasonable beliefs does not *require* having evidence for our beliefs. The reliability of a process or a procedure of belief formation is, so to speak, its *cognitive batting average*: the *ratio* of true beliefs to total beliefs that do, or would, under the appropriate conditions result from forming beliefs by means of that process or procedure. If, as we normally suppose, forming beliefs on the basis of *sensory perception* is a highly reliable belief-forming procedure, then beliefs formed by means of sensory perception are *by that very fact* reasonable for us whether or not we have any evidence for them. By contrast, we ordinarily suppose that *wishful thinking* does not result in reasonable beliefs. Reliabilism can explain this. According to reliabilism, the trouble with wishful thinking is that it is an insufficiently reliable belief-forming procedure because it lets in too many false beliefs. According to reliabilism, therefore, memory beliefs are reasonable just in case the processes or procedures that we follow in forming memory beliefs produce a sufficiently high ratio of true beliefs. The solution to the paradox of absent evidence, according to the reliabilist, is to reject premise (1): Knowledge does not require good evidence.[9]

A strength of reliabilism is that reliability is an important intellectual value. Given our interest in having as many true and as few false beliefs as possible on topics of interest to us, it matters whether the standards, processes, and procedures we use in forming beliefs are reliable or not. A very important contribution of the psychological research reported earlier in this volume is that it helps us to understand important factors that influence the reliability of eyewitness identification and testimony. Reliabilism can also explain how it is that we can have reasonable inconsistent beliefs and how memory can result in new beliefs that are reasonable because it does not imply that memory is merely a faculty by which we reactivate previously formed beliefs.

Unfortunately, there are good reasons for thinking that reliabilism does not provide a correct account of reasonable memory belief. One problem is based on the fact that *any* particular belief can be described as resulting from different procedures that have significantly different degrees of reliability. For example, suppose again that I recollect that "I had salad for dinner yesterday." There are various ways to describe the procedure I followed in activating this belief: forming beliefs by means of memory, forming beliefs by means of memory about what I have eaten in the past, forming beliefs by means of memory about what I have eaten on Thursdays, forming beliefs by means of memory about what I have eaten on the previous day, and so on. Because these procedures are quite likely to have different degrees of reliability—I am undoubtedly much more reliable about what I ate yesterday than about what I ate exactly 10 years ago—whether and to what extent my belief is reasonable according to reliabilism depends upon how my belief-forming procedure is described. Because my memory of last night's dinner is neither both reasonable and unreasonable nor both more and less reasonable, reliabilism requires that there be some *principled* way to pick out *the* procedure that I used in forming my belief about last night's dinner. Because it is not clear what this principled distinction might be, a major problem for reliabilism is to solve this *generality problem*.[10]

Even if this problem can be solved, there is a more serious one. This problem also involves the distinction between a particular belief and the process by means of which it is formed. Suppose that we have solved the generality problem and we have a canonical way of describing *the* procedure that a person uses in forming a memory belief. It seems, nevertheless, that any reliable process of belief formation will result in some beliefs that are more reasonable than others. The recollection of beliefs formed with ample time for study and reflection will be more reasonable than the recollection of beliefs about the identity of an assailant whose face was obscured, or that were formed in poor lighting conditions, in the presence of a weapon, or in a very short period of time, yet these beliefs might well be the result of *the very same process or procedure for recollection and that procedure might, on balance, be highly reliable*. Reliabilism implies that all beliefs formed by the same procedure are equally reasonable, but this is not so. Nor can this problem be solved by describing the canonical process in terms of the factors that are conducive to higher reliability, for some memory beliefs formed with ample time for study and reflection will be more reasonable than others formed under similar conditions. The problem, in brief, is that reliabilism implies that the reasonability of a belief is determined by the reliability of the procedure by which the belief was formed, hence that *all beliefs formed by the same process are equally reasonable*. But *any* process or procedure results in beliefs with different degrees of reasonability. So a major problem for reliabilism is that it implies that beliefs that result from the same procedure are equally reasonable, yet this is not correct (Feldman, 1985, 2003).

Nonevidentialist Coherentism

Gilbert Harman defends a nonevidentialist coherence theory. Harman's view avoids the fatal objections to evidentialist coherentism but faces problems of its own.

Harman's view holds that beliefs come to be reasonable in two ways. First, beliefs that we already hold are ipso facto reasonable whether or not we have a reason for them (*conservatism*). Second, changes in beliefs result in reasonable beliefs just in case those changes improve the overall coherence of our system of beliefs. Thus, Harman (1986) stated, "The coherence theory supposes one's present beliefs are justified just as they are in the absence of special reasons to change them, where changes are allowed only to the extent that they yield sufficient increases in coherence" (p. 32).

Coherence thus functions not as a necessary condition for reasonability but as a regulative ideal for improving our system of reasonable beliefs. We may state Harman's theory this way:

> A belief that P is reasonable for a person S at a time t if, and only if, either S already accepts P at t (*conservatism*) or S forms the belief that P at t and adding P to S's set of beliefs improves the overall coherence of S's system of beliefs at t (*rational change*).

One advantage of Harman's theory is that it does not require that reasonable beliefs be consistent: Coherence is a regulative ideal for belief change, not a necessary condition of reasonability. The beliefs that we hold at any time are quite likely to contain inconsistencies, but this does not make them unreasonable in the absence of specific reasons to doubt them. Indeed, rooting out subtle inconsistencies may take more cognitive effort than it is worth. Also, like reliabilism, the theory does not require that memory beliefs be reactivated beliefs or even that their contents have been previously thought about. Finally, nonevidentialist coherentism has an attractive solution to paradox of absent evidence: Because beliefs are innocent until proven guilty (by *conservatism*), reasonable beliefs do not require positive evidential support. So premise (1) of the paradox of absent evidence is false.

A major problem for the theory, however, is that it implies that *any* reactivated memory belief is reasonable. For suppose that a person S adds the belief that P to his system of beliefs at a time $t1$ despite the fact that adding this belief does not improve the coherence of S's beliefs at that time. According to Harman's theory, S's belief P is not reasonable at $t1$ because adding it has violated the principle governing rational change in view. Suppose, however, that at a later time $t2$, S recollects S's previously unreasonable belief P. By the principle of conservatism, P is reasonable for S at $t2$, provided only that S has no specific reason to doubt P. So Harman's view implies, wrongly, that just about any memory belief is reasonable.

A view like Harman's might attempt to identify an *ur*-time—a privileged time at which rational inquiry begins—such that beliefs held at that time are automatically reasonable whether or not they have evidential support. The point at which a person becomes reflective, for example, might be identified as the relevant *ur*-time. After that special time, new beliefs can be reasonable only by increasing the coherence of the person's system of beliefs. Beliefs that do not increase the coherence of the system are not made reasonable at later times simply by being held.

A problem for this view, however, is that identifying a point at which actual beliefs are innocent until proven guilty will be arbitrary. It is as likely that the beliefs we hold at a given point have genuine epistemic value as it is (in accordance with a view held by some theorists about justice) that there is a special time in the past at which property was justly distributed so that subsequent distributions are just provided that transfers of property after that point have all been conducted fairly.[11] For any such theory to work, we need an *independent* reason to think that the beliefs we hold at the *ur*-point have positive epistemic value, just as the corresponding theory of justice needs an independent reason for thinking that the distribution of property at a given point was fair.

Another problem for Harman's view is that we might well modify reasonable memory beliefs in ways that increase the coherence of our system of beliefs but that eliminate better beliefs. In the presence of authorities and other witnesses testifying to the identity of a criminal, a witness might well improve the coherence of his beliefs by changing his view about the identity of the culprit despite the fact that his own memory is better than the feedback provided by the authorities and by other witnesses. So despite the fact that it improves upon evidentialist coherentism, there are serious problems with nonevidentialist coherentism as an account of the epistemology of memory.

☐ Conclusion

Each of the theories of memory that we have surveyed calls attention to important intellectual virtues that any account of memory must take into consideration. However, each of the theories of reasonable memory belief that we have surveyed also faces significant challenges, so there is substantial work yet to be done in the epistemology of memory. The issues investigated in this book call attention to a range of factors that any successful account of the epistemology of memory will have to take into consideration.

☐ Endnotes

1. The claim that justified true belief is not sufficient for knowledge is due to Gettier (1963). For a detailed survey of early attempts to respond to the Gettier problem, see Shope (2000).
2. A stronger version of evidentialism holds that evidence is the only factor that contributes to epistemic justification. See Feldman and Conee (2004).
3. These objections are due to Huemer (1999).
4. In yet another sense, *justification* can refer to the property or set of properties that are necessary or sufficient for justification in the first sense. Huemer (1999) used the following notions more or less interchangeably: justified belief, justification for a belief (see esp. p. 347, where what justifies one in believing a proposition is associated with one's reason for believing it), doing one's epistemic best (e.g., p. 349), being epistemically responsible, rational belief, not being epistemically blameworthy, and having beliefs not likely-to-be-false (the opposite of blameworthy beliefs; p. 349).

5. *Strong evidentialism* (Feldman and Conee, 2004) is the view that the *only* factor that is relevant to its being epistemically permissible, virtuous, or otherwise good to hold a belief is having adequate evidence for it.

6. Huemer must be referring to evidence by *justification* here, on pain of being uninformative. If *justification* refers to the property of being good to believe, then the theory says that a belief is good to believe if, and only if, it started out good to believe and has remained good to believe, which is uniformatively circular.

7. The *two-Mikes problem* is our term, not Huemer's. Also, we have stated Huemer's objection using our own example.

8. One might object that this can happen only if S has retained the dispositional belief that "John has seen *Full Metal Jacket*" and that therefore this is not a case in which S has given up the relevant belief. This is implausible and seems to depend upon supposing that a person has the dispositional belief P, if S is able to form the belief P under possible circumstances. This is incorrect because it would imply that we dispositionally believe every proposition that we can come to believe. Because it is possible that S comes to believe a previously believed and subsequently withheld proposition P after an extended period of time in which S was not inclined to form the occurrent belief in question for purposes of thinking or acting—the hallmark of dispositional belief—the scenario does not require that S has the dispositional belief in question.

9. The foremost defender of reliabilism is Alvin Goldman. See especially his *Epistemology and Cognition* (1988).

10. This objection is due to Richard Feldman, "Reliability and Justification" (1985). See also Richard Feldman, *Epistemology* (2003, ch. 5).

11. Robert Nozick, in *Anarchy, State, and Utopia* (1977), defends a theory of this sort.

REFERENCES

Adcock, C., & Webberley, M. (1971). Primary mental abilities. *Journal of General Psychology, 84*, 229–243.

Adlam, A., Malloy, M., Mishkin, M., & Vargha-Khadem, F. (2009). Dissociation between recognition and recall in developmental amnesia. *Neuropsychologia, 47*, 2207–2210.

Alley, T. R., & Cunningham, M. R. (1991). Averaged faces are attractive, but very attractive faces are not average. *Psychological Science, 2*, 123–125.

Anastasi, J. S., & Rhodes, M. G. (2006). Evidence for an own-age bias in face recognition. *North American Journal of Psychology, 8*, 237–253.

Anderson, J. R. (1995). *Cognitive psychology and its implications.* San Francisco, CA: Freeman.

Atkinson, R. C., & Shiffrin, R. M. (1968). Human memory: A proposed system and its control processes. In K. W. Spence & J. T. Spence (Eds.), *The psychology of learning and motivation* (Vol. 2, pp. 89–195). New York: Academic Press.

Baddeley, A. D. (1996). Exploring the central executive. *Quarterly Journal of Experimental Psychology, 49A*, 5–28.

Baddeley, A. D. (2000). The episodic buffer: A new component of working memory? *Trends in Cognitive Science, 4*, 417–423.

Baddeley, A., Gathercole, S., & Papagno, C. (1998). The phonological loop as a language learning device. *Psychological Review, 105*, 158–173.

Baddeley, A. D., & Hitch, G. (1974). Working memory. In G. H. Bower (Ed.), *The Psychology of Learning and Motivation: Advances in Research and Theory* (Vol. 8, pp. 47–89). New York: Academic Press.

Baenninger, M. (1994). The development of face recognition: Featural or configurational processing? *Journal of Experimental Child Psychology, 57*, 377–396.

Balota, D., & Neely, J. (1980). Test-expectancy and word-frequency effects in recall and recognition. *Journal of Experimental Psychology: Human Learning and Memory, 6*, 576–587.

Barsalou, L. W. (2008). Representation and knowledge in long-term memory. In E. E. Smith & S. M. Kosslyn (Textbook authors). *Cognitive psychology: Mind and brain* (pp. 147–191). Upper Saddle River, NJ: Prentice Hall.

Bartlett, F. C. (1932). *Remembering: A Study in Experimental and Social Psychology.* New York: Macmillan.

Bartlett, J. C., Hurry, S., & Thorley, W. (1984). Typicality and familiarity of faces. *Memory & Cognition, 12*, 219–228.

Bartlett, J. C., & Leslie, J. (1986). Aging and memory for faces versus single views of faces. *Memory & Cognition, 14*(5), 371–381.

Barton, J. J. S., Press, D. Z., Keenan, J. P., & O'Connor, M. (2002). Lesions of the fusiform face area impair perception of facial configuration in prosopagnosia. *Neurology, 58*, 71–78

Bastin, C., Linden, M., Charnallet, A., Denby, C., Montaldi, D., Roberts, N., & Andrew, M. (2004). Dissociation between recall and recognition memory performance in an amnesic patient with hippocampal damage following carbon monoxide poisoning. *Neurocase, 10*, 330–344.

Beal, C., Schmitt, K., & Dekle, D. (1995). Eyewitness identification of children: Effects of absolute judgments, nonverbal response options, and event encoding. *Law and Human Behavior, 19,* 197–216.

Behrman, B., & Davey, S. (2001). Eyewitness identification in actual criminal cases: An archival analysis. *Law and Human Behavior, 25,* 475–491.

Behrman, B., & Richards, R. (2005). Suspect/foil identification in actual crimes and in the laboratory: A reality monitoring analysis. *Law and Human Behavior, 29,* 279–301.

Bekerian, D. A., & Dennett, J. L. (1997). Imagery effects in spoken and written recall. In D. Payne and F. Conrad (Eds.), *Intersections in basic and applied memory research* (pp. 175–191). Mahwah, NJ: Lawrence Erlbaum.

Bell, B., & Loftus, E. (1985). Vivid persuasion in the courtroom. *Journal of Personality Assessment, 49,* 659–664.

Bell, B., & Loftus, E. (1988). Degree of detail of eyewitness testimony and mock juror judgments. *Journal of Applied Social Psychology, 18,* 1171–1192.

Bell, B., & Loftus, E. (1989). Trivial persuasion in the courtroom: The power of (a few) minor details. *Journal of Personality and Social Psychology, 56,* 669–679.

Belli, R. F. (1988). Color blend retrievals: Compromise memories or deliberate compromise responses? *Memory & Cognition, 16,* 314–326.

Belli, R. F. (1989). Influences of misleading postevent information: Misinformation interference and acceptance. *Journal of Experimental Psychology: General, 118,* 72–85.

Bem, D. (1972). Self-perception theory. In L. Berkowitz (Ed.), *Advances in experimental social psychology* (Vol. 6). New York: Academic Press.

Benton, D., Owens, D., & Parker, P. (1994). Blood glucose influences memory and attention in young adults. *Neuropsychologia, 32,* 595–607.

Berman, G. L., Narby, D. J., & Cutler, B. L. (1995). Effects of inconsistent eyewitness statements on mock-jurors' evaluations of eyewitnesses, perceptions of defendant culpability and verdicts. *Law and Human Behavior, 19,* 79–88.

Bernstein, M., Young, S., & Hugenberg, K. (2007). The cross-category effect: Mere social categorization is sufficient to elicit an own-group bias in face recognition. *Psychological Science, 18,* 706–712.

Bothwell, R., Brigham, J., & Pigott, M. (1987). An exploratory study of personality differences in eyewitness memory. *Journal of Social Behavior & Personality, 2,* 335–343.

Bothwell, R., Deffenbacher, K., & Brigham, J. (1987). Correlation of eyewitness accuracy and confidence: Optimality hypothesis revisited. *Journal of Applied Psychology, 72,* 691–695.

Bower, G. H., Black, J. B., & Turner, T. J. (1979). Scripts in memory for text. *Cognitive Psychology, 11,* 177–220.

Bradfield, D. A., & Steblay, N. (2006). Memory distortion in eyewitnesses: A meta-analysis of the post-identification feedback effect. *Applied Cognitive Psychology, 20,* 859–869.

Brainerd, C., Payne, D., Wright, R., & Reyna, V. (2003). Phantom recall. *Journal of Memory and Language, 48,* 445–467.

Brainerd, C. J., & Reyna, V. F. (2002). Fuzzy-trace theory and false memory. *Current Directions in Psychological Science, 11,* 164–169.

Brainerd, C., Reyna, V., & Ceci, S. (2008). Developmental reversals in false memory: A review of data and theory. *Psychological Bulletin, 134,* 343–382.

Brainerd, C., Wright, R., Reyna, V., & Mojardin, A. (2001). Conjoint recognition and phantom recollection. *Journal of Experimental Psychology: Learning, Memory, and Cognition, 27*, 307–327.

Braje, W. L. (2003). Illumination encoding in face recognition: Effect of position shift. *Journal of Vision, 3*, 161–170.

Braje, W. L., Kersten, D., Tarr, M. J., & Troje, N. F. (1998). Illumination effects in face recognition. *Psychobiology, 26*, 371–380.

Brehm, J. W. (1966). *A theory of psychological reactance*. New York: Academic Press.

Brewer, N., & Burke, A. (2002). Effects of testimonial inconsistencies and eye-witness confidence on mock-juror judgments. *Law and Human Behavior, 26*, 353–364.

Brewer, N., Keast, A., & Rishworth, A. (2002). The confidence-accuracy relation-ship in eyewitness identification: The effects of reflection and disconfirma-tion on correlation and calibration. *Journal of Experimental Psychology: Applied, 8*, 44–56.

Brewer, N., Weber, N., & Semmler, C. (2005). Eyewitness identification. In N. Brewer & K. D. Williams (Eds.), *Psychology and law: An empirical perspec-tive* (pp. 177–221). New York: Guilford.

Brewer, N., Weber, N., & Semmler, C. (2007). A role for theory in eyewitness iden-tification research. In R. C. L. Lindsay, D. F. Ross, J. D. Read, & M. Toglia (Eds.), *Handbook of eyewitness psychology: Vol. 2. Memory for people* (pp. 210–218). Mahwah, NJ: Lawrence Erlbaum.

Brewer, N., & Wells, G. (2006). The confidence–accuracy relationship in eye-witness identification: Effects of lineup instructions, foil similarity, and target-absent base rates. *Journal of Experimental Psychology: Applied, 12*, 11–30.

Brigham, J. (1988). Is witness confidence helpful in judging eyewitness accuracy? In *Practical aspects of memory: Current research and issues: Vol. 1. Memory in everyday life* (pp. 77–82). Oxford: John Wiley & Sons.

Brigham, J. C., Bennett, L. B., Meissner, C. A., & Mitchell, T. L. (2007). The influ-ence of race on eyewitness memory. In R. Lindsay, D. Ross, J. Read, & M. Toglia (Eds.), *Handbook of eyewitness psychology* (pp. 257–281). Mahwah, NJ: Lawrence Erlbaum.

Brigham, J. C., & Cairns, D. L. (1988). The effect of mugshot inspections on eye-witness identification accuracy. *Journal of Applied Social Psychology, 18*, 1394–1410.

Brigham, J. C., & Malpass, R. S. (1985). The role of experience and contact in the recognition of faces of own- and other-race persons. *Journal of Social Issues, 41*, 139–155.

Brigham, J. C., & Ready, D. J. (1985). Own-race bias in lineup construction. *Law and Human Behavior, 9*, 415–424.

Brigham, J. C., Van Verst, M., & Bothwell, R. (1986). Accuracy of children's eyewit-ness identifications in a field setting. *Basic and Applied Social Psychology, 7*, 295–306.

Brigham, J. C., & WolfsKeil, M. (1983). Opinions of attorneys and law enforcement personnel on the accuracy of eyewitness identifications. *Law and Human Behavior, 7*, 337–349.

Brown, E. L., & Deffenbacher, K. A., & Sturgill, W. (1977). Memory for faces and the circumstances of encounter. *Journal of Applied Psychology, 62*, 311–318.

Bruce, V. (2002). Face perception. In L. Backman & C. von Hofsten (Eds.), *Psychology at the turn of the millennium: Vol. 1. Cognitive, biological and health perspectives* (pp. 201–217). New York: Psychology Press.

Bruce, V., Doyle, T., Dench, N., & Burton, M. (1991). Remembering facial configurations. *Cognition, 38*, 109–144.

Bruce, V., & Young, A. (1986). Understanding face recognition. *British Journal of Psychology, 77*, 305–327.

Bruce, V., & Young, A. (2000). *In the eye of the beholder: The science of face perception.* Oxford: Oxford University Press.

Burton, A. M., Bruce, V., & Johnston, R. A. (1990). Understanding face recognition with an interactive activation model. *British Journal of Psychology, 81*(Pt. 3), 361–380.

Cabezza, R., & Kato, T. (2001). Features are also important: Contributions of featural and configural processing to face recognition. *Psychological Science, 11*, 429–433.

Carey, S., & Diamond, R. (1977). From piecemeal to configurational representation of faces. *Science, 195*(4275), 312–314.

Carlson, C., Gronlund, S. D., & Clark, S. E. (2010). Lineup composition, suspect position, and the sequential lineup advantage. *Journal of Experimental Psychology: Applied, 14*, 118–128.

Carroo, A. W. (1987). Recognition of faces as a function of race, attitudes and reported cross-racial friendships. *Perceptual and Motor Skills, 64*, 319–325.

Cassia, V., Picozzi, M., Kuefner, D., Bricolo, E., & Turati, C. (2009). Holistic processing for faces and cars in preschool-aged children and adults: Evidence from the composite effect. *Developmental Science, 12*, 236–248.

Ceci, S. J., & Bruck, M. (1993). Suggestibility of the child witness: A historical review and synthesis. *Psychological Bulletin, 113*, 403–439.

Ceci, S. J., & Bruck, M. (1995). *Jeopardy in the courtroom: The scientific analysis of children's testimony.* Washington, DC: American Psychological Association.

Ceci, S., Ross, D., & Toglia, M. (1987). Suggestibility of children's memory: Psycholegal implications. *Journal of Experimental Psychology: General, 116*, 38–49.

Chan, J., & McDermott, K. (2006). Remembering pragmatic inferences. *Applied Cognitive Psychology, 20*, 633–639.

Chance, J. E., & Goldstein, A. G. (1981). Depth of processing in response to own and other race faces. *Personality and Social Psychology Bulletin, 7*, 475–480.

Chance, J., Goldstein, A. G., & McBride, L. (1975). Differential experience and recognition memory for faces. *Journal of Social Psychology, 97*, 243–253.

Chance, J. E., Turner, A. L., & Goldstein, A. G. (1982). Development of differential recognition for own and other race faces. *Journal of Psychology: Interdisciplinary and Applied, 112*, 29–37.

Charman, S. D., & Wells, G. L. (2007). Eyewitness lineups: Is the appearance–change instruction a good idea? *Law & Human Behavior, 31*, 3–22.

Charman, S. D., & Wells, G. L. (2008). Can eyewitnesses correct for external influences on their lineup identifications? *Journal of Experimental Psychology: Applied, 14*, 5–20.

Chen, C. C., Kao, K. L. C., & Tyler, C. W. (2006). Face configuration processing in the human brain: the role of symmetry. *Cerebral Cortex, 7*, 1423–1432.

Cheung, O. S., Richler, J. J., Palmeri, T. J., & Gauthier, I. (2008). Revisiting the role of spatial frequencies in the holistic processing of faces. *Journal of Experimental Psychology: Human Perception & Performance, 34*, 1327–1336.

Christiaansen, R., & Ochalek, K. (1983). Editing misleading information from memory: Evidence for the coexistence of original and postevent information. *Memory & Cognition, 11*, 467–475.

Christianson, S. A. (1992). Emotional stress and eyewitness memory: A critical review. *Psychological Bulletin, 112*, 284–309.

Christianson, S. A., Karlsson, I., & Persson, L. G. W. (1998). Police personnel as eyewitnesses to a violent crime. *Legal and Criminological Psychology, 3*, 59–72.

Christie, D., & Ellis, H. (1981). Photofit constructions versus verbal descriptions of faces. *Journal of Applied Psychology, 66*, 358–363.

Clark, S. E. (2003). A memory and decision model for eyewitness identification. *Applied Cognitive Psychology, 17*, 629–654.

Clark, S. E. (2005). A re-examination of the effects of biased lineup instructions in eyewitness identification. *Law and Human Behavior, 29*, 395–424.

Clark, S. E., Howell, R. T., & Davey, S. L. (2008). Regularities in eyewitness identification. *Law and Human Behavior, 32*, 187–203.

Clark, S. E., & Tunnicliff, J. L. (2001). Selecting lineup fillers in eyewitness identification: Experimental control and real-world simulation. *Law and Human Behavior, 25*, 199–216.

Clifford, B. R., & Hollin, C. R. (1981). Effects of the type of incident and the number of perpetrators on eyewitness memory. *Journal of Applied Psychology*, 364–370.

Clifford, B. R., & Richards, J. (1977). Comparison of recall by policemen and civilians under conditions of long and short durations of exposure. *Perceptual & Motor Skills, 45*, 503–512.

Clifford, B. R., & Scott, J. (1978). Individual and situational factors in eyewitness testimony. *Journal of Applied Psychology, 63*, 352–359.

Cohen, J. (1988). *Statistical power analysis for the behavioral sciences* (2nd ed.). Mahwah NJ: Lawrence Erlbaum.

Cohen, M. E., & Carr, W. J. (1975). Facial recognition and the von Restoff effect. *Bulletin of the Psychonomic Society, 6*, 383–384.

Collette, F., Germanin, S., Hogge, M., & van der Linden, M. (2009). Inhibitory control of memory in normal ageing: Dissociation between impaired intentional and preserved unintentional processes. *Memory, 17*, 104–122.

Colombo, J. (1982). The critical period concept: Research, methodology, and theoretical issues. *Psychological Bulletin, 91*, 260–275.

Costa, P. T., & McCrae, R. R. (1992). *NEO-PI-R: Professional Manual*. Odessa, FL: Psychological Assessment Resources.

Costanzo, L. S. (2007). *Physiology*. Hagerstown, MD: Lippincott Williams & Wilkins.

Cross, H., Schuck, J., & Dannemiller, E. (1972). Judgments of verticality as a function of exposure duration, luminance, frame tilt, and frame-rod interval. *Psychonomic Science, 26*(2), 65–68.

Cross, J. F., Cross, J., & Daly, J. (1971). Sex, race, age, and beauty as factors in recognition of faces. *Perception & Psychophysics, 10*, 393–396.

Crutchfield, R., Woodworth, D., & Albrecht, R. (1958). Perceptual performance and the effective person. *USAF Wright Air Development Center Technical Note, 58*, x.

Curran, T., & Hintzman, D. L. (1995). Violations of the independence assumption in process dissociation. *Journal of Experimental Psychology: Learning, Memory, and Cognition, 21*, 531–547.

Cutler, B. L., Dexter, H. R., & Penrod, S. D. (1989). Expert testimony and jury decision making: An empirical analysis. *Behavioral Sciences & the Law, 7*, 215–225.

Cutler, B. L., & Kovera, M. B. (Eds.). (2008). Commentaries on the Illinois Pilot Study of Lineup Reform. *Law and Behavior, 32*(1).

Cutler, B. L., & Penrod, S. D. (1988). Improving the reliability of eyewitness identification: Lineup construction and presentation. *Journal of Applied Psychology, 73*, 281–290.

Cutler, B. L., Penrod, S. D., & Dexter, H. R. (1990). Juror sensitivity to eyewitness identification evidence. *Law and Human Behavior, 14*, 185–191.

Cutler, B. L., Penrod, S. D., & Martens, T. (1987a). Improving the reliability of eyewitness identification: Putting context into context. *Journal of Applied Psychology, 72*, 629–637.

Cutler, B. L., Penrod, S. D., & Martens, T. (1987b). The reliability of eyewitness identification: The role of system and estimator variables. *Law and Human Behavior, 11*, 233–258.

Cutler, B. L., Penrod, S. D., O'Rourke, T., & Martens, T. (1986). Unconfounding the effects of contextual cues on eyewitness identification accuracy. *Social Behaviour, 1*, 113–134.

Darling, S., Valentine, T., & Memon, A. (2008). Selection of lineup foils in operational contexts. *Applied Cognitive Psychology, 22*, 159–169.

Daubert v. Merrell Dow Pharmaceuticals (92-102), 509 U.S. 579 (1993).

Davidoff, J., & Donnelly, N. (1990). Object superiority effects: Complete versus part probes. *Acta Psychologica, 73*, 225–243.

Davies, G. M., Ellis, H., & Shepherd, J. (1977). Cue saliency in faces as assessed by the Photofit technique. *Perception, 6*, 263–269.

Deffenbacher, K. A. (1980). Eyewitness accuracy and confidence: Can we infer anything about their relationship? *Law and Human Behavior, 4*, 243–260.

Deffenbacher, K. A. (1994). Effects of arousal on everyday memory. *Human Performance, 7*, 141–161.

Deffenbacher, K. A., Bornstein, B. H., McGorty, K., & Penrod, S. D. (2008). Forgetting the once-seen face: Estimating the strength of an eyewitness's memory representation. *Journal of Experimental Psychology: Applied, 14*, 139–150.

Deffenbacher, K. A., Bornstein, B. H., & Penrod, S. D. (2006). Mugshot exposure effects: Retroactive interference, mugshot commitment, source confusion, and unconscious transference. *Law and Human Behavior, 30*, 287–307.

Deffenbacher, K. A., Bornstein, B. H., Penrod, S. D., & McGorty, E. K. (2004). A meta-analytic review of the effects of high stress on eyewitness memory. *Law and Human Behavior, 28*, 687–706.

Deffenbacher, K. A., Carr, T., & Leu, J. (1981). Memory for words, pictures, and faces: Retroactive interference, forgetting, and reminiscence. *Journal of Experimental Psychology: Human Learning and Memory, 7*, 299–305.

Deffenbacher, K. A., & Loftus, E. F. (1982). Do jurors share a common understanding concerning eyewitness behavior? *Law and Human Behavior, 6*, 15–30.

Dehon, H., & Brédart, S. (2001). An "other-race" effect in age estimation from faces. *Perception, 30*, 1107–1113.

Devenport, J. L., & Cutler, B. L. (2004). Impact of defense-only and opposing eye-witness experts on juror judgments. *Law and Human Behavior, 28,* 569–576.

Devenport, J. L., Stinson, V., Cutler, B. L., & Kravitz, D. A. (2002). How effective are the expert testimony and cross-examination safeguards? Jurors' percep-tions of the suggestiveness and fairness of biased lineup procedures. *Journal of Applied Psychology, 87,* 1042–1054.

Diamond, R., & Carey, S. (1977). Developmental changes in the representation of faces. *Journal of Experimental Child Psychology, 23,* 1–22.

Diamond, R., & Carey, S. (1986). Why faces, are and are not special: An effect of expertise. *Journal of Experimental Psychology: General, 115,* 107–117.

Diana, R. A., Reder, L. M., Arndt, J., & Park, H. (2006). Models of recognition: A review of arguments in favor of a dual process account. *Psychonomic Bulletin and Review, 13,* 1–21.

DiNardo, L., & Rainey, D. W. (1989). Recognizing faces in bright and dim light. *Perceptual and Motor Skills, 68,* 836–838.

DiNardo, L., & Rainey, D. W. (1991). The effects of illumination level and exposure time on facial recognition. *Psychological Record, 41,* 329–334.

Dodson, C. S., & Johnson, M. K. (1996). Some problems with the process-dissoci-ation approach to memory. *Journal of Experimental Psychology: General, 125,* 181–194.

Donath, J. (2001, August 6–9). Mediated faces. In *Proceedings of Cognitive Technology,* Warwick, UK.

Douglas, A. B., Neuschatz, J. S., Imrich, J., & Wilkinson, M. (2010). Does post-iden-tification feedback affect evaluations of eyewitness testimony and identifica-tion procedures? *Law and Human Behavior, 34,* 282–294.

Douglas, A. B., Smith, C., & Fraser-Thill, R. (2005). A problem with double-blind photospread procedures: Photospread administrators use one eyewitness's confidence to influence the identification of another eyewitness. *Law and Human Behavior, 29,* 543–562.

Dunning, D., & Perretta, S. (2002). Automaticity and eyewitness accuracy: A 10- to 12-second rule for distinguishing accurate from inaccurate positive identifi-cations. *Journal of Applied Psychology, 87,* 951–962.

Dunning, D., & Stern, L. B. (1994). Distinguishing accurate from inaccurate eye-witness identifications via inquiries about decision processes. *Journal of Personality and Social Psychology, 67,* 818–835.

Durham, M. D., & Dane, F. C. (1999). Juror knowledge of eyewitness behavior: Evidence for the necessity of expert testimony. *Journal of Social Behavior and Personality, 14,* 299–308.

Dysart, J. E., & Lindsay, R. C. L. (2007a). Showup identifications: Suggestive tech-nique or reliable method? In R. C. L. Lindsay, D. R. Ross, J. D. Read, & M. P. Toglia (Eds.), *The handbook of eyewitness psychology: Vol. 2. Memory for people* (pp. 137–153). Mahwah, NJ: Lawrence Erlbaum.

Dysart, J. E., & Lindsay, R. C. L. (2007b). The effects of delay on eyewitness iden-tification accuracy: Should we be concerned? In R. C. L. Lindsay, D. R. Ross, J. D. Read, & M. P. Toglia (Eds.), *Handbook of eyewitness psychology : Vol. 2. Memory for people* (pp. 361–376). Mahwah, NJ: Lawrence Erlbaum,

Dysart, J. E., Lindsay, R. C. L., & Dupuis, P. R. (2006). Showups: The critical issue of clothing bias. *Applied Cognitive Psychology, 20,* 1009–1023.

Dysart, J. E., Lindsay, R. C. L., Hammond, R., & Dupuis, P. (2001). Mug shot exposure prior to lineup identification: Interference, transference, and commitment effects. *Journal of Applied Psychology, 86*, 1280–1284.

Dysart, J., Lindsay, R., MacDonald, T., & Wicke, C. (2002). The intoxicated witness: Effects of alcohol on identification accuracy from showups. *Journal of Applied Psychology, 87*, 170–175.

Eagle, M., Goldberger, L., & Breitman, M. (1969). Field dependence and memory for social vs. neutral and relevant vs. irrelevant incidental stimuli. *Perceptual and Motor Skills, 29*, 903–910.

Eakin, D. K., Schreiber, T. A., & Sergent-Marshall, S. (2003). The presence and absence of memory impairment as a function of warning and misinformation accessibility. *Journal of Experimental Psychology: Learning, Memory, and Cognition, 5*, 813–825.

Easterbrook, J. A. (1959). The effect of emotion on cue utilization and the organization of behaviour. *Psychological Review 66*, 183–201.

Ebbinghaus, E. (1885/1913). *Memory: A study in experimental psychology.* New York: Columbia University Press.

Elliott, E. S., Wills, E. J., & Goldstein, A. G. (1973). The effects of discrimination training on the recognition of white and oriental faces. *Bulletin of the Psychonomic Society, 2*, 71–73.

Ellis, H. D., Deregowski, J. B., & Shepherd, J. W. (1975). Descriptions of white and black faces by white and black subjects. *International Journal of Psychology, 10*, 119–123.

Ellis, H. D., Shepherd, J., & Davies, G. (1975). An investigation of the use of the photo-fit technique for recalling faces. *British Journal of Psychology, 66*, 29–37.

Enns, J. T. (2004). *The thinking eye, the seeing brain: Explorations in visual cognition.* New York: W. W. Norton.

Ericson, K., Isaacs, B., & Taylor, S. J. (2003). Eyewitness identification accuracy: A comparison of adults with and those without intellectual disabilities. *Mental Retardation, 41*, 161–173.

Erskine, A., Markham, R., & Howie, P. (2001). Children's script-based inferences: Implications for eyewitness testimony. *Cognitive Development, 16*, 871–887.

Ettlinger, G. (1990). "Object vision" and "spatial vision": The neuropsychological evidence for the distinction. *Cortex, 26*, 319–341.

Faigman, D. L., & Monahan, J. (2005). Psychological evidence at the dawn of the law's scientific age. *Annual Review of Psychology, 56*, 631–659.

Fallshore, M., & Schooler, J. W. (1995). The verbal vulnerability of perceptual expertise. *Journal of Experimental Psychology: Learning, Memory, and Cognition, 21*, 1608–1623.

Farah, M. J., Wilson, K. D., Drain, M., & Tanaka, J. N. (1998). What is "special" about face perception? *Psychological Review, 105*, 482–498.

Fazey, J. A., & Hardy, L. (1988). *The inverted-U hypothesis: A catastrophe for sport psychology* (British Association for Sports Sciences Monograph No. 1). Leeds, UK: National Coaching Foundation.

Fein, S., Hilton, J. L., & Miller, D. T. (1990). Suspicion of ulterior motivation: An antidote for the correspondence bias. *Journal of Personality and Social Psychology, 58*, 753–764.

Feingold, C. A. (1914). The influence of environment on identification of persons and things. *Journal of Criminal Law and Police Science, 5*, 39–51.

Feldman, R. (1985). Reliability and justification. *The Monist, 68*, 159–174.

Feldman, R. (2003). *Epistemology.* Upper Saddle River, NJ: Prentice Hall.

Feldman, R., & Conee, E. (2004). *Evidentialism.* Oxford: Oxford University Press.

Ferguson, D., Rhodes, G., Lee, K., & Sriram, N. (2001). "They all look alike to me": Prejudice and cross-race face recognition. *British Journal of Psychology, 92*, 567–577.

Ferris, S. H., Crook, T., Clark, E., McCarthy, M., & Rae, D. (1980). Facial recognition memory deficits in normal aging and senile dementia. *Journal of Gerontology, 35*, 707–714.

Finger K., & Pezdek, K. (1999). The effect of the cognitive interview on face identification accuracy: Release from verbal overshadowing. *Journal of Applied Psychology, 3*, 340–348.

Fisher, R. P., & Geiselman, R. (1992). *Memory enhancing techniques for investigative interviewing.* Springfield, IL: Charles Thomas.

Fisher, R. P., Geiselman, R. E., & Raymond, D. S. (1987). Critical analysis of police interview techniques. *Journal of Police Science & Administration, 15*, 177–185.

Fisher, R. P., McCauley, M., & Geiselman, R. E. (1994). Improving eyewitness testimony with the cognitive interview. Ross, D. F., Read, J. D., & Toglia, M. P. (Eds.). In *Adult eyewitness testimony: Current trends and developments* (pp. 245–269). New York, NY: Cambridge University Press.

Fisher, R. P., & Schreiber, N. (2005). Forensic psychiatry and forensic psychology: Forensic interviewing. In J. Payne-James, R. Byard, T. Corey, & C. Henderson (Eds.), *Encyclopedia of forensic and legal medicine* (pp. 371–378). Oxford: Elsevier Science.

Flin, R. (1985). Development of face recognition: An encoding switch? *British Journal of Psychology, 76*, 123–134.

Flowe, H., Ebbesen, E., Burke, C., & Chivabunditt, P. (2001). At the scene of the crime: An examination of the external validity of published studies on lineup identification accuracy. Paper Presented at the annual meeting of the American Psychological Society, Toronto, ON.

Foley, H. J. (1979). Justified inconsistent beliefs. *American Philosophical Quarterly, 16*, 247–257.

Foley, H. J., & Matlin, M. W. (2010). *Sensation and perception* (5th ed.). Boston: Allyn & Bacon.

Fong, G. T., Krantz, D. H., & Nisbett, R. E. (1986). The effects of statistical training on thinking about everyday problems. *Cognitive Psychology, 18*, 253–292.

Fox, S. G., & Walters, H. A. (1986). The impact of general versus specific expert testimony and eyewitness confidence upon mock juror judgment. *Law and Human Behavior, 10*, 215–228.

Freire, A., & Lee, K. (2001). Face recognition in 4- to 7-year-olds: Processing of configural, featural, and paraphernalia information. *Journal of Experimental Child Psychology, 80*, 347–371.

Frowd, C. D., Bruce, V., & Hancock, P. J. B. (2008). Helping the police to construct the face of a criminal. *The Psychologist, 21*, 670–672.

Frowd, C. D., Bruce, V., Smith, A., & Hancock, P. (2008). Improving the quality of facial composites using a holistic cognitive interview. *Journal of Experimental Psychology: Applied, 14*, 276–287.

Frowd, C. D., Carson, D., Ness, H., Richardson, J., Morrison, L., McLanaghan, S., et al. (2005). A forensically valid comparison of facial composite systems. *Psychology, Crime & Law, 11,* 33–52.

Frowd, C. D., Hancock, P., & Carson, D. (2004). EvoFIT: A holistic, evolutionary facial imaging technique for creating composites. *ACM Transactions on Applied Perception, 1,* 19–39.

Frowd, C. D., Mcquiston-Surrett, D., Anandaciva, S., Ireland, C., & Hancock, P. (2007). An evaluation of US systems for facial composite production. *Ergonomics, 50,* 1987–1998.

Fulero, S. M., & Wrightsman, L. S. (2009). *Forensic psychology.* Belmont, CA: Wadsworth.

Gabbert, F., Hope, L., & Fisher, R. (2009). Protecting eyewitness evidence: Examining the efficacy of a self-administered interview tool. *Law and Human Behavior, 33,* 298–307.

Galotti, K. M. (2004). *Cognitive psychology: In and out of the lab.* Belmont, CA: Wadsworth.

García-Bajos, E., & Migueles, M. (2003). False memories for script actions in a mugging account. *European Journal of Cognitive Psychology, 15,* 195–208.

Gardiner, J. M. (1988). Functional aspects of recollective experience. *Memory & Cognition, 16,* 309–313.

Gardiner, J. M., & Java, R. I. (1990). Recollective experience in word and nonword recognition. *Memory & Cognition, 18,* 23–30.

Gardiner, J. M., & Java, R. I. (1991). Forgetting in recognition memory with and without recollective experience. *Memory & Cognition, 19,* 617–623.

Garrioch, L., & Brimacombe, C. A. E. (2001). Lineup administrators' expectations: Their impact on eyewitness confidence. *Law and Human Behavior, 25,* 299–315.

Gauthier, I., & Bukach, C. M. (2007). Should we reject the expertise hypothesis? *Cognition, 103,* 322–330.

Geiselman, R. E., Putman, C., Korte, R., Shahriary, M., Jachimowicz, G., & Irzhevsky, V. (2002). Eyewitness expert testimony and juror decisions. *American Journal of Forensic Psychology, 20*(3), 21–36.

General Electric Co. v. Joiner, 522 U.S. 136 (1997).

George, R. (1991). A field and experimental evaluation of three methods of interviewing witnesses and victims of crime. Unpublished master's thesis, Polytechnic of East London, UK.

Gettier, E. (1963). Is justified true belief knowledge? *Analysis* 23, 121–123.

Goffaux, V., & Rossion, B. (2006). Faces are "spatial": Holistic face perception is supported by low spatial frequencies. *Journal of Experimental Psychology/: Human Perception and Performance, 32,* 1023–1039.

Going, M., & Read, J. D. (1974). Effects of uniqueness, sex of subject, and sex of photograph on facial recognition. *Perceptual and Motor Skills, 39,* 109–110.

Goldberg, L. R. (1990). An alternative "description of personality": The Big-Five factor structure. *Journal of Personality and Social Psychology, 59,* 1216–1229.

Goldman, A. (1988). *Epistemology and cognition.* Cambridge, MA: Harvard University Press.

Goldstein, A. (1975). Recognition of inverted photographs of faces by children and adults. *Journal of Genetic Psychology, 127,* 109–123.

Goldstein, A. G. (1979a). Race-related variation of facial features: Anthropometric data I. *Bulletin of the Psychonomic Society, 13,* 187–190.

Goldstein, A. G. (1979b). Facial features variation: Anthropometric data: II. *Bulletin of the Psychonomic Society, 13,* 191–193.

Goldstein, A. G., & Chance, J. E. (1978). Judging face similarity in own and other races. *The Journal of Psychology, 98,* 185–193.

Goldstein, A. G., & Chance, J. E. (1985). Effects of training on Japanese face recognition: Reduction of the other-race effect. *Bulletin of the Psychonomic Society, 23,* 211–214.

Goldstein, E. B. (2007). *Sensation and perception* (7th ed.). Belmont, CA: Thomson Wadsworth.

Goodale M. A., & Milner, A. D. (1992). Separate visual pathways for perception and action. *Trends Neuroscience, 15,* 20–25.

Goodenough, D. (1976). The role of individual differences in field dependence as a factor in learning and memory. *Psychological Bulletin, 83,* 675–694.

Goodsell, C. A., Neuschatz, J. S., & Gronlund, S. D. (2009). Effects of mugshot commitment and choosing on lineup performance in young and older adults. *Applied Cognitive Psychology, 23,* 788–803.

Gorenstein, G. W., & Ellsworth, P. C. (1980). Effect of choosing an incorrect photograph on a later identification by an eyewitness. *Journal of Applied Psychology, 65,* 616–622.

Graf, P., & Komatsu, I. (1995). The process dissociation procedure: Handle with caution. *European Journal of Cognitive Psychology, 6,* 113–129.

Grass, E., & Sporer, S. L. (1991). *Richtig oder falsch? Zur Vorhersage von Identifizierungsleistungen durch weitere Aussagen von Zeugen* [Correct or false? Post-dicting eyewitness identification accuracy from verbal statements]. Paper presented at the 33rd Tagung experimentell arbeitender Psychologen in Giesen, Germany.

Greenberg, M., Westcott, D., & Bailey, S. (1998). When believing is seeing: The effect of scripts on eyewitness memory. *Law and Human Behavior, 22,* 685–694.

Grill-Spector, K., Knouf, N., & Kanwisher, N. (2004). The fusiform face area subserves face perception, not generic within-category identification. *Nature Neuroscience, 7,* 555–562.

Gross, C. G., Roche-Miranda, C. E., & Bender, D. B. (1972). Visual properties of neurons in inferotemporal cortex of the macaque. *Journal of Neurophysiology, 35,* 96–111.

Gross, S. R., Jacoby, K., Matheson, D. J., Montgomery, N., & Patel, S. (2005). Exonerations in the United States, 1989–2003. *Journal of Criminal Law and Criminology, 95,* 523–560.

Habak, C., Wilkinson, F., & Wilson, H. (2008). Aging disrupts the neural transformations that link facial identity across views. *Vision Research, 48*(1), 9–15.

Hacking, I. (1998). *Rewriting the soul: Multiple personality and the sciences of memory.* Princeton, NJ: Princeton University Press.

Hafstad, G., Memon, A., & Logie, R (2004). The effects of post-identification feedback on children's memory. *Applied Cognitive Psychology, 18,* 901–912.

Hall, J., Gonder-Frederick, L., Chewning, W., & Silveira, J. (1989). Glucose enhancement of performance on memory tests in young and aged humans. *Neuropsychologia, 27*(9), 1129–1138.

Hannigan, S. L., & Reinitz, M. T. (2001). A demonstration and comparison of two types of inference-based memory errors. *Journal of Experimental Psychology: Learning, Memory, and Cognition, 27,* 931–940.

Hannigan, S. L., & Reinitz, M. T. (2003). Migration of objects and inferences across episodes. *Memory and Cognition, 31,* 434–444.

Harman, G. (1986). *Change in view: Principles of reasoning.* Cambridge, MA: MIT Bradford.

Harrison, Y., & Horne, J. A. (2000). Sleep loss and temporal memory. *Quarterly Journal of Experimental Psychology, 53A,* 271–279.

Hasel, L., & Kassin, S. (2009). On the presumption of evidentiary independence: Can confessions corrupt eyewitness identifications? *Psychological Science, 20,* 122–126.

Hasel, L. E., & Wells, G. L. (2007). Catching the bad guy: Morphing composite faces helps. *Law and Human Behavior, 31,* 193–208.

Haw, R. M., & Fisher, R. P. (2004). Effects of administrator-witness contact on eyewitness identification accuracy. *Journal of Applied Psychology, 89,* 1106–1112.

Haxby, J. V., Hoffman, E. A., & Gobbini, M. I. (2000). The distributed human neural system for face perception. *Trends Cognitive Science, 4,* 223–233.

Hinz, T., & Pezdek, K. (2001). The effect of exposure to multiple lineups on face identification accuracy. *Law and Human Behavior, 25,* 185–198.

Hoffman, C., & Kagan, S. (1977). Field dependence and facial recognition. *Perceptual and Motor Skills, 44*(1), 119–124.

Hole, G. J. (1994). Configurational factors in the perception of unfamiliar faces. *Perception, 23,* 65–74.

Hole, G. J., George, P. A., & Dunsmore, V. (1999). Evidence for holistic processing of faces viewed as photographic negatives. *Perception, 28,* 341–359.

Holliday, R., Brainerd, C., Reyna, V., & Humphries, J. (2009). The cognitive interview: Research and practice across the lifespan. *Handbook of psychology of investigative interviewing: Current developments and future directions* (pp. 137–160). Malden, MA: Wiley-Blackwell.

Holst, V., & Pezdek, K. (1992). Scripts for typical crimes and their effects on memory for eyewitness testimony. *Applied Cognitive Psychology, 6*(7), 573–587.

Hope, L., & Wright, D. (2007). Beyond unusual? Examining the role of attention in the weapon focus effect. *Applied Cognitive Psychology, 21,* 951–961.

Horry, R., & Wright, D. B. (2008). I know your face but not where I saw you: Context memory is impaired for other race faces. *Psychonomic Bulletin and Review, 15,* 610–614.

Hosch, H. M., Beck, E. L., & McIntyre, P. (1980). Influence of expert testimony regarding eyewitness accuracy on jury decisions. *Law and Human Behavior, 4,* 287–296.

Hosch, H. M., Leippe, P., & Cooper, D. (1984). Victimization, self-monitoring, and eyewitness identification. *Journal of Applied Psychology, 69,* 280–288.

Hubel, D. H., & Wiesel, T. N. (1959). Receptive fields of single neurones in the cat's striate cortex. *Journal of Physiology, 148,* 574–591.

Hubel, D. H., & Wiesel, T. N. (1962). Receptive fields, binocular vision and the functional architecture in the cat's visual cortex. *Journal of Physiology, 160,* 106–154.

Huemer, M. (1999). The problem of memory knowledge. *Pacific Philosophical Quarterly, 80,* 346–357.

Hugenberg, K., Miller, J., & Claypool, H. (2007). Categorization and individuation in the cross-race recognition deficit: Toward a solution to an insidious problem. *Journal of Experimental Social Psychology, 43,* 334–340.

Hugenberg, K., & Sacco, D. (2008). Social categorization and stereotyping: How social categorization biases person perception and face memory. *Social and Personality Psychology Compass, 2,* 1052–1072.

Innocence Project. (2010). The Innocence Project. Retrieved from http://www.innocenceproject.org

Jackiw, L., Arbuthnott, K., Pfeifer, J., Marcon, J., & Meissner, C. (2008). Examining the cross-race effect in lineup identification using Caucasian and First Nations samples. *Canadian Journal of Behavioural Science/Revue canadienne des sciences du comportement, 40,* 52–57.

Jacoby, L. L. (1992). A process dissociation framework: Separating automatic from intentional uses of memory. *Journal of Memory and Language, 30,* 513–541.

Jacoby, L. L. (1997). Invariance in automatic influences of memory: Toward a user's guide for the process-dissociation procedure. *Journal of Experimental Psychology: Learning, Memory, and Cognition, 24,* 3–26.

Jacoby, L. L., & Dallas, M. (1981). On the relationship between autobiographical memory and perceptual learning. *Journal of Experimental Psychology: General, 3,* 306–340.

Jacoby, L. L., Lindsay, D. S., & Toth, J. P. (1992). Unconscious influences revealed: Attention, awareness, and control. *American Psychologist, 47,* 802–809.

Jacoby, L. L., Yonelinas, A. P., & Jennings, J. (1997). The relation between conscious and unconscious (automatic) influences. A declaration of independence. In J. Cohen & J. W. Schooler (Eds.), *Scientific approaches to consciousness* (pp. 13–47). Mahwah, NJ: Erlbaum.

John, O. P. (1990). The "Big Five" factor taxonomy: Dimensions of personality in natural language and in questionnaires. In L. A. Pervin (Ed.), *Handbook of personality: Theory and research* (pp. 66–100). New York: Guilford Press.

Johnson, C. (1976). Effects of luminance and stimulus distance on accommodation and visual resolution. *Journal of the Optical Society of America, 66,* 138–142.

Johnson, K. (2006). Erasing race: Positive emotions eliminate recognition differences between own-race and other-race faces.

Johnson, M. K., Hashtroudi, S., & Lindsay, D. S. (1993). Source monitoring. *Psychological Bulletin, 114,* 3–28.

Johnson, M. K., & Raye, C. (1981). Reality monitoring. *Psychological Review, 88,* 67–85.

Joordens, S., & Hockley, W. E. (2000). Recollection and familiarity through the looking glass: When old does not mirror new. *Journal of Experimental Psychology: Learning, Memory, and Cognition, 26,* 1534–1555.

Juslin, P., Olsson, N., & Winman, A. (1996). Calibration and diagnosticity of confidence in eyewitness identification: Comments on what can be inferred from the low confidence–accuracy correlation. *Journal of Experimental Psychology: Learning, Memory, and Cognition, 22*(5), 1304–1316.

Kahneman, D. (1973). *Attention and effort.* Englewood Cliffs, NJ: Prentice Hall.

Kanwisher, N. G., McDermott, J., & Chun, M. M. (1997). The fusiform face area: A module in human extrastriate cortex specialized for face perception. *Journal of Neuroscience, 17,* 4302–4311.

Karlsen, P., & Snodgrass, J. (2004). The word-frequency paradox for recall/recognition occurs for pictures. *Psychological Research, 68*, 271–276.

Kassin, S. (1984). Eyewitness identification: Victims versus bystanders. *Journal of Applied Social Psychology, 14*(6), 519–529.

Kassin, S. (1985). Eyewitness identification: Retrospective self-awareness and the accuracy–confidence correlation. *Journal of Personality and Social Psychology, 49*, 878–893.

Kassin, S. (1998). Eyewitness identification procedures: The fifth rule. *Law and Human Behavior, 22*(6), 649–653.

Kassin, S. M., & Barndollar, K. A. (1992). The psychology of eyewitness testimony: A comparison of experts and prospective jurors. *Journal of Applied Social Psychology, 22*, 1241–1249.

Kassin, S. M., Ellsworth, P. C., & Smith, V. L. (1989). The "general acceptance" of psychological research on eyewitness testimony: A survey of the experts. *American Psychologist, 44*, 1089–1098.

Kassin, S., Tubb, V., Hosch, H., & Memon, A. (2001). On the "general acceptance" of eyewitness testimony research: A new survey of the experts. *American Psychologist, 56*, 405–416.

Kazén, M., & Solís-Macías, V. (1999). Recognition hypermnesia with repeated trials: Initial evidence for the alternative retrieval pathways hypothesis. *British Journal of Psychology, 90*, 405–424.

Kebbell, M. R., Milne, R., & Wagstaff, G. F. (1999). The cognitive interview: A survey of its forensic effectiveness . *Psychology, Crime and Law, 5*, 101–115.

Kelly, D., Quinn, P., Slater, A., Lee, K., Ge, L., & Pascalis, O. (2007). The other-race effect develops during infancy: Evidence of perceptual narrowing. *Psychological Science, 18*(12), 1084–1089.

Kintsch, W. (1968). Recognition and free recall of organized lists. *Journal of Experimental Psychology, 78*, 481–487.

Kleider, H., Pezdek, K., Goldinger, S., & Kirk, A. (2008). Schema-driven source misattribution errors: Remembering the expected from a witnessed event. *Applied Cognitive Psychology, 22*, 1–20.

Klobuchar, A., Steblay, N. K. M., & Caligiuri, H. L. (2006). Improving eyewitness identifications: Hennepin County's blind sequential lineup pilot project. *Cardozo Public Law, Policy, and Ethics Journal, 2*, 381–414.

Kneller, W., Memon, A., & Stevenage, S. (2001). Simultaneous and sequential lineups: Decision processes of accurate and inaccurate eyewitnesses. *Applied Cognitive Psychology, 15*, 659–671.

Konecni, V. J., & Ebbesen, E. B. (1986). Courtroom testimony by psychologists on eyewitness identification issues: Critical notes and reflections. *Law and Human Behavior, 10*, 117–125.

Kovera, M. B., & McAuliff, B. D. (2000). The effects of peer review and evidence quality on judge evaluations of psychological science: Are judges effective gatekeepers? *Journal of Applied Psychology, 85*, 574–586.

Kovera, M. B., McAuliff, B. D., & Hebert, K. S. (1999). Reasoning about scientific evidence: Effects of juror gender and evidence quality on juror decisions in a hostile work environment case. *Journal of Applied Psychology, 84*, 362–375.

Kovera, M. B., Russano, M. B., & McAuliff, B. D. (2002). Assessment of the commonsense psychology underlying *Daubert*: Legal decision makers' abilities to evaluate expert evidence in hostile work environment cases. *Psychology, Public Policy, and Law, 8*, 180–200.

Krall, K. (1912). *Denkende Tiere*. Leipzig, Germany: Engelmann.

Kramer, T., Buckhout, R., & Eugenio, P. (1990). Weapon focus, arousal, and eyewitness memory: Attention must be paid. *Law and Human Behavior, 14*(2), 167–184.

Krouse, F. (1981). Effects of pose, pose change, and delay on face recognition performance. *Journal of Applied Psychology, 66*(5), 651–654.

Kuefner, D., Cassia, M., Viola, Picozzi, M., & Bricolo, E. (2002). Do all kids look alike? Evidence for an other-age effect in adults. *Journal of Experimental Psychology: Human Perception and Performance, 34*, 811–817.

Kumho Tire Co. v. Carmichael (97-1709) 526 U.S. 137 (1999).

Kurtzman, H. S. (1983). Modern conceptions of memory. *Philosophy and Phenomenological Research, 44*, 1–19.

Lamberts, K., & Freeman, R. P. J. (1999). Building object representations from parts: Tests of a stochastic sampling model. *Journal of Experimental Psychology: Human Perception and Performance, 25*, 904–926.

Lampinen, J. M., Arnal, J. D., & Hicks, J. L. (2008). Prospective person memory. In M. Kelley (Ed.), *Applied Memory*. Hauppauge NY: Nova.

Lampinen, J. M., Copeland, S. M., & Neuschatz, J. S. (2001). Recollections of things schematic: Room schemas revisited. *Journal of Experimental Psychology: Learning, Memory, and Cognition, 27*, 1211–1222.

Lampinen, J. M., Faries, J. M., Neuschatz, J. S., & Toglia, M. P. (2000). Recollections of things schematic: The influence of scripts on recollective experience. *Applied Cognitive Psychology, 14*, 543–554.

Lampinen, J. M., Judges, D. P., & Odegard, T. N. (2002). Recommendations for Eyewitness Evidence Procedures: The View from the Street. Biennial meeting of the American Psychology Law Society. Austin, TX.

Lampinen, J. M., Leding, J. K., Reed, K. B., & Odegard, T. N. (2006). Global gist extraction in children and adults. *Memory, 14*, 952–964.

Lampinen, J. M., Meier, C., Arnal, J., & Leding, J. (2005). Compelling untruths: Content borrowing and vivid false memories. *Journal of Experimental Psychology: Learning, Memory, and Cognition, 31*, 954–963.

Lampinen, J. M., & Neuschatz, J. S. (2008). Reconstructive memory. In B. Cutler (Ed.), *Encyclopedia of psychology and the law* (pp. 675–678). Thousand Oaks, CA: Sage.

Lampinen, J. M., Neuschatz, J. S., & Payne, D. G. (1998). Memory illusions and consciousness: Exploring the phenomenology of true and false memories. *Current Psychology, 16*, 181–224.

Lampinen, J. M., Odegard, T. N., Blackshear, E., & Toglia, M. P. (2005). Phantom ROC. In D. T. Rosen (Ed.), *Progress in experimental psychology research* (pp. 235–267). Hauppauge, NY: Nova.

Lampinen, J. M., Ryals, D. B., & Smith, K. (2008). Compelling untruths: The effect of retention interval on content borrowing and vivid false memories. *Memory, 16*, 149–156.

Lampinen, J. M., Scott, J., Leding, J. K., Pratt, D., & Arnal, J. D. (2007). "Good, you identified the suspect...but please ignore this feedback": Can warnings eliminate the effects of post-identification feedback? *Applied Cognitive Psychology*, 1037–1056.

Lampinen, J. M., & Smith, V. L. (1995). The incredible (and sometimes incredulous) child witness: Child eyewitnesses' sensitivity to source credibility cues. *Journal of Applied Psychology, 80*, 621–627.

Lampinen, J. M., Watkins, K. N., & Odegard, T. N. (2006). Phantom ROC: Recollection rejection in a hybrid conjoint recognition signal detection model. *Memory, 14*, 655–671.

Langlois, J. H., & Roggman, L. A. (1990). Attractive faces are only average. *Psychological Sciences, 1*, 115–121.

LaVoie, D. J., Mertz, H. K., & Richmond, T. L. (2007). False memory susceptibility in older adults: Implications for the elderly eyewitness. In M. Toglia, J. Read, D. Ross, & R. Lindsay. (Eds.), *Handbook of eyewitness psychology* (pp. 605–626). New York: Erlbaum.

Lavrakas, P., Buri, J., & Mayzner, M. (1976). A perspective on the recognition of other-race faces. *Perception & Psychophysics, 20*, 475–481.

Le Grand R., Mondloch, C. J., Maurer, D., & Brent, H. P. (2004). Impairment in holistic face processing following early visual deprivation. *Psychological Science, 15*, 762–768.

Leder, H., & Bruce, V. (2000). When inverted faces are recognized: The role of configural information in face recognition. *Quarterly Journal of Experimental Psychology, 53A*, 513–536.

Leippe, M. R. (1980). Effects of integrative memorial and cognitive processes on the correspondence of eyewitness accuracy and confidence. *Law and Human Behavior, 4*, 261–274.

Leippe, M. R. (1995). The case for expert testimony about eyewitness memory. *Psychology, Public Policy, and Law, 1*, 909–959.

Leippe, M. R., & Eisenstadt, D. (2007). Eyewitness confidence and the confidence–accuracy relationship in memory for people. In R. C. L. Lindsay, D. F. Ross, J. D. Read, & M. P. Toglia (Eds.), *Handbook of eyewitness psychology* (Vol. 2, pp. 377–425). Mahwah, NJ: Erlbaum.

Leippe, M. R., Eisenstadt, D., Rauch, S. M., & Seib, H. M. (2004). Timing of eyewitness expert testimony, jurors' need for cognition, and case strength as determinants of trial verdicts. *Journal of Applied Psychology, 89*, 524–541.

Leippe, M. R., Manion, A. P., & Romanczyk, A. (1992). Eyewitness persuasion: How and how well do fact finders judge the accuracy of adults' and children's memory reports? *Journal of Applied Personality and Social Psychology, 63*, 181–197.

Leippe, M. R., Romanczyk, A., & Manion, A. (1991). Eyewitness memory for a touching experience: Accuracy differences between child and adult witnesses. *Journal of Applied Psychology, 76*, 367–379.

Leippe, M. R., Wells, G. L., Ostrom, T. M. (1978). Crime Seriousness as a Determinant of Accuracy in Eyewitness Identification. *Journal of Applied Psychology, 63*, 345– 351.

Levett, L. M., & Kovera, M. B. (2008). The effectiveness of educating jurors about unreliable expert evidence using an opposing witness. *Law and Human Behavior, 32*, 363–374.

Levi, A. M. (1998). Are defendants guilty if they were chosen in a lineup? *Law and Human Behavior, 22,* 389–407.

Levin, D. T. (2000). Race as a visual feature: Using visual search and perceptual discrimination tasks to understand face categories and the cross-race recognition deficit. *Journal of Experimental Psychology: General, 129,* 559–574.

Lewin, C., & Herlitz, A. (2002). Sex differences in face recognition: Women's faces make the difference. *Brain & Cognition, 50,* 121–128.

Lewin, K. (1952). *Field theory in social science: Selected theoretical papers by Kurt Lewin.* London: Tavistock.

Light, L. (1991). Memory and aging: Four hypotheses in search of data. *Annual Review of Psychology, 42,* 333–376.

Light, L. L., Hollander, S., & Kayra-Stuart, F. (1981). Why attractive people are harder to remember. *Personality and Social Psychology Bulletin, 7,* 269–276.

Light, L. L., Kayra-Stuart, F., & Hollander, S. (1979). Recognition memory for typical and unusual faces. *Journal of Experimental Psychology: Human Learning and Memory, 5*(3), 212–228.

Lilienfeld, S. O., Lynn, S. J., & Lohr, J. M. (2003). *Science and pseudoscience in clinical psychology.* New York: Guilford Press.

Lindholm, T., Christianson, S., & Karlsson, I. (1997). Police officers and civilians as witnesses: Intergroup biases and memory performance. *Applied Cognitive Psychology, 11,* 431–444.

Lindsay, D. S. (1990). Misleading suggestions can impair eyewitnesses' ability to remember event details. *Journal of Experimental Psychology: Learning, Memory, and Cognition, 16,* 1077–1083.

Lindsay, D. S. (1993). Eyewitness suggestibility. *Current Directions in Psychological Science, 2*(3), 86–89.

Lindsay, D. S., Jack, P. C., & Christian, M. A. (1991). Other-race face perception. *Journal of Applied Psychology, 76,* 587–589.

Lindsay, D. S., & Johnson, M. (1989). The eyewitness suggestibility effect and memory for source. *Memory & Cognition, 17,* 349–358.

Lindsay, R. C. L., Lea, J., Nosworthy, G., Fulford, J., Hector, J., LeVan, V., et al. (1991). Biased lineups: Sequential presentation reduces the problem. *Journal of Applied Psychology, 76,* 796–802.

Lindsay, D. S., Nilsen, E., & Read, J. (2000). Witnessing-condition heterogeneity and witnesses' versus investigators' confidence in the accuracy of witnesses' identification decisions. *Law and Human Behavior, 24,* 685–697.

Lindsay, R. C. L., Martin, R., & Webber, L. (1994). Default values in eyewitness descriptions: A problem for the match-to-description lineup foil selection strategy. *Law and Human Behavior, 18,* 527–541.

Lindsay, R. C. L., Nosworthy, G. J., Martin, R. R., & Martynuck, C. (1994). Finding suspects in mugshots. *Journal of Applied Psychology, 79,* 121–130.

Lindsay, R. C. L., Pozzulo, J. D., Craig, W., Lee, K., & Corber, S. (1997). Simultaneous lineups, sequential lineups, and showups: Eyewitness identification decisions of adults and children. *Law and Human Behavior, 21,* 391–404.

Lindsay, R. C. L., Semmler, C., Weber, N., Brewer, N., & Lindsay, M. R. (2008). How variations in distance affect eyewitness reports and identification accuracy. *Law and Human Behavior, 32,* 526–535.

Lindsay, R. C. L, Wallbridge, H., & Drennan, D. (1987). Do the clothes make the man? An exploration of the effect of lineup attire on eyewitness identification accuracy. *Canadian Journal of Behavioural Science, 19,* 464–478.

Lindsay, R. C. L., & Wells, G. L. (1980). What price justice? Exploring the relationship of lineup fairness to identification accuracy. *Law and Human Behavior, 4,* 303– 313.

Lindsay, R. C. L., & Wells, G. L. (1985). Improving eyewitness identification from lineups: Simultaneous versus sequential lineup presentations. *Journal of Applied Psychology, 70,* 556–564.

Lindsay, R. C.L., Wells, G. L., & O'Connor, F. J. (1989). Mock-juror belief of accurate and inaccurate eyewitnesses: A replication and extension. *Law & Human Behavior, 13,* 333–339.

Lindsay, R. C. L., Wells, G. L., & Rumpel, C. (1981). Can people detect eyewitness identification accuracy within and between situations? *Journal of Applied Psychology, 66,* 79–89.

Liu, C. H., Collin, C. A., Burton, A. M., & Chaudhuri, A. (1999). Lighting direction affects recognition of untextured faces in photographic positive and negative. *Vision Research, 39,* 4003–4009.

Loftus, E. F. (1974, December). The incredible eyewitness. *Psychology Today.* 117–119.

Loftus, E. F. (1975). Leading questions and the eyewitness report. *Cognitive Psychology, 7,* 560–572.

Loftus, E. F. (1977). Shifting human color memory. *Memory & Cognition, 5(6),* 696–699.

Loftus, E. F. (1979). The malleability of human memory. *American Scientist, 67,* 312–320.

Loftus, E. F. (1980). Impact of expert psychological testimony on the unreliability of eyewitness identification. *Journal of Applied Psychology, 65,* 9–15.

Loftus, E. F. (1984). Eyewitness: Essential but unreliable. *Psychology Today,* 22–26.

Loftus, E. F. (1991). Made in memory: Distortions in recollection after misleading information. *Psychology of Learning and Motivation, 27,* 187–215.

Loftus, E. F. (2003). Make-believe memories. *American Psychologist, 58,* 864–873.

Loftus, E. F., & Greene, E. (1980). Warning: Even memory for faces may be contagious. *Law and Human Behavior, 4,* 323–334.

Loftus, E. F., & Hoffman, H. (1989). Misinformation and memory: The creation of new memories. *Journal of Experimental Psychology: General, 118,* 100–104.

Loftus, E. F., & Loftus, G. R. (1980). On the permanence of stored information in the human brain. *American Psychologist, 35,* 400–420.

Loftus, E. F., Loftus, G. R., & Messo, J. (1987). Some facts about "weapon focus." *Law and Human Behavior, 11,* 55–62

Loftus, E. F., Miller, D. G., & Burns, H. J. (1978). Semantic integration of verbal information into a visual memory. *Journal of Experimental Psychology: Human Learning and Memory, 4,* 19–31.

Loftus, G. R., & Harley, E. M. (2005). Why is it easier to identify someone closer than far away? *Psychonomic Bulletin and Review 12,* 43–65.

Loftus, G. R., & Loftus, E. F. (1976). *Human Memory: The Processing of Information.* New York, NY: Routledge.

Logie, R. H. (1995). *Visuo-spatial Working Memory.* Hove, UK: Lawrence Erlbaum.

Lopez, J. C. 2000. Shaky memories in indelible ink. *Nature Reviews Neuroscience, 1*, 6–7.

Luna, K., & Migueles, M. (2008). Typicality and misinformation: Two sources of distortion. *Psicológica, 29*, 171–187.

Lupien S. J., & McEwen, B. S. (1997). The acute effects of corticosteroids on cognition: integration of animal and human model studies. *Brain Research Review, 24*, 1–27.

Luus, C. A. E., & Wells, G. L. (1991). Eyewitness identification and the selection of distracters for lineups. *Law and Human Behavior, 15*, 43–57.

Luus, C. A. E., & Wells, G. L. (1994). The malleability of eyewitness confidence: Co-witness and perseverance effects. *Journal of Applied Psychology, 79*, 714–724.

Lyle, K., Bloise, S., & Johnson, M. (2006). Age-related binding deficits and the content of false memories. *Psychology and Aging, 21*, 86–95.

Maass, A., & Köhnken, G. (1989). Eyewitness identification: Simulating the 'weapon effect.'. *Law and Human Behavior, 13*(4), 397–408.

MacLin, O., MacLin, M., & Malpass, R. (2001). Race, arousal, attention, exposure and delay: An examination of factors moderating face recognition. *Psychology, Public Policy, and Law, 7*, 134–152.

MacLin, O., Meissner, C., & Zimmerman, L. (2005). PC. *Behavior Research Methods, 37*, 324–334.

MacLin, O., Zimmerman, L., & Malpass, R. (2005). PC. *Law and Human Behavior, 29*, 303–321.

Magnussen, S., Wise, R., Raja, A., Safer, M., Pawlenko, N., & Stridbeck, U. (2008). What judges know about eyewitness testimony: A comparison of Norwegian and US judges. *Psychology, Crime & Law, 14*, 177–188.

Malpass, R. S. (1990). An excursion into utilitarian analysis. *Behavior Science Research, 24*(1), 1–15.

Malpass, R. S., & Devine, P. G. (1981). Eyewitness identification: Lineup instructions and the absence of the offender. Journal of Applied Psychology, 66, 482–489.

Mandler, G. (1980). Recognizing: The judgment of previous occurrence. *Psychological Review, 87*, 252–271.

Manson v. Braithwaite. (1977). 432 U.S. 98.

Martin, K. A. C. (1994). A brief history of the "feature detector." *Cerebral Cortex, 4*, 1–7.

Mather, G. (2008). *Foundations of sensation and perception* (2nd ed.). New York: Psychology Press.

Maurer, D., & Barrera, M. (1981). Infants' perception of natural and distorted arrangements of a schematic face. *Child Development, 52*(1), 196–202.

Mayer, E., & Rossion, B. (2007). Prosopagnosia. In O. Godefroy and J. Bogousslavsky (Eds.), *The behavioral and cognitive neurology of stroke* (pp. 315–334). Cambridge: Cambridge University Press.

McAllister, H., (2007). Mug books: More than just large photospreads. In R. C. Lindsay, D. F. Ross, J. D. Read, M. P. Toglia. (Eds.), *The handbook of eyewitness psychology: Vol. 2. Memory for people* (pp. 35–58). Mahwah, NJ: Lawrence Erlbaum.

McAllister, H. A., Bearden, J. N., Kohlmaier, J. R., & Warner, M. D. (1997). Computerized mug books: Does adding multi-media help? *Journal of Applied Psychology, 82*, 688–698.

McAllister, H. A., Blair, M. J., Cerone, L. G., & Laurent, M. J. (2000). Multimedia mug books: How multi should the media be? *Applied Cognitive Psychology*, 14, 277–291.

McAllister, H. A., Stewart, H. A., & Loveland, J. (2003). Effects of mug book size and computerized pruning on the usefulness of dynamic mug book procedures. *Psychology, Crime, & Law*, 9, 265–278.

McAuliff, B. D., & Kovera, M. B. (2003). *Need for cognition and juror sensitivity to methodological flaws in psychological science*. Unpublished manuscript, Florida International University, Miami, FL.

McCloskey, M., Egeth, H., & McKenna, J. (1986). The Experimental psychologist in court: The ethics of expert testimony. *Law and Human Behavior*, 10, 1–13.

McCloskey, M., & Zaragoza, M. (1985a). Misleading postevent information and memory for events: Arguments and evidence against memory impairment hypotheses. *Journal of Experimental Psychology: General*, 114, 1–16.

McCloskey, M., & Zaragoza, M. (1985b). Postevent information and memory: Reply to Loftus, Schooler, and Wagenaar. *Journal of Experimental Psychology: General*, 114, 381–387.

McKone, E., Kanwisher, N., & Duchaine, B. C. (2007). Can generic expertise explain special processing for faces? *Trends in Cognitive Sciences*, 11, 8–15.

McQuiston, D. E., & Malpass, R. S. (2002). Validity of the mock witness paradigm: Testing the assumptions. *Law and Human Behavior*, 26, 439–453.

Mecklenburg, S. H., Malpass, R. M., & Ebbeson, E. (2006). The Illinois pilot program on sequential double blind identification procedures. In *Report to the Legislature of the State of Illinois*. Springfield: State of Illinois.

Meissner, C. A. (2002). Applied aspects of the instructional bias effect in verbal overshadowing. *Applied Cognitive Psychology*, 16, 911–928.

Meissner, C. A., & Brigham, J. C. (2001). Thirty years of investigating the own-race bias in memory for faces: A meta-analytic review. *Psychology, Public Policy, & Law*, 7, 3–35.

Meissner, C. A., Brigham, J. C., & Kelley, C. M. (2001). The influence of retrieval processes in verbal overshadowing. *Memory & Cognition*, 29, 176–186.

Meissner, C. A., Sporer, S., & Schooler, J. (2007). Person descriptions as eyewitness evidence. In M. P. Toglia, Read, D., Ross, D. F., & Lindsay, R. C. L. (Eds.), *Handbook of eyewitness psychology: Vol. 1. Memory for people* (pp. 2–34). Mahwah, NJ: Erlbaum.

Meissner, C. A., Sporer, S., & Susa, K. (2008). A theoretical review and meta-analysis of the description-identification relationship in memory for faces. *European Journal of Cognitive Psychology*, 20, 414–455.

Meissner, C. A., Tredoux, C. G., Parker, J. F., & MacLin, O. H. (2005). Eyewitness decisions in simultaneous and sequential lineups: A dual-process signal detection theory analysis. *Memory & Cognition*, 33, 783–792.

Memon, A., Bartlett, J. C., Rose, R., & Gray, C. (2003). The aging eyewitness: The effects of face-age and delay upon younger and older observers. *Journal of Gerontology*, 58, 338–345.

Memon, A., Hope, L., Bartlett, J., & Bull, R. (2002). Eyewitness recognition errors: The effects of mugshot viewing and choosing in young and old adults. *Memory & Cognition*, 30, 1219–1227.

Memon, A., Hope, L., & Bull, R. (2003). Exposure duration: Effects on eyewitness accuracy and confidence. *British Journal of Psychology*, 94, 339–354.

Messick, S., & Damarin, F. (1964). Cognitive styles and memory for faces. *The Journal of Abnormal and Social Psychology, 69*, 313–318.

Metcalfe, J. (1990). Composite holographic associative recall model (CHARM) and blended memories in eyewitness testimony. *Journal of Experimental Psychology: General, 119*, 145–160.

Metzger, M. M. (2000). Glucose enhancement of a facial recognition task in young adults. *Physiology Behavior*, 549–553.

Metzger, M. M. (2006). Face distinctiveness and delayed testing: Differential effects on performance and confidence. *Journal of General Psychology, 133*, 209–216.

Metzger, M., & Flint, R. (2003). Glucose enhancement of face recognition is unaffected by alterations of face features. *Neurobiology of Learning and Memory, 80*, 172–175.

Michel, C., Rossion, B., Han, J., Chung, C-S., & Caldara, R. (2006). Holistic processing is finely tuned for faces of our own race. *Psychological Science, 17*, 608–615.

Miller, G. A. (1956). The magical number seven, plus or minus two: Some limits on our capacity for processing information. *Psychological Review, 63*, 81–97.

Miller, L., McFarland, D., Cornett, T., & Brightwell, D. (1977). Marijuana and memory impairment: Effect on free recall and recognition memory. *Pharmacology, Biochemistry and Behavior, 7*, 99–103.

Mishkin, M., & Ungerleider, L. G.(1982). Contribution of striate inputs to the visuospatial functions of parieto-preoccipital cortex in monkeys. *Behavorial Brain Research, 6*, 57–77.

Mitchell, K., Johnson, M., & Mather, M. (2003). Source monitoring and suggestibility to misinformation: Adult age-related differences. *Applied Cognitive Psychology, 17*(1), 107–119.

Mitchell, K., Livosky, M., & Mather, M. (1998). The weapon focus effect revisited: The role of novelty. *Legal and Criminological Psychology, 3*, 287–303.

Morgan, C. A., Hazlett, G., Baranoski, M., Doran, A., Southwick, S., & Loftus, E. (2007). Accuracy of eyewitness identification is significantly associated with performance on a standardized test of face recognition. *International Journal of Law and Psychiatry, 30*, 213–223.

Morgan, C. A., Hazlett, G., Doran, A., Garrett, S., Hoyt, G., Thomas, P., et al. (2004). Accuracy of eyewitness memory for persons encountered during exposure to highly intense stress. *International Journal of Law and Psychiatry, 27*, 265–279.

Morris, N. (2008). Elevating blood glucose level increases the retention of information from a public safety video. *Biological Psychology, 78*(2), 188–190.

Näsänen, R. (1999). Spatial frequency bandwidth used in the recognition of facial images. *Vision Research, 23*, 3824–3833.

Navon, D. (1992). Selection of lineup foils by similarity to the suspect is likely to misfire. *Law and Human Behavior, 16*(5), 575–593.

Neath, I., & Brown, G. (2007). Making distinctiveness models of memory distinct. *The foundations of remembering: Essays in honor of Henry L. Roediger, III* (pp. 125–140). New York, NY: Psychology Press.

Neil v. Biggers, 409 U.S. 188 (1972).

Neuschatz, J. S., & Cutler, B. L. (2008). Eyewitness identification. In H. L. Roediger III (Ed.), *Learning and memory: A comprehensive reference: Vol. 2. Cognitive psychology of memory* (pp. 845–865). Oxford: Elsevier.

Neuschatz, J. S., Lampinen, J. M., Preston, E. L., Hawkins, E. R., & Toglia, M. P. (2002). The effect of memory schemata on memory and the phenomenological experience of naturalistic situations. *Applied Cognitive Psychology, 16,* 687–708.

Neuschatz, J. S., Neuschatz, J. S., Lawson, D. S., Powers, R. A., Fairless, A. H., Goodsell, C. A., & Toglia, M. P. (2007).The mitigating effects of suspicion on post-identification feedback and on retrospective eyewitness memory. *Law and Human Behavior, 31,* 231–247.

Neuschatz, J. S., Preston, E. L., Burkett, A. D., Toglia, M. P., Lampinen, J. M., Neuschatz, J. S., Fairless, A. H., Lawson, D. S., Powers, R. A., & Goodsell, C. A. (2005). The effects of post-identification feedback and age on retrospective eyewitness memory. *Applied Cognitive Psychology, 19,* 435–453.

Newcomer, J. W., Selke, G., Melson, A. K., Hershey, T., Craft, S., Richards, K., & Alderson, A. L. (1999). Decreased memory performance in healthy humans induced by stress-level cortisol treatment. *Archives of General Psychiatry, 56,* 527–533.

Nisbett, R. E. (1993). Violence and U. S. regional culture. *American Psychologist, 48,* 441–449.

Nisbett, R. E., Krantz, D. H., Jepson, D., & Kunda, Z. (1983). The use of statistical heuristics in everyday reasoning. *Psychological Review, 90,* 339–363.

Noon, E., & Hollin, C. (1987). Lay knowledge of eyewitness behaviour: A British survey. *Applied Cognitive Psychology, 1,* 143–153.

Nozick, R. (1977). *Anarchy, state, and utopia.* New York: Basic.

O'Toole, A. J., Roark, D., & Abdi, H. (2002). Recognition of moving faces: A psychological and neural framework. *Trends in Cognitive Sciences, 6,* 261–266.

Odegard, T. N., & Lampinen, J. M. (2004). Memory conjunction errors for autobiographical events: More than just familiarity. *Memory, 12,* 288–301.

Ogloff, J. R. P., & Rose, V. G. (2005). The comprehension of judicial instructions. In N. Brewer & K. Williams (Eds.), *Psychology and law: An empirical perspective.* New York, Guilford.

O'Hagan, C. J. (1993). When seeing is not believing: The case for eyewitness expert testimony. *Georgetown Law Journal, 81,* 741–772

Okado, Y., & Stark, C. (2005). Neural activity during encoding predicts false memories created by misinformation. *Learning & Memory, 12,* 3–11.

Pallak, S., Murroni, E., & Koch, J. (1983). Communicator attractiveness and expertise, emotional versus rational appeals, and persuasion: A heuristic versus systematic processing interpretation. *Social Cognition, 2,* 122–141.

Parker, J., & Ryan, V. (1993). An attempt to reduce guessing behavior in children's and adults' eyewitness identifications. *Law and Human Behavior, 17*(1), 11–26.

Parks, T. (1966). Signal-detectability theory of recognition-memory performance. *Psychological Review, 73,* 44–58.

Passarotti, A. M., Smith, J., DeLano, M., & Huang, J. (2007). Developmental differences in the neural bases of the face inversion effect show progressive tuning of face-selective regions to the upright orientation. *NeuroImage, 34,* 1708–1722.

Paterson, H. M., & Kemp, R. I. (2006). Comparing methods of encountering post-event information: The power of co-witness suggestion. *Applied Cognitive Psychology, 20,* 1083–1099.

Penrod, S., & Cutler, B. (1995). Witness confidence and witness accuracy: Assessing their forensic relation. *Psychology, Public Policy, & Law, 1,* 817–845.

Pezdek, K., & Blandon-Gitlin, I. (2005). When is an intervening lineup most likely to affect eyewitness identification accuracy? *Legal and Criminological Psychology, 10,* 247–263.

Pezdek, K., & Roe, C. (1995). The effect of memory trace strength on suggestibility. *Journal of Experimental Child Psychology, 60,* 116–128.

Pfungst, O. (1911). *Clever Hans (The horse of Mr. von Osten): A contribution to experimental animal and human psychology* (Trans. C. L. Rahn). New York: Henry Holt.

Phillips, M. R., Geiselman, R. E., Haghighi, D., & Lin, C. (1997). Some boundary conditions for bystander misidentification. *Criminal Justice and Behavior, 24,* 370–390.

Phillips, M. R., McAuliff, B. D., Kovera, M. B., & Cutler, B. L. (1999). Double-blind photoarray administration as a safeguard against investigator bias. *Journal of Applied Psychology, 84,* 940–951.

Pickel, K. L. (1998). Unusualness and threat as possible causes of "weapon focus." *Memory, 6,* 277–295.

Pickel, K. L. (1999). The influence of context on the "weapon focus" effect. *Law and Human Behavior, 23,* 299–311.

Pickel, K. L. (2007). Remembering and identifying menacing perpetrators: Exposure to violence and the weapon focus effect. In R. C. L. Lindsay, D. F. Ross, & M. P. Toglia (Eds.), *The handbook of eyewitness psychology: Vol. 2. Memory for people* (pp. 339–360). Mahwah NJ: Erlbaum.

Pickel, K. L., Ross, S., & Truelove, R. (2006). Do weapons automatically capture attention? *Applied Cognitive Psychology, 20,* 871–893.

Pigott, M. A., & Brigham, J. C. (1985). Relationship between accuracy of prior description and facial recognition. *Journal of Applied Psychology, 70,* 547–555.

Pigott, M. A., Brigham, J. C., & Bothwell, R. K. (1990). Field study of the relationship between quality of eyewitnesses' descriptions and identification accuracy. *Journal of Police Science and Administration, 17,* 84–88.

Pike, G., Brace, N., & Kynan, S. (2002). *The visual identification of suspects: Procedures and practice* (Briefing Note 2/02). London: Home Office.

Platz, S., & Hosch, H. (1988). Cross-racial/ethnic eyewitness identification: A field study. *Journal of Applied Social Psychology, 18,* 972–984.

Pollock, J. L., & Cruz, J. (1999). *Contemporary theories of knowledge* (2nd ed.). Lanham, MD: Rowman & Littlefield.

Poon, L. W. (1985). Differences in human memory with aging: Nature, causes, and clinical implications. In J. E. Birren & K. W. Schaie (Eds.), *Handbook of the psychology of aging* (2nd ed., pp. 427–462). New York, NY: Van Nostrand Reinhold.

Poston, A. (2000). Static adult human physical characteristics of the adult head. Department of Defense Human Factors Engineering Technical Advisory Group (DOD HFE TAG). *Human Engineering Design Data Digest.*

Pozzulo, J., & Lindsay, R. (1998). Identification accuracy of children versus adults: A meta-analysis. *Law and Human Behavior,* 549–570.

Pozzulo, J., & Lindsay, R. (1999). Elimination lineups: An improved identification procedure for child eyewitnesses. *Journal of Applied Psychology, 84,* 167–176.

Psychological Corporation. (1997). *Weschler Memory Scale III: Faces I.* San Antonio, TX: Harcourt Brace.

Putnam, W. H. (1979). Hypnosis and distortions in eyewitness memory. *International Journal of Clinical and Experimental Hypnosis, 27,* 437–448.

Quinlivan, D. S., Neuschatz, J. S., Jimenez, A., Cling, A. D., Douglass, A. B., & Goodsell, C. A. (2009). Do prophylactics prevent inflation? Post-identification feedback and the effectiveness of procedures to protect against confidence-inflation in earwitnesses. *Law and Human Behavior, 33,* 111–121.

Quinlivan, D. S., Neuschatz, J. S., Cutler, B. L., Wells, G. L., McClung, J., & Harker, D. L. (2011). Do pre-admonition suggestions moderate the effect of the unbiased-lineup instructions? *Legal and Criminological Psychology, 16,* no. doi:10.1348/135532510X53554.

Quinlivan, D. S., Wells, G. L., & Neuschatz, J. S. (2010). Is manipulative intent necessary to mitigate the eyewitness post-identification feedback effect? *Law and Human Behavior, 34,* 186–197.

Rajaram, S. (1993). Remembering and knowing: Two means of access to the personal past. *Memory & Cognition, 21,* 89–102.

Rajaram, S. (1998). The effects of conceptual salience and perceptual distinctiveness on conscious recollection. *Psychonomic Bulletin & Review, 5,* 71–78.

Rapus-Benton, Ross, D. F., McDonnell, S., Thomas, N., & Bradshaw, M. (2006). Eyewitness memory is still not common sense: Comparing jurors, judges and law enforcement to eyewitness experts. *Applied Cognitive Psychology, 20,* 115–129.

Ratcliff, R., Sheu, C. F., & Gronlund, S. D. (1992). Testing global memory models using ROC curves. *Psychological Review, 99,* 518–536.

Ratcliff, R., & Starns, J. (2009). Modeling confidence and response time in recognition memory. *Psychological Review, 116,* 59–83.

Read, J.D. (1995). The availability heuristic in person identification: The sometimes misleading consequences of enhanced contextual information. *Applied Cognitive Psychology, 9,* 91–121.

Reingold, E. M. (2002). On the perceptual specificity of memory representations. *Memory, 10,* 365–379.

Reyna V. F., & Titcomb, A. L. (1997). Constraints on the suggestibility of eyewitness testimony: A fuzzy-trace theory analysis. In D. G. Payne & F. G. Conrad (Eds.), *A synthesis of basic and applied approaches to human memory* (pp. 157–174). Hillsdale, NJ: Lawrence Erlbaum.

Rhodes, G., Brake, S., Taylor, K., & Tan, S. (1989). Expertise and configural coding in face recognition. *British Journal of Psychology, 80,* 313–331.

Richler, J., Gauthier, I., Wenger, M., & Palmeri, T. (2008). Holistic processing of faces: Perceptual and decisional components. *Journal of Experimental Psychology: Learning, Memory, and Cognition, 34*(2), 328–342.

Roark, D., Barrett, S. E., Spence, M. J., Abdi, H., & O'Toole, A. J. (2003). Psychological and neural perspectives on the role of facial motion in face recognition. *Behavioral and Cognitive Neuroscience Reviews, 2,* 15–46.

Robbins, R., & McKone, E. (2007). No face-like processing for objects-of-expertise in three behavioural tasks. *Cognition, 103,* 34–79.

Roediger, H., & McDermott, K. (2000). Tricks of memory. *Current Directions in Psychological Science, 9,* 123–127.

Rosenthal, R. (1966). *Experimenter effects in behavioral research.* New York: Appleton-Century-Crofts.

Rosenthal, R. (1967). Covert communication in the psychological experiment. *Psychological Bulletin, 67,* 356–367.

Rosenthal, R. (2002). Covert communication in classrooms, clinics, courtrooms, and cubicles. *American Psychologist, 57,* 839–849.

Ross, D. F., Ceci, S. J., Dunning, D., & Toglia, M. P. (1994). Unconscious transference and mistaken identity: When a witness misidentifies a familiar but innocent person. *Journal of Applied Psychology, 79,* 918–930.

Ross, S. J., & Malpass, R. S. (2008). Moving forward: Responses to "Studying eyewitness investigations in the field." *Law and Human Behavior, 32,* 16–21.

Rudy, L., & Goodman, G. S. (1991). Effects of participation on children's reports: Implications for children's testimony. *Developmental Psychology, 27,* 1–26.

Rushton, W. A. H.(1965). The rod dark adaptation curve measured above cone threshold. *Journal of Physiology, 181,* 641–644.

Sadler, L. L. (1986). Scientific art and the milk carton kids. Paper presented at the 7th Annual Guild of Scientific Illustrators, Washington, DC.

Salthouse, T. A., & Babcock, R. L. (1991). Decomposing adult age differences in working memory. *Developmental Psychology, 27,* 763–776.

Sanders, G. S., & Simmons, W. L. (1983). Use of hypnosis to enhance eyewitness accuracy: Does it work? *Journal of Applied Psychology, 68,* 70–77.

Sangrigoli, S., Pallier, C., Argenti, A., Ventureyra, V., & de Schonen, S. (2005). Reversibility of the other-race effect in face recognition during childhood. *Psychological Science, 16,* 440–444.

Sapolsky, R., Krey, L., & McEwen, B. (1985). Prolonged glucocorticoid exposure reduces hippocampal neuron number: Implications for aging. *Journal of Neuroscience, 5,* 1221–1226.

Sauerland, M., & Sporer, S. (2009). Fast and confident: Postdicting eyewitness identification accuracy in a field study. *Journal of Experimental Psychology: Applied, 15,* 46–62.

Savaskan, E., Müller, S., Böhringer, A., Philippsen, C., Müller-Spahn, F., & Schächinger, H. (2007). Age determines memory for face identity and expression. *Psychogeriatrics, 7,* 49–57.

Schacter, D. L. (1996). *Searching for memory: The brain, the mind, and the past.* New York: Basic Books.

Schacter, D. L., Dawes, R., Jacoby, L. L., Kahneman, D., Lempert, R., Roediger, H. L., & Rosenthal, R. (2008). Policy forum: Studying eyewitness investigations in the field. *Law and Human Behavior, 32,* 3–5.

Scheck, B., Neufeld, P., & Dwyer, J. (2000). *Actual innocence.* New York: Random House.

Schmechel, R. S., O'Toole, T. P., Easterly, C., & Loftus, E. F. (2006). Beyond the ken: Testing jurors' understanding of eyewitness reliability evidence. *Jurimetrics Journal, 46,* 177–214.

Schooler, J. W., & Engstler-Schooler, T. Y. (1990). Verbal overshadowing of visual memories: Some things are better left unsaid. *Cognitive Psychology, 22,* 36–71.

Schooler, J. W., Foster, R. A., & Loftus, E. F. (1988). Some deleterious consequences of the act of recollection. *Memory & Cognition, 16,* 243–251.

Schooler, J. W., Gerhard, D., & Loftus, E. F. (1986). Qualities of the unreal. *Journal of Experimental Psychology: Learning, Memory, and Cognition, 12,* 171–181.

Searcy, J., Bartlett, J., & Memon, A. (1999). Age differences in accuracy and choosing in eyewitness identification and face recognition. *Memory & Cognition, 27,* 538–552.

Searcy, J., Bartlett, J., & Memon, A. (2000). Influence of postevent narratives, lineup conditions and individual differences on false identification of young and older eyewitnesses. *Legal and Criminological Psychology, 5,* 219–235.

Searcy, J., Bartlett, J., Memon, A., & Swanson, K. (2001). Aging and lineup performance at long retention intervals: Effects of metamemory and context reinstatement. *Journal of Applied Psychology, 86,* 207–214.

Seeleman, V. (1940). The influence of attitude upon the remembering of pictorial material. *Archives of Psychology,* (258), 69.

Sekunova A., & Barton J. J. S.(2008). The effects of face inversion on the perception of long-range and local spatial relations in eye and mouth configuration. *Journal of Experimental Psychology: Human Perception and Performance, 34,* 1129–1135.

Servos. P., Engel, S. A., Gati, J., & Menon, R. (1999). fMRI evidence for an inverted face representation in human somatosensory cortex, *NeuroReport, 10,* 1393–1395.

Shapiro, P., & Penrod, S. D. (1986). A meta-analysis of the facial identification literature. *Psychological Bulletin, 100,* 139–156.

Shaw, J. I., & Skolnick, P. (1999). Weapon focus and gender differences in eyewitness accuracy: Arousal versus salience. *Journal of Applied Social Psychology, 29,* 2328–2341.

Shaw, J. S., Garven, S., & Wood, J. M. (1997). Co-witness information can have immediate effects on eyewitness memory reports. *Law and Human Behavior, 21,* 503–523.

Shepherd, J. W., Davies, G., & Ellis, H. (1981). Studies of cue saliency. In G. Davies, H. Ellis, & J. Shepherd (Eds.), *Perceiving and remembering faces* (pp. 105–131). London: Academic Press.

Shepherd, J. W., & Deregowski, J. B. (1981). Races and faces: A comparison of the responses of Africans and Europeans to faces of the same and different races. *British Journal of Psychology, 20,* 125–133.

Sheperd, J. W., Gibling, F., & Ellis, H. D. (1991). The effects of distinctiveness, presentation time, and delay on face recognition. *European Journal of Cognitive Psychology, 3,* 137–145.

Shiffrin, R. M., & Atkinson, R. C. (1969). Storage and retrieval processes in long term memory. *Psychological Review, 76,* 179–193.

Shoemaker, S. (1967). Memory. S.v. in *The encyclopedia of philosophy* (Ed. P. Edwards) (p. 274). New York: MacMillan.

Shope, R. (2000). *The analysis of knowing: A decade of research.* Princeton, NJ: Princeton University Press.

Shriver, E., Young, S., Hugenberg, K., Bernstein, M., & Lanter, J. (2008). Class, race, and the face: Social context modulates the cross-race effect in face recognition. *Personality and Social Psychology Bulletin, 34*(2), 260–274.

Simmons v. United States, 390 U.S. 377 (1968).

Singer, M. (2009). Strength-based criterion shifts in recognition memory. *Memory & Cognition, 37,* 976–984.

Singer, M., & Remillard, G. (2008). Veridical and false memory for text: a multiprocess analysis. *Journal of Memory and Language, 59,* 18–35.

Skagerberg., E. M. (2007). Co-witness feedback in line-ups. *Applied Cognitive Psychology, 21,* 489–497.

Skagerberg, E. M., & Wright, D. B. (2008). The prevalence of co-witnesses and co-witness discussions in real eyewitnesses. *Psychology, Crime and Law, 14,* 513–521.

Slater, A. (1994). *Identification parades: A scientific evaluation.* London, Home Office.

Slone, A., Brigham, J., & Meissner, C. (2000). Social and cognitive factors affecting the own-race bias in Whites. *Basic and Applied Social Psychology, 22*(2), 71–84.

Smith, S. M., Lindsay, R. C. L., & Pryke, S. (2000). Postdictors of eyewitness errors: Can false identifications be diagnosed? *Journal of Applied Psychology, 85,* 542–550.

Smith, S. M., Lindsay, R. C. L., Pryke, S., & Dysart, J. E. (2001). Postdictors of eyewitness errors: Can false identifications be diagnosed in the cross race situation? *Psychology, Public Policy, and Law, 7,* 153–169.

Smith, V. L., & Ellsworth, P. C. (1987). The social psychology of eyewitness accuracy: Misleading questions and communicator expertise. *Journal of Applied Psychology, 72,* 294–300.

Smith, V. L., & Studebaker, C. A. (1996). What do you expect: The influence of people's prior knowledge of crime categories on fact-finding. *Law and Human Behavior, 20,* 517–532.

Snodgrass, J. G., & Corwin, J. (1988). Pragmatics of measuring recognition memory: Applications to dementia and amnesia. *Journal of Experimental Psychology: General, 117,* 34–50.

Snyder, M. (1974). Self-monitoring of expressive behavior. *Journal of Personality and Social Psychology, 30*(4), 526–537.

Solano, D. (2010, July 30). Innocent man released after 27 years in prison. *KIAH Online.* Retrieved from http://www.39online.com/news/local/kiah-finally-released-story,0,479819.story

Sporer, S. (1992). Post-dicting eyewitness accuracy: Confidence, decision-times and person descriptions of choosers and non-choosers. *European Journal of Social Psychology, 22,* 157–180.

Sporer, S. (1993). Eyewitness identification accuracy, confidence, and decision times in simultaneous and sequential lineups. *Journal of Applied Psychology, 78,* 22–33.

Sporer, S. (1994). Decision times and eyewitness identification accuracy in simultaneous and sequential lineups. In D. F. Ross, J. D. Read, & M. P. Toglia (Eds.), *Adult eyewitness testimony: Current trends and developments* (300–327). New York : Cambridge University Press.

Sporer, S., Penrod, S. D., Read, D., & Cutler, B. L. (1995). Gaining confidence in confidence: A new meta-analysis on the confidence-accuracy relationship in eyewitness identification studies. *Psychological Bulletin, 118,* 315–327.

Stahl, C., & Klauer, K. (2009). Measuring phantom recollection in the simplified conjoint recognition paradigm. *Journal of Memory and Language, 60,* 180–193.

Steblay, N. (1992). A meta-analytic review of the weapon focus effect. *Law and Human Behavior, 16,* 413–424.

Steblay, N. M. (1997). Social influences in eyewitness recall: A meta-analytic review of lineup instruction effects. *Law and Human Behavior, 21,* 283–297.

Steblay, N. M., Dysart, J., Fulero, S., & Lindsay, R. C. L. (2003). Eyewitness accuracy rates in police showup and lineup presentations: A meta-analytic comparison. *Law and Human Behavior, 27,* 523–540.

Steblay, N., Hosch, H., Culhane, S., & McWethy, A. (2006). The impact on juror verdicts of judicial instruction to disregard inadmissible evidence: A meta-analysis. *Law and Human Behavior, 30,* 469–542.

Steblay, N. K., Tix, R. W., & Benson, S. L. (under review). Double exposure: The effects of repeated identification lineups on eyewitness accuracy.

Steele, C., & Josephs, R. (1990). Alcohol myopia: Its prized and dangerous effects. *American Psychologist, 45,* 921–933.

Stewart, H. A., & McAllister, H. A. (2001). One-at-a-time versus grouped presentation of mug book pictures: Some surprising results. *Journal of Applied Psychology , 86,* 1300–1305.

Stovall v. Denno. (1967). 388 U.S. 293.

Sünram-Lea, S., Foster, J., Durlach, P., & Perez, C. (2002). Investigation into the significance of task difficulty and divided allocation of resources on the glucose memory facilitation effect. *Psychopharmacology, 160,* 387–397.

Taylor, K. T. (2001). *Forensic art and illustration.* Boca Raton FL: CRC Press.

Taylor, M. J., Batty, M., & Itier, R. J. (2004). The faces of development: a review of early processing over childhood. *Journal of Cognitive Neuroscience, 16,* 1–17.

Technical Working Group for Eyewitness Evidence. (1999). *Eyewitness evidence: A guide for law enforcement.* Washington DC: U.S. Department of Justice.

Thompson-Cannino, J. (2009, April 20). Transcript: Gates PSL Speaker Series "Picking cotton." University of Washington School of Law. Retrieved from http://www.law.washington.edu/Multimedia/2009/Cotton/Transcript. aspx

Tollestrup, P. A., Turtle, J. W., & Yuille, J. C. (1994). Actual victims and witnesses to robbery and fraud: An archival analysis. In D. F. Ross, J. D. Read, and M. P. Toglia (Eds), *Adult eyewitness testimony: Current trends and development* (144–160). New York: Cambridge University Press.

Tooley, V., Brigham, J., Maass, A., & Bothwell, R. (1987). Facial recognition: Weapon effect and attentional focus. *Journal of Applied Social Psychology, 17*(10), 845–859.

Tousignant, J. P., Hall, D., & Loftus, E. F. (1986). Discrepancy detection and vulnerability to misleading postevent information. *Memory and Cognition, 14,* 329–338.

Tredoux, C. G. (2002). A direct measure of facial similarity and its relation to human similarity perceptions. *Journal of Experimental Psychology: Applied, 8,* 180–193.

Treisman, A., & Souther, J. (1985). Search asymmetry: A diagnostic for preattentive processing of separable features. *Journal of Experimental Psychology: General, 114,* 285–310.

Tuckey, M., & Brewer, N. (2003). The influence of schemas, stimulus ambiguity, and interview schedule on eyewitness memory over time. *Journal of Experimental Psychology: Applied, 9,* 101–118.

Tulving, E. (1972). Episodic and semantic memory. In E. Tulving & W. Donaldson (Eds.), *Organization and memory* (pp. 381–403). New York: Academic Press.

Tulving, E. (1974). Cue-dependent forgetting. *American Scientist, 62,* 74–82.

Tulving, E. (1983). *Elements of episodic memory.* London: Oxford University Press.

Tulving, E. (1985). Memory and consciousness. *Canadian Psychology, 26,* 1–12.

Tulving, E. (1999). Study of memory: Processes and systems. In J. K. Foster & M. Jelicic (Eds.), *Memory: Systems, process, or function?* (pp. 11–30). New York: Oxford University Press.

Tulving, E. (2002). Episodic memory: From mind to brain. *Annual Review of Psychology, 53,* 1–25.

Tulving, E., & Thomson, D. (1973). Encoding specificity and retrieval processes in episodic memory. *Psychological Review, 80,* 352–373.

Tulving, E., & Wiseman, S. (1975). Relation between recognition and recognition failure of recallable words. *Bulletin of the Psychonomic Society, 6,* 79–82.

Turk, D., Handy, T., & Gazzaniga, M. (2005). Can perceptual expertise account for the own-race bias in face recognition? A split-brain study. *Cognitive Neuropsychology, 22*(7), 877–883.

Turtle, J. W., & Wells, G. L. (1988). Children versus adults as eyewitnesses: Whose testimony holds up under cross examination? In M. W. Gruneberg et al. (Eds.), *Practical aspects of memory* (pp. 27–33). New York: Wiley.

Tversky, B., & Tuchin, M. (1989). A reconciliation of the evidence on eyewitness testimony: Comments on McCloskey and Zaragoza. *Journal of Experimental Psychology: General, 118,* 86–91.

United States v. Ash (1973). 413 US 300.

Valentine, T. (1991). A unified account of the effects of distinctiveness, inversion, and race in face recognition. *Quarterly Journal of Experimental Psychology, 43A,* 161–204.

Valentine, T. (1995). *Cognitive and computational aspects of face recognition: Explorations in face space.* London: Routledge.

Valentine, T., & Bruce, V. (1986). Recognizing familiar faces: The role of distinctiveness and familiarity. *Canadian Journal of Psychology, 40,* 300–305.

Valentine, T., Davis, J., Thorner, K., Solomon, C., & Gibson, S. (2010). Evolving and combining facial composites: Between-witness and within-witness morphs compared. *Journal of Experimental Psychology: Applied, 16,* 72–86.

Valentine, T., & Mesout, J. (2009). Eyewitness identification under stress in the London Dungeon. *Applied Cognitive Psychology, 23,* 151–161.

Valentine, T., Pickering, A., & Darling, S. (2003). Characteristics of eyewitness identification that predict the outcome of real lineups. *Applied Cognitive Psychology, 17,* 969–993.

Vornik, L., Sharman, S. J., & Garry, M. (2003). The power of the spoken word: Sociolinguistic cues influence the misinformation effect. *Memory, 11,* 101–109.

Wagenaar, W. A., & Schrier, van der J. H. (1996). Face recognition as a function of distance and illumination: A practical tool for use in the courtroom. *Psychology, Crime & Law, 2,* 2321–2332.

Wagstaff, G. (1989). Forensic aspects of hypnosis. In G. Wagstaff, *Hypnosis: The cognitive-behavioral perspective* (pp. 340-357). Amherst, NY: Prometheus.

Wagstaff, G., Vella, M., & Perfect, T. (1992). The effect of hypnotically elicited testimony on jurors' judgments of guilt and innocence. *The Journal of Social Psychology, 132*(5), 591–595.

Walker, L., & Monahan, J. (1996). *Daubert* and the reference manual: An essay on the future of science in law. *Virginia Law Review, 82,* 837.

Walker, P. M., & Hewstone, M. (2008). The influence of social factors and implicit racial bias on a generalized own-race effect. *Applied Cognitive Psychology, 22,* 441–453.

Weber, N., Brewer, N., Wells, G. L., Semmler, C., & Keast, A. (2004). Eyewitness identification accuracy and response latency: The unruly 10–12 second rule. *Journal of Experimental Psychology: Applied, 10,* 139–147.

Weinstein, C., & Mayer, R. (1986). The teaching of learning strategies. In M. Wittrock (Ed.), *Handbook of research on teaching* (3rd ed.). New York: MacMillan.

Wells, G. L. (1978). Applied eyewitness testimony research: System variables and estimator variables. *Journal of Personality and Social Psychology, 36,* 1546–1557.

Wells, G. L. (1984). The psychology of lineup identifications. *Journal of Applied Social Psychology, 14,* 89–103.

Wells, G. L. (1985). Verbal descriptions of faces from memory: Are they diagnostic of identification accuracy? *Journal of Applied Psychology, 70,* 619–626.

Wells, G. L. (1993). What do we know about eyewitness identification? *American Psychologist, 48,* 553–571.

Wells, G. L. (2006). Comments on the Mecklenburg Report. Retrieved from http://www.psychology.iastate.edu/~glwells/Illinois_Project_Wells_comments.pdf

Wells, G. L. (n.d.-a). Frequently asked questions of Gary Wells. Retrieved from http://www.psychology.iastate.edu/~glwells/faqs.htm

Wells, G. L.(n.d.-b). Bad and good lineups. Retrieved from http://www.psychology.iastate.edu/~glwells/badandgoodlineups.htm

Wells, G. L. (2008). Field experiments on eyewitness identification: Towards a better understanding of pitfalls and prospects. *Law & Human Behavior, 32,* 6–10.

Wells, G. L., & Bradfield, A. L. (1998). "Good, you identified the suspect": Feedback to eyewitnesses distorts their reports of the witnessing experience. *Journal of Applied Psychology, 83,* 360–376.

Wells, G. L., Charman, S. D., & Olson, E. A. (2005). Building face composites can harm lineup identification performance. *Journal of Experimental Psychology: Applied, 11,* 147–157.

Wells, G. L., & Hasel, L. E. (2007). Facial composite production by eyewitnesses. *Current Directions in Psychological Science, 16,* 6–16.

Wells, G. L., & Olson, E. (2003). Eyewitness identification. *Annual Review of Psychology, 54,* 277–295.

Wells, G. L., & Murray, D. M. (1984). Eyewitness confidence. In G. L. Wells & E. F. Loftus (Eds.), *Eyewitness testimony: Psychological perspectives* (pp. 155–170). New York: Cambridge University Press.

Wells, G. L., Leippe, M. R., & Ostrom, T. M. (1979). Guidelines for empirically assessing the fairness of a lineup. *Law and Human Behavior, 3,* 285–293.

Wells, G. L., & Lindsay, R. (1980). On estimating the diagnosticity of eyewitness nonidentifications. *Psychological Bulletin, 88,* 776–784.

Wells, G. L., Lindsay, R. C. L., & Ferguson, T. J. (1979). Accuracy confidence and juror perceptions in eyewitness identification. *Journal of Applied Psychology, 64,* 440–448.

Wells, G. L., Lindsay, R. C., & Tousignant, J. P. (1980). Effects of expert psychological advice on human performance in judging the validity of eyewitness testimony. *Law and Human Behavior, 4,* 275–285.

Wells, G. L., & Luus, C. A. E. (1990). Police lineups as experiments. *Personality and Social Psychology Bulletin, 16,* 106–117.

Wells, G. L., Malpass, R. S., Lindsay, R. C. L., Fisher, R. P., Turtle, J. W., & Fulero, S. (2000). From the lab to the police station: A successful application of eyewitness research. *American Psychologist, 55,* 581–598.

Wells, G. L., Olson, E. A., & Charman, S. D. (2002). The confidence of eyewitnesses in their identifications from lineups. *Current Directions in Psychological Science, 11,* 151–154.

Wells, G. L., Olson, E. A., & Charman, S. D. (2003). Distorted retrospective eyewitness reports as functions of feedback and delay. *Journal of Experimental Psychology: Applied, 9,* 42–52.

Wells, G. L., Rydell, S. M., & Seelau, E. P. (1993). On the selection of distractors for eyewitness lineups. *Journal of Applied Psychology, 78,* 835–844.

Wells, G. L., & Seelau, E. P. (1995). Eyewitness identification: Psychological research and legal policy on lineups. *Psychology, Public Policy, and Law, 1,* 765–791.

Wells, G. L., Small, M., Penrod, S. J., Malpass, R. S., Fulero, S. M., & Brimacombe, C. A. E. (1998). Eyewitness identification procedures: Recommendations for lineups and photospreads. *Law and Human Behavior, 22,* 603–647.

Wells, G. L., & Quinlivan, D. S. (2009). Suggestive eyewitness identification procedures and the Supreme Court's reliability test in light of the eyewitness science: 30 years later. *Law and Human Behavior, 33,* 1–24.

Wells, G. L., Wright, E. F., & Bradfield, A.L. (1999). Witnesses to crime: Social and cognitive factors governing the validity of people's reports. In R. Roesch & S. Hart (Eds.), *Psychology and law: State of the discipline* (pp. 53–87). New York: Plenum Press.

Wickelgren, W. A. (1974). Single-trace fragility theory of memory dynamics. *Memory & Cognition, 2,* 775–780.

Wickham, L. H. V., & Morris, P. (2003). Attractiveness, distinctiveness, and recognition of faces: Attractive faces can be typical or distinctive but are not better recognized. *American Journal of Psychology, 116,* 455–468.

Wickham, L. H. V., Morris, P. E., & Fritz, C. O. (2000). Facial distinctiveness: Its measurement, distribution and influence on immediate and delayed recognition. *British Journal of Psychology, 91,* 99–123.

Wiese, H., Schweinberger, S. R., & Hansen, K. (2008). The age of the beholder: ERP evidence of an own-age bias in face memory. *Neuropsychologia, 46,* 2973–2985.

Winograd, E. (1981). Elaboration and distinctiveness in memory for faces. *Journal of Experimental Psychology: Human Learning & Memory, 7,* 181–190.

Wise, R. A., Meyer, D., Pawlenko, N. B., & Safer, M. A. (2007, November). A survey of defense attorneys' knowledge and beliefs about eyewitness testimony. *The Champion,* 18.

Wise, R. A., & Safer, M. A. (2003). A survey of judges' knowledge and beliefs about eyewitness testimony. *Court Review, 40*(1), 6–16.

Wise, R. A., & Safer, M. A. (2004). What U.S. judges know and believe about eyewitness testimony. *Applied Cognitive Psychology, 18,* 427–443.

Witkin, H. A., Moore, C., Goodenough, D., & Cox, P. (1977). Field-dependent and field-independent cognitive styles and their educational implications. *Review of Educational Research, 47*(1), 1–64.

Witkin, H. A. Oltman, P. A. Raskin, E., & Karp, S. A. (1971/2002). *Group embedded figures test manual* (3rd ed.). Menlo Park, CA: Mind Garden.

Wogalter, M. S., Malpass, R. S., & Berger, M. A. (1993). How police officers construct lineups: A national survey. In *Proceedings of the Human Factors and Ergonomics Society* (pp. 640–644). Santa Monica, CA: Human Factors and Ergonomics Society.

World Bank. (2010). Life expectancy at birth, total (years). Retrieved from http://data.worldbank.org/indicator/SP.DYN.LE00.IN?cid=GPD_10

Wright, D. B., Boyd, C., & Tredoux, C. (2003). Inter-racial contact and the own-race bias for face recognition in South Africa and England. *Applied Cognitive Psychology, 17*, 365–373.

Wright, D. B., & McDaid, A. T. (1996). Comparing system and estimator variables using data from real line-ups. *Applied Cognitive Psychology ,10*, 75–84.

Wright, D. B., & Skagerberg, E. M. (2007). Post-identification feedback affects real eyewitnesses. *Psychological Science, 18*, 172–178.

Wright, D. B., & Sladden, B. (2003). An own gender bias and the importance of hair in face recognition. *Acta Psychologica, 114*, 101–114.

Xu, Y. (2005). Revisiting the role of the fusiform and occipital face areas in visual expertise. *Cerebral Cortex, 15*, 1234–1242.

Yarmey, A., & Kent, J. (1980). Eyewitness identification by elderly and young adults. *Law and Human Behavior, 4*(4), 359–371.

Yarmey, A. D., & Jones, H. P. T. (1983). Is the psychology of eyewitness identification a matter of common sense? In S. Lloyd-Bostock & B. R. Clifford (Eds.), *Evaluating witness evidence* (pp. 13–40). Chichester, UK: Wiley.

Yarmey, A. D., Yarmey, A. L., & Yarmey, M. J. (1994). Face and voice identifications in showups and lineups. *Applied Cognitive Psychology, 8*, 453–464.

Yarmey, A. D., Yarmey, A. L., & Yarmey, M. J. (1996). Accuracy of eyewitness identification in showups and lineups. *Law and Human Behavior, 20*, 459–477.

Yerkes, R. M., & Dodson, J. D. (1908). The relation of strength of stimulus to rapidity of habit-formation. *Journal of Comparative Neurology and Psychology, 18*, 459–482.

Yin, R. K. (1969). Looking at upside-down faces. *Journal of Experimental Psychology, 81*, 141–145.

Yonelinas, A. P. (1994). Receiver-operating characteristics in recognition memory: Evidence for a dual-process model. *Journal of Experimental Psychology: Learning, Memory, and Cognition, 20*, 1341–1354.

Yonelinas, A. (2001). Consciousness, control, and confidence: The 3 Cs of recognition memory. *Journal of Experimental Psychology: General, 130*, 361–379.

Young, A. W., Hellawell, D., & Hay, D. C. (1987). Configural information in face perception. *Perception, 16*, 747–759.

Yuille, J. C. (1993). We must study forensic eyewitnesses to know about them. *American Psychologist, 48*, 572–573.

Yuille, J. C. (1986). Meaningful research in the police context. In J. C. Yuille (Ed.), *Police selection and training: The role of psychology* (pp. 225–246). Dordrecht, the Netherlands: Martinus Nijhoff.

Yuille, J., & McEwan, N. (1985). Use of hypnosis as an aid to eyewitness memory. *Journal of Applied Psychology, 70*, 389–400.

Yuille, J., & Tollestrup, P. (1990). Some effects of alcohol on eyewitness memory. *Journal of Applied Psychology, 75*, 268–273.

Yuille, J., Tollestrup, P., Marxsen, D., Porter, S., & Herve, H. (1998). An exploration on the effects of marijuana on eyewitness memory. *International Journal of Law and Psychiatry, 21*(1), 117–128.

Zaragoza, M., & Lane, S. (1994). Source misattributions and the suggestibility of eyewitness memory. *Journal of Experimental Psychology: Learning, Memory, and Cognition, 20,* 934–945.

Zaragoza, M., & McCloskey, M. (1989). Misleading postevent information and the memory impairment hypothesis: Comment on Belli and reply to Tversky and Tuchin. *Journal of Experimental Psychology: General, 118,* 92–99.

Zaragoza, M. S., McCloskey, M., & Jamis, M. (1987). Misleading postevent information and recall of the original event: Further evidence against the memory impairment hypothesis. *Journal of Experimental Psychology: Learning, Memory, and Cognition, 13,* 36–44.

AUTHOR INDEX

321

SUBJECT INDEX